AF793177

Widows Under Hindu Law

ROCHER INDOLOGY SERIES

Series editor: Patrick Olivelle

Widows Under Hindu Law
David Brick

Mirror of Nature, Mirror of Self
Models of Consciousness in Sāṃkhya, Yoga, and Advaita Vedānta
Dimitry Shevchenko

Widows Under Hindu Law

DAVID BRICK

OXFORD
UNIVERSITY PRESS

OXFORD
UNIVERSITY PRESS

Oxford University Press is a department of the University of Oxford. It furthers the University's objective of excellence in research, scholarship, and education by publishing worldwide. Oxford is a registered trade mark of Oxford University Press in the UK and certain other countries.

Published in the United States of America by Oxford University Press
198 Madison Avenue, New York, NY 10016, United States of America.

© Oxford University Press 2023

Some rights reserved. No part of this publication may be reproduced, stored in a retrieval system, or transmitted, in any form or by any means, for commercial purposes, without the prior permission in writing of Oxford University Press, or as expressly permitted by law, by licence or under terms agreed with the appropriate reprographics rights organization.

This is an open access publication, available online and distributed under the terms of a Creative Commons Attribution – Non Commercial – No Derivatives 4.0 International licence (CC BY-NC-ND 4.0), a copy of which is available at http://creativecommons.org/licenses/by-nc-nd/4.0/.

All rights reserved. No part of this publication may be reproduced, stored in a retrieval system, or transmitted, in any form or by any means, without the prior permission in writing of Oxford University Press, or as expressly permitted by law, by license, or under terms agreed with the appropriate reproduction rights organization. Inquiries concerning reproduction outside the scope of the above should be sent to the Rights Department, Oxford University Press, at the address above.

You must not circulate this work in any other form
and you must impose this same condition on any acquirer.

Library of Congress Cataloging-in-Publication Data
Names: Brick, David J., author.
Title: Widows under Hindu Law / David Brick.
Description: New York, NY : Oxford University Press, [2023] |
Series: Rocher Indology |
Includes bibliographical references and index.
Identifiers: LCCN 2022044083 (print) | LCCN 2022044084 (ebook) |
ISBN 9780197664544 (hardback) | ISBN 9780197664568 (epub)
Subjects: LCSH: Widows (Hindu law)
Classification: LCC KNS550 .B75 2023 (print) | LCC KNS550 (ebook) |
DDC 346.5401/3082—dc23/eng/20230106
LC record available at https://lccn.loc.gov/2022044083
LC ebook record available at https://lccn.loc.gov/2022044084

DOI: 10.1093/oso/9780197664544.001.0001

Printed by Integrated Books International, United States of America

Contents

Preface

My academic interest in widows began with a seminar that I took as part of my graduate coursework. Cynthia Talbot was the instructor, and the topic was historical memory in South Asia with a particular focus on the memory and construction of premodern Indian history during the colonial and later periods. At the time I had already studied Sanskrit for quite a few years and had a burgeoning scholarly focus on classical Hindu law or Dharmaśāstra, as it is called in Sanskrit. Aware of this, Dr. Talbot suggested that I write my term paper on the well-known colonial debate on sati, or widow burning, since it involved a great many Dharmaśāstra texts and ideas. As a place to start, she suggested that I read Lata Mani's book, *Contentious Traditions*, which examines this debate in detail and was at the time still fairly new. This proved to be an extremely fruitful suggestion, for which I am especially grateful in hindsight.

When I read Mani's book, I was impressed by her nuanced, empathetic, multifaceted, and generally insightful analysis of the early colonial debate on sati. Even at the time, however, it was apparent to me that her understanding of premodern India and Dharmaśāstra in particular was not very strong, despite its obvious relevance to the subject matter of her book. One simple way to illustrate the extent to which Mani's book ignores Dharmaśāstra is to point out the startling fact that it nowhere cites or even mentions P. V. Kane's voluminous and magisterial *History of Dharmaśāstra*—a five-volume work that has long been the starting place for virtually all serious studies of classical Hindu law, including the present one. It was clear to me as a graduate student—and it is even clearer to me now—that if Mani had read Kane's work and been more knowledgeable about Dharmaśāstra, her work would have greatly benefited in numerous ways (for specific cases, see note 9 in the Introduction).

Having said this, I do not see Mani's unawareness of premodern India as severely vitiating the significant contribution of her work; nor do I see a general neglect of Dharmaśāstra sources as by any means unique to her among scholars of colonial South Asia. However, I do see in such neglect of Dharmaśāstra an opportunity for a scholar of the subject to provide crucial context for those working on colonial South Asia, for it is simply impossible to discern what changed under colonialism without a detailed knowledge of what preceded it. Hence, it is impossible to fully understand the colonial debate on sati, as well as the important colonial debate on widow remarriage, without a detailed knowledge of the Dharmaśāstra tradition and its discussions of these same topics. Thus, my hope is that, by providing a detailed history of widows under Hindu law, this book will be of interest and use not only to classical Indologists but also—perhaps especially—to scholars of colonial South Asia.

As a rather old-fashioned philologist who has dedicated his life to the study of ancient and medieval Indian texts, I generally assume that the audience for my work will be a small one and that my work's influence outside of academe will be negligible. However, given the intense controversies around Hindu widows that have arisen in colonial and even modern India, I recognize that this book may have a notably wider audience than I am accustomed to. Indeed, as explained above, my hope is that it will to some degree. Hence, while I realize that authors inevitably have limited control over the ways in which their works are used and interpreted, I feel obligated to lay out my personal feelings about the matters addressed in this book.

It probably goes without saying, but I certainly do not wish to see a revival of anything like the treatment of widows prescribed in Dharmaśāstra sources; nor do I wish to embarrass or defame modern Hindus by drawing attention to the historical reality of certain clearly misogynistic practices that they themselves likely consider to have no place in their religion. My firm belief is that religions, like all human institutions, change and that Hinduism is no exception. This book provides just one illustration of this. As such, I consider it a mistake to dismiss sati and the other widow-related practices prescribed in classical Hindu sources as mere customs or cultural practices irrelevant to true Hindu religion, for to do so is to capriciously make classical Hindu sources—or at least those of them that one does not like—irrelevant to genuine Hinduism. At the same time, I also consider it a mistake to regard sati and the other widow-related practices discussed in this book as essential and timeless Hindu institutions, for to do so is not only to privilege scriptural religion over lived religion but also to imagine a unanimity of scriptural voices that simply does not exist and to ignore an array of significant historical changes that took place during the premodern period—changes that I try to delineate in this book.

Acknowledgments

In bringing this scholarly project to completion, I naturally owe thanks to many people and institutions who have lent me great assistance over the years. At the institutional level, I owe thanks first to the University of Washington, where I received my bachelor's degree and began to study Indology, and to the University of Texas at Austin, where I earned my master's and doctoral degrees. I especially wish to thank the residents of Washington and Texas as well as other parts of the United States, whose tax dollars helped to fund my education. These anonymous persons are my greatest benefactors, to whom I extremely grateful. I hope that this book offers some return on the considerable investment that they have made in me. The other two institutions that I wish to single out for special thanks are my former employer, Yale University, and my current employer, the University of Michigan. I am grateful to these institutions for providing me with the means to live and work as a full-time Indologist since finishing my schooling. I especially wish to thank the many wonderful students that I have had over the years at Yale and the University of Michigan and all those persons (e.g., tuition-paying parents) who have helped sustain the study of Indology at these fine institutions.

Of course, universities are nothing without teachers. Thus, I owe an enormous debt of gratitude not only to the universities with which I have been associated but also to specific persons employed by them, learned and accomplished scholars, who have devoted considerable amounts of time and energy to teaching, guiding, and supporting me at various stages in my career. Although I have had many wonderful teachers and mentors, I would single out four for special thanks: Patrick Olivelle, who has taught me more than anyone not only about Sanskrit but also about what it means to be a scholar and a fine human being; Richard Salomon, my first Sanskrit teacher and a regular source of guidance and support ever since; Joel Brereton, who tried to teach me Vedic and has offered crucial advice and support in times of doubt; and Phyllis Granoff, who was the best colleague and mentor a newly minted PhD in Sanskrit could hope to have. Without each of these four individuals I would be doing something else entirely with my life, I am sure. So I thank them all from the bottom of my heart. In addition, I wish to thank

Ludo and Rosane Rocher, for teaching my teachers and for making North America a center of Dharmaśāstra studies today. I am thrilled to have my work included in this monograph series in their honor.

Other colleagues I wish to thank especially are Donald Davis, Timothy Lubin, and Harald Wiese—three friends and great scholars of classical Indian law who closely read and provided crucial feedback on an earlier draft of this book. Their help in writing this book has been immense. I also feel obliged to acknowledge the many interlocutors with whom I have shared portions of this book as conference papers and the like and whose comments and insights have improved my work in ways big and small. Of these I would single out for special recognition my close friend and colleague Mark McClish.

Last and most importantly, I must offer very special thanks to my wife, Nicki, who has been a constant source of love and support since before I ever thought to study Sanskrit and who has sacrificed more on behalf of my career—financially, emotionally, socially, and geographically—than anyone.

Abbreviations

AiB	*Aitareya Brāhmaṇa*
ĀpDh	*Āpastamba Dharmasūtra*
AŚ	*Arthaśāstra* of Kauṭilya
AV	*Atharvaveda* (Śaunaka recension)
BDh	*Baudhāyana Dharmasūtra*
BSm	*Bṛhaspati Smṛti*
GDh	*Gautama Dharmasūtra*
ĪU	*Īśa Upaniṣad*
KSm	*Kātyāyana Smṛti*
KSS	*Kathāsaritsāgara*
MBh	*Mahābhārata*
MDh	*Mānava Dharmaśāstra*
NSm	*Nārada Smṛti*
PMS	*Pūrvamīmāṃsāsūtra*
PSm	*Parāśara Smṛti*
Rām	*Rāmāyaṇa*
ṚV	*Ṛgveda Saṃhitā*
ŚPB	*Śatapatha Brāhmaṇa* (Mādhyaṃdina recension)
ṢV	*Ṣaḍviṃśa Brāhmaṇa*
TĀ	*Taittirīya Āraṇyaka*
TB	*Taittirīya Brāhmaṇa*
TS	*Taittirīya Saṃhitā*
VaDh	*Vasiṣṭha Dharmasūtra*
ViDh	*Vaiṣṇava Dharmaśāstra*
YDh	*Yājñavalkya Dharmaśāstra*

Introduction

When employees of the British East India Company first became aware of the treatment of widows within high-caste Hindu society, many of them were aghast, for high-caste Hindu widows at the time could often be quite young due to the prevalence of child marriages and the general vicissitudes of life before modern medicine, yet they were strictly forbidden from ever remarrying. Beyond this, these widows were also faced with a stark choice between two seemingly grim options. On the one hand, they could live on after their husbands, but as stigmatized and socially marginalized persons, adopting a mandatory lifestyle of harsh asceticism, according to which they had to keep their heads perpetually shaved, observe a demanding regimen of vows and fasts, and eschew such pleasurable things as festivals, flavorful foods, dyed garments, and jewelry. Or, on the other hand, they could kill themselves by ascending their husbands' funeral pyres in a celebrated act of wifely devotion known since the colonial period as sati. This essentially was the choice facing the high-caste Hindu widow as the British encountered her in the eighteenth and early nineteenth centuries; and if contemporaneous sources are to be believed, it may not always have been a real choice for the Hindu widow.[1]

Given this situation and the nature of British culture and colonial rule, it is unsurprising that various legal issues centered on the figure of the Hindu widow—meaning specifically the high-caste Hindu widow—became the subject of considerable public attention and deeply contentious debate during the early to mid-nineteenth century. Moreover, as is widely known, colonial administrators, Christian missionaries, and Hindu intellectuals all played prominent roles in these heated debates. Undoubtedly the most well-known instance of such legalistic contention in colonial India is the early nineteenth-century debate on the traditional Hindu practice of widow

[1] See in this regard Rammohan Roy's criticism of contemporaneous proponents of sati: "[T]he widow should voluntarily quit life, ascending the flaming pile of her husband. But, on the contrary, you first bind down the widow along with the corpse of her husband and then heap over her such a quantity of wood that she cannot rise" (Ghose 1901, 135).

Widows Under Hindu Law. David Brick, Oxford University Press. © Oxford University Press 2023.
DOI: 10.1093/oso/9780197664544.003.0001

self-immolation, or sati, as it is commonly called—a debate involving a fascinating array of legal arguments both for and against the practice that culminated in the prohibition of sati throughout most of British India in 1829.[2] The most celebrated participant in this debate is without doubt the enormously influential Hindu reformer Rammohan Roy. Another well-known instance of legal contention regarding widows from the colonial period is the mid-nineteenth-century debate on the right of Hindu widows to remarry—widow remarriage having long been prohibited among high-caste Hindus throughout essentially all of South Asia.[3] In this case, the reform-minded Bengali Sanskrit scholar Ishvarchandra Vidyasagar led a spirited campaign in favor of Hindu widow remarriage, both as a legal right and as a praiseworthy practice fully sanctioned by recognized Hindu scriptures; and this campaign played a major role in the passage of the Hindu Widows' Remarriage Act of 1856, which granted all Hindu widows in British India the right to remarry.[4]

The work of modern scholars (Bandyopadhyay 1995; Hatcher 1996; Mani 1998) has shed considerable light on these colonial debates around widows, as well as their legacies in modern India, interrogating the aims and motives of the various parties involved. These scholars have, for instance, shown how the pitiable figure of the Hindu widow was used to illustrate the purportedly backward nature of Indian culture and, thereby, justify British colonial rule. Moreover, they have crucially revealed how "the generation of law from brahmanic scriptures extended a more restrictive high-caste law to women to whom it had not previously applied" (Mani 1998, 38) and how the work of early Indologists was complicit in this (R. Rocher 2010). Despite this important work, however, scholars have managed to shed little light on a related set of important historical questions, namely, when, where, and why did the salient social practices governing the lives of high-caste Hindu widows during the eighteenth and nineteenth centuries first arise and become so widespread throughout South Asia. Indeed, when it comes to answering this set of questions, we are still very much in the dark, being dependent upon the broad and loosely substantiated conjectures of past generations of scholars.[5]

[2] On this, see Mani (1998) and Fisch (2006, 364–438).

[3] See Chapter 1.

[4] For a modern English translation of Vidyasagar's writings in favor of Hindu widow remarriage and a study thereof, see Hatcher (2012).

[5] For examples of such conjectures, one may consult the chapters on widows in Altekar ([1959] 1989, 135–95) and Kane (1962, 2:583–636). Although these authors' statements about the treatment and status of widows in classical India are largely accurate, their discussions of the topic are necessarily quite cursory, given the ambitious scope of their works, and, thus, fail to delineate important

Nevertheless, it would seem that premodern India provides us with a more than ample set of sources to answer these questions. These sources are the abundant and voluminous works of the pan-Indian tradition of classical Hindu law known as Dharmaśāstra—a tradition spanning more than two millennia of Indian history, from roughly the third century BCE to the eighteenth century CE, and addressing in detail virtually every aspect of social practice relevant to Brahmanical Hinduism. Hence, it is fair to say that, when read critically and historically, works of Dharmaśāstra provide a long and detailed record of the prevailing legal and social norms of high-caste Hindu society, including those pertaining to widows.

This book is an attempt to construct the first exhaustive history of widows under Hindu law, that is, a history of how widows are presented and treated in Dharmaśāstra sources. The reasons for writing such a history may not be obvious to readers and, therefore, warrant some explanation before proceeding. First, I will explain why widows in early India are or should be a topic of interest to scholars of South Asia, both modern and premodern. Then I will explain why Dharmaśāstra literature constitutes the best available lens for studying such women and constructing a large-scale history of them.

Although the most famous examples of legal debate concerning Hindu widows come from the colonial period, it is by no means the case that such debates begin in the colonial period. It is simply that ancient and medieval debates on widows in South Asia remain largely unknown, even to many classical Indologists. Despite the limited attention that they have received, however, debates concerned with various aspects of the legal status and treatment of widows abound in works of Dharmaśāstra, particularly in Dharmaśāstra commentaries. For instance, Dharmaśāstra literature attests to considerable controversy regarding the practice of *niyoga*, that is, the ancient Brahmanical version of levirate, whereby a man would beget a son for his sonless kinsman upon that kinsman's widow. It also contains record of a debate on the validity of sati as a customary practice—a debate with significant, but unnoticed echoes in the much more famous colonial debate on the same topic. Thus, it is clear that the Hindu widow was the subject of deep and multifaceted legal contention during precolonial periods as much as the colonial one.

shifts in Brahmanical opinion. Mitra (1881) provides probably the most extensive discussion of widows under Hindu law. However, his work is now badly outdated and misleading in places, such as when he (1881, 104) asserts that the practice of sati was certainly known during the Vedic period and distinctly referred to in certain Vedic passages.

The reason that widows aroused such controversy in premodern South Asia likely stems from orthodox Brahmanical culture's strong emphasis on the control—especially the sexual control—of the women within its communities (probably as a marker of high social standing[6]). Throughout Indian history, the institution of marriage constituted the primary means by which such control was exercised; and, among the various social roles that a woman might assume in premodern India, Brahmanical culture was clearly most comfortable with that of wife. Thus, one can discern rather obvious efforts made by authors within the Dharmaśāstra tradition to strengthen and extend the institution of marriage, for example, by denying the possibility of divorce and stressing the importance of marrying girls prior to their first menstruation.[7] However, the circumstances of real life in ancient India—no different than today—would have meant that women frequently outlived their husbands, especially since they would have generally been much younger than them.[8] Hence, one can rather safely assume that widowed women would have been common in classical India. In other words, there would have been at the time a class of adult women outside of the controlling bonds of marriage. And it is easy to see how these women would have been deeply and uniquely problematic from the perspective of orthodox Brahmanical men. For this reason, attention to the treatment of widows under Hindu law promises to provide crucial insights into dominant male views of women in classical India and, importantly, into how these views changed over time. In comparison with widows, wives and prepubescent girls—the only other types of women recognized as socially respectable—are unproblematic within Dharmaśāstra. Hence, the treatment of them in Dharmaśāstra texts is relatively consistent and uncontroversial. It is primarily only when confronted with the inescapable fact of sexually mature women within their communities who are outside of the controlling bonds of marriage—the fact of widows—that Brahmin jurists are faced with a serious problem. And how they choose to deal with this problem reveals a great deal about their underlying views of women.

[6] On this, see the concluding section of Chapter 1.

[7] On divorce in classical Hindu law, see Kane (1962, 2:619–23) and Lariviere (1991). For texts stressing the importance of marrying a girl prior to her first menstruation, see GDh 18.21–22, VaDh 17.70, and YDh 1.64. For a discussion of the appropriate age of marriage for girls in early India, see Jamison (1996, 237–40) and Kane (1962, 2:439–47).

[8] See, e.g., MDh 9.94: "A man thirty years in age should marry a charming girl twelve years in age" (*triṃśadvarṣo vahet kanyāṃ hṛdyāṃ dvādaśavārṣikīm |*).

Furthermore, Dharmaśāstra texts comprise a uniquely well-suited set of sources upon which to construct a large-scale history of widows in ancient and medieval South Asia. The reasons for this have already been alluded to. To begin with, works of Dharmaśāstra provide far more abundant and detailed evidence about the status and treatment of widows than any other set of classical Indian sources. They are also the products of a remarkably coherent, pan-Indian tradition of legal thought that remained unbroken, although it certainly evolved, over two millennia (c. 300 BCE–1800 CE). Consequently, a history of widows in Dharmaśāstra has the advantage of being simultaneously bounded by a discrete genre of Sanskrit texts and yet uniquely full in its detail, long in its duration, and broad in its geographic scope. Moreover, since traditional Dharmaśāstric notions and the interpretation of Dharmaśāstra texts played a central role in important colonial debates about Hindu widows, a detailed examination of classical Dharmaśāstra discussions of widows will provide useful context for understanding these debates.[9]

However, despite the unparalleled amount of information about widows in early India that Dharmaśāstra sources provide, a history of widows based upon them is necessarily limited in two crucial ways that must be explicitly acknowledged at the outset. The first limitation of such a history is that it will not be a history of Indian widows in general or even Hindu widows. Instead, it must be specifically a history of Brahmin widows and, to some extent, other high-caste widows whose families observed or aspired to observe Brahmanical norms. The reason for this limitation is simply that, with only a few late exceptions,[10] the Dharmaśāstra tradition shows remarkably little concern with how members of the lower castes conducted their private lives. Indeed, ordinarily the authors of Dharmaśāstra texts do not even intend for their rules concerning widows to apply to low-caste women. Thus, although

[9] A more thorough knowledge of Dharmaśāstra, for instance, would have improved Lata Mani's (1998) otherwise excellent analysis of the colonial debate on sati. In her work, for example, Mani (1998, 69–70) notes that Hindu elites in nineteenth-century Bengal held the Veda to be of greater authority than Smṛti, and Smṛti to be of greater authority than custom, but she is seemingly unaware that this very same position had long been established within Dharmaśāstra. As a result, she implausibly sees in this ranking of sources of authority the influence of specifically British colonial ideas. Moreover, had she known more about Dharmaśāstra, she would likely not have imagined traditional pundits to have a "lack of concern about textual contradictions" (37), but instead have been aware that the harmonizing of seemingly contradictory scriptures had for more than a thousand years been *the* major goal of Dharmaśāstra commentators. Beyond this, she may also have recognized that many specific details of the colonial debate on sati go back to much earlier Dharmaśāstra sources, such as the rule that Brahmin widows can only perform sati on the same funeral pyre as their husbands (Mani 1998, 19, 35)—a rule first proposed in the twelfth-century *Mitākṣara* as a way to harmonize certain scriptures (see Chapter 4).

[10] On these, see Vajpeyi (2010).

it would be interesting to know about the lives of such women in classical India, the available evidence sadly makes this effectively impossible.

The second limitation of a history of widows based upon Dharmaśāstra texts is that it will be a history of how elite men believed women should act and be treated, not a history of what women themselves believed or how they actually acted and were treated. The reason for this is the prescriptive nature of Dharmaśāstra literature, like all legal literature, combined with the fact that all known Dharmaśāstra authors were either Brahmin men or, much more rarely, Kṣatriya men. Thus, unfortunately, the marginality of women, the absence of their perspectives, and the lack of recognition of their agency, which Mani (1998, 1, 26–28, 31–32, etc.) rightly decries in the case of the colonial debate on sati, are all equally present in Dharmaśāstric treatments of widows. The extent to which people in premodern South Asia actually followed the dictates of Dharmaśāstra works and, thus, the extent to which we can reliably reconstruct historical social practice from them are matters of long and contentious debate among scholars of Hindu law. I will address these issues below. But there can be no doubt that, in general, Dharmaśāstra works express their authors' genuine opinions about how people—mainly high-caste people and especially Brahmins—should act. Hence, a history of widows under Hindu law is by nature more a history of elite male ideology than a history of social practice, although one might reasonably imagine that these two things bear at least some relation to one another.

Dharmaśāstra Literature

At this point, it is worth taking some space to give a general account of the Dharmaśāstra tradition and its literature so that nonspecialist readers will be better able to follow the subsequent chapters of this book. From an emic perspective, Dharmaśāstra is the *śāstra* or expert Brahmanical tradition that takes as its subject *dharma*, a term denoting in this context the rules of right conduct governing virtually all aspects of Brahmanical Hindu life. As such, Dharmaśāstra prescribes sets of specific normative rules for a massive and varied array of topics, including, among other things, statecraft (*rājadharma*), the adjudication of lawsuits (*vyavahāra*), pilgrimage (*tīrthayātrā*), life-cycle rites (*saṃskāra*), and world renunciation (*saṃnyāsa*). Moreover, this prodigious tradition spans over two millennia of Indian history from roughly the third century BCE to the eighteenth century CE; and during this time, important Dharmaśāstra works were composed in virtually all areas of the subcontinent. Thus, taken in its entirety, Dharmaśāstra literature is incredibly vast, surprisingly so to most nonspecialists. Broadly speaking, however, it can be divided into two periods: the period of the Smṛtis and the period of the commentaries. These are equivalent to a period of scriptural composition and a period of scriptural exegesis, respectively.

The period of the Smṛtis extends from approximately the third century BCE to the seventh century CE. It is so named, because during this time authors working within the Dharmaśāstra tradition composed works that came to be regarded as Smṛtis, that is, as sacred scriptures second in authority only to the earlier Vedas. It is noteworthy, however, that the early works of the Dharmaśāstra tradition are not the only works classified as Smṛtis. Important Smṛti texts of other literary genres include, for instance, the two great Sanskrit epics, the *Mahābhārata* and *Rāmāyaṇa*, and the various *Purāṇas*. The Dharmaśāstra tradition produced dozens of Smṛti works known from citations in later commentaries. However, only nine of these works survive in their entireties today as independent treatises. Of these, the earliest four are known as Dharmasūtras. They are ascribed to the authors Āpastamba, Gautama, Baudhāyana, and Vasiṣṭha. Today scholars generally consider them to have been composed in this order.[11] After the four Dharmasūtras come the so-called Dharmaśāstras (confusingly also the name for the genre as a whole). By all accounts the first of these is the *Mānava Dharmaśāstra*, also referred to as the *Manu Smṛti*. Ascribed to Manu, who is the first man and king in Hindu mythology, this watershed text is by all accounts the single most important and influential Dharmaśāstra work ever composed. Following the *Mānāva Dharmaśāstra* are, in roughly chronological order, the *Yājñavalkya Dharmaśāstra*, *Nārada Smṛti*, *Vaiṣṇava Dharmaśāstra*, and *Parāśara Smṛti*.[12]

The second great period of Dharmaśāstra, that of the commentaries, covers more or less the eighth to eighteenth centuries. Scholars often loosely refer to this period as "medieval." During this time, Dharmaśāstra authors composed primarily exegetical works that strive to create clear, comprehensive, and systematic accounts of the rules of right conduct (*dharma*) prescribed in the earlier Smṛtis. The harmonization of the various recognized scriptures is

[11] For the influential arguments regarding the relative and absolute dates of the Dharmasūtras, see Olivelle (2000, 4–10).

[12] On the dating of these texts, see Olivelle (2010, 42–52, 56–57). Alternative names for these four texts are the *Yājñavalkya Smṛti*, *Nārada Dharmaśāstra*, *Viṣṇu Smṛti*, *Viṣṇu Dharmasūtra*, and *Parāśara Dharmaśāstra*. The names used for them in this book are those used in the most reliable printed editions.

a major aim of many Dharmaśāstra works of this period. The earliest exegetical works of the Dharmaśāstra tradition are true commentaries. That is, they are texts organized around and dedicated to explaining a single root Smṛti, which they follow from beginning to end. The most important such texts are commentaries on either Manu or Yājñavalkya. Beginning around the twelfth century, however, a new genre of exegetical Dharmaśāstra work develops: the *nibandha* or legal digest. Works of this genre, unlike proper commentaries, do not focus on a single root Smṛti, but rather on a specific topic or set of topics falling within the broad rubric of *dharma*. They then gather together passages from assorted Smṛti texts on their chosen topic or set of topics, logically arrange these passages, and comment upon them as their authors see fit. For the purposes of this book, the distinction between a commentary and a *nibandha* or legal digest is just a formal one.

For ease of reference, following are what I deem to be the most likely dates of the major Dharmaśāstra works and authors cited and discussed in this book:

Āpastamba Dharmasūtra	300–200 BCE
Gautama Dharmasūtra	200–150 BCE
Baudhāyana Dharmasūtra	150–100 BCE
Vasiṣṭha Dharmasūtra	100 BCE–100 CE
Mānava Dharmaśāstra	100–200 CE
Yājñavalkya Dharmaśāstra	300–500 CE
Nārada Smṛti	400–600 CE
Vaiṣṇava Dharmaśāstra	600–700 CE
Parāśara Smṛti	600–800 CE
Bhāruci on Manu	600–650 CE
Tantravārttika of Kumārila Bhaṭṭa	560–620 CE
Viśvarūpa on Yājñavalkya	800–850 CE
Medhātithi on Manu	850–900 CE
Unpublished commentary on Yājñavalkya	900–1000 CE
Mitākṣarā of Vijñāneśvara on Yājñavalkya	1075–1125 CE
Dāyabhāga of Jīmūtavāhana	1075–1125 CE
Aparārka on Yājñavalkya	1125–1175 CE
Kṛtyakalpataru of Lakṣmīdhara	1110–1150 CE
Smṛtyarthasāra of Śrīdhara	1150–1200 CE
Smṛticandrikā of Devaṇa Bhaṭṭa	1175–1225 CE
Madanapārijāta of Madanapāla	1300–1400 CE

Parāśaramādhava of Mādhava on Parāśara	1300–1400 CE
Śuddhitattva of Raghunandana	1510–1580 CE
Nirṇayasindhu of Kamalākara Bhaṭṭa	1612 CE
Saṃskāra- & Śuddhimayūkhā of Nīlakaṇṭha	1610–1650 CE
Dharmasindhu of Kāśīnātha Upādhyāya	1790–1791 CE

References to scholarly discussions of the dates of these works and authors can be found within the chapters of this book, as can information about their geographical provenances.

Dharmaśāstra and Social Reality

Given the nature and sheer size of Dharmaśāstra sources, one might wonder about the precise relationship between these sources and the historical societies in which they were composed and preserved. And as I mentioned earlier, this question has, indeed, been the subject of long and intense debate among scholars of Hindu law. At stake is the fundamental usefulness of the vast Dharmaśāstra corpus for reconstructing the social history of premodern South Asia. On one extreme in this debate, there is the view that works of Dharmaśāstra accurately reflect the prevailing laws of the land at the time they were composed. According to this view, Dharmaśāstra literature paints a detailed and generally reliable picture of early Indian society. On the other extreme, there is the view that works of Dharmaśāstra are essentially just a scholastic or theological exercise or reflect simply the wishful thinking of a small minority of pious Brahmins. According to this view or set of related views, Dharmaśāstra literature bears little relation to actual social practices in early India.

If one wishes to understand the current state of the scholarly debate on the relationship between Dharmaśāstra and social practice, the best place to begin is with an influential essay by Richard Lariviere (1997). There Lariviere (1997, 98) takes the bold position that "*dharmaśāstra* literature represents a peculiarly Indian record of local social norms and traditional standards of behavior. It represents in very definite terms the law of the land." This position of Lariviere, which departs radically from that once taken by his influential teacher Ludo Rocher,[13] has been enthusiastically endorsed by Albrecht Wezler (2004). In the introduction to his critical edition of the *Mānava*

[13] See L. Rocher (2012, 52–57, 103–17) for his views on the relationship between Dharmaśāstra and law on the ground in early India.

Dharmaśāstra, Patrick Olivelle (2005, 62), undoubtedly the most important living scholar of Dharmaśāstra, also expresses general support for Lariviere's thesis, although he places greater stress on the scholastic or theoretical nature of Dharmaśāstra, arguing that it "represents an expert tradition and, therefore, presents not a 'record' of custom but a jurisprudential, or in Indian terms, a śāstric *reflection* on custom." More recently, Donald Davis (2012, 18–21) has similarly defended Rocher's emphasis on the deeply and fundamentally scholastic nature of Dharmaśāstra, while acknowledging the value of Lariviere's thesis.

My personal position on this matter is fairly close to those articulated by Olivelle and Davis. Specifically, I believe that Dharmaśāstra must be understood, first and foremost, as a specialized tradition of legal scholasticism rather than as a tradition of practical or applied law or as a record of custom. My reason for this is that such a view best accounts for an especially salient feature of Dharmaśāstra literature that is central to Rocher's (2012, 53–54) understanding of it: the remarkable degree to which this literature restricts itself to discussing pre-established themes in pre-established ways with pre-established terms and lists. Thus, for instance, once Āpastamba (1.17.37) in the third century BCE introduces the theme of exceptional "five-nailed animals" (*pañcanakhāḥ*) that are permissible to eat, most later Dharmaśāstra authors also take up this exact theme, although sometimes writing more than a millennium later.[14] Moreover, the list of permissible "five-nailed animals" is incredibly consistent throughout Dharmaśāstra literature: rabbit, hedgehog, porcupine, monitor lizard, tortoise, and rhinoceros.[15] Such remarkable thematic consistency over so many centuries is unlikely to be a reflection of dietary consistency, especially given that orthodox Brahmins today uniformly eschew the eating of any five-nailed animals. Instead, it is in all likelihood simply a reflection of the deeply conservative nature of the Dharmaśāstra tradition. Once a Smṛti text introduces a particular theme into the tradition and, thus, imbues it with scriptural authority, later authors feel a strong compulsion to include that same theme in their works, regardless of whether it has any practical bearing on their lives. And this literary practice accounts for much of the contents of Dharmaśāstra works.

[14] See GDh 17.27, BDh 1.12.5, VaDh 14.39, MDh 5.18, YDh 1.176, ViDh 51.6, Viśvarūpa (on YDh 1.176), and Medhātithi (on MDh 5.18).

[15] For an insightful analysis of this puzzling list, which includes the three-toed rhinoceros, see Jamison (1998).

However, this practice can by no means account for all of the contents of Dharmaśāstra works. And in these other contents one can often discern the influence of forces external to the Dharmaśāstra tradition itself, sometimes specifically the influence of contemporaneous social practice. In my experience, there are principally four situations in which one might reasonably attribute the content of a Dharmaśāstra work to a contemporaneous custom. The first of these is when a text introduces an entirely new theme without precedent in the earlier literature. For example, when Viṣṇu (25.14) first prescribes the practice of sati in perhaps the seventh century, it is reasonable to interpret this as a reflection of contemporaneous custom. The second situation is when a text radically departs from the preceding literature in its treatment of an established topic. Thus, for instance, when Yājñavalkya (2.139–40) lists the wife of a sonless man as the primary heir to his entire estate and in this directly contradicts all earlier authors, a change in custom or at least the views of a significant segment of Brahmanical society is likely responsible. The third situation where contemporaneous custom plausibly accounts for the contents of a Dharmaśāstra work is when the treatment of a topic is unusually long, such as when Manu (5.157–62) dedicates six consecutive verses to saying nothing more than that widows should remain celibate. In such cases it would seem that something more than academic is at stake and that the text reflects a heated controversy about proper behavior within at least segments of contemporaneous society. The fourth situation where a Dharmaśāstra text likely reflects contemporaneous social practice applies only to exegetical works. It is when a commentary or digest engages in an especially tortured interpretation of the accepted scriptures, such as when Viśvarūpa (on YDh 1.69) interprets all of the Smṛtis that enjoin *niyoga* (levirate) as applying only to Śūdra or low-caste women. Such tortured interpretations would again seem to be more than academic and to reveal cases where Brahmanical society at the time of a particular commentator differs from that at the time of the Smṛtis. Of course, these four basic situations that I have given, where one can see the influence of custom upon Dharmaśāstra, are nothing more than generalizations. One must critically read each Dharmaśāstra passage on its own, bearing in mind both the deeply scholastic nature of the literature and the genuine belief of its various authors in the rightness of Dharmaśāstra rules. When this is done, I believe it is possible to construct a generally reliable and detailed history of Brahmanical norms and customs on the basis of Dharmaśāstra sources.

Before moving on, it is also worth briefly addressing a related issue, namely, the possible influence of Dharmaśāstra on social practice, as opposed to the influence of social practice upon Dharmaśāstra, which has just been discussed. Here the leading theory remains that of Sanskritization, which was first proposed over sixty years ago by the anthropologist M. N. Srinivas.[16] The theory of Sanskritization holds that one way in which communities in South Asia attempt to increase their social standing is by adopting attitudes and behaviors that more closely conform to the great pan-Indian tradition of Sanskrit literature, including importantly Dharmaśāstra. However, the extent to which Sanskritization existed in premodern India is quite uncertain due to the dearth of confirming or disconfirming evidence. Nevertheless, it perhaps bears mentioning that, in a recent article (Brick 2021, 50–52), I have identified an unambiguous case where an argument developed in one particular work of Dharmaśāstra, the *Smṛticandrikā*, directly influenced the practice of cross-cousin marriage in fifteenth-century South India, albeit only slightly. Moreover, the recent work of Timothy Lubin (2015) has shown how the Dharmaśāstra tradition influenced local charters of statutes and other legal documents in South and Southeast Asia; and Donald Davis, Jr. (2004) has similarly shed light on the complex interaction between Dharmaśāstra and customary law in medieval Kerala. Together this work shows that Dharmaśāstra likely had at least some impact on some people's actual behavior in premodern South Asia.

Structure of the Book

There are four general areas where Dharmaśāstra literature talks specifically and in substantial detail about widows. First, there is widow remarriage and the related issue of *niyoga*, which is the ancient Brahmanical version of levirate. Second, there is a widow's right to inherit property. Third, there are the rules governing the general lifestyle of a widow, which we may collectively refer to as "widow asceticism." And, finally, there is the issue of sati, or widow self-immolation. Each of these issues was a topic of sustained and heated discussion within the Dharmaśāstra tradition during certain historical periods, and no widow-related issue other than these ever was, with the

[16] For the original formulation of this theory and the coinage of the term for it, see Srinivas ([1952] 1965, 1956).

partial exception of a widow's right to adopt sons, which I will touch upon below. An analysis of these four issues in Dharmaśāstra is, therefore, tantamount to a complete analysis of the widow under classical Hindu law. As a result, one chapter of this book has been dedicated to examining each of these issues. Thus, the book has four chapters.

Each of the book's chapters will begin by examining the earliest Dharmaśāstra texts that address the widow-related issue on which it focuses. In most cases, these will be among the earliest texts of the Dharmaśāstra tradition, but in the case of sati, they will be markedly later works. The chapter will then proceed chronologically forward and trace historical shifts in the thinking of Hindu jurists and, by implication, Brahmanical society at large. Each chapter will end with an examination of the most recent Dharmaśāstra texts that show significant intellectual or ritual developments on the topic that is its focus. Given this approach and the nature of the primary sources involved, the book will abound in lengthy citations and technical discussions of particular Dharmaśāstra works. Without these, it would surely be a much shorter and more easily accessible book, but also one that fails to convey the complex inner workings of classical Hindu law.

None of the widow-related issues that was a topic of heated discussion within Dharmaśāstra was a topic of such discussion throughout anything approaching the tradition's entire history. Instead, each of these issues was a hot topic for only a limited period of time, albeit a period of centuries, before becoming essentially a settled matter. The order of the chapters in this book is a reflection of this fact. That is, the first chapter deals with the first widow-related issue to become the subject of heated discussion within Dharmaśāstra, the second with the next one, and so on. As a result, the first chapter of the book deals with widow remarriage and the related issue of *niyoga*; the second with a widow's right to inherit; the third with widow asceticism; and the fourth with sati. Following this, there is a short conclusion, where I summarize and attempt to synthesize the salient findings of the book's four main chapters.

To the main body of the book I have also added a single appendix, where I analyze a fifth widow-related issue that was the topic of some discussion within classical Hindu law, namely, a widow's right to adopt a son. There are several reasons that I have relegated treatment of this issue to an appendix and not made it into an additional chapter of its own. The most important of these is that a widow's right to adopt is discussed in far fewer Dharmaśāstra texts and, even there, in more cursory fashion than any of the four widow-related issues that are the subjects of separate chapters of this book. Thus, a chapter on widows' rights of adoption would be a conspicuously short one—far shorter than any of the four extant chapters. Moreover, treatment of the issue in Dharmaśāstra sources is a fairly late phenomenon, apparently arising no earlier than the fifteenth century, although it became a major topic of litigation in colonial Hindu law.[17] Therefore, if a widow's right to adopt were to be the subject of its own chapter, it would have to be the fifth and final chapter of this book and, as a result, give the work a rather anticlimactic conclusion.

Finally, it is worth explaining how the contents of this book differ from my previous shorter publications on widows under Hindu law. None of my previously published writings concern widow remarriage, levirate, or a widow's right to inherit. Therefore, everything in Chapters 1 and 2 is new material. I have, however, published an article and a book chapter on sati (Brick 2010, 2018) and an article on widow asceticism (Brick 2014). All of the materials dealt with and the ideas proposed in these shorter publications can be found in Chapters 3 and 4 of this book, albeit presented in somewhat different fashion. However, a significant amount of material in both of these chapters is new. In Chapter 3, most of the new material concerns evidence for a previously unrecognized type of Brahmanical widow ascetic—evidence that comes from outside of the Dharmaśāstra tradition, but allows one to better contextualize the treatment of widow asceticism within Dharmaśāstra sources. In Chapter 4, I have incorporated a somewhat broader range of textual sources on sati than in my previous writings. Specifically, I discuss the following in detail: an early unpublished commentary on the *Yājñavalkya Dharmaśāstra*; sections of Dharmaśāstra texts prescribing the ritual performance of sati; and juridical attempts to explain how the special otherworldly benefits of sati do not violate the accepted laws of *karma*. Furthermore, I have been able to connect the changing views on sati and widow asceticism within the Dharmaśāstra tradition to changing views on inheritance—something that I have not done and, indeed, was unable to do in my previous writings.

[17] On this, see note 1 in the Appendix.

1
Widow Remarriage and *Niyoga*

This chapter deals with two conceptually distinct, yet related legal issues concerning widows. The first of these is widow remarriage; the second is *niyoga*, which is the Sanskrit term for the specific version of levirate practiced in classical India. The common noun *niyoga* in Sanskrit has the general meaning of "appointment" and can be used in a wide array of contexts. However, in the technical usage of the term that concerns us here, it denotes specifically the appointment of a man to beget a child upon a woman, who is typically the wife of his deceased brother. As such, *niyoga* is a euphemistic word for a historical practice easily recognizable as a form of levirate—the modern anthropological term used to designate a set of diverse cultural practices found in many parts of the world, all centered on the sexual union of a woman and her deceased husband's male kinsman, typically his brother.[1] The reason that these two distinct issues jointly comprise the focus of a single chapter of this book is that, despite the concerted effort of the Hindu legal tradition to dissociate them, they are in fact rather closely related. Indeed, as I will argue, the strong and discernible effort on the part of many Brahmanical jurists to dissociate *niyoga* from widow remarriage suggests that, in the minds of many ancient Indians, the former practice was apt to be taken as a particular instantiation of the latter. The reason that these two issues comprise the focus of the first chapter of this book is that *niyoga* in particular is the first widow-related issue to become the subject of considerable debate within Dharmaśāstra and, thus, the first such issue where we can see a major shift in Brahmanical opinion over time. By contrast, the Dharmaśāstra tradition widely opposes the practice of widow remarriage from its inception until at least the major Hindu reforms of the nineteenth century; and those classical authors that support widow remarriage always constitute a small minority.

[1] On the definition of levirate and the diversity of practices classified as levirate, see Weisberg (2009, 1–22).

Widows Under Hindu Law. David Brick, Oxford University Press. © Oxford University Press 2023.
DOI: 10.1093/oso/9780197664544.003.0002

Before examining how Dharmaśāstra sources treat the issues of *niyoga* and widow remarriage, however, it is worth taking a little space to discuss the general views on these issues discernible in Vedic sources, for the authors of our early Dharmaśāstra works were undoubtedly Brahmins steeped in the Vedas, who felt a profound personal commitment to them as foundational scriptures and to their attendant religious culture. Indeed, although the advent of Dharmaśāstra is likely not a natural, organic outgrowth of the preceding Vedic tradition as past generations of scholars tended to believe,[2] Dharmaśāstra literature still is, in many substantive ways, deeply indebted to the Vedas. Consequently, it is reasonable to assume that Vedic opinions on widow remarriage and levirate would have influenced early Dharmaśāstric opinions on these same issues—an assumption that the available evidence broadly confirms.

The *Ṛgveda*, our earliest surviving Indian text, contains a line of verse that several later Dharmaśāstra commentators cite as providing tacit support for the legitimacy of *niyoga*. This line comes from a hymn addressed to the Aśvins, twin Vedic deities associated with miraculous cures and rescues. The specific line in question (ṚV 10.40.2cd) reads:

> Who invites you into his home, like a widow her husband's brother into her bed, like a young lady a man?
>
> *kó vāṃ śayutrā́ vidhávevа devā́raṃ máryaṃ ná yóṣā kṛṇute sadhástha ā́ ||*

Here, amid various queries about the Aśvins' wanderings, the poet asks who it is that invites them to his home, presumably with the intention of making a ritual offering to them; and, significantly, he compares this act of inviting the Aśvins to a widow inviting her husband's brother into her bed. Thus, this incidental remark provides evidence that, in early Vedic times, some variety of levirate was customarily practiced, for it makes a seemingly positive allusion to the typical practice of sexual union between a woman and her deceased husband's brother. Moreover, there appears to be nothing in subsequent Vedic literature to indicate that later Vedic society adopted a more negative view of levirate than early Vedic society. Beyond this, a few Vedic passages even suggest a more accepting attitude toward widow remarriage in general—as opposed strictly to levirate—than one typically encounters in

[2] On this, see Olivelle (2005; 2019, 15–20).

post-Vedic Brahmanical society.[3] These facts will provide useful context for understanding the views regarding widow remarriage and *niyoga* expressed in our earliest Dharmaśāstra works—the four Dharmasūtras ascribed to Āpastamba, Gautama, Baudhāyana, and Vasiṣṭha.

The Dharmasūtras

In his views and treatment of *niyoga* and widow remarriage, Āpastamba differs markedly from the authors of the three other Dharmasūtras, who are in broad agreement with one another on these issues. In other words, Āpastamba represents something of an outlier on these topics. Consequently, although he is the author of probably the very earliest surviving Dharmaśāstra work, I will set him aside for the moment and instead first examine the views on *niyoga* and widow remarriage of the slightly later authors Gautama, Baudhāyana, and Vasiṣṭha, who collectively seem to represent the mainstream of early Dharmaśāstra thought on these matters. Since these authors all discuss *niyoga* in greater detail and with greater clarity than they do widow remarriage, I will discuss their views on that topic first.

Gautama, Baudhāyana, and Vasiṣṭha all generally permit *niyoga* for widows, which is unsurprising, given that the preceding Vedic literature seems to similarly approve of the practice. The passages of these authors' works that prescribe *niyoga* read as follows:

> A widow may seek to obtain a child from her husband's brother, provided her elders command it. She should not go to him outside of her fertile season. She may instead seek to obtain a child from another man related to her husband through ancestral offerings, patrilineal clan, or a common ancestral seer or from someone simply related to her husband by birth. According to some, it cannot be anyone other than her husband's brother. She should not obtain more than a second child in this way.
>
> *apatir apatyalipsur devarāt* | *guruprasūtā nartum atīyāt* | *piṇḍagotrarṣisaṃbandhebhyo yonimātrād vā* | *nādevarād ity eke* | *nātidvitīyam* | (GDh 18.4–8)

[3] See, e.g., AV 9.5.27–28. For a discussion of this and other Vedic passages pertaining to widow remarriage, see Kane (1962, 2:614–19).

> After this (= period of mourning), a sonless widow may, with her elders' permission, conceive a child through her husband's brother. Now, they also quote:
>
> > One should not appoint to beget a son a woman who is barren, who has already given birth to a son, who has gone through menopause, whose children have died, or who is unwilling—the sort of woman in whom the effort will not bear fruit.
>
> *ata ūrdhvaṃ gurubhir anumatā devarāj janayet putram aputrā | athāpy udāharanti—*
>
> > *vaśā cotpannaputrā ca nīrajaskā gataprajā |*
> > *nākāmā saṃniyojyā syāt phalaṃ yasyāṃ na vidyata iti* || (BDh 2.4.9–10)
>
> After six months (= period of mourning), a woman should bathe and make a funerary offering to her deceased husband. Then his father or brother should assemble the elders, who taught and performed rites for him, and his blood-relatives and have them issue the appointment (*niyoga*). One should not appoint a widow who is insane, barren, or sick as well as one who is too old, meaning sixteen years past puberty. Nor should one appoint a man if he is sickly. At Prajāpati's hour (= shortly before dawn), the man should approach the woman like a husband, but without laughter or verbal or physical roughness.
>
> *ūrdhvaṃ ṣaḍbhyo māsebhyaḥ snātvā śrāddhaṃ ca patye dattvā vidyākarmaguruyonisaṃbandhān saṃnipātya pitā bhrātā vā niyogaṃ kārayet | na sonmādām avaśāṃ vyādhitāṃ vā niyuñjyāt | jyāyasīm api | ṣoḍaśa varṣāṇi | na ced āmayāvī syād | prājāpatye muhūrte pāṇigrāhavad upacared anyatra saṃprahāsyavākpāruṣyadaṇḍapāruṣyāt* | (VaDh 17.56–61)

From these passages, we learn an array of important details about the practice of *niyoga* in the early Dharmaśāstra tradition.

To begin with, we gain a fairly detailed picture of the sort of woman who is supposed to engage in *niyoga*. Obviously, she is a widow, but she must also be sonless, according to Baudhāyana (2.4.9), or at least have no more than one child, according to Gautama (18.8).[4] Furthermore, it must be reasonably safe to assume that she will be capable of bearing and caring for a child.

[4] Vasiṣṭha oddly makes no mention of any such restriction. However, the fact that he clearly understands *niyoga* to be solely for the purpose of procreation suggests that he assumes one.

Thus, the woman cannot be barren, sickly, too old, or mentally ill. In addition to being of sound mind, she must also want to engage in *niyoga* (BDh 2.9.10). Indeed, Gautama and Baudhāyana present *niyoga* as something brought about essentially at the behest of widows rather than an unwanted sexual union foisted upon them, although they both explicitly require the permission of her elders—likely specifically elder members of her husband's family—for *niyoga* to be lawful. Vasiṣṭha, by contrast, seems to hold the deceased husband's father or brother responsible for initiating *niyoga*[5] and does not explicitly require that the widow be a willing participant, although he may well have assumed as much.

As for the levir, that is, the man charged with fathering a child upon the widow, he is in all cases a relative of the deceased. Baudhāyana assigns this task specifically to the woman's husband's brother (*devara*) and mentions no other possible appointees, whereas Gautama regards the husband's brother as the ideal appointee, but states that, at least according to some authorities, a more distant male relative can fill this role instead.[6] None of the Dharmasūtras indicates any basis for choosing between a man's brothers if he had more than one, although some later texts (e.g., AŚ 3.4.38–39) address this issue, as we will see. Vasiṣṭha differs somewhat from Gautama and Baudhāyana in that he does not specify whom a man's relatives should appoint as levir, only that he should not be sickly or diseased. However, judging from other early Dharmaśāstra works, it is fairly safe to assume that the levir would have been a relative of the deceased man and typically his brother.

Let us turn now to the nature of the union between the widow and the levir under *niyoga*. Does their union comprise a form of marriage, or is it merely a sexual union with the goal of producing a child, ideally a son, for a woman with one or no children or at least no sons? A number of explicit

[5] However, if one accepts the grammatically more plausible, but less well-attested variant *pitrā bhrātrā vā* for *pitā bhrātā vā*, the widow initiates *niyoga* in Vasiṣṭha as well, for VaDh 17.56 would then mean: "After six months, a woman should bathe; make a funerary offering to her deceased husband; assemble the elders who taught him and performed rites for him and his blood-relatives; and have his father or brother make the appointment."

[6] Technically, these relatives comprise, in order of closeness, a man's *sapiṇḍas*, *sagotras*, *samānapravaras*, and other generic blood relatives. A *sapiṇḍa* is literally a person with whom one has *piṇḍas* or ancestral offerings in common. Generally speaking, a person's *sapiṇḍas* are those descended from his great-grandfather purely patrilineally. For a detailed discussion of this important Brahmanical kinship term, see Kane (1962, 2:452–78) and especially Trautmann (1981, 246–71). A *sagotra* is a person who belongs to one's *gotra* or Brahmanical clan, each of which ostensibly originates from a particular ancient Vedic seer. Membership in a *gotra* is passed down indefinitely through patrilineal descent. A person is one's *samānapravara* if the set of more distant Vedic seers from which he claims descent, technically called a *pravara*, contains some of the same seers as one's own *pravara*. For a detailed discussion of *gotra* and *pravara*, see Kane (1962, 2:479–99).

textual statements in the Dharmasūtras make clear that it must be the latter. Such statements include Gautama's prohibition against sexual intercourse between a widow and her husband's kinsman outside of her fertile season (18.5)[7]; his strict limit on the number of children conceived through *niyoga* (18.8); Baudhāyana's prohibition against appointing a woman who is barren, past menopause, or sickly (2.4.10); and Vasiṣṭha's similar set of prohibitions (17.57–59). Particularly revealing in this regard is Vasiṣṭha's statement (17.61) that sexual intercourse between the widow and the male appointee must take place at a specific sacred hour of the day and be free from the playful laughter, bites, scratches, dirty talk, and the like that frequently accompany sex. For it reveals a juridical attempt to stress the solemn, somber nature of *niyoga* and to dispel any suspicions that those who participate in the practice do so simply out of sexual lust.

Thus, given that the aim of *niyoga* is to provide a childless widow with a son, it is easy to understand the practice as a means of mitigating the serious financial and social precariousness that such women would have faced in classical Brahmanical society. The financial precariousness of a childless widow in early India would have stemmed from the combination of essentially three features of traditional Brahmanical society. The first of these is that widow remarriage was generally condemned. The second is that, at least during the period of the Dharmasūtras, inheritance was restricted almost entirely to male members of a person's patriline. Thus, as I will discuss in detail in the next chapter, widows had little or no right to inherit their husbands' estates. The third feature of classical Brahmanical society that would have contributed to the financial precariousness of childless widows is that, as in most traditional societies, women were effectively barred from all but a few income-generating activities; and these few occupations open to women either were deemed disgraceful (e.g., prostitute) or earned only meager wages (e.g., yarn spinner). Thus, a childless widow in Brahmanical society would have been almost entirely dependent upon her male relatives to support her; and these relatives might often have resented this, especially when she would have contributed nothing to the family either financially or through the addition of new male members. If modern ethnographies are any guide, this

[7] Precisely what constitutes a woman's "fertile season" (*ṛtu*) is the topic of several verses in important later Dharmaśāstras (MDh 3.46–47, YDh 1.78) and some scholarly disagreement. For a discussion of this issue, see Olivelle (2005, 257). In GDh 18.5, it is likely that the term *ṛtu* refers to a period of sixteen days starting from the onset of menstruation and that, even during this period, sexual intercourse was prohibited on numerous days, including especially the days of menstruation itself.

would perhaps have been especially true of a woman's affines, with whom a strong personal and emotional connection would often have taken many years to develop.[8] Consequently, one can plausibly view the institution of *niyoga* as a sort of lifeline for childless widows faced with the prospects of destitution and social ostracism and understand why Dharmaśāstra texts present it as an option that widows would actively pursue.

The fact that Gautama, Baudhāyana, and Vasiṣṭha all hold a son begotten through *niyoga* to be a legitimate heir to a man's property and rank him quite high among the various types of sons that a man might have further supports the position that *niyoga* would have been an attractive option to many widows. Specifically, both Gautama (28.32) and Vasiṣṭha (17.14) list a son fathered upon a woman through *niyoga* among a man's heirs, second in rank only to a son that the man himself fathered upon his lawfully wedded wife; and Baudhāyana (2.3.31) differs only slightly from these authors in that he lists the son begotten through *niyoga* third rather than second.[9] Hence, these three Dharmasūtras present *niyoga* not only as a legitimate means for a childless widow to acquire offspring but also as a means to provide a man with a legitimate son and heir.

Of course, this then raises an important question to ask of all leviratic practices, including *niyoga*: to whom does the resulting child legally belong, the widow's dead husband or the levir? If a boy begotten through *niyoga* is a legitimate son and heir, it is still necessary to determine whether he is the legitimate son and heir of his mother's deceased husband or his biological father. Dharmaśāstra literature often addresses this question through the metaphor of a crop grown in a field. It frames the legal issue of the ownership of a child conceived through *niyoga* as a question of whether a crop belongs to the man who owned the seed from which it grew or the man who owns the field in which it grew. If a crop belongs to the owner of the seed, a child conceived through *niyoga* belongs to its biological father, the levir. If instead it belongs to the owner of the field, the child belongs to the widow's husband. This metaphor of a crop grown in a field is implicit in the very term used throughout Dharmaśāstra literature to designate a son begotten through *niyoga*, which is *kṣetraja*, meaning literally "one born of a field."

[8] See, e.g., Lamb (2000, 71–74).

[9] Like Gautama (28.32) and Vasiṣṭha (17.13), Baudhyāyana (2.3.31) lists first an *aurasa* son (i.e., a son begotten by a man upon his lawfully wedded wife). However, before listing a *kṣetraja* son (i.e., the son begotten through *niyoga*), he lists a *putrikāputra* (i.e., the son of a daughter appointed as legal son). Metrical exigencies might partially account for the order of Baudhāyana's list. For a discussion of the various types of sons recognized in Dharmaśāstra, see Kane (1962, 2:643–61).

Different Dharmaśāstra texts offer different answers to this crucial question of whether a boy is legally the son of his mother's husband or his biological father. Vasiṣṭha (17.63–64), for instance, states the following:

> They say that a son born of a woman who was not appointed belongs to the man who fathered him. But if she was appointed, he belongs to both men involved in the appointment.
>
> *aniyuktāyām utpanna utpādayituḥ putro bhavatīty āhuḥ | syāc cen niyoginoḥ |*

Thus, for Vasiṣṭha a son conceived through lawful *niyoga* belongs to both his biological father and his mother's husband.[10] Baudhāyana (2.3.18), for his part, fundamentally agrees with Vasiṣṭha, stating that a *kṣetraja* son has two fathers, belongs to two *gotras* (patrilineal clans), and offers ancestral offerings to and receives inheritance from both the man who fathered him and his mother's husband.

Gautama's discussion of paternity (18.9–14), however, is more cryptic:

> A child belongs to the man who fathered it, except when there is an agreement or it is begotten on the appointed wife of a living man. If it is begotten by a stranger, it belongs to him; or else to both of them. However, if the woman's husband takes care of the child, it belongs to him alone.
>
> *janayitur apatyam | samayād anyatra | jīvataś ca kṣetre | parasmāt tasya | dvayor vā | rakṣaṇāt tu bhartur eva |*

Here Gautama begins by stating that a child belongs to its biological father, but he makes two exceptions to this rule. The first of these is in the event of some sort of agreement. The second is if the child is fathered upon the *kṣetra* ("appointed wife") of a living man.

The decision to use the word *kṣetra*, which ordinarily means "field," to denote a man's wife in this passage is quite telling, for it undoubtedly alludes to the standard metaphor of a crop grown in a field used in Dharmaśāstric discussions of the paternity of a child begotten through *niyoga*, the *kṣetraja*

[10] Earlier in his text, however, Vasiṣṭha (17.6–11) addresses this issue but does not seem to take a personal position.

son. Thus, referring to a man's wife as a *kṣetra* strongly implies the context of *niyoga*. And the fact that Gautama prescribes *niyoga* immediately before the passage under discussion confirms this context. Hence, we incidentally learn from Gautama's second exception an unusual feature of *niyoga* that sets it apart from most other forms of levirate practiced throughout the world: the woman involved did not have to be a widow. Instead, she could be a married woman, whose husband was unable to father children himself due to impotency or disease. This is made clear, for instance, by Baudhāyana, who explicitly defines a *kṣetraja* son as "the son of a dead man or an impotent or diseased man that another man, after receiving permission, begets upon his wife."[11] Thus, Gautama's second exception to his general rule that a child belongs to its biological father comprises cases of *niyoga* where the woman involved is not a widow. In such cases, according to Gautama, the resulting child belongs to the woman's husband. And this only makes sense, for why would a man permit his brother to have sex with his wife, if it wasn't a viable means for him to acquire a lawful son and heir?

Moreover, if Gautama's second exception is *niyoga* involving a nonwidow, it would make sense if his first exception comprises cases of *niyoga* involving a widow. In other words, it is reasonable to understand the *samaya* ("agreement") that Gautama refers to as *niyoga*, which is precisely how his extant commentators do.[12] The reason why Gautama uses the generic term *samaya* instead of the more standard *niyoga* may be that, in his day, the technical usage of the term to denote levirate had not yet developed.[13] In any case, it is fairly clear that, in Gautama's opinion, the father of a child begotten through *niyoga* is its mother's husband. It is unclear, however, whether he considers such a child's biological father to be a second legal father, as do Baudhāyana and Vasiṣṭha.

Beyond this, in the above passage Gautama addresses the issue of a woman who conceives a child with a man from outside of her husband's family. Such a child, he holds, belongs only to its biological father or else to both its

[11] BDh 2.3.17: *mṛtasya prasūto yaḥ klībavyādhitayor vānyenānumatena sve kṣetre sa kṣetrajaḥ* |

[12] According to Maskarin, "the agreement takes the form: you get sexual pleasure, I get the kid" (*tava ratir mamāpatyam iti evaṃrūpaḥ samayaḥ*), while Haradatta explains the situation as follow: "if relatives appoint a man after making the agreement that the child will belong to the woman's husband" (*yadi jñatayaḥ samayaṃ kṛtvā niyuñjate kṣetriṇo 'patyam astv iti*).

[13] Within the context of levirate, the term *niyoga* appears to be first used by Vasiṣṭha (17.56, 64–65). However, a participial form of *ni* + √*yuj* ("to appoint") with the additional preverb *sam* is used slightly earlier in this context by Baudhāyana (2.4.10).

biological father and its mother's husband. However, if the woman's husband looks after it, then it belongs to him alone.

In light of what we have seen about the paternity of children begotten through *niyoga* according to Gautama, Baudhāyana, and Vasiṣṭha, it is worth considering what the two men most associated with the practice—the levir and the woman's husband—might have gotten out of it. Sexual pleasure, of course, is a plausible motive for the levir, although Vasiṣṭha along with several later authors attempts to rule this out. A feeling of obligation to obey one's elders and to help a sonless brother or sister-in-law might also have motivated levirs. In addition, at least according to Baudhāyana and Vasiṣṭha, through *niyoga* a levir has the potential to acquire a son, albeit one that he must share with his deceased kinsman. Hence, the increased social standing and greater financial security in old age that came with sons in premodern India would have provided strong motivations for a levir as well as for the woman's husband, if he was alive at the time of *niyoga*.

It is noteworthy, however, that while Dharmaśāstra literature frequently stresses the importance of sons to a man, it generally attributes this importance not to the worldly benefits of social status and financial security, but rather to otherworldly, religious benefits.[14] Thus, for example, Vasiṣṭha (17.2) cites a passage from a Vedic text, the *Aitareya Brāhmaṇa* (33.1), which states:

> If a father sees the face of his son born and living, he pays off a debt and attains immortality in him.
>
> *ṛṇam asmin saṃnayati amṛtatvaṃ ca gacchati |*
> *pitā putrasya jātasya paśyec cej jīvato mukham ||*

This verse alludes to two major Vedic beliefs concerning the importance of sons. The first of these is that a man is born with an innate debt to his ancestors which he must pay off through fathering sons.[15] The second is that a man is reborn in his son and, thereby, attains immortality. Hence, an important current in early Brahmanical thought held that sons are essential for a man's prosperity in the hereafter. And it is all but certain that this widely

[14] See Kane (1962, 3:641–43).
[15] On the early history of this concept, see Jamison (2014).

attested line of thinking would have provided another powerful incentive for the practice of *niyoga*—one that Brahmanical jurists, deeply concerned as they were with soteriology, would have found especially important.

Although Gautama, Baudhāyana, and Vasiṣṭha all lay down a number of rules governing the practice of *niyoga*, these rules do not appear to be so restrictive that they would render the lawful practice of *niyoga* especially rare or difficult.[16] Furthermore, none of these authors addresses any possible objections to *niyoga* or expresses any personal misgivings about the practice. The only possible exception to this is the following statement of Vasiṣṭha (17.65–66):

> There is no *niyoga* out of greed for inheritance. According to some, however, one might appoint a woman after assigning her a penance.
>
> *rikthalobhān nāsti niyogaḥ | prāyaścittaṃ vāpy upadiśya niyuñjyād ity eke |*

It seems, however, that Vasiṣṭha's intent here is not to discourage *niyoga*, but merely to rule out the financial security that a woman gains by having a son as a motive for *niyoga*, just as he elsewhere (VaDh 17.61) attempts to rule out sexual lust as a motive for the practice. Hence, Gautama, Baudhāyana, and Vasiṣṭha all clearly regard *niyoga* as an unproblematic means for a sonless woman, a dead man, and even a living man incapable of fathering children to acquire a lawful son.

Having examined how these authors treat *niyoga*, it is now necessary to consider how they view widow remarriage. It is noteworthy that none of these authors' works contains anything like a straightforward prohibition against widows remarrying. Nevertheless, passages in all of their works strongly suggest that they understood the practice to be generally prohibited. For instance, there are the following passages of Baudhāyana and Vasiṣṭha that allow widows to remarry under quite restricted conditions:

> If a girl's husband dies after she has been given away or after the nuptial offering has been made and she returns home after going away, provided that

[16] In this regard, I disagree with Kane's view (1962, 2:601–2) that "the practice of niyoga was hedged round with so many restrictions that it must not have been very much prevalent and instances must have been rather rare."

she is a virgin, she can undergo the rite of marriage again following the procedure for a remarried woman.

nisṛṣṭāyāṃ hute vāpi yasyai bhartā mriyeta saḥ |
sā ced akṣatayoniḥ syād gatapratyāgatā satī |
paunarbhavena vidhinā punaḥ saṃskāram arhati || (BDh 4.1.16)

If a young girl has been given with words and the pouring of water, but her fiancée dies beforehand and she was never married with the recitation of mantras, then she belongs only to her father.[17] A girl who has been forcibly taken, if she is not married with the recitation of mantras, may be given to another man according to the prescribed rules. She is like a virgin in every way. When the man who took her hand dies, a girl who has merely been consecrated with mantras, provided she is still a virgin, can undergo the rite of marriage again.

adbhir vācā ca dattāyāṃ mriyetādau varo yadi |
na ca mantropanītā syāt kumārī pitur eva sā ||
balāc cet prahṛtā kanyā mantrair yadi na saṃskṛtā |
anyasmai vidhivad deyā yathā kanyā tathaiva sā ||
pāṇigrāhe mṛte bālā kevalaṃ mantrasaṃskṛtā |
sā ced akṣatayoniḥ syāt punaḥ saṃskāram arhati || (VaDh 17.72–74)

Broadly speaking, these passages allow young women to remarry, if their first marriage rite was never properly completed or their marriage was never consummated. Hence, it would seem that their authors understand widows to be prohibited from remarrying once their marriages have been ritually performed in their entirety and consummated. In other words, the authors of these passages assume a general prohibition against widow remarriage.

Furthermore, although the above passage of Baudhāyana comes from what scholars have long recognized to be a significant later addition to his text,[18] one can discern a similarly negative attitude toward widow remarriage in earlier sections of the *Baudhāyana Dharmasūtra*. In particular, such an attitude is evident in Baudhāyana's treatment of a standard Dharmaśāstric category of son called *paunarbhava*, which he (2.3.27) defines as follows:

[17] The implication is that her father is free to give her in marriage to another man.
[18] See Bühler ([1879–1882] 1969, 2:xxxiii–xxxv), Kane (1962, 1:42–43), and Olivelle (2000, 191).

A *paunarbhava* is a son born of a woman, called "remarried" (*punarbhū*), who takes another husband after abandoning her first husband, as he is either impotent or an outcaste.

klībaṃ tyaktvā patitaṃ vā yānyaṃ patiṃ vindet tasyāṃ punarbhvāṃ yo jātaḥ sa paunarbhavaḥ |

Thus, a *paunarbhava* is a son born of a remarried woman, for which the Sanskrit term is *punarbhū*. And although Baudhāyana presents her first husband's impotency or loss of caste as the reasons why a woman might seek to remarry, Vasiṣṭha provides a longer list of such reasons and includes among them specifically the death of her first husband.[19] Hence, the treatment of the *paunarbhava* ("son of a remarried woman") in Dharmaśāstra provides an important lens through which to understand how classical Brahmanical society viewed widow remarriage, at the same time that it informs us that widows did, in fact, remarry in early India with some regularity. Baudhāyana (2.3.32) considers a *paunarbhava* to be entitled to membership in his father's *gotra* or patrilineal clan, but devoid of any rights of inheritance. From this his fundamentally negative attitude toward widow remarriage is apparent. Gautama, for his part, likewise seems to disapprove of widow remarriage, for he (15.18) includes a *paunarbhava* among those unfit to be fed at a Śrāddha rite, the classical form of Brahmanical ancestor worship. However, he may not have disapproved of widow remarriage quite as strongly as Baudhāyana does, given that he (28.33–34) considers a *paunarbhava* to be entitled to a quarter of his father's estate in the absence of sons of more prestigious types.

Although the previously cited passage of Vasiṣṭha (17.72–74) indicates that he understood widow remarriage to be generally prohibited by providing exceptions to this rule, at least one passage of his work suggests a more tolerant attitude toward the practice. Specifically, Vasiṣṭha departs notably from Gautama and Baudhāyana in his treatment of a *paunarbhava*, whom he includes among the categories of sons that are "heirs, relatives, and saviors from great danger."[20] Therefore, he clearly holds the sons of remarried

[19] VaDh 17.19–20: "A remarried woman (*punarbhū*) is a woman who abandons the husband of her childhood, consorts with other men, and then returns to his house. Or instead a remarried woman (*punarbhū*) can be a woman who abandons a husband who is impotent, an outcaste, or insane and takes another husband or who does so after her husband's death." (*punarbhūr yā kaumāraṃ bhartāram utsṛjyānyaiḥ saha caritvā tasyaiva kuṭumbam āśrayati sā punarbhūr bhavati* | *yā vā klībaṃ patitam unmattaṃ vā bhartāram utsṛjyānyaṃ patiṃ vindate mṛte vā sā punarbhūr bhavati* |)

[20] VaDh 17.25: *ity ete dāyādā bāndhavās trātāro mahato bhayād ity āhuḥ* |

women, including remarried widows, in markedly higher regard than Gautama and Baudhāyana do and grants them considerably greater rights of inheritance.

Beyond this, Vasiṣṭha's work also contains the following vexing passage, germane to a discussion of widow remarriage:

> A woman whose husband has gone abroad should wait five years for him. After five years, she should go to her husband's presence. But if she does not wish to live abroad for religious or financial reasons, she may act as if he were dead. Thus, a Brahmin woman who has given birth should wait five years and one who has not, four; a Kṣatriya woman who has given birth should wait five years and one who has not, three; a Vaiśya woman who has given birth should wait four years and one who has not, two; and a Śūdra woman who has given birth should wait three years and one who has not, one. After this period, each preceding member of this list is worthier than each subsequent one: a man who shares in the same property as her husband, a man of his same parentage, a man who shares in the same ancestral offerings of food or of water, and a man of the same patrilineal clan. However, when a member of her husband's family is available, she should not go to a stranger.
>
> *proṣitapatnī pañca varṣāṇy upāsīta | ūrdhvaṃ pañcabhyo varṣebhyo bhartṛsakāśaṃ gacchet | yadi dharmārthābhyāṃ pravāsaṃ praty anukāmā na syād yathā preta evaṃ vartitavyaṃ syāt | evaṃ brāhmaṇī pañca prajātāprajātā catvāri rājanyā prajātā pañcāprajātā trīṇi vaiśyā prajātā catvāry aprajātā dve śūdrā prajātā trīṇy aprajātaikam | ata ūrdhvaṃ samān ārthajanmapiṇḍodakagotrāṇāṃ pūrvaḥ pūrvo garīyān | na tu khalu kulīne vidyamāne paragāminī syāt* | (VaDh 17.75–80)

As one can see, here Vasiṣṭha lays down rules for a woman whose husband has traveled abroad.[21] After waiting a period of between one and five years, depending upon her caste and whether she has given birth to any children, such a woman is supposed to go to her husband unless concerns related to her religious (*dharma*) or material (*artha*) well-being dissuade her. In this event, Vasiṣṭha effectively prescribes that a woman should have recourse to

[21] Gautama (18.15–17) lays down a similar, but less detailed set of rules. Unlike Vasiṣṭha, however, he neglects to explain what a woman is supposed to do, if she does not go to her husband after a period of waiting.

her husband's closest available male relative and that, failing all such relatives, she may even have recourse to a stranger. Unfortunately, Vasiṣṭha fails to spell out the exact nature of the recourse he here intends, but it is almost certainly sexual, given that the waiting period is shorter for a woman who has not borne any children and longer for higher-caste women, of whom Brahmanical society expected greater chastity. Moreover, although the passage above strictly addresses a woman whose husband has gone abroad rather than a widow, it is reasonable to assume that if a woman whose husband may still be alive is allowed to have sex with another man, a woman whose husband is definitely dead would be permitted to do the same. Consequently, this passage of Vasiṣṭha is implicitly germane to the sexual behavior of widows.

Some confirmation of this comes from the following passage of the *Arthaśāstra* (3.4.37–42):

> The wife of a man who has taken a long trip abroad, become a renunciant, or died should wait for seven menstrual periods or for a year, if she has borne children. Then she should go to her husband's uterine brother. If there are many, she should go to the one closest in age, a righteous one, one capable of supporting her, the youngest one, or one without a wife. In the absence of uterine brothers, she may go to a *sapiṇḍa* relative who is not her husband's uterine brother or to a more distant family-member who is nearby. This is the precise order of them.
>
> If she remarries or takes a lover, passing over these heirs, the lover, the woman, the man who gives her, and the man who marries her all receive the punishment for adultery.
>
> *dīrghapravāsinaḥ pravrajitasya pretasya vā bhāryā sapta tīrthāny ākāṅkṣeta saṃvatsaraṃ prajātā | tataḥ patisodaryaṃ gacchet | bahuṣu pratyāsannaṃ dhārmikaṃ bharmasamarthaṃ kaniṣṭham abhāryaṃ vā | tadabhāve 'py asodaryaṃ sapiṇḍaṃ kulyaṃ vāsannam | eteṣām eṣa eva kramaḥ |*
> *etān utkramya dāyādān vedane jārakarmaṇi |*
> *jārastrīdātṛvettāraḥ saṃprāptāḥ saṃgrahātyayam ||*

As one can see, this passage of the *Arthaśāstra* lays down rules for a woman whose husband is traveling abroad just like the preceding passage of Vasiṣṭha. However, it also specifies that these rules apply equally to a woman whose husband has become a renunciant or died. Therefore, it makes explicit what I have argued can be reasonably inferred from Vasiṣṭha's passage: that its rules for women whose husbands have gone abroad also broadly apply to widows. Furthermore, the *Arthaśāstra* spells out quite clearly that the rules it lays down concern marriage (*vedana*) and the taking of a lover (*jārakarman*) rather than *niyoga*. And this in turn supports Stephanie Jamison's (2006, 211) position that the passage of Vasiṣṭha under discussion prescribes remarriage.

However, there is a serious problem with this interpretation of Vasiṣṭha: it seemingly conflicts with at least two other passages of his work. One of these is the set of three verses (VaDh 17.72–74) that I cited and discussed earlier, where Vasiṣṭha lays down special circumstances under which widows can remarry: essentially if their marriages were not sanctified with mantras or not consummated. It is not obvious how to reconcile these verses with VaDh 17.79–80, if it is interpreted as prescribing remarriage, for it clearly lays down rules for women whose marriages have been properly performed and who are not virgins. One possible way to resolve this apparent conflict is to understand these two passages of Vasiṣṭha as concerned with notably different forms of marriage. Specifically, the former passage (VaDh 17.72–74) may address cases where control over a girl reverts to her father, who is then free to give her to another man of his choosing from any family, whereas the latter passage (VaDh 17.79–85) deals with so-called widow inheritance, that is, the remarriage of a widow within her husband's family by his co-heirs. The other passage of Vasiṣṭha that seemingly conflicts with VaDh 17.79–80, if it is understood to enjoin remarriage, is the previously discussed passage (17.56–61) where he prescribes *niyoga* and takes pains to stress the solemn, strictly procreative nature of the institution. For it is hard to understand why Vasiṣṭha would do this, if he actually approves of widow remarriage. Moreover, it seems unlikely that VaDh 17.79–80 prescribes *niyoga* rather than remarriage, given that it explicitly includes among its intended subjects women who have already borne children.[22] Consequently, there appears to be a genuine conflict between VaDh 17.79–80 and certain other passages of Vasiṣṭha (17.56–61, 72–74). Perhaps the best way to account for this is by assuming that these passages constitute separate textual layers of the *Vasiṣṭha Dharmasūtra*, unsatisfying as this solution may be to some readers.

In any case, it is worth noting at this point that the men clearly prescribed as second husbands in the *Arthaśāstra* (3.4.38–40) closely match the men

[22] One might attempt to explain this away by noting that, unlike other authors, Vasiṣṭha nowhere requires a woman engaging in *niyoga* to be sonless or childless. This, however, feels rather like special pleading and ignores the obviously procreative goal of *niyoga* according to Vasiṣṭha.

prescribed as levirs in Gautama (18.4–6) and other Dharmaśāstra texts. Specifically, as we have seen, the ideal levir within Dharmaśāstra is a woman's husband's brother, and this is precisely the ideal second husband prescribed in the *Arthaśāstra*. Furthermore, the general principle in both *niyoga* and widow remarriage as presented in the *Arthaśāstra* seems to be that, if her husband has no available brother, a woman is supposed to seek out his next closest available kinsman. This suggests that these two practices were not nearly so distinct from one another in early India as Dharmaśāstra sources would lead one to believe. In this regard, the fact that the *Arthaśāstra*—a text that deals with many of the same topics as Dharmaśāstra works, but from a less moralistic perspective—makes essentially no mention of *niyoga*[23] is extremely telling. From this it would appear that the institution of *niyoga* is a distinctive and intentional Brahmanical creation—a reformed version of widow remarriage, if you will—designed with the specific aim of making the practice appear wholly different from widow remarriage at a time when it was increasingly frowned upon for women to remarry. This origin of *niyoga* in widow remarriage would then explain the increasing efforts taken by many Dharmaśāstra authors to dissociate these practices, as we will see.

Finally, before moving on from the Dharmasūtras, let us turn to Āpastamba, the author of probably the earliest surviving Dharmaśāstra text. Unlike Gautama, Baudhāyana, and Vasiṣṭha, Āpastamba regards *niyoga* as a completely illegitimate practice that is contrary to *dharma*. The relevant passage of his work (ĀpDh 2.27.2–3) begins by presenting an argument in favor of *niyoga* or probably more accurately widow inheritance:

> One should not introduce to strangers a woman who has assumed a place among the members of one's patrilineal clan, for a woman is given to a family—so they teach.
>
> *sagotrasthānīyāṃ na parebhyaḥ samācakṣīta | kulāya hi strī pradīyata ity upadiśanti |*

The argument here is quite different from what one encounters in later Dharmaśāstra literature, where the debate is between *niyoga* and lifelong

[23] The closest exception to this is AŚ 5.6.40, which concerns the failure of a royal line and puts forth as a possible remedy that a future king might be sired upon the dead king's daughter by a man of the same caste.

celibacy for widows. Instead, the issue in this passage is whether one "should introduce" (*samācakṣīta*) a widowed woman who has married into one's family to men outside of one's family. The verb *sam* + *ā* + √*cakṣ* ("to introduce") is an unusual one to use here, as its translation implies, but context makes clear that it must mean one of two things: "to give in marriage" or "to appoint" in the sense of *niyoga*. Consequently, it is somewhat ambiguous whether Āpastamba's passage deals with *niyoga* per se or with widow remarriage. Given that the levirs involved in *niyoga* are always the female participant's affines,[24] the latter seems more likely. Assuming this to be correct, the position taken in this passage is that a widow cannot remarry outside of her husband's family, but must remarry inside of it. And the justification provided for this is the belief that a bride is given to an entire family.

Āpastamba agrees with the aforementioned position insofar as he opposes widows remarrying outside of their husbands' families. However, he also opposes widows remarrying within their husbands' families and makes his case against such remarriages as follows:

> This position is rejected on account of people's weakness vis-à-vis their sense-organs, for any other man's hand is that of stranger with no difference between them. Moreover, for such a transgression both the man and the woman go to hell, for the good fortune resulting from self-restraint is superior to a child resulting from such behavior.
>
> *tad indriyadaurbalyād vipratipannam | aviśiṣṭaṃ hi paratvaṃ pāṇeḥ | tadvyatikrame khalu punar ubhayor narakaḥ | niyamārambhaṇo hi varṣīyān abhyudaya evamārambaṇād apatyāt* | (ĀpDh 2.27.4–7)

Here Āpastamba holds that widows should not remarry even within their husbands' families on the basis of two arguments. The first of these is that people are naturally given over to sensual pleasures and, thus, presumably might be sullied, if they sought to marry their husbands' kinsmen or their kinsmen's wives. Here Āpastamba perhaps alludes to the established principle of Brahmanical hermeneutics (Mīmāṃsā) that only an action without a perceptible, worldly motive can qualify as *dharma*. His second argument

[24] The only exception to this comes from the very late (c. 700–800 CE) *Vaiṣṇava Dharmaśāstra* (15.3), which allows an unrelated Brahmin to be the levir.

against widow remarriage even within one's husband's family is that the hand of a stranger and her husband's kinsman are equally foreign to a virtuous wife. Having made these arguments against widow remarriage, Āpastamba then warns of the hellish afterlife that awaits those who engage in the practice and proclaims lifelong celibacy to yield greater otherworldly rewards than any resulting offspring might produce. From this it is clear that, uniquely among the authors of the Dharmasūtras, Āpastamba opposes not only widow remarriage but also *niyoga* and considers lifelong celibacy to be the only legitimate option for widows.

That Āpastamba takes such a unique position is rather unsurprising, when one notes the uniquely strong restrictions that he places upon polygyny. For whereas Baudhāyana (1.16.2–5) and Vasiṣṭha (1.24) both explicitly allow high-caste men to marry multiple wives and Gautama issues no prohibitions against it, Āpastamba allows polygyny only if a man has not yet established his sacred fires and his wife fails to fulfill her religious duties (*dharma*) or to bear children.[25] Hence, Āpastamba appears to have held an especially strong belief in monogamy and the indissolubility of marriage, which may explain why he prohibits women from any sort of sexual activity after their husbands' deaths. Beyond this, his complete opposition to *niyoga* and widow remarriage further explains his position that a child belongs only to the man who fathered it.[26]

To briefly summarize then, the Dharmasūtras of Gautama, Baudhāyana, and Vasiṣṭha all prescribe *niyoga* as a perfectly legitimate option for widows with few or no children or at least no sons. Moreover, Gautama and Baudhāyana both clearly oppose widow remarriage, while seemingly recognizing it as a common practice in early India. And certain passages of Vasiṣṭha (17.56–61, 72–74) likewise seem to imply opposition to widow remarriage. At least one passage of Vasiṣṭha's work (17.79–80), however, apparently allows or even enjoins widows to remarry. Āpastamba, for his part, differs markedly from the authors of the other Dharmasūtras in his views on the sexual behavior of widows. Specifically, he is unique in his opposition to

[25] ĀpDh 2.11.12–14: "When his wife successfully participates in religious rites and bears children, a man may not take another wife. However, if she fails in either of these duties, he may take another wife before establishing his sacred fires, for a woman involved in the establishment of the sacred fires is connected with all the rites of which this establishment is a prerequisite part." (*dharmaprajāsaṃpanne dāre nānyāṃ kurvīta | anyatarābhāve kāryā prāg agnyādheyāt | ādhāne hi satī karmabhiḥ saṃbadhyate yeṣām etad aṅgam |*)

[26] See, e.g., ĀpDh 2.13.5: "A son belongs to the man who begat him—so states a Brāhmaṇa." (*utpādayituḥ putra iti hi brāhmaṇam |*)

not only widow remarriage but also *niyoga* and in his advocacy of lifelong celibacy for widows.

Manu

After the four Dharmasūtras, the next oldest work of Hindu law is almost certainly the *Mānava Dharmaśāstra*, by all accounts the single most important and influential text in the entire Hindu legal tradition. Although ascribed to Manu, the mythical first man and king, it is undoubtedly indebted to the earlier Dharmasūtras and probably dates to around the second century CE (Olivelle 2005, 25). Like most of the Dharmasūtras, Manu's work denies the legitimacy of widow remarriage, but unlike most of them, it also rejects *niyoga*. I will begin by examining Manu's views on the former issue before turning to the latter.

Manu flatly prohibits widows from remarrying and advocates that they should instead practice lifelong celibacy in the following passage (5.157–62):

> A woman may emaciate her body as she desires by living on auspicious flowers, roots, and fruits, but she should never even mention the name of another man, when her husband has died. Until death, she should remain forbearing, self-restrained, and celibate, pursuing the unsurpassable law of those women who take only one husband. Many thousands of Brahmins who were celibate from youth have gone to heaven without continuing their family-lines. A virtuous woman who remains celibate after her husband has died goes to heaven, even if sonless, just like those men who were celibate. A woman who transgresses against her husband out of greed for children obtains scorn in his world and is deprived of the world of her husband. There is no legitimate offspring in this world that is begotten by another man or upon another man's wife. A second husband is nowhere taught for virtuous women.

kāmaṃ tu kṣapayed dehaṃ puṣpamūlaphalaiḥ śubhaiḥ |
na tu nāmāpi gṛhṇīyāt patyau prete parasya tu ||
āsītā maraṇāt kṣāntā niyatā brahmacāriṇī |
yo dharma ekapatnīnāṃ kāṅkṣantī tam anuttamam ||
anekāni sahasrāṇi kumārabrahmacāriṇām |
divaṃ gatāni viprāṇām akṛtvā kulasaṃtatim ||

mṛte bhartari sādhvī strī brahmacarye vyavasthitā |
svargaṃ gacchaty aputrāpi yathā te brahmacāriṇaḥ ||
apatyalobhād yā tu strī bhartāram ativartate |
seha nindām avāpnoti patilokāc ca hīyate ||
nānyotpannā prajāstīha na cāpy anyaparigrahe |
na dvitīyaś ca sādhvīnāṃ kvacid bhartopadiśyate ||

Virtually the only purpose of this entire passage is to establish and to stress that women must not engage in sexual intercourse after their husbands' deaths. One important implication of this, of course, is that widows in second-century North India were, in fact, often sexually active, or at least that Brahmanical jurists at the time, like Manu, worried deeply about this possibility. Another perhaps more obvious implication is that Manu himself strongly opposes widow remarriage. And in keeping with this sentiment, he elsewhere bars the sons of remarried women from attending divine and ancestral rites (3.155); discourages giving gifts to them (3.181); and denies them the right to inherit their fathers' estates (9.160). Thus, he clearly condemns widow remarriage in general as a practice contrary to *dharma*.

There are, however, a few verses of Manu that allow widows to remarry under restricted conditions. For example, the following passage (MDh 9.175–76) permits a widow to take another husband apparently via some special remarriage ceremony, provided that she is still a virgin:

> If a woman who is abandoned by her husband or widowed gets remarried of her own desire and bears a son, he is called a "son of a remarried woman" (*paunarbhava*). Such a woman or one who has gone away and come back, provided that she is a virgin, can be married again to her husband following the procedure for remarriage.

yā patyā vā parityaktā vidhavā vā svayecchayā |
utpādayet punar bhūtvā sa paunarbhava ucyate ||
sā ced akṣatayoniḥ syād gatapratyāgatāpi vā |
paunarbhavena bhartrā sā punaḥ saṃskāram arhati ||

Consequently, Manu permits remarriages for what must have been a numerically small group of widows: young girls whose marriages were never consummated. However, considering his negative attitude toward sons born of remarried women, it would seem that he rather discourages even remarriages of this type.

Similarly, earlier in his text, Manu (9.97) mentions another scenario in which widow remarriage is permissible:

> If a girl has had a bride-price paid for her and the giver of that bride-price dies, she should be given to her fiancée's brother, if she consents.
>
> *kanyāyāṃ dattaśulkāyāṃ mriyeta yadi śulkadaḥ |*
> *devarāya pradātavyā yadi kanyānumanyate ||*

This verse imagines a case where a man has paid a bride price for a girl and subsequently dies, presumably before marrying her.[27] In such an event, it lays down that the girl should be given instead to her would-be husband's brother, if she consents. Thus, the verse effectively prescribes a limited form of so-called widow inheritance applicable specifically in bride-price marriages. It is notable, however, that the immediately following verse of Manu condemns bride-price marriages even among Śūdras.[28] Olivelle (2005, 31) compellingly argues that we reconcile the apparent contradiction between these verses by interpreting the latter as an expression of Manu's moral voice and the former as an expression of his legal voice. In other words, he suggests that while Manu was personally opposed to both bride-price marriages and widow remarriage, he recognized the reality of these practices and, thus, provides legal rules governing them despite his misgivings.

One final passage of Manu (9.75–76), where he seemingly takes a rather tolerant view of widow remarriage, merits special discussion:

> If a woman's husband has gone abroad after providing for her livelihood, she should live observing self-restraint. However, if he has gone abroad without providing for her livelihood, she should live by means of respectable crafts. She should wait eight years for a husband who has gone abroad

[27] Some confirmation of this comes from MDh 9.99, which seemingly refers to a similar case where a father receives a bride price for his daughter from one man, but then gives her in marriage to another. Note that, in this case, there is an understood period of time between the giving of the bride price and the wedding ceremony, during which legally significant events may take place. On the interpretation of this verse, see Olivelle (2005, 327).

[28] MDh 9.98: "Even a Śūdra giving his daughter should not accept a bride-price." (*ādadīta na śūdro 'pi śulkaṃ duhitaraṃ dadat |*)

to carry out a religious duty; six years for one who has gone abroad for the purpose of knowledge or fame; and three years for one who has gone abroad to fulfill a desire.

vidhāya proṣite vṛttiṃ jīven niyamam āsthitā |
proṣite tv avidhāyaiva jīvec chilpair agarhitaiḥ ||
proṣito dharmakāryārthaṃ pratīkṣyo 'ṣṭau naraḥ samāḥ |
vidyārthaṃ ṣaḍ yaśorthaṃ vā kāmārthaṃ trīṃs tu vatsarān ||

As one can see, this passage deals with a theme that we have encountered and discussed earlier in this chapter in the Dharmasūtra of Vasiṣṭha, namely, the proper period of waiting for women whose husbands have gone abroad. Indeed, the inclusion of a passage on this theme within Manu is likely a reflection of his participation in a conservative expert tradition of jurisprudence, wherein the treatment of certain established topics was fully expected, almost required. Furthermore, although this passage does not, strictly speaking, concern widows, it is fairly safe to draw implications about widows from it, as I argued earlier with respect to a similar passage of Vasiṣṭha (17.75–80). And, significantly, this passage of Manu appears to allow women to remarry after a period of waiting for their husbands. At least, this seems to be the implication.[29] However, Manu notably refrains from stating it outright, presumably because he is personally very much opposed to widow remarriage, as Olivelle (2005, 326) notes. Thus, here again we are perhaps experiencing the difference between Manu's moral voice, which denies the legitimacy of widow remarriage, and his legal or juridical voice, which compels him to include certain traditional themes in his work.

Let us turn now to Manu's views on *niyoga*. Although Manu mentions and alludes to *niyoga* in numerous places in his work, he most directly addresses

[29] Interestingly, only Nandana among Manu's commentators admits this. He states: "The intended meaning is that, after this period, there is no sin in taking another husband. And this does not conflict with the passage prescribing celibacy for widows as that applies to women who desire an especially great reward, not to others." (*ūrdhvaṃ bhartrantaraparigrahe na doṣo 'stīty abhiprāyaḥ | yat tu mṛtabhartṛkāṇāṃ brahmacaryavacanaṃ tat phalātiśayakāmānāṃ nānyāsām ity avirodhaḥ* |) Manu's other commentators, by contrast, engage in tortured reasoning of various sorts to arrive at more acceptable interpretations of his verse. For example, Bhāruci argues: "This time limit applies only to a woman whose husband has provided no livelihood for her insofar as she must live by means of respectable crafts. After this time period, she may instead live even by means of contemptible crafts." (*tasyā evāyaṃ kālaniyamaḥ agarhitaśilpajīvanena | ūrdhvaṃ tu kālād etasmād garhitenāpi jīvec chilpena* |)

the legitimacy of the practice in a single lengthy passage (9.57–71). The first section of this passage (9.57–63) reads as follows:

> An older brother's wife is an elder's wife to his younger brother, whereas a younger brother's wife is held to be a daughter-in-law to his older brother. If an older brother has sex with his younger brother's wife or a younger brother has sex with his older brother's wife when no calamity threatens, they both become outcastes, even if they were properly appointed. However, a duly appointed woman may obtain from her husband's brother or *sapiṇḍa* relative desirable progeny, if his family-line would die out. A man who has been appointed to a widow should at night smear himself with ghee and, refraining from speech, beget upon her a single son, never a second. Some who are knowledgeable about this, seeing that the couple have not thereby fulfilled the purpose of *niyoga* under the law, prescribe begetting a second child upon appointed women. However, when the purpose of the appointment (*niyoga*) to the widow has been fulfilled in accordance with the rules laid down, the couple should behave toward one another like an elder and a daughter-in-law. But if the appointed couple forsakes the prescribed rules and acts out of lust, they both become outcastes—the one for sleeping with his daughter-in-law, the other for sleeping with her elder.

bhrātur jyeṣṭhasya yā bhāryā gurupatny anujasya sā |
yavīyasas tu yā bhāryā snuṣā jyeṣṭhasya sā smṛtā ||
jyeṣṭho yavīyaso bhāryāṃ yavīyān vāgrajastriyam |
patitau bhavato gatvā niyuktāv apy anāpadi ||
devarād vā sapiṇḍād vā striyā saṃyaṅ niyuktayā |
prajepsitādhigantavyā saṃtānasya parikṣaye ||
vidhavāyāṃ niyuktas tu ghṛtākto vāgyato niśi |
ekam utpādayet putraṃ na dvitīyaṃ kathaṃcana ||
dvitīyam eke prajanaṃ manyante strīṣu tadvidaḥ |
anivṛttaṃ niyogārthaṃ paśyanto dharmatas tayoḥ ||
vidhavāyāṃ niyogārthe nivṛtte tu yathāvidhi |
guruvac ca snuṣāvac ca varteyātāṃ parasparam ||
niyuktau yau vidhiṃ hitvā varteyātāṃ tu kāmataḥ |
tāv ubhau patitau syātāṃ snuṣāgagurutalpagau ||

This passage begins by stating the general rule that a man may not have sex with his brother's wife before prescribing in detail an important exception: a woman may have sexual intercourse with her husband's brother or other *sapiṇḍa* relative for the purpose of conceiving a child, provided that she has been duly appointed and that the family line would otherwise come to end. In this regard, the passage closely resembles those passages of the Dharmasūtras that prescribe *niyoga*. However, it adds a few restrictive rules governing the levir's behavior that are not seen in these earlier texts, specifically, that he must smear himself with ghee, refrain from talking, and approach the appointed woman at night. These details are similar to Vasiṣṭha's requirement (17.61) that sexual intercourse between the widow and the male appointee must take place at a sacred hour before dawn (*prājāpatye muhūrte*) and be free from the playful laughter, bites, scratches, dirty talk, and the like that often accompany sex. Thus, like Vasiṣṭha, Manu appears determined to emphasize the solemn, somber nature of *niyoga* and to dispel any suspicions that those who participate in the practice do so simply out of sexual lust. And, to this end, he places additional unprecedented restrictions around the sexual intercourse that is the central part of *niyoga*. One finds additional confirmation of Manu's desire to stress the solemn ritual nature of *niyoga* in the fact that, more than any of his predecessors, he takes pains to warn of the dire consequences of violating the rules governing the practice. From all of this one gets the impression that Manu basically approves of *niyoga*, but with notable apprehension.

However, the immediately following passage of Manu's text (9.64–68) directly contradicts this, for it harshly and unambiguously condemns *niyoga*:

> Twice-born men should never appoint a widowed woman to another man, for those who appoint such a woman to another man kill the eternal law. *Niyoga* is nowhere spoken of in the wedding mantras nor is widow remarriage ever prescribed in the rules of marriage. It is a law for beasts reviled by educated twice-born men. It became a law for men as well when Vena reigned as king. Long ago, when he ruled the entire earth, that greatest of royal sages brought about a mixing of the social classes, his mind overcome by lust. Since that time, good people revile any man who out of delusion appoints a woman whose husband has died to beget a child.

nānyasmin vidhavā nārī niyoktavyā dvijātibhiḥ |
anyasmin hi niyuñjānā dharmaṃ hanyuḥ sanātanam ||
nodvāhikeṣu mantreṣu niyogaḥ kīrtyate kvacit |
na vivāhavidhāv uktaṃ vidhavāvedanaṃ punaḥ ||
ayaṃ dvijair hi vidvadbhiḥ paśudharmo vigarhitaḥ |

manuṣyāṇām api prokto vene rājyaṃ praśāsati ||
sa mahīm akhilāṃ bhuñjan rājarṣipravaraḥ purā |
varṇānāṃ saṃkaraṃ cakre kāmopahatacetanaḥ ||
tadāprabhṛti yo mohāt pramītapatikāṃ striyam |
niyojayaty apatyārthe taṃ vigarhanti sādhavaḥ ||

In this passage, as one can see, Manu argues that virtuous people or at least twice-born men should not participate in *niyoga*, as it—like widow remarriage—lacks a basis in scripture and, in fact, originated during the ancient reign of the deluded king Vena. Hence, the passage clearly conflicts with the earlier passage of Manu, where he enjoins *niyoga*. Therefore, some explanation of this glaring contradiction within his text is necessary. To this end, Olivelle (2005, 326) suggests that the earlier section of Manu's text (9.57–63) expresses an opponent's view or what is called a *pūrvapakṣa* in Sanskrit, whereas the later one (9.64–68) expresses the author's own view. Given that such a textual practice would be entirely in keeping with the typical mode of argumentation in classical India and that it is discernible elsewhere in Manu's work (e.g., 3.13–14), even if scholars have not often recognized it,[30] I am persuaded by Olivelle's explanation.

After the preceding passage, Manu concludes his discussion of *niyoga* with a pair of verses (MDh 9.69–70) expressing the view that when a girl's fiancée dies after her betrothal, his brother should copulate with her once each fertile season until she bears a child:

> When a girl has been verbally promised in marriage and her husband dies, her husband's brother should take her in accordance with this rule. Following the prescribed rules, he should approach that girl whose vows are pure, when she is dressed in white, and copulate with her once each fertile season until she begets a child.

yasyā mriyeta kanyāyā vācā satye kṛte patiḥ |
tām anena vidhānena nijo vindeta devaraḥ ||
yathāvidhy adhigamyaināṃ śuklavastrāṃ śucivratām |
mitho bhajetā prasavāt sakṛt sakṛd ṛtāv ṛtau ||

[30] On contradictions within Manu and scholarly attempts to account for them, see Olivelle (2005, 29–36).

Thus, these verses effectively prescribe *niyoga* for women who have merely been betrothed, but not married. Hence, considering that they occur right after Manu's prohibition against the practice, they apparently constitute a minor exception to his general opposition to *niyoga*, at least among the twice-born classes.

That Manu should be understood to basically oppose *niyoga* harmonizes well with his lengthy statement that we examined earlier in this chapter (MDh 5.157–62), where he argues that widows should practice lifelong celibacy. Other statements of Manu, however, suggest—at least on the surface—a more tolerant attitude toward *niyoga*. For instance, like Gautama (28.32), Baudhāyana (2.3.31), and Vasiṣṭha (17.14), Manu (9.145, 159) grants sons lawfully conceived through *niyoga*—so-called *kṣetraja* sons—the right to inherit their fathers' estates. More specifically, he apparently considers them to be the legal sons and heirs of their mothers' husbands rather than their biological fathers.[31] Elsewhere, however, Manu (9.163–64) stipulates that in the unusual event that a man has both a *kṣetraja* and an *aurasa* son (i.e., a son that he fathered himself upon his lawfully wedded wife),[32] the *aurasa* son inherits his entire estate, but should give a sixth or fifth of it to his *kṣetraja* brother. Therefore, like his predecessors in the Dharmaśāstra tradition aside from Āpastamba, Manu appears to hold *kṣetraja* sons in fairly high esteem, but to regard them as notably inferior to *aurasa* sons. From this it would, indeed, seem that he possesses a fairly tolerant attitude toward *niyoga*. In Manu's positive statements about *kṣetraja* sons, however, I suggest that we are seeing simply another reflection of his legal—as opposed to moral—voice. That is, Manu treats *kṣetraja* sons the way he does, despite his considerable misgivings about the practice whereby they are conceived, both because they were a social reality in his day and because the Dharmaśāstra tradition had set a precedent in dealing with them from which he, as an expert jurist, was loathe to diverge.

[31] Manu discusses this issue in a lengthy and complex passage (9.32–56), where he first presents an argument that a child belongs to its biological father (9.35–40) before presenting an argument that it belongs to its mother's husband instead (9.41–56). I agree wholeheartedly with Olivelle's (2005, 324) position that "Manu is here following the classical Indian form of argumentation, presenting first the opinion of the opponent (*pūrvapakṣa*) and then the opinion of the author (*uttarapakṣa*)."

[32] Such an event would seem to be impossible given the rules governing *niyoga*. Medhātithi (on MDh 9.162) plausibly imagines a scenario where an impotent man first acquires a *kṣetraja* son and then later, when his impotency is somehow medically cured, fathers an *aurasa* son.

Later Smṛtis

After Manu, only four Dharmaśāstra works classified as Smṛtis or post-Vedic scriptures still survive intact. In approximate chronology order (Olivelle 2010, 57), these are the Dharmaśāstras ascribed to Yājñavalkya, Nārada, Viṣṇu, and Parāśara. A huge number of other Dharmaśāstra texts regarded as Smṛtis undoubtedly once existed as evidenced by the copious citations ascribed to them found in later commentaries and digests. Nevertheless, I exclude these lost Dharmaśāstras from consideration in this section, because there is no available way to determine their original dates or contents with reasonable precision and confidence. Consequently, in this chapter and elsewhere in this book, I will treat the various lost Smṛtis ascribed to Bṛhaspati, Kātyāyana, and others largely within the context of the commentaries and digests that cite them.

Considering Manu's opposition to *niyoga* and his immense influence on the Hindu legal tradition, one might imagine that subsequent Dharmaśāstra works would similarly prohibit *niyoga*. This, however, turns out not to be the case. In fact, not a single surviving Smṛti composed after Manu opposes *niyoga*. Yājñavalkya (1.68–69), for instance, straightforwardly enjoins the practice:

> If permitted by his elders, a man's brother, his *sapiṇḍa* relative, or a member of his patrilineal clan may approach his sonless wife in her fertile season with the desire for a son, after smearing himself with ghee. He should so approach her until she conceives a child. If he does so otherwise, he becomes an outcaste. A son born in accordance with this procedure belongs to the woman's husband.

> *aputrāṃ gurvanujñānād devaraḥ putrakāmyayā |*
> *sapiṇḍo vā sagotro vā ghṛtābhyakta ṛtāv iyāt ||*
> *ā garbhasaṃbhavād gacchet patitas tv anyathā bhavet |*
> *anena vidhinā jātaḥ kṣetriṇaḥ sa bhavet sutaḥ ||*

As readers can see, this passage introduces no new ideas concerning *niyoga*. Instead, it simply and concisely states the fundamental rules regarding the practice that we have already encountered in earlier texts: that the woman engaged in *niyoga* must be sonless and act out of a desire for a son; that her elders' permission is required; that the ideal levir is her husband's brother, but a more distant male relative of her husband will also suffice; that the levir should smear himself with ghee and have sex with the woman only during her fertile season until she conceives a child; that he falls from caste for violating the rules governing *niyoga*; and that any resulting boy is the legal son and heir of his mother's husband. Hence, Yājñavalkya undoubtedly approves of *niyoga*. And one finds confirmation of this in the fact that he ranks a *kṣetraja* son third among the twelve types of sons (2.132) and grants him the right to inherit his father's estate in the absence of sons of the two more prestigious types (2.136).[33]

However, although Yājñavalkya clearly permits *niyoga*, he seems to have a negative view of widow remarriage of any kind. Thus, he defines a remarried woman (*punarbhū*) broadly as any woman who is remarried whether or not she is a virgin[34] and explicitly regards the sons of such women as unfit to be invited to ancestral Śrāddha rites (1.220). Yājñavalkya also ranks the sons of remarried women relatively lowly, as only sixth among the twelve recognized types of sons (2.134), and especially praises a widow who never resorts to another man (1.75). Such statements further confirm his basic opposition to women's remarriage—a position that is unsurprising, as there is almost no support for such marriages in the preceding Dharmaśāstra tradition.

Interestingly, however, both Nārada (12.97) and Parāśara (4.30) contain an identical verse that seemingly enjoins a woman to remarry in the event that her husband is lost, dead, or impotent or has become an outcaste or an ascetic:

> When her husband is lost, dead, a renunciant, impotent, or an outcaste—in these five calamities another husband is enjoined for women.
>
> *naṣṭe mṛte pravrajite klībe ca patite patau |*
> *pañcasv āpatsu nārīṇāṃ patir anyo vidhīyate ||*

[33] These two types of more prestigious sons are the *aurasa*, that is, the son fathered by a man upon his lawfully wedded wife, and the *putrikāputra*, or son of a daughter who has been appointed as a legal son. On these, see Kane (1962, 3:655–59). In addition to granting the *kṣetraja* son a general right to receive his father's property, Yājñavalkya adds two specific rules regarding his inheritance rights. First, if the levir was sonless, a *kṣetraja* son inherits the property of and makes ancestral offerings to both his mother's husband and his biological father (2.131). Second, although men who are impotent, lame, insane, mentally incompetent, blind, or afflicted with an incurable disease receive no share of their paternal estate, a *kṣetraja* son of theirs does (2.144–45).

[34] YDh 1.67: *akṣatā ca kṣatā caiva punarbhūḥ saṃskṛtā punaḥ |*

Within the context of Parāśara, this verse is followed by three others, of which the first (4.31) proclaims the heavenly reward of a widow who remains celibate and the next two (4.32–33) extol the even greater heavenly reward of a widow who follows her husband in death. Hence, the verse is conceivably a *pūrvapakṣa* or opponent's view that is refuted by the immediately following verses, much like we have seen in certain passages of Manu. At the very least, context suggests that Parāśara deems remarriage to be an inferior option to lifelong celibacy and especially self-immolation for widows. Consequently, Parāśara may not be quite the proponent of widow remarriage that the above verse makes him appear to be. It is noteworthy, however, that numerous later commentators who oppose women's remarriage clearly find this particular verse to be problematic, for they offer various interpretations of it designed to explain away its seeming approval of widow remarriage, as we will see. Conversely, it was this verse of Parāśara that Ishvarchandra Vidyasagar, the great nineteenth-century Hindu reformer, seized upon and used as the crucial piece of scriptural evidence in his juridical defense of widow remarriage (Hatcher 2012, 61–62, 73–74).

In Nārada, unlike Parāśara, however, the above verse does not occur within a context that suggests it is a *pūrvapakṣa* or that otherwise might diminish its import. Indeed, as Lariviere (1991) argues, textual evidence suggests that Nārada was a rare proponent of widow remarriage within the Dharmaśāstra tradition. Thus, after laying down the five calamitous conditions under which a woman is enjoined to take another husband, he (12.98–102) states:

> A Brahmin woman should wait eight years for her husband when he has gone abroad, but if she has not borne a child, only four. After this, she should seek refuge in another man. A Kṣatriya woman should wait six years, but only three, if she has not borne a child. A Vaiśya woman who has given birth should wait four years, but otherwise just two. No period of waiting is prescribed for a Śūdra woman nor can she violate the law for seeking another man, especially if she has not borne a child. She should wait at most one year. This is held to be the law governing the celibacy of women whose husbands have gone abroad. However, if her husband lives and is heard from, the prescribed number of years is doubled. Prajāpati created beings in this world so that they might beget offspring. Therefore, women commit no sin by approaching other men in this way.

aṣṭau varṣāṇy udīkṣeta brāhmaṇī proṣitaṃ patim |
aprasūtā tu catvāri parato 'nyaṃ samāśrayet ||
kṣatriyā ṣaṭ samās tiṣṭhed aprasūtā samātrayam |
vaiśyā prasūtā catvāri dve same tv itarā vaset ||
na śūdrāyāḥ smṛtaḥ kālo na ca dharmavyatikramaḥ |
viśeṣato 'prasūtāyāḥ saṃvatsaraparā sthitiḥ ||
apravṛttau smṛto dharma eṣa proṣitayoṣitām |
jīvati śrūyamāṇe tu syād eṣa dviguṇo vidhiḥ ||
prajāpravṛttau bhūtānāṃ sṛṣṭir eṣā prajāpateḥ |
ato 'nyagamane strīṇām evaṃ doṣo na vidyate ||

Here Nārada, like Gautama (18.15–17), Vasiṣṭha (17.75–80), and Manu (9.76), prescribes a period of waiting for a woman whose husband has gone abroad. Unlike Gautama and Manu, however, he explicitly instructs such a woman to take another husband. And, in this regard, Nārada's instruction is perhaps even clearer than the similar instruction of Vasiṣṭha (17.79–80). Furthermore, unlike Vasiṣṭha and the *Arthaśāstra* (3.4.38–42), Nārada does not restrict a widow's choice of a new husband to members of her first husband's family, although he may well have assumed such a restriction. Thus, in this passage at least, Nārada seems to be a uniquely strong proponent of women's remarriage within the Dharmaśāstra tradition, including implicitly the remarriage of widows. Moreover, the general permissibility of widow remarriage in his view explains why he elsewhere (NSm 1.18–19) lays down the rule that a man who marries a widow is responsible for paying off her first husband's debts.

Nevertheless, other passages of Nārada seemingly conflict with this stance, for elsewhere he is an unambiguous advocate of *niyoga*, a practice that he clearly distinguishes from any form of remarriage. Nārada (12.79–88) discusses *niyoga* in great detail in the following passage:

> If the husband of a woman who has borne no children should die, she, after being appointed by her elders, should approach her husband's brother with a desire for a son. And he should approach her accordingly until she bears a son. When a son is born, he should stop. Otherwise there will be disaster. The man should smear his limbs with ghee or unrefined oil, keep his mouth from hers, and not touch her limbs with his. He should not approach a woman who has a son, is barren or past menopause, does not consent, is pregnant or blameworthy, or has not been appointed by her relatives. If a woman who has not been appointed bears a son with her husband's brother,

men versed in the law declare that boy to be born of a paramour and unfit for inheritance.

Similarly, both a younger brother who has sex with his older brother's wife, although not appointed to her, and an older brother who has sex with his younger brother's wife commit the sin of sleeping with an elder's wife. But when he is the only remaining male in the family and has been appointed by his elders, a man may approach his younger brother's wife in order to continue his family-line, not out of lust.

When no elder is available, however, the king should be told about the family's imminent destruction. Then, having been verbally ordered by him, a man should have sex with his brother's wife. Following the aforementioned rules, he should go to her once or until she becomes pregnant, when she has bathed after menstruation and he has been purified for begetting a son. Once she becomes pregnant, she is like a daughter-in-law to him. The king must severely punish any man or woman who engages in this practice out of lust or in any other way than prescribed. If he fails to restrain them, he is guilty of a sin.

anutpannaprajāyās tu patiḥ preyād yadi striyāḥ |
niyuktā gurubhir gacched devaraṃ putrakāmyayā ||
sa ca tāṃ pratipadyeta tathaivā putrajanmataḥ |
putre jāte nivarteta viplavaḥ syād ato 'nyathā ||
ghṛtenābhyajya gātrāṇi tailenāvikṛtena vā |
mukhān mukhaṃ pariharan gātrair gātrāṇy asaṃspṛśan ||
striyaṃ putravatīṃ vandhyāṃ nīrajaskām anicchantīm |
na gacched garbhiṇīṃ nindyām aniyuktāṃ ca bandhubhiḥ ||
aniyuktā tu yā nārī devarāj janayet sutam |
jārajātam arikthīyaṃ tam āhur dharmavādinaḥ ||
tathāniyukto bhāryāyāṃ yavīyāñ jyāyaso vrajet |
yavīyaso vā yo jyāyān ubhau tau gurutalpagau ||
kule tadavaśeṣe tu saṃtānārthaṃ na kāmataḥ |
niyukto gurubhir gacched bhrātṛbhāryāṃ yavīyasaḥ ||
avidyamāne tu gurau rājño vācyaḥ kulakṣayaḥ |
tatas tadvacanād gacched anuśiṣya striyā saha ||
pūrvoktenaiva vidhinā snātāṃ puṃsavane śuciḥ |
sakṛd ā garbhādhānād vā kṛte garbhe snuṣaiva sā ||
ato 'nyathā vartamānaḥ pumān strī vāpi kāmataḥ |
vineyau subhṛśaṃ rājñā kilbiṣī syād anigrahāt ||

Here Nārada prescribes *niyoga* in a way that is similar to what we have seen elsewhere. He does, however, add a few interesting new details regarding the practice. In particular, he explicitly prefers the levir to be the deceased man's younger brother, allowing his older brothers to act as levirs only as a last resort. He also explains that when no elders are available, the local king is responsible for authorizing *niyoga* and ensuring its lawful performance. Hence, Narāda is certainly an advocate of *niyoga*—a practice that he, like other Dharmaśāstra authors, clearly differentiates from widow remarriage.

Further confirmation of Nārada's positive view of *niyoga* comes from the following passage, where he (12.45–53) gives a taxonomical account of the various possible sorts of wives who have previously been with other men:

> There are, however, other wives, who have been with other men before. They are said to be of seven types in order. Among these, the remarried woman (*punarbhū*) comprises three types and the loose woman (*svairiṇī*) four.
>
> The first type of remarried woman is said to be a girl who is still a virgin, but has been defiled by a man taking her hand in marriage. She is fit to be married again. The second type is said to be a woman who abandons the husband of her youth, resorts to another man, and then returns to her husband's home. The third is said to be a woman whom her relatives give to a man who is of her husband's social class, but not his *sapiṇḍa* relative, when her husband has no brothers.
>
> The first type of loose woman is a woman who may or may not have borne children, but resorts to another man out of lust while her husband is alive. The second is said to be a woman who after her husband's death ignores his brothers, although they are fitting, and goes to another man out of lust. The third is said to be a woman who has come from another country, whom a man has purchased for money, or who has approached a man, stricken with thirst and hunger, saying "I am yours." The last type of loose woman is held to be a woman who has been raped and, thereafter, given by her elders to another man in conformity with regional laws.
>
> Here have been stated the rules for remarried women and for loose women. Among them each preceding type is inferior and each subsequent one superior.[35]

[35] As Lariviere (2003, 390) observes, the commentator Bhavasvāmin rejects interpreting this line in the way that I have, arguing: "Some interpret the text exactly as it reads, but this cannot be correct, for how can a virgin be inferior to the other two types of remarried women? Therefore, it must be understood that among remarried women, each preceding type in order is *not* inferior."

parapūrvāḥ striyas tv anyāḥ sapta proktā yathākramam |
punarbhūs trividhā tāsāṃ svairiṇī tu caturvidhā ||
kanyaivākṣatayonir yā pāṇigrahaṇadūṣitā |
punarbhūḥ prathamā soktā punaḥ saṃskāram arhati ||
kaumāraṃ patim utsṛjya yānyaṃ puruṣam āśritā |
punaḥ patyur gṛhaṃ yāyāt sā dvitīyā prakīrtitā ||
asatsu devareṣu strī bāndhavair yā pradīyate |
savarṇāyāsapiṇḍāya sā tṛtīyā prakīrtitā ||
strī prasūtāprasūtā vā patyāv eva tu jīvati |
kāmāt samāśrayed anyaṃ prathamā svairiṇī tu sā ||
mṛte bhartari yā prāptān devarān apy apāsya tu |
upagacchet paraṃ kāmāt sā dvitīyā prakīrtitā ||
prāptā deśād dhanakrītā kṣutpipāsāturā ca yā |
tavāham ity upagatā sā tṛtīyā prakīrtitā ||
deśadharmān apekṣya strī gurubhir yā pradīyate |
utpannasāhasānyasmai sāntyā vai svairiṇī smṛtā ||
punarbhuvām eṣa vidhiḥ svairiṇīnāṃ ca kīrtitaḥ |
pūrvā pūrvā jaghanyāsāṃ śreyasī tūttarottarā ||

Notably absent from the above lists of loose and remarried women is a woman who engages in *niyoga* with her husband's brother or other *sapiṇḍa* relative. This is a clear indication that Nārada considers such women to be neither "remarried" (*punarbhū*) nor "loose" (*svairiṇī*). Instead, he apparently holds them in markedly higher esteem. And this is confirmed by the fact that he ranks the son of a remarried woman seventh among the twelve types of sons (13.44) and includes them among those who do not inherit (13.45), whereas he ranks a *kṣetraja* son second (13.43) and grants him strong rights of inheritance (13.45–46).

Thus, Nārada is, in various places, a proponent of both widow remarriage and *niyoga*. And although these two practices stand in obvious contrast to the lifelong celibacy of widows advocated by certain Dharmaśāstra authors, they also seem to conflict with one another to a notable degree. For as I argued earlier, *niyoga* is essentially a reformed version of widow

(*eke yathāpāṭham evecchanti | na tad upapannam | katham akṣatayonir itarābhyāṃ jaghanyā syāt | tasmāt krameṇa punarbhuvāṃ pūrvā pūrvā ajaghanyā |*). Although I share Bhavasvāmin's puzzlement, I cannot accept his interpretation on grammatical grounds. Instead, I tentatively suggest that the pronoun "them" (*āsām*) in the line be understood to refer only to loose women (*svairiṇī*) and not also to remarried women (*punarbhū*).

remarriage, designed to preserve a limited form of the practice at a time when it was increasingly condemned within Brahmanical society. Hence, given that Nārada allows widows and even certain other types of women to remarry, it is unclear why he also prescribes *niyoga*. One might argue that, in Nārada's view, *niyoga* significantly differs from widow remarriage in that it alone is a means for a dead man to attain a son.[36] Even if one grants this, however, it is still puzzling why Nārada lays down rules clearly designed to stress the unpleasurable, dispassionate nature of *niyoga* (12.81) and issues so many warnings against violating these rules (12.80, 84, 88). Perhaps the key to resolving this conundrum lies in the fact that Nārada first enjoins *niyoga* (12.79–88) and then, shortly afterward, prescribes widow remarriage (12.97–102). Thus, his intent in arranging his discussion this way might be to show that he not only allows *niyoga* as traditionally prescribed, but even goes so far as to allow widows to remarry.

Lastly, before concluding our examination of *niyoga* and widow remarriage in the Smṛtis, we must briefly look at the *Vaiṣṇava Dharmaśāstra*, a work composed in Kashmir likely around the seventh century (Olivelle 2007). In comparison with the other Smṛtis of the Dharmaśāstra tradition, Viṣṇu is remarkably silent on the issues of *niyoga* and widow remarriage. Indeed, the only place in his work where he seems to mention them at all is in his discussion of the twelve types of sons. There, in standard Dharmaśāstra fashion, he defines and ranks the *kṣetraja* and *paunarbhava* son, that is, the son born through *niyoga* and the son born of a remarried woman, respectively. Viṣṇu defines the latter specifically as the son of a remarried virgin,[37] which may explain why he ranks him fourth, notably higher than any author other than Vasiṣṭha.[38] Of the former type of son, Viṣṇu (15.3) states:

> Second is the *kṣetraja* son, who is begotten upon an appointed woman by a *sapiṇḍa* relative or a man of the highest social class (i.e., a Brahmin).
>
> *niyuktāyāṃ sapiṇḍenottamavarṇena votpāditaḥ kṣetrajo dvitīyaḥ* |

[36] Note that, unlike the son of a remarried woman (*paunarbhava*), a *kṣetraja* son is considered to be the legal son and heir of a widow's deceased husband.

[37] ViDh 15.8: *akṣatā bhūyaḥ saṃskṛtā punarbhūḥ* |

[38] The *paunarbhava* is ranked fourth at VaDh 17.18 and ViDh 15.7; sixth at YDh 2.134; seventh at NSm 13.44; eighth at AŚ 3.7.12; ninth at GDh 28.33; tenth at MDh 9.160; and eleventh at BDh 2.3.27.

Thus, like most Dharmaśāstra authors, Viṣṇu ranks the *kṣetraja* son second, behind only the *aurasa* son.[39] As Kane (1962, 2:603) observes, however, he uniquely adds the detail that the levir need not be a relative of the woman's husband, but can instead be any Brahmin. It is unlikely that Viṣṇu's inclusion of this particular detail stems from the unique way in which *niyoga* was practiced in his day, especially considering the fact that he nowhere even discusses the practice in the way that all of his predecessors do. Instead, it seems more likely that Viṣṇu lists Brahmins as possible levirs because of a well-known event narrated in the *Mahābhārata*. For there Vyāsa, the epic's mythical Brahmin author, sires the princes Dhṛtarāṣṭra and Pāṇḍu upon the widows of king Vicitravīrya.[40] If correct, this suggests that Viṣṇu did not know *niyoga* as a living social institution, but rather only as a practice of a bygone era read about in the scriptures and as an inherited feature of Dharmaśāstra literature. Therefore, even though he grants *kṣetraja* and *paunarbhava* sons the right to inherit in the absence of sons of more prestigious types (15.28–29), it is reasonable to doubt whether he personally supports the practices of *niyoga* and widow remarriage. Indeed, the fact that Viṣṇu elsewhere (25.14) lists celibacy and sati as the only two options for a widow strongly suggests that he does not.

Consequently, it is clear that the surviving Smṛtis of the Dharmaśāstra tradition for the most part support *niyoga*, although from Vasiṣṭha onward some discomfort with the practice is perhaps discernible, as authors increasingly lay down specific rules to dissociate it from remarriage and to stress its solemn, unpleasurable nature. The sole opponents of *niyoga* within the early Dharmaśāstra tradition are Āpastamba in the third century BCE and Manu in the second century CE. In addition, Viṣṇu also likely opposes the practice, but nowhere explicitly speaks against it. When it comes to widow remarriage, by contrast, most of the Hindu legal tradition strongly opposes it. The major exception to this is Nārada, although one passage of Vasiṣṭha (17.75–80) and one verse of Parāśara (4.30) likewise appear to support the practice.

The Commentaries

Having examined all of the surviving Smṛtis or foundational treatises of the Dharmaśāstra tradition, we must now turn to those exegetical works

[39] The *kṣetraja* is ranked second at GDh 28.32, VaDh 17.14, MDh 9.159, NSm 13.43, and ViDh 15.3 and third at BDh 2.3.17, AŚ 3.7.6, and YDh 2.132.
[40] See MBh 1.99.1–100.30.

that strive to explain and frequently harmonize the various Smṛtis—works classified as commentaries, if they focus on a single root Smṛti, or as digests or *nibandhas*, if they do not, but instead treat a specific topic or set of topics within Dharmaśāstra. As we will see, with the significant exception of Bhāruci, the earliest surviving Dharmaśāstra commentator to discuss *niyoga*, these exegetical works almost uniformly reject the legitimacy of *niyoga* and widow remarriage; and none of them fully endorses these practices. They, therefore, reflect what appears to have been a decisive historical shift against *niyoga* and widow remarriage within Brahmanical culture. However, the number of surviving Dharmaśāstra commentaries and digests that contain discussions of *niyoga* is quite large. Hence, it would be extremely time-consuming and repetitive to examine all or even most of them here. Thus, my analysis will focus only on those exegetical Dharmaśāstra works that were likely composed during the late first millennium, when the decisive turn against *niyoga* and widow remarriage within Brahmanical society seems to have taken place.[41] Unsurprisingly, these works contain the lengthiest and most detailed arguments against *niyoga* within the entire Dharmaśāstra tradition. Moreover, although they generally devote little separate space to arguing specifically against widow remarriage, it is clear that all of them oppose the practice, as one might reasonably infer from their opposition to *niyoga*. After examining the Dharmaśāstra commentaries of the late first millennium and explaining their intricate arguments against *niyoga*, I will briefly discuss several later commentaries and digests before concluding the chapter.

Bhāruci

The earliest surviving commentator within the Dharmaśāstra tradition to discuss *niyoga* appears to be Bhāruci, who, according to Derrett (1975, 1:9), likely wrote his commentary on the *Mānava Dharmaśāstra* during the first half of the seventh century. Unlike all other extant commentators, Bhāruci considers *niyoga* to be a perfectly legitimate option for widows. This is clear

[41] Although Maskarin's commentary on Gautama likely dates to the tenth century (Olivelle 2000, 116) and, thus, belongs to the late first millennium, I do not discuss it here, because it does not engage with the issue of *niyoga*'s legitimacy or attempt to harmonize conflicting scriptural statements on the topic. Instead, it simply explains the meaning of Gautama's text (18.4–17) in isolation. Incidentally, this is also true of the later commentaries on Gautama (18.4–17) and Āpastamba (2.27.2–7) ascribed to Haradatta.

from the way he harmonizes Manu's seemingly conflicting statements regarding the practice:

> Since it is both prescribed and prohibited, *niyoga* is optional. We do not much care whether the Smṛti prescribing the practice or the one prohibiting it is superior, but can say this, that both lead to good results, for in one case there is offspring and in the other self-restraint. Moreover, both are especially sanctified, since *niyoga* also leads to good results on the grounds that the woman's husband, whether dead or alive, and the man who appoints the levir derive no sensual pleasure from the practice, nor do the husband's forebears. Further, one understands from the force of the injunction prescribing the practice that *niyoga* leads to good results for a man's forebears as well. And because of the force of the prohibition against *niyoga*, it is not a sin not to practice it.
>
> *uktapratiṣiddhatvāc ca niyogasya vikalpaḥ | anayos tu smṛtyoḥ katarā jyāyasīti kiṃ na etena | śakyate tv etad evaṃ vaktum | ubhayatrābhyudayaḥ yenaikatrāpatyam anyatra saṃyamaḥ | ubhayaṃ ca viśeṣataḥ saṃskṛtaṃ yato niyogo 'py abhyudayāya | na hi mṛtasya jīvato vā patyur niyoktuḥ [vā] kācid indriyaprītir asti nāpi pitrādīnām | vidhānasāmarthyāc ca pitrādīnām api niyogo 'bhyudayāyeti gamyate | pratiṣedhasāmarthyāc cāniyoge 'py anatyayaḥ* | (on MDh 9.68)

As one can see, Bhāruci's fundamental position here is that *niyoga* is optional, since Manu both enjoins and prohibits the practice. More specifically, he holds that it is, for all intents and purposes, an equal option to lifelong celibacy for widows, since both options lead to good results for the woman who carries them out. From this incidentally it is clear that Bhāruci does not consider remarriage to be a legitimate option for widows, even if he supports *niyoga*.

Beyond this, Bhāruci also argues that, like lifelong celibacy, *niyoga* is an especially meritorious undertaking and cites as evidence of this the fact that various men connected with the practice—the woman's husband, his ancestors, and the elder who appoints the levir—all derive no sensual pleasure from it. The implication here is that since these men derive no worldly enjoyment from *niyoga*, it must have for them an unseen or otherworldly benefit. And in order to appreciate this argument one must be aware of an established principle of Brahmanical hermeneutics that we will see invoked numerous times throughout this book: only an action that is *adṛṣṭārtha*, that is, lacking a seen or worldly purpose (such as sexual pleasure), can qualify as *dharma*. In other words, the Dharmaśāstra tradition holds that actions can yield either visible or otherworldly benefits, but not both. Commentators typically use this principle to divest scriptural statements of injunctive force by identifying a visible purpose behind them. Here, however, Bhāruci uses it quite differently to argue that *niyoga* is an especially meritorious practice in that it benefits an array of men in addition to the widow herself. Hence, he unambiguously regards *niyoga* as a lawful, but not mandatory practice for widows. And the considerable extent to which he approves of *niyoga* is further evident from the fact that he personally considers it better for women to conceive two sons through *niyoga* rather than just one.[42]

Kumārila

Kumārila Bhaṭṭa, an approximate contemporary of Bhāruci and famous author within the Mīmāṃsā tradition of Brahmanical hermeneutics, also expresses his opinion on the practice of *niyoga*. Unfortunately, it remains uncertain precisely when and where Kumārila wrote his celebrated works.[43] Nevertheless, whatever his provenance may have been, it appears from a fairly brief statement in his *Tantravārttika* that he rejects the legitimacy of *niyoga* and, thus, by implication widow remarriage as well. Therefore, some discussion of him is warranted, although his writings technically do not belong to the Dharmaśāstra tradition.

Kumārila's discussion of *niyoga* occurs within the context of his lengthy commentary on *Pūrvamīmāṃsāsūtra* 1.3.7. The more specific context within which he discusses the practice is a particular hypothetical objection

[42] On MDh 9.61, Bhāruci comments: "Of these two Smṛtis (MDh 9.60–61), the one prescribing the fathering of a second son is superior, for it better promotes the continuance of a family-line." (*anayoḥ smṛtyor dvitīyaputrajananasmṛtir jyāyasī saṃtānānugrahāt* |)

[43] Recently, Yoshimizu (2015, 43n) has argued that Kumārila likely lived in the general vicinity of the coastal city of Lāṭa in southeastern Gujarat. He also assigns the date 560–620 for Kumārila's literary activity.

to the view that the conduct of good people (*sadācāra*) constitutes a legitimate source of *dharma*. The *Tantravārttika* (p. 127) phrases this objection as follows:

> In the behaviors of good people, one sees the violation of the law and rash acts carried out by great beings such as Prajāpati, Indra, Vasiṣṭha, Viśvāmitra, Yudhiṣṭhira, Vyāsa, Bhīṣma, Dhṛtarāṣṭra, Kṛṣṇa, and Arjuna and also by many people today.
>
> *sadācāreṣu hi dṛṣṭo dharmavyatikramaḥ sāhasaṃ ca mahatāṃ prajāpatīndravasiṣṭhaviśvāmitrayudhiṣṭhirakṛṣṇadvaipāyanabhīṣmadhṛtarāṣṭravāsudevārjunaprabhṛtīnāṃ bahūnām adyatanānāṃ ca* |

Thus, the hypothetical objection here to accepting the conduct of good people as a source of *dharma* is that when one examines the behaviors of both revered figures of the past—as described in Brahmanical scriptures—and contemporaneous peoples, one sees abundant cases where the actions of good people, in fact, violate *dharma*. And following the above statement, Kumārila goes on to cite many examples of this, including undoubtedly the most well-known instance of *niyoga* in Sanskrit epic literature: the events in the opening book of the *Mahābhārata* where Vyāsa—the epic's legendary author—fathers two sons upon the wives of his departed half-brother Vicitravīrya.[44] Consequently, it is clear that at least the hypothetical objector in this section of the *Tantravārttika* regards *niyoga* as a prohibited practice.

Furthermore, it appears from Kumārila's later response to this objection that he himself agrees about the general illegitimacy of *niyoga*:

> Vyāsa begat sons upon the wives of his brother, related through his mother, by the appointment of his elders in accordance with the scripture that states: a widow wishing to obtain a child from her husband's brother, whom his elders have compelled, should approach him in her fertile season. This was not very hard for Vyāsa to do, given the power of his past and future

[44] See *Tantravārttika* (p. 128): "Vyāsa, who had undertaken lifelong celibacy, engaged in siring children upon the wives of Vicitravīrya." (*kṛṣṇadvaipāyanasya gṛhītanaiṣṭhikabrahmacaryasya vicitravīryadāreṣv apatyotpādanaprasaṅgaḥ* |) These events are told in full at MBh 1.99.1–100.30.

asceticism. And should another man arise who possesses such ascetic power, he could certainly do the same.

dvaipāyanasyāpi guruniyogād apatir apatyalipsur devarād gurupreritād ṛtumatīyād ity evam āgamān mātṛsaṃbandhabhrātṛjāyāputrajananaṃ prākkṛtapaścātkariṣyamāṇatapobalena nātiduṣkaram | anyo 'pi yas tādṛktapobalo nirvahet sa kuryād eva | (*Tantravārttika*, p. 134)

Here Kumārila attempts to justify Vyāsa's engagement in *niyoga* in the *Mahābhārata* through essentially two different arguments. The first of these is that Vyāsa acted in accordance with certain authoritative scriptures that prescribe *niyoga*. To substantiate this claim, Kumārila offers what appears to be a paraphrase of Gautama's prescription of the practice (18.4–5), which we discussed earlier in this chapter. From this it would seem that Kumārila accepts the general legitimacy of *niyoga*. However, the second argument he uses to justify Vyāsa's behavior suggests otherwise, for Kumārila argues—or at least implies—that it was Vyāsa's immense power derived from his ascetic practices that allowed him to engage in *niyoga* unsullied. Consequently, Kumārila seems to regard *niyoga* as a practice that only a person endowed with nearly superhuman ascetic powers could legitimately perform.[45] Thus, like all commentators within the Dharmaśāstra tradition aside from Bhāruci, he appears to understand *niyoga* to be effectively prohibited among respectable people in his time.

Viśvarūpa

After Bhāruci, the earliest commentator within the Dharmaśāstra tradition itself to discuss *niyoga* appears to be Viśvarūpa, who likely wrote his commentary *Bālakrīḍā* on the *Yājñavalkya Dharmaśāstra* in the first half of the ninth century, perhaps in the region of Malwa.[46] As we have seen,

[45] For some early passages expressing this same idea (i.e., that it was the great sanctity of the ancients that allowed them to perform acts forbidden for ordinary men today), see ĀpDh 2.13.7–9 and GDh 1.3.

[46] On the date of Viśvarūpa, see Kane (1962, 1:562–64). On the basis of Viśvarūpa's commentary on YDh 1.162, where he notes that in Malwa, *vaiśvadevika* is a common term for a *grāmayājin* ("sacrificer for a village"), Kane (1962, 1:564) suggests that he may have been an inhabitant of that region.

Yājñavalkya accepts the general legitimacy of *niyoga* for sonless widows, but devotes only two verses (1.68–69) to the practice. Therefore, it is natural and unsurprising that Viśvarūpa's exceptionally long and meandering discussion of the topic comprises his commentary on these two verses, particularly the second of them.

After making a few remarks intended to clarify the meaning of Yājñavalkya's verses, Viśvarūpa takes up the crucial issue of whether *niyoga* is a lawful practice. This he does by presenting the view that it is, in fact, contrary to *dharma* in that it conflicts with both scripture and custom:

> On this issue, some insist that the position taken here of allowing *niyoga* cannot be right, for it conflicts with both the Smṛtis and customary practice. And, thus, Manu (9.64) states:
>
> > Twice-born men should not appoint a widowed woman to another man, for those who appoint such a woman to another man kill the eternal law.
>
> Moreover, after describing a previous age of the world, he (MDh 9.68) concludes:
>
> > Since that time, good people revile any man who out of delusion appoints a woman whose husband has died to beget children.
>
> Hence, there can be no *niyoga*. And the conduct of learned men further supports this.

> *atra codayanti—nāyaṃ niyogapakṣaḥ śreyān smṛtyācāravirodhāt | tathā cāha manuḥ—*
>
> *nānyasmin vidhavā nārī niyoktavyā dvijātibhiḥ |*
> *anyasmin hi niyuñjānā dharmaṃ hanyuḥ sanātanam iti ||* (MDh 9.64)
>
> *purākalpaṃ copanyasyopasaṃhṛtam—*
>
> *tadāprabhṛti yo mohāt pramītapatikāṃ striyam |*
> *niyojayaty apatyārthe taṃ vigarhanti sādhava iti ||* (MDh 9.68)
>
> *ato nāsti niyogaḥ | tathā ca śiṣṭasamācāraḥ |*

As one can see, the opponents of *niyoga* whose views are presented here support their position by citing several verses of Manu (9.64, 68) that condemn the practice and noting the fact that learned men (*śiṣṭa*) similarly refrain from engaging in it.

At this point, Viśvarūpa temporarily assumes the viewpoint of a hypothetical adversary and argues in favor of this adversary's position. That is, he begins a *pūrvapakṣa*. This particular *pūrvapakṣa* of Viśvarūpa is extremely long and tangential, so long, in fact, that it comprises the bulk of the commentator's exceptionally long discussion of *niyoga*. Thus, it is sometime before Viśvarūpa resumes his own voice and presents his own views on the topic. The *pūrvapakṣa* in defense of *niyoga* found in Viśvarūpa begins as follows:

> [Opponent:] But doesn't the very Smṛti text under discussion (YDh 1.68–69), which allows a man's brother to approach "his sonless wife with his elders' permission" and so forth, support *niyoga*? Manu's work also contains a statement (MDh 9.59) that "a duly appointed woman may obtain desirable progeny from her husband's brother or *sapiṇḍa* relative." And it cannot be said that these Smṛtis are rooted in greed or the like, for they completely prohibit any emotion in the practice of *niyoga*. Thus, it is said that a man engaging in the practice must "smear himself with ghee." (YDh 1.68) And Manu (9.60) also says the same:
>
> A man who has been appointed to a widow should at night smear himself with ghee and, refraining from speech, beget upon her a single son.
>
> Hence, the Smṛtis prescribing *niyoga* cannot be false scriptures. And if one were to contend that the motive behind the practice is a woman's desire for her father-in-law's wealth or the like, this too is refuted by the statement (MDh 9.59) that a duly appointed woman "may obtain desirable progeny . . . *if the family-line would die out*." Moreover, it is said (MDh 9.58):
>
> If they have sex when no calamity threatens, they both become outcastes, even if they were properly appointed.
>
> Vasiṣṭha (17.65) also states: "There is no *niyoga* out of greed for wealth." Hence, the practice is unobjectionable. However, the prohibitions against *niyoga* found in the scriptures result in it being optional, for there is no distinction between those scriptures enjoining the practice and those prohibiting it. In this way, there is no conflict between them.

nanv ayam api smṛtir eva aputrāṃ gurvanujñānād ity ādi (YDh 1.68) | *mānave 'pi devarād vā sapiṇḍād vā striyā saṃyaṅniyuktayety ādi* (MDh 9.59) | *na ceyaṃ lobhādimūleti śakyaṃ vaktuṃ sarvathā vikārapratiṣedhāt* | *tad uktaṃ ghṛtābhyakta iti* (YDh 1.68) | *manunāpi ca—*

vidhavāyāṃ niyuktas tu ghṛtākto vāgyato niśīti | (MDh 9.60) *ato neyam apasmṛtiḥ* | *atha śvaśuradhanādīcchayā lobha āśaṅkyeta* | *tad api prajepsitādhigantavyā saṃtānasya parikṣaya ity* (MDh 9.59) *anenaiva nirastam* | *tathā coktam—*

patitau bhavato gatvā niyuktāv apy anāpadīti |
vasiṣṭhenāpi—dhanalobhān nāsti niyoga iti (VaDh 17.65) | *ato nirdoṣaḥ* | *śāstrāviśeṣāt tu pratiṣedho vikalpāya* | *ato na virodhaḥ* |

The basic position of the *pūrvapakṣa*, as one can see, is that *niyoga* is a lawful practice when a man's family line would otherwise die out. Viśvarūpa's hypothetical opponent arrives at this position on the basis of Manu (9.59), who explicitly enjoins *niyoga* in such an event. However, according to this opponent, since other scriptures of equal authority to Manu clearly prohibit *niyoga*, the practice is strictly optional, not mandatory. Beyond this, the opponent defends his position against one possible objection to it: those Smṛti passages that enjoin *niyoga* are motivated either by greed for inheritance or sexual lust. The implication of this is that the Smṛtis in question lack the unseen or otherworldly purpose (*adṛṣṭārtha*) necessary for any behavioral rule to qualify as *dharma* according to classical Brahmanical thought. In order to refute this objection, Viśvarūpa's opponent argues that by requiring a man engaged in *niyoga* to smear himself with ghee, Manu (9.60) and Yājñavalkya (1.68) effectively prohibit the involvement of any passionate emotions, such as lust or greed, in the performance of the practice. The hypothetical opponent also notes that Vasiṣṭha (17.65) specifically forbids engaging in *niyoga* out of greed for wealth.

Having laid out his fundamental position on *niyoga*, Viśvarūpa's imagined opponent refutes an alternative view on the conditions under which *niyoga* is permissible:

> Others, however, hold that the right to engage in *niyoga* occurs when a girl's husband dies prior to marriage in accordance with the maxims (A) that a particular rule overrides a general one and (B) that the conclusion of a text clarifies its beginning.[47] For Manu (9.69) states at the end of his discussion of *niyoga*:
>
>> When a girl has been verbally promised in marriage and her husband dies, her own husband's brother should take her in accordance with this rule.

[47] On these maxims, see Kane (1962, 5:1341).

However, this position is refuted by the fact that Manu (9.60) speaks of a "man who has been appointed to a *widow*." One might respond that, surely, even a girl whose husband has died prior to marriage can be called a widow. But this is not true, for it conflicts with other Smṛtis. For instance, Vasiṣṭha (17.55–56) first speaks of the "wife (*patnī*) of a dead man for six months, observing her vow," and concludes by saying that she "should have her father or brother appoint a man for her." And it is not the case that even an unmarried woman can be the "wife (*patnī*) of a dead man," if her husband dies, for the word "wife" (*patnī*) is not applied to a woman prior to marriage, as the Smṛti of Lord Pāṇini (4.1.33) prescribes the use of the word "wife" (*patnī*) specifically for a woman involved in the performance of sacrifices.[48] Hence, by using the conclusion of Manu's text to clarify its beginning, these people have construed something that doesn't exist (i.e., a widow/wife who was never married).

anye tu prāg vivāhād uparate bhartari niyogādhikāraṃ varṇayanti sāmānyaviśeṣopasaṃhṛtinyāyāt | yathā manuḥ—

> *yasyā mriyeta kanyāyā vācā satye kṛte patiḥ |*
> *tām anena vidhānena nijo vindeta devara iti* || (MDh 9.69)

tat tu vidhavāyāṃ niyuktas tv ity anenaiva nirastam | nanu ca sāpi vidhaveti śakyaṃ vaktum | na smṛtyantaravirodhāt | yathā vasiṣṭhaḥ pretapatnī ṣaṇmāsaṃ vratacāriṇīty upakramya pitrā bhrātrā vā niyogaṃ kārayed ity ādi (VaDh 17.55–56) | *nanv anūḍhāpi prete patyau pretapatny eva | maivam | na hi prāg vivāhāt patnīśabdapravṛttir iti | evaṃ hi bhagavataḥ pāṇineḥ smaraṇam—patyur no yajñasaṃyoga iti* (4.1.33) | *ato 'satkalpanam upakramopasaṃhārāt* |

Here the idea is presented that *niyoga* is permissible only for a betrothed girl, whose fiancée dies prior to marriage. Significantly, several later commentators, such as Vijñāneśvara and the author of an unpublished early commentary on Yājñavalkya that will be discussed later in this chapter, endorse precisely this view, although not on the exact grounds presented here. In the above passage, an attempt is made to justify this view based upon the position within Manu of a particular verse (9.69) that prescribes either *niyoga*

[48] Technically *Aṣṭādhyāyī* 4.1.33 prescribes the form *patnī* ("wife") as the feminine equivalent of *pati* ("husband, lord") with the unusual *n* infix, when there is a connection with sacrifice (*yajñasaṃyoge*).

or remarriage with her husband's brother for a girl whose intended husband dies prior to marriage, when she has merely been verbally promised. Since this verse occurs after those passages of Manu (9.59–61) that seemingly enjoin *niyoga* and it is an accepted principle of Brahmanical hermeneutics that the later parts of a text tend to clarify its earlier parts, it is argued that the passages prescribing *niyoga* in Manu and elsewhere really apply only to betrothed girls.

The *pūrvapakṣa* refutes this position on the grounds that, in the context of enjoining *niyoga*, Manu (9.60) speaks specifically of a "widow" (*vidhavā*), a term that cannot reasonably be applied to a girl who has never been married, but simply betrothed. In addition, it is pointed out that Vasiṣṭha (17.55–56) prescribes *niyoga* for the "wife" (*patnī*) of a dead man, yet the revered grammarian Pāṇini (4.1.33) prescribes use of the word *patnī* only for a woman connected with Vedic sacrifices—rites in which only fully married women are entitled to participate. Hence, Viśvarūpa's hypothetical opponent argues that to hold *niyoga* to be permissible only for women who are merely betrothed is to hold that it is permissible only for a class of women that is a contradiction in terms: wives and widows who have never been married!

After refuting the position that *niyoga* is lawful only for betrothed women, Viśvarūpa's opponent then offers his own interpretation of the verse of Manu (9.69) that has led to this erroneous conclusion:

> How then do we explain Manu's verse (9.69) about a girl whose husband dies when she has been verbally promised in marriage? It should be explained as applying to marriages where a bride-price is paid. If after giving a bride-price for a girl the giver of that bride-price dies and the girl is willing, she may be given to her would-be husband's brother as per the prior arrangement. If she is unwilling, then she should have her husband's brother himself engage in *niyoga*. Alternatively, because of the phrase "her own" in Manu's statement (9.69) that "*her own* husband's brother should take her," it could be that a husband's brother, who is specifically her husband's full brother, should take her in accordance with this rule prescribing either *niyoga* or marriage. However, if her husband's brother has a different mother than her husband, the girl must consent to him. And, thus, Manu (9.97) states:
>
>> If a girl has had a bride-price paid for her and the giver of that bride-price dies, she should be given to her husband's brother, if she consents.

If, however, a girl's fiancée should die and he has not in fact paid a bride-price for her, then after his death, if she is still a young girl and so desires, her father may give her to another man according to the prescribed rules, as Vasiṣṭha (17.72) states:

> If a young girl has been given with words and the pouring of water, but her fiancée dies beforehand and she was never married with the recitation of mantras, then she belongs only to her father.

From the use of the word "beforehand" here, it is understood that, although she was verbally given in the context of a marriage, the girl is not yet of adolescent age.

katham tarhi yasyā mriyetety ayaṃ ślokaḥ | āsuravivāhaviṣayatayā vyākhyeyaḥ | yasyāḥ kanyāyāḥ śulkaṃ dattvā śulkado mriyeta sā yadīcchet tato devarāya pūrvavat pradātavyā | na cen niyogaṃ devareṇaiva kārayet | yad vā nijo vindeteti nijagrahaṇāt sodaryo devaro 'nena vidhinā naiyogikena vaivāhikena vā vindetaiva | sāpatnas tu kanyānumataḥ | tathā cāha—

> *kanyāyāṃ dattaśulkāyāṃ mriyeta yadi śulkadaḥ |*
> *devarāya pradātavyā yadi kanyānumanyata iti ||* (MDh 9.97)

yadā tv adattaśulka eva mriyeta tadā tasmin prete kumāry eva satīcchayānyasmai pitrā vidhivad deyā | yathāha vasiṣṭhaḥ—

> *adbhir vācā ca dattā yā mriyetādau varo yadi |*
> *na ca mantropanītā syāt kumārī pitur eva sā ||* (VaDh 17.72)

ādāv iti vacanād vivāhasaṃnidhau vāgdattāpy akanyaketi jñāyate |

Here, as one can see, the imagined opponent argues that the verse of Manu in question (9.69) actually applies specifically to marriages where, prior to his death, the groom paid a bride price to his future father-in-law. In such cases, either *niyoga* or marriage to the deceased groom's brother—depending upon the bride's inclination and one's interpretation of the relevant texts—is prescribed.

Following this minor tangent, Viśvarūpa's opponent then begins another longer tangent, which is strictly irrelevant to the issue of *niyoga*, but instead addresses a number of Smṛtis that seemingly allow widows to remarry under restricted conditions:

> Furthermore, this is the meaning of Vasiṣṭha's statement (17.73) about giving to another man "a girl who has been forcibly taken." The word "taken" in this statement means "defiled," for the particular form of the

word "taken" here has this force.[49] And one should understand that this statement applies to cases other than the rules governing Kṣatriyas, since it is impossible for a girl forcibly taken by them to be defiled.[50] If the girl in question has not been married with the recitation of mantras, then one may give her to another man according to the prescribed rules after having her perform a penance. And it is to be understood that once the girl has performed this penance, she is like a virgin in every way.

However, Vasiṣṭha addresses a different scenario in his statement (17.74) about the remarriage of "a girl who has merely been consecrated with mantras" "when the man who took her hand dies." The meaning of this statement is as follows. In accordance with a certain village law, a man might take a girl's hand even before their wedding ceremony. When a man who has taken a girl's hand in this fashion dies and only her nuptial offering prior to the ritual taking of her hand has been offered, that girl can, nevertheless, undergo the rite of marriage again with another husband, provided that she is still a virgin.

Thus, there is no remarriage for a girl once she has been fully married. Hence, it is said: "Widow remarriage is never prescribed in the rules of marriage." (MDh 9.65) And, therefore, Baudhāyana (4.1.16) speaks of remarriage "if a girl's husband dies after she has been given away or after the nuptial offering has been made." The meaning of this is that she can be married again even if she was given away and even if the nuptial offering was made, but not if she was fully married. The fact that the text stipulates "provided that she is a virgin" makes clear what I have just explained.

balāc cet prahṛtā kanyety (VaDh 17.73) *asya punar ayam arthaḥ | prahṛtā dūṣitā praśabdasāmarthyāt | kṣātrāc ca vidher anyatraiva draṣṭavyaṃ tatra dūṣaṇāsaṃbhavāt | yadi mantrair na saṃskṛtā tato 'nyasmai vidhivat prāyaścittaṃ kārayitvā deyā | kṛtaprāyaścittā ca yathā kanyā tathaiva seti mantavyam | idaṃ tu kalpāntaram—*

pāṇigrāhe mṛte kanyā kevalaṃ mantrasaṃskṛteti | (VaDh 17.74)

[49] The standard Sanskrit word for "taken" is *hṛta* from the root √*hṛ* ("to take"). However, the word used here is *prahṛta* with the additional preverb *pra*; and the combination *pra* + √*hṛ* often does not mean simply "to take," but rather "to assault." Viśvarūpa literally says that the word *prahṛta* ("taken") in Vasiṣṭha's statement must mean *dūṣita* ("defiled") because of the force of the preverb *pra*.

[50] Kṣatriyas are uniquely permitted to perform *rākṣasa* marriages, which are marriages where the groom forcibly abducts his bride. On this, see MDh 3.26, 33.

asyārthaḥ | *grāmadharmeṇa pūrvam api vivāhāt pāṇigrahaṇam* | *tasmin pāṇigrāhe* | *mṛte kanyā hut[aiva]*[51] *prāk pāṇigrahaṇād yady akṣatayoniḥ* | *tathāpy anyena bhartrā punar vivāhasaṃskāram arhatīti* | *sarvathā pariṇītāyāḥ punaḥ pariṇayanābhāvaḥ* | *tad uktam—*

na vivāhavidhāv uktaṃ vidhavāvedanaṃ kvacid iti | (MDh 9.65)

tathā ca baudhāyanaḥ—

nisṛṣṭāyāṃ hute vāpi yasyai bhartā mriyeta sa iti | (BDh 4.1.16)

api nisṛṣṭāyām api hute na pariṇītāyām ity arthaḥ | *sā ced akṣatayoniḥ syād ity etad eva spaṣṭīkaroti yad upavarṇitam asmābhiḥ* |

In this passage, the *pūrvapakṣa* first addresses a particular verse of Vasiṣṭha (17.73) that allows young women who were forcibly abducted and raped, but not properly married to marry other men and that stipulates that such women are ritually and legally equivalent to virgins. After presenting a fairly straightforward interpretation of this verse, Viśvarūpa's opponent then goes on to offer a more tortured interpretation of another verse of Vasiṣṭha (17.74), which permits a girl to remarry if the "man who took her hand" (*pāṇigrāha*) dies while she is still a virgin and has "merely been consecrated with mantras" (*kevalaṃ mantrasaṃskṛtā*). The problematic aspect of this verse, from Viśvarūpa's perspective, appears to involve the use of the term *pāṇigrāha*, which literally means "hand grasper," but conventionally means "husband," because a central event in traditional Hindu weddings is the groom's grasping of the bride's hand. The issue with this term seems to be that the grasping of the bride's hand at Brahmanical weddings—as Viśvarūpa understood them—takes place after the offering of the nuptial oblation at which mantras are recited. Thus, if the groom dies in the middle of the wedding immediately after the recitation of the mantras, he wouldn't yet have taken the bride's hand. So how can Vasiṣṭha refer to him as a "hand grasper" (*pāṇigrāha*)? In order to solve this technical ritual issue, Viśvarūpa's opponent notes that it is the custom of certain villages for men to take their fiancées' hands even before the wedding ceremony. He argues that it is this sort of hand grasping that Vasiṣṭha's verse alludes to. Hence, the *pūrvapakṣa* holds that, despite the appearance of certain Smṛtis (e.g., BDh 4.1.16), the authoritative scriptures completely forbid women whose wedding ceremonies

[51] The printed edition reads *huter vā*, which I have tentatively emended to *hutaiva*, since the printed reading is unintelligible, at least to me, and this portion of the text presumably contains Viśvarūpa's gloss of *kevalaṃ mantrasaṃskṛtā* ("merely been consecrated with mantras") in VaDh 17.74.

have been fully performed from remarrying. And it is noteworthy that Viśvarūpa's later comments give us no reason to believe that he disagrees with the *pūrvapakṣa* on this particular point.

After the above tangent, which makes a case against widow remarriage, Viśvarūpa's imagined opponent returns to the issue of *niyoga* proper:

> Hence, the Smṛtis prescribing *niyoga* do not apply to virgins. To what then do they apply? They apply to cases where the husband has died and his family-line will die out. And due to the force of the scriptural prohibitions against it, *niyoga* is optional. Moreover, the Veda (AiB 12.12) states:
>
> > Therefore, a single man has many wives; a single woman does not have many co-husbands.
>
> And from the fact that specifically "co-husbands" are here prohibited, it is understood that a woman can have multiple husbands sequentially (but not simultaneously). The Veda (ŚPB 4.1.5.9) also states:
>
> > I will not abandon the man to whom my father gives me so long as he lives.
>
> And from this statement prohibiting the abandonment of a living husband, one understands that *niyoga* occurs after a woman's husband has died. Beyond this, the practice of *niyoga* is especially clear from the following mantra (ṚV 10.40.2):
>
> > Who invites you into his home, like a widow her husband's brother into her bed, like a young lady a man?
>
> For the meaning of this is that Indra, having seen the Aśvins after a long time, says to them: "You are hard to find. Where are you off to again? Does someone invite—i.e., attend upon—you, like a widowed woman bringing into her bed, the place of pleasure, her husband's mortal—i.e., having a human nature—brother?" Therefore, the text makes the practice of *niyoga* quite clear. And, thus, Vasiṣṭha (17.61) states: "At Prajāpati's hour, the appointed man should approach her like a husband." Hence, *niyoga* is a blameless practice.
>
> *ato na kanyāviṣayā niyogasmṛtiḥ | kas tarhi viṣayaḥ | prete patyau saṃtānaparikṣaye ca | pratiṣedhasāmarthyāc ca vikalpaḥ | tathā cāmnāyaḥ—*
>
> > *tasmād ekasya bahvyo jāyā bhavanti naikasyai bahavaḥ sahapataya iti |* (AiB 12.12)
>
> *sahapratiṣedhāc ca krameṇa bhavantīti jñāyate | tathā—*

yasmai māṃ pitā dadyān naivāhaṃ taṃ jīvantaṃ hāsyāmīti | (ŚPB 4.1.5.9) *jīva[d]ahānavacanāc*[52] *ca mṛte bhartari niyogo 'stīti jñāyate* |
ko vāṃ śayutrā vidhaveva devaraṃ maryaṃ na yoṣā sadhastha ā || (ṚV 10.40.2)
ity asmāt punar mantravarṇāt spaṣṭataro niyogaḥ | *evaṃ hīndreṇa cirād dṛṣṭāv aśvināv uktau durdarśau yuvāṃ kva punar vidhaveva yoṣā devaraṃ maryaṃ manuṣyabhāvaṃ śayane harṣasthāne āpādayantī kaccid ā kurute vām upacaratīty arthaḥ* | *anena niyogaṃ spaṣṭīkaroti* | *tathā ca vasiṣṭhaḥ—prājāpatye muhūrte pāṇigrāhavad upacared iti* (VaDh 17.61) | *ato 'navadyo niyogaḥ* |

Here Viśvarūpa's opponent returns to the topic of *niyoga* by drawing a pertinent conclusion from his preceding discussion of widow remarriage: since certain scriptures allow betrothed virgins to marry again, those Smṛtis that enjoin *niyoga* cannot apply strictly to such women. He then proceeds to reiterate his own position on *niyoga*, namely, that it is an optional practice, permissible to widows in general, but only when their husbands' family lines are threatened with extinction. Following this, the hypothetical opponent cites three Vedic passages that confirm his position on *niyoga*. The first two of these (AiB 12.12, ŚPB 4.1.5.9) speak against a woman having multiple husbands simultaneously and abandoning her husband while he lives. Thus, at least according to Viśvarūpa's *pūrvapakṣa*, these passages implicitly permit women to engage in *niyoga* after their husbands' deaths. The third Vedic passage cited by the *pūrvapakṣa* is the line of the *Ṛgveda* (10.4.2) presented at the beginning of this chapter as early evidence of the practice of levirate in South Asia. As readers may recall and can see from the above passage, this line compares a person inviting the Aśvins to his home with a widow inviting her husband's brother into her bed.

At this point, Viśvarūpa's lengthy and meandering *pūrvapakṣa* finally comes to an end. Thereafter, the commentator attempts to rebut the position of his hypothetical opponent and offers his own opinion on the practice of *niyoga*:

[Author:] To this I reply that the Smṛtis prescribing *niyoga* should not be explained in this way, for such an explanation conflicts with customary practice and it is illogical to regard *niyoga* as optional. To what then do the

[52] The printed edition reads *jīvannahānavacanāc*.

Smṛtis prescribing *niyoga* apply? They apply to Śūdra women. Why is this? Because Manu (9.64) states the following:

> Twice-born men should not appoint a widowed woman to another man.

Consequently, the prohibition against the practice applies specifically to members of the twice-born classes, whereas the injunction for it is issued generally such that it applies to Śūdras. Therefore, there is no grounds for it being optional. And, thus, it is said about *niyoga*:

> This is a law for beasts reviled by educated twice-born men. It was prescribed for men as well when Vena reigned as king. (MDh 9.66)

The phrase "for men as well" means "also for Śūdras." And customary practice confirms this.

atrocyate | naivaṃ niyogasmṛtir vyākhyeyā samācāravirodhād vikalpasya cānyāyyatvāt | kathaṃ tarhi | śūdrāviṣayā niyogasmṛtiḥ | kuta etat | manuvacanāt—

> *nānyasmin vidhavā nārī niyoktavyā dvijātibhir iti* | (MDh 9.64)

dvijātisaṃbaddhaḥ pratiṣedhaḥ | sāmānyataḥ śūdrasaṃbandhitayā vidhiḥ | tasmād avikalpaḥ | tathā coktam—

> *ayaṃ dvijair hi vidvadbhiḥ paśudharmo vigarhitaḥ |*
> *manuṣyāṇām api prokto vene rājyaṃ praśāsatīti* || (MDh 9.66)

manuṣyāṇām api śūdrāṇām apīty arthaḥ | tathā ca samācāraḥ |

Here, at long last, Viśvarūpa states his fundamental position on the issue of *niyoga*: it is a lawful practice for Śūdras and only Śūdras. Hence, since the Dharmaśāstra tradition is concerned almost exclusively with the behavior of high-caste Hindus, especially Brahmins, and decidedly disinterested in the customary practices of the lower castes, his position on *niyoga* is tantamount to a prohibition against it.

As readers can see, Viśvarūpa argues for his position on the basis of both custom and scriptural exegesis. Regarding the former, he provides no details. However, one may reasonably infer from context that Viśvarūpa understands widow remarriage to be essentially a low-caste practice, as in fact it has often been in more recent times.[53] Regarding the latter, Viśvarūpa makes a specific argument as to why scripture supports his position: since scriptural injunctions to engage in *niyoga* are issued generally,

[53] See Kane (1962, 2:615).

yet Manu's prohibition against the practice (9.64) is directed specifically at twice-born men, it follows that the scriptures enjoin *niyoga* only for non-twice-born people, that is, Śūdras. In order to appreciate Viśvarūpa's argument here, it is necessary to recall a particular axiom of Brahmanical hermeneutics, namely, that a specific rule overrides a general one. Consequently, according to Viśvarūpa, there is no reason to construe the practice of *niyoga* as optional, as his opponent proposes, for an option only arises when an injunction and prohibition apply to the same set of subjects with equal force.

After establishing his basic position that *niyoga* is permissible only for Śūdras, Viśvarūpa then adds another numerically small class of people for whom it may be permissible: kings of the Kṣatriya class whose dynasties are threatened with extinction. This he does in the following passage:

> As for the fact that Vyāsa sired children upon the wives of Vicitravīrya, one should pay no heed to that, just like Draupadī's marriage to five men. Alternatively, it could be that *niyoga* is permitted also for Kṣatriyas in order to protect their kingdoms, when their family-lines would otherwise die out. And, in that case, the practice is permissible only for kings specifically, as it accords only with their duties. Moreover, because of what Vyāsa has said, only a Brahmin should be appointed to sire children for kings. And, this being the case, certain Vedic passages must also apply only to Kṣatriyas, such as the statement (ŚPB 4.1.5.9): "I will not abandon the man to whom my father gives me so long as he lives." The meaning of this Vedic statement is that a woman should not abandon her living, capable husband. However, the statement (AiB 12.12) that "a single woman does not have many co-husbands" concerns remarriage (not *niyoga*). The word "husband" in it is to be taken literally. By contrast, one should interpret the previously quoted mantra (ṚV 10.40.2) as applying only to Śūdras. One should also interpret other statements mentioning husbands' brothers and the like in this fashion. And, thus, Manu the Elder states:
>
> > This law of resorting to another man when one's husband dies is for Śūdras alone. It is also practiced by uneducated Kṣatriyas, deluded by greed.
>
> And, after stating this, he says:
>
> > On this issue, wise men quote a hymn spoken by Vāyu. Among Brahmins, there is neither *niyoga* nor remarriage after a woman's husband has died.
>
> The hymn referred to here is this:

Neither of these things should Brahmins do: appoint a widow to beget children or marry a woman when her husband has died, especially if one is her husband's brother.

yat punar vyāsena vicitravīryabhāryāsv apatyotpādanaṃ tad draupadīvivāhavad anādṛtyam | atha vā kṣatriyāṇām apy anvayakṣaye rājyaparipālanāya niyogo 'bhyanujñāyate | sa ca rājñām eva kāryānurodhāt | vyāsavacanāc ca rājñāṃ brāhmaṇenaiva kārayitavyam | evaṃ ca saty āmnāyā api kṣatriyaviṣayā eva naivāhaṃ taṃ jīvantaṃ hāsyāmīty ādi (ŚPB 4.1.5.9) | *jīvan samartho na hātavya ity āmnāyārthaḥ* | *naikasyai bahavaḥ sahapataya iti* (AiB 12.12) *tu punaḥsaṃskāraviṣayam* | *tatra mukhyaḥ patiśabdaḥ* | *mantravarṇas tu śūdraviṣaya eva vyākhyeyaḥ* | *evaṃ devarādivākyāny anyāny api vyākhyeyāni* | *tathā ca vṛddhamanuḥ—*

śūdrāṇām eva dharmo 'yaṃ patyau prete 'nyasaṃśrayaḥ |
lobhān mūḍhair avidvadbhiḥ kṣatriyair api caryate ||

ity uktvāha—

vāyuproktāṃ tathā gāthāṃ paṭhanty atra manīṣiṇaḥ |
viprāṇāṃ na niyogo 'sti prete patyau na vedanam ||

iyaṃ sā gāthā—

akāryam etad viprāṇāṃ vidhavā yan niyujyate |
uhyate vā mṛte patyau devareṇa viśeṣataḥ ||

Here, as one can see, Viśvarūpa cites Vyāsa's behavior in the *Mahābhārata* as a justification for extending the right to engage in *niyoga* to the widows of certain kings, specifically those whose dynasties would otherwise come to end. Additionally, since Viśvarūpa's opponent might still defend his position on the basis of the Vedic passages that he argued tacitly support *niyoga*, Viśvarūpa subsequently explains these passages as variously applying to Kṣatriyas (ŚPB 4.1.5.9), Śūdras (ṚV 10.40.2), or remarriage rather than *niyoga* (AiB 12.12). In this way, he fully refutes the earlier *pūrvapakṣa*.

Next Viśvarūpa raises and responds to a hypothetical objection to his own position on *niyoga*, an objection based upon a verse ascribed to Vasiṣṭha, but not found in the extant *Vasiṣṭha Dharmasūtra*. Although Viśvarūpa does not provide a full uninterrupted quotation of the relevant verse, a close reading of his commentary allows one to reconstruct it with some confidence as follows:

When his brother is teaching,[54] a man should never learn from him without an excuse on account of possibly sleeping with his teacher's wife, for a husband's brother becomes a husband in calamities.

bhrāṭary avyapadeśena nādhyetavyaṃ kadā cana |
gurutalpasya nimittaṃ bhartā hy āpatsu devaraḥ ||

My translation here is intended to convey a natural interpretation of this admittedly cryptic verse. As one can see, it prohibits a man from having his brother as his teacher without a good excuse. Furthermore, it provides a perfectly understandable reason for this prohibition: if his brother dies and he is appointed to beget a child upon his widow in accordance with the rules of *niyoga*, he would then be compelled to sleep with his teacher's wife—one of the five most heinous sins in Dharmaśāstra literature.[55] The particular problem that this verse poses for Viśvarūpa is that it seemingly allows a teacher's widow to engage in *niyoga*, yet Dharmaśāstra texts allow only Brahmins to act as teachers.

Viśvarūpa explains his solution to this problem as follows:

[Objection:] But how then does Vasiṣṭha state the following?

When his brother is teaching, a man without his designation should never learn from him [on account of possible sexual impropriety involving a teacher, for a lord is a husband's brother in calamities.]

For one understands from this that Brahmins also have the right to engage in *niyoga*, since they alone are connected with teaching.

[Author:] I say that this interpretation is incorrect, for the text states the logic underlying it. Moreover, it is better to hold that a single passage with a contrary intent is nullified than to render many more passages with harmonious intent pointless. And this passage of Vasiṣṭha applies to Kṣatriyas, for they have the right to engage in *niyoga* in the event of a calamity; and I have already explained that only a Brahmin may act as levir in their case. Therefore, Vasiṣṭha's statement should be construed as

[54] From Viśvarūpa's commentary it is clear that the "brother" (*bhrātari*) in this verse is teaching, although nothing in the verse itself indicates this. Thus, it is necessary to supply a locative participle, such as *adhyāpayati* ("teaching"), which Viśvarūpa himself supplies.

[55] These five sins are technically called *mahāpātakas* ("great sins causing loss of caste"). In addition to sleeping with a teacher or other elder's wife, they are as follows: killing a Brahmin, drinking liquor, stealing a Brahmin's gold, and associating with an outcaste. On these, see, e.g., MDh 11.55 and YDh 3.228.

follows. Even when his brother is teaching, a man should not learn from him. What man specifically? "A man without his designation." A man who is not designated by the same term as another is a "man without his designation." He is, in other words, a man of a different caste. Why would this be a rule? One can discern the answer: "on account of possible sexual impropriety involving a teacher," that is, because the brother who teaches might be obliged to have sex with his student's wife, "for a lord is a husband's brother in calamities." The "lord" referred to here is a Brahmin, because etymologically the word means "supporter"[56] and a Brahmin is the highest. Since he becomes the husband's brother, i.e., is appointed to a woman, in calamities, therefore his Kṣatriya brother should not learn from him. The phrase "in calamities" refers to just a single calamity. The plural is used to the show the seriousness of it, as that calamity is none other than the one characterized by the dying out of a family-line. In addition, given that the text should say that the Kṣatriya brother "should not be taught," the fact that it says that he "should not learn" is intended to communicate that a son begotten through *niyoga* belongs to the woman's husband.[57] Besides, how could it be right that Vasiṣṭha's statement applies to Brahmins? For it is impossible for full brothers to engage in *niyoga*. Why is this? Even if such a brother without a son were to be appointed to beget sons, he would beget a son only for himself. Now, suppose instead the brother had a son. In that case, why would *niyoga* occur? For his full brother's family-line would not die out on the account the statement (MDh 9.182):

> If just one brother among several brothers born from a single source has a son, then through that son they all have a son—so Manu has declared.

If, however, Vasiṣṭha's statement applies to Kṣatriyas, this conflict does not occur. One might argue that the statement applies to any brothers with different mothers. That would be the same in the case of a Kṣatriya half-brother as well. However, when the phrase "born from a single source" is understood to mean "born of a single caste," then it is absolutely clear that Vasiṣṭha's statement applies to Kṣatriyas.

[56] The word here translated as "lord" (*bhartṛ*), which frequently also means "husband," is etymologically an agent noun from √*bhṛ* ("to support").

[57] Viśvarūpa's reasoning here is unclear to me. Perhaps he imagines that the use of the active verb "to learn" in preference to the passive verb "to be taught" somehow connotes agency on the part of the woman's husband in the practice of *niyoga*.

katham idānīm etad vasiṣṭhavacanam—
bhrātary avyapadeśena nādhyetavyaṃ kadā caneti |
anena hy adhyāpanasaṃbandhād brāhmaṇānām api niyogādhikāro 'stīti gamyate |
ucyate | naitad yuktam uktatvān nyāyasya | bhūyasām ananyaparāṇāṃ cānarthakyād varam ekasyānyaparasya ca bādhakalpanā | kṣatriyaviṣayaṃ caitad vākyaṃ teṣāṃ hy āpadi niyogādhikārāt | sa ca brāhmaṇenaivety uktam | tenaivaṃ yojanā bhrātary adhyāpayaty api nādhyetavyam | kena | avyapadeśena | na vyapadiśyate 'nenety avyapadeśaḥ | anyajātīya ity arthaḥ | kimartham | boddhavyaṃ gurutalpasya nimittaṃ bhrātuḥ śiṣyabhāryāgamanāt | bhartā hy āpatsu devaraḥ | bharteti bharaṇayogāc chraiṣṭhyāc ca brāhmaṇaḥ | sa yasmād āpatsu devaro bhavati niyojyata ity arthas tasmāt tato nādhyetavyam | āpatsv iti caikasyām evāpadi | bahuvacanaṃ gauravārthaṃ saṃtānaparikṣayalakṣaṇaivāpad yathā syāt | nādhyāpayitavya iti ca vaktavye nādhyetavyam ity uktaṃ kṣetriṇaḥ putra iti jñāpanārtham |
kathaṃ vāsya brāhmaṇaviṣayatvopapattiḥ | na hi sodaryayor niyogasaṃbhavaḥ | kathaṃ kṛtvā | yadi tāvan niyojyo 'py aputras tadātmana evotpādayet | atha tasya putro 'sti | tadā
bhrātṝṇām ekajātānāṃ yady ekaḥ putravān bhavet |
sarve te tena putreṇa putriṇo manur abravīt || (MDh 9.182)
iti vacanād akṣīṇatvāt saṃtānasya kuto niyogaḥ | kṣatriyaviṣayatve tu naiṣa virodhaḥ | atha sāpatnaviṣayatocyeta | tat kṣatriye 'pi samānam | yadā tv ekajātānām ity asyaikavarṇajātānām ity arthas tadā spaṣṭaiva kṣatriyaviṣayatā |

Here Viśvarūpa proposes two different ways of dealing with Vasiṣṭha's problematic verse. First, he invokes a hermeneutic principle attested elsewhere in Dharmaśāstra literature: it is right to nullify a single incongruous scriptural passage when it directly conflicts with many other scriptural passages that are in harmony with one another.[58] Thus, Viśvarūpa suggests that one might simply consider this particular verse of Vasiṣṭha to be nullified or overruled by other Smṛtis. Second, he offers his own rather tortured interpretation of Vasiṣṭha's verse, which I have attempted to reflect in my translation.

This interpretation starts with the word *avyapadeśa*, which one might take to mean "without excuse or pretext," but which Viśvarūpa takes to mean

[58] On this, see Kane (1962, 5:1266).

"without one's title or designation" and, thus, to denote a brother of a different caste, specifically, in the context of Vasiṣṭha's verse, a Kṣatriya half-brother. Viśvarūpa argued earlier in his commentary on the basis of Vyāsa's behavior in the *Mahābhārata* that in cases of *niyoga* involving a Kṣatriya, a Brahmin must act as the levir. Consequently, he holds that, in Vasiṣṭha's verse, it is the Brahmin teacher, rather than the Kṣatriya student, whom the rules of *niyoga* would compel to engage in sexual impropriety. Thus, according to Viśvarūpa, the word *gurutalpa* in the verse does not denote the sin of a student having sex with his teacher's wife, as it usually does. Instead, it denotes the opposite sin of a teacher having sex with his student's wife. And this in turn forces Viśvarūpa to inventively reinterpret two key terms in the final *pāda* of Vasiṣṭha's verse. The first of these is *bhartṛ*, which one would naturally interpret as "husband." Viśvarūpa, however, takes it to mean "Brahmin," since the word can also mean "lord" and "supporter"—sensible descriptions of a Brahmin in Viśvarūpa's mind. The second reinterpreted term is *devara*, which ordinarily refers to a husband's brother, but Viśvarūpa effectively takes to mean "levir." In this way, Viśvarūpa constructs an alternative reading of Vasiṣṭha's verse that suits his purpose, even if it is unlikely to be convincing to modern readers.

Furthermore, in order to support his alternative reading, Viśvarūpa argues that Vasiṣṭha's verse cannot refer to full brothers or brothers of the same caste, for Manu (9.182) states that when there are several brothers of the same caste and one of them fathers a son, all of them have a son. Therefore, since *niyoga* is permissible only when a man's family line would die out according to Viśvarūpa, there would be no reason for a man to act as a levir for his full brother or for a brother of the same caste. For if the man has a son, his deceased brother will likewise have a son; and if he doesn't have a son, he would father a child for himself, not his brother.

Finally, before concluding his exceptionally long discussion of *niyoga* and widow remarriage, Viśvarūpa addresses the period of waiting prescribed in certain texts for a Brahmin woman whose husband has gone abroad:

> As for those scriptural statements that enjoin a Brahmin woman to wait for a certain period of time when her husband has gone abroad, one must conclude upon careful examination that their purpose is to instruct a woman to go to her husband after this period, not to engage in *niyoga*. Therefore, I have properly stated how one should construe the spheres of applicability

of various scriptures dealing with *niyoga*. Thus, the right to engage in *niyoga* is prescribed for Śūdras.

> *yat tu brāhmaṇyāḥ proṣite bhartari kālapratīkṣaṇavacanaṃ tad bhartur antikagamanārthaṃ na niyogārtham iti vivicya vacanīyam | tasmāt sūktā niyogavākyānāṃ viṣayakalpanā | evaṃ tāvac chūdrāṇāṃ niyogādhikāra uktaḥ |*

Here Viśvarūpa argues—not very convincingly—that when certain Smṛtis (e.g., GDh 18.15–17, VaDh 17.75–80, MDh 9.76) prescribe a period of waiting for a Brahmin woman whose husband has gone abroad, their intention is not that, after this period, a woman should engage in *niyoga* much less remarry, but simply that she should go to her husband. Thereafter, Viśvarūpa suitably ends his lengthy discussion of *niyoga* by reiterating his fundamental position on the practice: it is permissible only for Śūdras. This, as I have said, is tantamount to a prohibition against the practice within the context of Dharmaśāstra. Hence, despite his exceptionally long and intricate treatment of the topic, Viśvarūpa arrives at a position on *niyoga* effectively no different from that of any Dharmaśāstra commentator other than Bhāruci. Simply put, he holds that it is wrong.

Medhātithi

After Viśvarūpa, the next Dharmaśāstra author to discuss *niyoga* appears to be Medhātithi, who likely wrote his celebrated commentary on the *Mānava Dharmaśāstra* in ninth-century Kashmir.[59] Like Manu, Medhātithi unambiguously opposes widow remarriage. This is clear, for instance, from the following statement (on MDh 5.163–64), where he succinctly expresses his understanding of women's duties to their husbands according to Manu:

> These verses of Manu summarize a woman's duties and a woman's duties are straightforward. Therefore, I will take the trouble to explain them here. This is the gist of the teachings on this topic: a woman cannot remarry[60]

[59] On the provenance of Medhātithi, see Kane (1962, 1:574–75, 583).

[60] The Sanskrit phrase for remarriage here, *punaḥ saha pravṛtti*, is rather unusual. Literally, it means "starting again with."

another man in this world as a man remarries another woman on account of the rule that she "should not transgress against her deceased husband." (MDh 5.151)

strīdharmopasaṃhāraślokā ṛjavaś ca strīdharmā ity ato mayātra vyākhyānādaraḥ kṛtaḥ | etāvat tatropadeśārthaḥ | yathā puṃso 'nyayā saha punaḥpravṛttikarma neha saṃsthitaṃ ca na laṅghayed ity (MDh 5.151) *anena nyāyena punaḥ saha pravṛttir iti* |

Unfortunately, however, Medhātithi does not express his personal position on *niyoga* as clearly and as forthrightly as he does his position on widow remarriage. Nevertheless, a careful examination of his commentary leads to the conclusion that he effectively opposes the practice. Thus, his basic position on the topic broadly resembles those of other Dharmaśāstra exegetes, although the specific details of his views on *niyoga* are generally unique to him.

Like the root text on which he comments, Medhātithi mentions the practice of *niyoga* in a number of different places. However, he discusses the issue most in earnest in his commentary on the following verse of Manu (9.64), which effectively prohibits *niyoga* among the twice-born classes:

> Twice-born men should never appoint a widowed woman to another man, for those who appoint such a woman to another man kill the eternal law.

nānyasmin vidhavā nārī niyoktavyā dvijātibhiḥ |
anyasmin hi niyuñjānā dharmaṃ hanyuḥ sanātanam ||

As discussed earlier, this verse comes immediately after a series of verses (9.57–63), where Manu prescribes *niyoga* for a widow whose husband's family line will otherwise die out. These verses, therefore, seem to represent a sort of *pūrvapakṣa* or opponent's view in Manu's text; and the verse cited above appears to constitute the start of Manu's personal view on *niyoga* and of his refutation of the preceding *pūrvapakṣa*. Consequently, it is a very natural place for Medhātithi to discuss the legitimacy of the practice in detail.

Medhātithi begins his commentary by noting that the verse under discussion constitutes a prohibition against *niyoga*, a practice that was previously enjoined.[61] He then presents one possible way to explain away this seeming contradiction within Manu and between various Smṛtis:

> On this issue, some hold that because this verse speaks of a widow, the prohibition against *niyoga* applies only to a woman whose husband has died. An impotent husband, by contrast, may appoint his wife to another man. Thus, the injunction for and prohibition against *niyoga* apply to different subjects.
>
> *tatra ke cid vidhavāgrahaṇān mṛtabhartṛkāyāḥ pratiṣedhaḥ klībena tu patyā niyoktavyeti vidhipratiṣedau vibhaktaviṣayāv iti pratipannāḥ* |

Here it is noted that Manu explicitly forbids widows from engaging in *niyoga*, but earlier enjoins the practice for women more generally. Based upon this, it is suggested that the cumulative effect of Manu's rules regarding *niyoga* is to prohibit it for widows, but to allow it for other eligible women, namely, the wives of impotent and diseased men.

Following this, Medhātithi lays out an alternative position ascribed to certain unnamed others. This position is rather detailed and lengthy and takes up the bulk of his discussion of the legitimacy of *niyoga*. And although he presents it as a *pūrvapakṣa* or opponents' view, Medhātithi himself seems to agree with it to a significant extent, as we will see. As presented by Medhātithi, this *pūrvapakṣa* first refutes the previously mentioned attempt to harmonize Manu's rules concerning *niyoga*:

> Others, however, argue the following: One hears in the statement containing the injunction to perform *niyoga* that the breaking of the man's family-line is the cause of the practice. From this it follows that *niyoga* is appropriate when a husband is impotent or diseased as well as dead. Moreover, like the injunction, the prohibition against the practice is also indeed unqualified. A woman whose connection to her husband has ceased is called a "widow." Thus, the term fits equally the wives of both kinds of men (i.e., the impotent or diseased and the dead). And one should certainly understand the use of the term in this way. Otherwise, when a woman is appointed to another man by an impotent husband, the restrictive rules that the man must smear himself with ghee, etc. would not apply, for in the case of these rules as well,

[61] Medhātithi on MDh 9.64: *pūrveṇa vihitasya niyogasya pratiṣedho 'yam* |

scripture says that a "man who has been appointed to *a widow* should smear himself with ghee." (MDh 9.60) Therefore, the prohibition of what has been enjoined without qualification is also unqualified.

anye tu—vidhivākye saṃtānavicchedasya nimittaśravaṇāt tasya ca klībavyādhitayor mṛtasyāpy upapattiḥ | tathā ca vidhivat pratiṣedho 'py aviśiṣṭa eva | apetadhavasaṃbandhā vidhavety ucyate | tat tulyam ubhayatrāpi | avaśyaṃ caitad evaṃ vijñeyam | itarathā ghṛtāktādiniyamo 'pi klībena niyujyamānāyā na syāt | tatrāpi hy āmananti vidhavāyāṃ niyuktaś ca ghṛtākta iti (MDh 9.60) | *tasmād vihitasyāviśeṣeṇa pratiṣedho 'py aviśiṣṭaḥ* |

Here it is argued that since Manu prescribes *niyoga* in the event that a man's lineage will otherwise come to end and an impotent man, a diseased man, and a dead man might all equally be faced with this calamity, he enjoins *niyoga* for widows as well as the wives of impotent and diseased men. It is then argued that, like the injunction to perform *niyoga*, the prohibition against it must also be unqualified, that is, apply equally to the wives of dead, diseased, and impotent men. The reason for this is that the word "widow" (*vidhavā*) supposedly denotes any woman whose connection to her husband has ceased and, as such, must be applicable not only to women whose husbands have died but also to those whose husbands are sickly or impotent. Otherwise, if the word "widow" applied only to women whose husbands are dead, Manu's rule (9.60) requiring a levir to smear himself with ghee would not apply in instances of *niyoga* involving the wife of a sickly or impotent man, for Manu explicitly prescribes this rule for a man appointed to a widow. From this the *pūrvapakṣa* concludes that, in the case of *niyoga*, both the scriptural prohibition and the scriptural injunction have the same generic sphere of applicability and, consequently, that they cannot be harmonized by construing them as applying to different subjects, as proposed.

At this point, the *pūrvapakṣa* explains what it regards as the right way to reconcile Manu's injunction to perform *niyoga* with his prohibition against the practice:

Consequently, given that the injunction for and the prohibition against *niyoga* apply to the same range of subjects, the practice is optional. And it is fitting that the obligatory injunction to beget children become subject to an option, like the conflicting instructions to grasp and not grasp the *ṣoḍaśin* cup. But when the injunction to beget children promises such rewards as that one will "win worlds through a son," (MDh 9.137) how can there be an option between the injunction and the prohibition as they yield different rewards? For if a man has no child, he cannot receive the help in the hereafter that a child would render. Some hold that, in the case of the grasping and not grasping of the *ṣoḍaśin* cup, the injunction and the prohibition, both of which apply to the same subject, become options toward the same end. It has been said, however, that the more components there are in a rite, the greater the rite's reward, but that when it comes to accomplishing the main rite itself, there is no difference. Therefore, in the position he lays out in this verse (9.64), Manu states that one does not receive the help that a son would render. However, if a woman engages in *niyoga* with the goal of receiving this special help in violation of the textual prohibition, her behavior is analogous to performing the *śyena* rite.

ataś ca viṣayasamatve vidhiniṣedhayor vikalpaḥ | ayaṃ ca nityo 'patyotpādanavidhir vikalpa eva kalpate grahaṇāgrahaṇavat | yadā tu putreṇa jayatīty (MDh 9.137) *evamādiphalotpādanavidhis tadāsaty apatye tatkār yasyaurdhvadehikasyopakārasyābhāvād bhinnaphalayoḥ kuto vikalpaḥ | samānaviṣayau vidhiniṣedhāv ekārthe vikalpyete ṣoḍaś[i]grahaṇāgrahaṇayor iti ke cit | uktam aṅgabhūyastve phalabhūyastvam | pradhānakāryasiddhau tv aviśeṣaḥ | tasmād asmin pakṣe putropakārābhāvam āha | upakāraviśeṣārthenāsya pravṛttau pratiṣedhātikrameṇa śyenatulyatā |*

Here, as one can see, it is argued, in keeping with the standard rules of Brahmanical hermeneutics, that since there is an injunction to perform *niyoga* and a prohibition against the practice and both the injunction and prohibition have the same sphere of applicability, *niyoga* must be optional. And it is noteworthy that although this is presented as the view of a *pūrvapakṣa* or unnamed others, it is in fact Medhātithi's own personal view as well. This is clear, for instance, from a passage found much earlier in his commentary (on MDh 5.163–64), where he states:

The statement that "even a sonless woman goes to heaven" (MDh 5.160) prohibits a widow from bearing children in the event of a calamity. A scriptural passage prescribing *niyoga*, however, will permit it later on. Therefore, since it is both prescribed and prohibited, bearing children is optional for widows.

tathā svargaṃ gacchaty aputrāpīty (MDh 5.160) *anenāpatyajananam āpadi pratiṣidhyate | niyogasmṛtyā tu tat punar abhyanujñāsyate | tad etad apatyotpādanam uktapratiṣiddhatvād vikalpyate |*

However, the *pūrvapakṣa* is obviously not content simply to establish *niyoga* as optional, for it goes on to mention the specific additional otherworldly rewards that a son is held to bring his parents. Noting this, it asks how lifelong celibacy and *niyoga* can be equal options for a widow, when the latter potentially bestows far greater benefit. In order to answer this question, the *pūrvapakṣa* discusses the standard Mīmāṃsā example of an injunction and prohibition that together result in an option: the *śoḍaśin* cup in the Atirātra rite, which one Vedic passage instructs the sacrificer to grasp and another instructs him not to grasp.[62] Specifically, it notes that while a person can complete the Atirātra rite either way, the rite is held to yield a greater reward if the *śoḍaśin* cup is taken up due to the principle that a rite yields a greater reward the more ritual elements are incorporated into it. Based upon this Vedic example and the hermeneutic principles derived therefrom, the *pūrvapakṣa* argues that, by engaging in *niyoga*, a woman gains the extra benefits that come with a son. In other words, it argues that *niyoga* is effectively a superior option to celibacy, which gives the temporary appearance that it supports *niyoga*.

Immediately after this, however, the *pūrvapakṣa* draws upon another hermeneutic principle often invoked in Dharmaśāstra commentaries: any action that people are naturally inclined to perform cannot qualify as *dharma*, even if an authoritative scripture enjoins it. In practice, this principle is used to divest certain scriptural passages of injunctive force. Here the *pūrvapakṣa* uses it to remove the injunctive force of those passages of Manu and other Smṛtis that prescribe *niyoga*, for it is argued that people are naturally inclined to seek the special otherworldly rewards that a son bestows. Therefore, if a woman engages in *niyoga* for this reason, her behavior does not qualify as *dharma*.[63] Worse, there remains in effect a scriptural prohibition against the

[62] On this, see Śabara's commentary on PMS 10.8.6.

[63] As Pollock (1997, 411–12) notes, Brahmanical literature offers surprisingly little discussion of what constitutes a natural or mundane motive for an action and, thus, disqualifies an action as *dharma*. In general, actions done to attain benefits in the hereafter are not held to have natural or mundane motives. However, in cases where scripture specifies a particular otherworldly reward

practice. Thus, by engaging in *niyoga* to acquire a son, a woman is actively violating *dharma*.

Consequently, according to the *pūrvapakṣa*, *niyoga* is analogous to the infamous *śyena* rite, a Vedic ritual whose explicit result is the death of the sacrificer's enemies. According to the traditional interpretation developed within the Mīmāṃsā tradition,[64] the performance of the *śyena* rite is a violation of *dharma*, since there is a general prohibition against violence and no true injunction for it. The Veda simply states that if a person wants to kill his enemies, the *śyena* rite is one means of accomplishing his goal. It does not prescribe such violence. Similarly, for the *pūrvapakṣa*, Manu simply states that if a person wants the otherworldly benefits of a son, *niyoga* is one means of attaining them. He does not actually enjoin the practice for such a person, but does prohibit it. Thus, the *pūrvapakṣa* holds that, like the *śyena* rite, *niyoga* is prohibited, at least for anyone who engages in the practice out of a desire for a son. And this prohibits *niyoga* for almost all women, the presumably rare exceptions being those who engage in the practice not out of a desire for sons, but rather because their elders have instructed them to. Furthermore, it is important to note that although Medhātithi presents this position on *niyoga* as that of other people, it is again clear that he himself subscribes to it, for earlier he comments that Manu "in his ninth chapter enjoins *niyoga* at the behest of a man's elders, not at the personal initiative of a woman seeking a son."[65]

Having explained that *niyoga* is strangely both optional and prohibited for women seeking sons, the *pūrvapakṣa* next addresses the issue of the levir's participation in the practice:

> Moreover, it is worth examining this: Why does a man who has been appointed to sire a child on his kinsman's wife do so? For there is no injunction for him to do so of the form "an appointed man must have sex." For a woman, however, Manu (9.59) issues such an injunction, when he says that a "duly appointed woman" should obtain a child. And one should not respond that the meaning of this statement is that only when her husband's brother or the like participates can a woman carry out *niyoga* and, thus,

for an action, commentators sometimes ascribe to that action a mundane or natural motive, as Medhātithi does here.

[64] See Śabara on PMS 1.1.2.

[65] Medhātithi on MDh 5.157: *niyogas tu navame gurvicchayā vihito nātmatantratayā putrārthinyāḥ* |

that the man participates in begetting the desired *kṣetraja* son also because of the woman's injunction. For it is perfectly reasonable that a man would participate in this out of a natural desire (for sex). If one then argues that the restrictive injunctions requiring the man to smear himself with ghee, etc. become pointless, this is untrue. They do not become pointless, for the designation "*kṣetraja* son" applies only to a boy begotten by a man observing these restrictions, not any other.

Some say instead that the reason a man participates in *niyoga* is the rule that a person must do what his elders command. But were this the case, it would follow that a person must also drink liquor and the like if his elders wished it. Moreover, a person is not one's elder, if he compels one to do things that one should not do, for there is a Smṛti that states:

> One is enjoined to abandon even one's elder, if he is proud, does not know the difference between what one should and should not do, and holds to a wrong path.

And the phrase "to abandon" here means "to desist from one's duties to an elder."

This[66] also refutes the argument that Manu's statement (9.63) about those involved in *niyoga* losing caste for violating restrictive rules—i.e., "they both become outcastes"—must permit behavior in conformity with those restrictive rules. For otherwise a man who engages in *niyoga* in any way would lose caste and, thus, it would not be right for Manu to make his loss of caste subject to certain conditions, as he does. It refutes this argument, because Manu's text speaks of the loss of caste of not only the man, but also the woman; and *niyoga* is enjoined for her if she does not seek to obtain a son. Thus, Manu's statement (9.63) about those involved in *niyoga* losing caste for violating the rules—i.e., "they both become outcastes"—applies to her. Indeed, it emerges by implication from Manu's text that if no violation occurs, only the man becomes an outcaste, but if a violation does occur, both the man and the woman become outcastes. Therefore, one must question how the participation in *niyoga* of a husband's brother, etc. can be characterized by an injunction directed at him.

idaṃ tv atra nirūpyam | yo 'sau niyujyate sa kimiti pravartate | na hi tasya vidhir asti niyuktena gantavyam iti | striyā[ḥ] punar vidyate saṃyak

[66] "This" must refer not to the immediately preceding discussion, but rather to the earlier argument that the restrictive rules governing a man engaged in *niyoga* do not become pointless without an injunction, as they are necessary elements in the definition of a *kṣetraja*.

striyā niyuktayeti (MDh 9.59) | *na ca devarādiṣu pravartamāneṣu striyā niyogasiddhir ity arthaḥ | teṣām api pravṛttis tadvidhinā kṣetraja īpsita iti vācyam | yato rāgataḥ pravṛttir upapadyate | ghṛtāktādiniyamavidhānam anarthakam iti cen nānarthakam | tathāniyamair utpanne kṣetrajavyapadeśo nānya iti |*

yad api guruvacanaṃ kartavyam iti ke cit pravṛttinibandhanam āhuḥ | evaṃ sati surāpānādiṣv api gurvicchayā pravṛttiḥ prāpnoti | na cāsau gurur akārye yaḥ pravartayati |

guror apy avaliptasya kāryākāryam ajānataḥ |
utpathapratipannasya parityāgo vidhīyate ||

iti smaraṇāt | parityāgaś ca gurukāryān nivṛttiḥ |

etenaitad api pratyuktaṃ yan niyamātikramapātityavacanaṃ niyamapūrvikāṃ vṛttim anujānāti tāv ubhau patitau syātām iti (MDh 9.63) | *itarathā sarvaprakāraṃ gacchataḥ pātityam iti viśeṣapātityam anupapannam | yatas tan na kevalasya puṃsaḥ śrūyate kiṃ tarhi striyā iti | tasyāś c[ā]putrārthinyā*[67] *niyogo vihitaḥ | tadapekṣaṃ hi vyatikrame patita[tva]vacanaṃ tāv ubhau patitau syātām iti* (MDh 9.63) | *asati vyatikrama ekaḥ patitaḥ pumān evātikrame tu dvāv apīty evam api liṅgān nirgacchaty eva | tasmād devarādividhilakṣaṇā pravṛttiḥ katham iti vaktavyam |*

Here the *pūrvapakṣa* contends that there is no legitimate reason for a man to participate as a levir in *niyoga*, for no text enjoins him to do so. One might be tempted to object that a woman obviously cannot carry out *niyoga* without a man's participation and, therefore, the injunction for a woman to engage in *niyoga*[68] must somehow apply to the levir as well. However, the *pūrvapakṣa* points out that sexual lust is a perfectly natural reason for a man to engage in *niyoga* and, consequently, an injunction directed at him is entirely unnecessary. Thus, there is no need to engage in such a tortured interpretation of the injunction to perform *niyoga*. Of course, the absence of such an injunction means that, by engaging in *niyoga*, a man is committing

[67] The reading in both Jha and Mandlik is *ca putrārthinyāḥ*, which means "seeking a son" rather than "not seeking a son." But this seems directly at odds with what Medhātithi says earlier in his commentary on MDh 9.64 (*upakāraviśeṣārthenāsya pravṛttau pratiṣedhātikrameṇa śyenatulyatā*) and on MDh 5.157 (*niyogas tu navame gurvicchayā vihito nātmatantratayā putrārthinyāḥ*).

[68] Note that the *pūrvapakṣa* identifies this injunction specifically as MDh 9.59, which is directed at a "duly appointed woman" (*striyā saṃyaṅ niyuktayā*). This detail is perhaps significant, given that the *pūrvapakṣa* apparently considers the urging of one's elders to be a legitimate reason to engage in *niyoga*, but not a personal desire for a son.

the serious sin of sleeping with his kinsman's wife. Consequently, the Smṛti passages requiring that he smear himself with ghee and so on seemingly become pointless, as he is committing a grevious sin whether he observes them or not. The *pūrvapakṣa* responds that these scriptural requirements are not pointless, since observing them is necessary for the resulting child to qualify as a *kṣetraja* son and to possess the considerable legal rights thereof. After this, the hypothesis is put forward that men participate in *niyoga* because of their duty to obey their elders. But the *pūrvapakṣa* refutes this by arguing that anyone who urges a person to act contrary to *dharma* cannot be his elder and should not be obeyed. Lastly, the *pūrvapakṣa* refutes an objection based upon a particular verse of Manu (9.63), which says that both the man and woman involved in *niyoga* become outcastes, if they violate the prescribed rules. This objection holds that, by speaking of outcasting for violating the rules, Manu implicitly permits behavior that conforms to the rules. The *pūrvapakṣa* answers this objection by arguing that the implication of Manu's verse is not that if the levir obeys all of the restrictive rules placed upon him, he commits no sin, but rather that if he obeys all of the rules, only he—and not the woman as well—loses caste.

At this point, Medhātithi's lengthy *pūrvapakṣa*, with which he agrees on many points, finally comes to an end. He then gives his own refutation of those parts of the *pūrvapakṣa* with which he actually disagrees:

> I reply that because of what one sees in the case of Vyāsa and others, a man's *sapiṇḍa* relatives should respect their elders' order to beget a *kṣetraja* son for him as they would an order to make ancestral offerings for children. It must then be granted that a man does not fall from caste for having sex with a woman in this way, for it is not right to hold that great men engaged in such behavior out of passionate desire. Furthermore, the purported implication of Manu's statement (9.63) about those involved in *niyoga* losing caste for violating restrictive rules cannot be correct, since the begetting of a son through *niyoga* then becomes pointless, given that the man involved always loses caste, for a child born of an outcaste has no rights. Therefore, there is here the appearance of an injunction for husbands' brothers, etc. to participate in *niyoga*.
>
> *ucyate—vyāsādidarśanenāpatyapiṇḍadāna iva kṣetrajotpattyarthaṃ sapiṇḍānāṃ guruniyogāpekṣā | tadā nopagamane cyutir astīty anumantavyam | na hi mahātmanāṃ rāgalakṣaṇapravṛttir abhyupagantuṃ*

nyāyyā | yac coktaṃ niyamātikrame patitatvavacan[e][69] *liṅgam iti tad ayuktaṃ yataḥ puṃsaḥ patitatve patitotpannasyādhikārābhāvād utpādanam anarthakam | tasmād asti devarādividher ābhāso 'yam |*

Here Medhātithi only bothers to refute the final section of the *pūrvapakṣa*, where it is argued that a man's participation in *niyoga* as a levir always results in his loss of caste. This again confirms that he himself personally agrees with the earlier sections of the *pūrvapakṣa*, where it is argued that a woman cannot lawfully engage in *niyoga* in order to acquire a son, only out of a desire to obey her elders.

Medhātithi contends that if a man's elders appoint him to act as a levir, then he is obliged to obey them and commits no sin in doing so. He presents two arguments in support of this view. The first of these is that certain revered figures of the past, such as Vyāsa, engaged in *niyoga* and it strains credulity to imagine that these pious and holy men acted sinfully out of sexual lust. The second is that all levirs cannot lose caste, because the children of outcastes lack any legal right to inherit property, perform ancestral rites, and the like. Consequently, if any man who engages in *niyoga* necessarily becomes an outcaste, the whole reason for the practice—obtaining a legal son and heir—disappears. On the basis of these two arguments, Medhātithi concludes that there is the *ābhāsa* ("appearance") of an injunction directed at certain men to participate in *niyoga*. And although Dharmaśāstra commentators typically use the word *ābhāsa* to denote specifically the false or erroneous appearance of something, Medhātithi does not seem to use the word in this sense here. Instead, he seemingly wants to remain noncommittal. While he cannot identify a specific scriptural passage enjoining men to act as levirs, it seems to him that there must be one.

This position of Medhātithi is a rather curious one for him to adopt, given that he appears not to be a genuine supporter of *niyoga*, for he considers it to be prohibited for women seeking sons, as we have seen. And one finds further evidence of Medhātithi's personal opposition to *niyoga* in the fact that he explicitly prohibits a man from marrying a woman begotten through the practice.[70] Therefore, it is necessary to ask why he seeks to defend men's

69 The editions of Jha and Mandlik both read *vacanaṃ*.

70 MDh 3.5 lists some of the qualities required of a twice-born man's bride: she cannot be a *sapiṇḍa* relative, a member of his *gotra*, or "born of mere copulation" (*maithunī*). Explaining the significance of this last quality, Medhātithi states: "*Niyoga* is enjoined and the previously listed qualities do not prohibit a man from marrying a woman begotten thereby. Hence, such a woman is separately prohibited by the requirement that a man's bride must be a woman 'not born of mere copulation.' Therefore,

participation in *niyoga*, albeit in a rather noncommittal fashion. I believe the answer is that, like Kumārila before him, Medhātithi is really concerned here not with defending *niyoga*, but rather with defending Vyāsa's behavior in the *Mahābhārata* and the similar behavior of other revered figures of the mythical past. Hence, he wants to leave some room for the practice of *niyoga* without properly allowing it as a contemporary custom.[71] And while many later Dharmaśāstra commentators achieve this goal by arguing that *niyoga* is among those practices permissible in past ages, but not in the present one, as we will see, Medhātithi holds a more complex and convoluted view: *niyoga* is permissible for those dispassionately following their elders' orders (like Vyāsa in the *Mahābhārata*), but prohibited for women seeking the benefits of a son (like ordinary women). Of course, this position of Medhātithi shifts the power to legitimately initiate *niyoga* from the widow herself to her male elders. Thus, one may be tempted to interpret it more as an effort to deprive widows of reproductive agency than as a stance against *niyoga*. In all likelihood, however, Medhātithi assumed that, in practice, Brahmin men would never instruct a kinsman's widow to engage in *niyoga*, for Brahmanical society appears to have turned decisively against the practice by his time. Thus, after Bhāruci, not a single Dharmaśāstra commentator, including Medhātithi, allows *niyoga* to serve as a means for Brahmin widows, seeking sons, to obtain sons, which is the obviously intended purpose of the practice.

Unpublished Commentary on the *Yājñavalkya Dharmaśāstra*

After the commentaries of Bhāruci, Viśvarūpa, and Medhātithi, the next Dharmaśāstra work to contain a detailed discussion of *niyoga* is a still unpublished commentary on the *Yājñavalkya Dharmaśāstra*. This commentary,

one cannot willfully marry a woman begotten through *niyoga*." (*niyogo vihitaḥ* | *tata utpannāyā nāsti pūrvoktaviśeṣaṇair niṣedhaḥ* | *ataḥ pṛthaṅ niṣidhyate amaithunīti* | *tato niyogotpannā kāmato na vivāhyā* |).

[71] This may explain why Medhātithi (on MDh 9.66) freely admits that the *Ṛgveda* implicitly allows *niyoga*: "It has been said that there are no implications of *niyoga* in the mantras recited at weddings. Elsewhere, however, one sees them, such as in the mantra (ṚV 10.40.2): 'Who invites you into his home, like a widow her husband's brother into her bed, like a young lady a man?'" (*udvāhakeṣu mantreṣu na santīty uktam* | *anyatra tu dṛśyate ko vāṃ [śayutrā] vidhaveva devaraṃ maryaṃ na yoṣā kṛṇute sadhastha ā ity ādi* |)

the name of whose author remains unknown, survives only in a single palm-leaf manuscript written in an early Nepalese script known as *bhujīmola* and in a modern Devanāgarī transcription of this manuscript.[72] Although the *bhujīmola* manuscript covers only the first 195 verses of Yājñavalkya, it contains a colophon. This gives the year in which it was written as 122. Since the era to which this date refers is likely the *Nepāla Saṃvat*, the manuscript appears to have been written in 1002 CE.[73] Moreover, it is highly unlikely that the manuscript was penned by the text's author himself, given that it clearly does not contain a completed work, yet contains a colophon. Based upon his recent study of the textual history of the *Yājñavalkya Dharmaśāstra*, Olivelle (2019, xxx) suggests that this unpublished commentary dates to the tenth century, which seems to be a reasonable guess.

Like Viśvarūpa, the unknown author of this commentary discusses *niyoga* in the most obvious and natural place, namely, when commenting upon the verses of Yājñavalkya (1.68–69) that prescribe the practice. The relevant portion of the text reads as follows[74]:

> If the fiancée of a betrothed girl should die, then his brother or, failing him, his *sapiṇḍa* relative or, failing him, a member of his patrilineal clan should approach her with his elders' permission, provided that the girl's fiancée had no son. Under these circumstances, he should approach her in her fertile season, which will be explained later on (YDh 1.79), with the desire for a son, after smearing himself with ghee, until she conceives a child. If he approaches her again after this or approaches her in any other way, he becomes an outcaste. It is with precisely this intention of addressing a girl who has been betrothed that Manu (9.60) states:
>
> > A man who has been appointed to a widow should at night smear himself with ghee and, refraining from speech, beget upon her a single son, never a second.
>
> However, Manu did not state this with the intention of addressing a girl who is no longer a virgin, for he (MDh 5.162) says:
>
> > A second husband is nowhere taught for virtuous women.

[72] These manuscripts were microfilmed as part of the Nepal-German Manuscript Preservation Project and are housed in the National Archives in Kathmandu, Nepal. The number for the *bhujīmola* manscript is 5-696/dharmaśāstra65 (Reel No. A51/12). The number for the Devanāgarī transcription is 5.2125/dharmaśāstra788 (Reel No. B432/19).

[73] On this assessment, see Olivelle (2019, xxx).

[74] The following transcription is based upon the *bhujīmola* manuscript. I have used notes and brackets to indicate where and how I have the emended the manuscript's reading.

And this practice of *niyoga* should not take place when a woman's husband (rather than fiancée) has died, for the following text (MDh 9.64) prohibits it:

> Wise men should not appoint a widowed woman to another man, for those who appoint such a woman to another man kill the eternal law.

Moreover, one should not engage in this practice for the sake of someone else, for Manu (9.66) says the following:

> This is a law for beasts that is reviled by educated twice-born men. It became a law for men when Vena reigned as king.

And, thereafter, he (MDh 9.68) states:

> Since that time, good people revile any man who out of delusion appoints a woman whose husband has died to beget children.

As for the origin of the Pāṇḍavas that is taught in the beginning of the *Mahābhārata*, Gautama (1.3) explicitly rejects precisely that on the grounds that lesser men are too weak, when he states: "One sees in the scriptures violations of the law and acts of rashness committed by great beings, but these are not examples to be followed due to the weakness of lesser men." It is for this very reason that Likhita states:

> Their bodies and sense-organs are composed of splendor. Sins do not stain them, just as water does not stain a lotus petal.

Āpastamba (2.13.8–9) also states: "Due to their special splendor there is no sin among them, but a person who sees this and engages in the same behaviors sinks down on account of his lesser birth." Therefore, one should understand this statement of Yājñavalkya (1.68–69) to apply only to a girl who has merely been betrothed. Hence, Manu (9.69) first says:

> When a girl has been verbally promised in marriage and her husband dies, her husband's brother should take her in accordance with this rule.

And, thereafter, he (MDh 9.70) says:

> Following the prescribed rules, he should approach that girl whose vows are pure, when she is dressed in white, and copulate with her once each fertile season until she begets a child.

It is with precisely this intention of addressing a girl who has been betrothed that it is said:

> When her husband is lost, dead, a renunciant, impotent, or an outcaste—in these five calamities another husband is enjoined for women. (NSm 12.97, PSm 4.30)

Otherwise, this statement would conflict with statements such as these:

> Wise men should not appoint a widowed woman to another man. (MDh 9.64)
>
> A second husband is nowhere taught for virtuous women. (MDh 5.162)

Furthermore, one should not engage in this practice of *niyoga* out of greed for sons, for the following text (MDh 5.161) prohibits that:

> A woman who transgresses against her husband out of greed for children obtains scorn in his world and is deprived of the world of her husband.

And it is not the case that a husband and wife who have no sons cannot reach heaven, for the following Smṛti (MDh 5.160) states:

> A virtuous woman who remains celibate after her husband has died goes to heaven, even if sonless, just like those men who have remained celibate.

There is, however, the following statement (NSm 12.98):

> A Brahmin woman should wait for eight years for her husband when he has gone abroad, but if she has not given birth to a child, only for four. After this, she should seek refuge in another man.

But this is intended to sanction merely seeking refuge, not marital infidelity, for the Smṛti of Manu (9.75) states:

> If a woman's husband has gone abroad after providing for her livelihood, she should live observing self-restraint. However, if he has gone abroad without providing for her livelihood, she should live by means of respectable crafts.

Therefore, it is established that the practice of *niyoga* applies only to a girl who has merely been betrothed.

yadi vāgdattāyā[75] *mriyate*[76] *tadā devaraḥ sapiṇḍaḥ sagotras*[77] *tasya varasya pūrvapūrvābhāve gurubhir anujñāto yady aputro bhavati tadā putrakāmyayā ghṛtākto ṛtukāle vakṣyamāṇe gacched ā garbhasaṃbhavāt | ūrdhvaṃ punar gacchann anyena vā prakāreṇa patito bhavati | amunaivābhiprāyeṇa manunoktam—*

> *vidhavāyāṃ niyuktas tu ghṛtākto vāgyato niśi*[78] |
> *ekam utpādayet putraṃ na dvitīya[ṃ] kathaṃcaneti* || (MDh 9.60)

na punaḥ kṣatayonyabhiprāye[ṇa] |

[75] Ms. *vāgdattāyāṃ*
[76] Ms. *mṛyate*
[77] Ms. *sagotro*
[78] Ms. *niśiḥ*

dvitī[ya]ś ca na sādhvīnāṃ kvacid bhartopadiśyata iti || (MDh 5.162)
na ca mṛte bhartari bhaviṣyati |
nānyasmin vidhavā nārī niyoktavyā manīṣibhiḥ |
anyasmin hi niyuñjānāḥ dharmaṃ hanyuḥ sanātanam iti || (MDh 9.64)
pratiṣedhāt | *na cānyārthā pravṛttiḥ* |
ayaṃ dvijair hi vidvadbhiḥ paśudharmo vigarhitaḥ |
manuṣy[ā]ṇām ayaṃ dharmo vene rājyaṃ praśāsatīti || (MDh 9.66)
uktvoktam—
tataḥ prabhṛti yo mohāt pramītapatikā[ṃ] striyam |
niyojayaty apatyārthe taṃ vigarh[a]nti[79] *sādhava iti* || (MDh 9.68)
yā punaḥ pāṇḍavā[nā]m utpatti[r] [bhārat]ādau pradarśitā[80] *sā svayam eva gautame[na]*[81] *śakyaṃ nirākṛtā—dṛṣṭo dharma[vy]atikramaḥ*[82] *sāhasaṃ ca mahatāṃ na tu dṛṣṭārthe 'varadaurbalyād iti* | (GDh 1.3) *avarāṇā[ṃ] durbalatvāt* | *ata eva likhitaḥ—*
tejomayāni teṣāṃ tu śarīrāṇīndriyāṇi ca |
lipyante naiva pāpais t[u][83] *padmapatram ivāmbubhir iti* ||
āpastambe 'pi—tejoviśeṣāt tatra pratya[v]āyo[84] *na vidyate* | *tad anvīkṣya pravartamānaḥ sīdaty avarajanmana iti* | (ĀpDh 2.13.8–9) *tasmād vāgdattāviṣayam etad veditavyam* | *ata eva manuḥ—*
yasyā mriyeta[85] *kanyāyā vācā satye kṛte patiḥ* |
tām anena vidhānena nijo vindeta devara iti || (MDh 9.69)
ukt[v]oktam—
yathāvidhy adhigamyaināṃ śuklavastrāṃ śucivratām[86] |
mitho bhajetā prasavāt sakṛt sakṛd ṛtāv ṛtāv iti || (MDh 9.70)
anenaivābhiprāyeṇoktam—
naṣṭe mṛte pravrajite klībe 'tha patite patau |
pañcasv āpatsu nārīṇāṃ patir anyo vidhīyata iti || (NSm 12.97, PSm 4.30)
anyathā
nānyasmin vidhavā nārī niyoktavyā manīṣibhiḥ | (MDh 9.64)
na dvitīyaś ca sādhvīnāṃ kvacid bhartopadiśyate | (MDh 5.162)
ity ādibhiḥ saha virodhaḥ | *na ca putralobhād etat kā[r]yaṃ* |

[79] Ms. *vigarhinti*
[80] Ms. *bhrātarādau pradarśitāḥ*
[81] Ms. *gautamekā*
[82] Ms. *dharmam atikramaḥ*
[83] Ms. *te*
[84] Ms. *pratyayāyo*
[85] Ms. *priyeta*
[86] Ms. adds (before *śuklavastrāṃ*) *śuklavarṇāṃ śucivratāṃ*

apatyalobhād yā tu strī bhartāram ativartate |
seha nindām avāpnoti patilok[ā]c ca hīyata iti || (MDh 5.161)
niṣedh[āt][87] | *na cāputrayoḥ svargo nāsti* |
mṛte bhartari sādhvī strī brahmacarye vyavasthitā[88] |
svargaṃ gacchaty aputrāpi yathā te brahmacāriṇa iti || (MDh 5.160)
smaraṇāt | *yat punar uktam—*
aṣṭau varṣāṇy [ud]īkṣeta[89] *brāhmaṇī proṣitaṃ patim* |
aprasūtā tu catvāri parato 'nyaṃ samāśrayed iti || (NSm 12.98)
tad api saṃśrayamātrārtha[ṃ] na vyabhicārāya|
vidhāya proṣite vṛtti[ṃ] jīven niyamam āsthitā |
proṣite tv avidhāyaiva jīvec chilpair agarhitair iti || (MDh 9.75)
manusmaraṇāt | *ato vā[gd]attāviṣayo*[90] *niyoga iti sthitam* |

From this passage the commentator's basic position on *niyoga* is clear: it is a valid practice only for women who have been betrothed or, more literally, "verbally given" (*vāgdattā*). That is, according to the commentator, those Smṛtis that prescribe *niyoga* apply strictly to women whose fiancées (not husbands) have died after they have been promised in marriage, but prior to their actual weddings. And a passage of Manu (9.69–70) is cited as explicit support for this position. Hence, like all published Dharmaśāstra commentaries aside from Bhāruci, this unpublished commentary on Yājñavalkya effectively considers *niyoga* to be prohibited.

Before citing positive support for its own position, however, the commentary rejects an alternative position on *niyoga*, namely, that it is permissible for any woman who is still a virgin. It rejects this position on the basis of another verse of Manu (5.162), which notes that the scriptures nowhere prescribe a second husband for respectable women. In addition, the commentary declares that one should not engage in *niyoga* for another person's sake and cites as evidence for this position yet another verse of Manu (9.68). Given that this verse condemns those who appoint a man to father a child upon a widow, the commentary's intent seems to be that although a betrothed woman might lawfully engage in *niyoga*, it is enitrely forbidden for elders to appoint a levir for her and perhaps also for a man to act as her levir, although this point is less clear. In any case, this further shows that, for the

[87] Ms. *niṣodho*
[88] Ms. *vyavasthitāḥ*
[89] Ms. *avīkṣeta*
[90] Ms. *vāsvattāviṣayo*

author of this commentary, *niyoga* was effectively forbidden. Lastly, like Kumārila, Viśvarūpa, and Medhātithi, the commentator addresses the issue of instances of *niyoga* in the *Mahābhārata*. Unlike these authors, however, he refers not to the story of Vyāsa fathering children upon the wives of his half-brother Vicitravīrya, but rather to the well-known story of the origin of the Pāṇḍavas, who were sired by gods upon the wives of king Pāṇḍu.[91] As one can see, the commentary explains away the practice of *niyoga* in the *Mahābhārata* by arguing that, due their immense sanctity, certain figures of the past could do things that would sully a modern person and by citing a number of scriptural passages (e.g., GDh 1.3, ĀpDh 2.13.8–9) that express precisely this.

Then, after citing a passage of Manu (9.69–70) as support for his own position that only betrothed women can engage in *niyoga*, the commentator addresses a particular verse, found in both Nārada (12.97) and Parāśara (4.30), that apparently allows a woman to remarry under certain conditions. This he explains as applying only to betrothed women, just as those Smṛti passages that prescribe *niyoga* do. Later on, the commentator also explains away another verse of Nārada (12.98) that enjoins a Brahmin woman to resort to another man, if her husband has been abroad for four or eight years, depending upon whether or not she has borne children. Since this verse undeniably deals with married women, the commentator cannot argue that it applies merely to betrothed women. Thus, instead, he argues that it enjoins resorting to a man merely for a livelihood and protection, not as a lover or new husband. Finally, the commentary notes that it is forbidden for women to engage in *niyoga* out of a desire for sons and that even sonless women who remain celibate can reach heaven according to Manu (5.160). Hence, like most earlier exegetes in the Dharmaśāstra tradition and virtually all later ones, the author of this unpublished commentary clearly opposes both *niyoga* and widow remarriage.

Later Digests and Commentaries

Let us turn now to the Dharmaśāstra commentaries and digests of the early second millennium. As mentioned earlier, all of these works effectively deny the legitimacy of *niyoga* and widow remarriage. Therefore, their authors

[91] This story is told in detail at MBh 1.113.21–115.26.

fundamentally agree with the earlier Dharmaśāstra commentators (with the notable exception of Bhāruci, of course). However, their discussions of the legitimacy of *niyoga* are invariably rather brief, far shorter and less detailed than the lengthy treatments of Viśvarūpa, Medhātithi, and even the unpublished commentary on Yājñavalkya. This fundamental unanimity of juridical opinion and general lack of interest in detailed argumentation with respect to *niyoga* suggest that to a significant extent the earlier turn against the practice within the Dharmaśāstra tradition was successful and enduring.

Nevertheless, although orthodox Brahmanical society seems to have decisively rejected *niyoga* during the late second millennium, almost no subsequent commentator or digest writer subscribes to any of the precise legal arguments against the practice formulated by earlier commentators. Indeed, the long tracts on *niyoga* by Medhātithi and Viśvarūpa seem to have gone completely ignored within the later tradition. Perhaps the sole exception to this pattern of ignoring earlier exegetes is Vijñāneśvara, author of the *Mitākṣarā*, an enormously influential commentary on Yājñavalkya, likely composed around the turn of the twelfth century.[92] For when discussing the passage of Yājñavalkya (1.68–69) prescribing *niyoga*, Vijñāneśvara states: "This statement applies to girls who have merely been betrothed, according to the teachers."[93] As readers may note, this position is identical to that advocated in the unpublished commentary on Yājñavalkya that was just cited and discussed.[94] Consequently, it is reasonable to assume that the author of that work, whoever he may have been, is among the unnamed teachers that Vijñāneśvara refers to here. Moreover, although Vijñāneśvara ascribes this position to certain unnamed teachers (*ācāryāḥ*), there can be no doubt that he himself basically subscribes to it for two reasons. First, he clearly regards *niyoga* as prohibited, given that later on (at YDh 2.135–36) he explicitly describes any woman who engages in the practice as "condemned by both scripture and popular opinion" (*smṛtilokaninditā*). Second, he presents no other argument against *niyoga*.

Although Vijñāneśvara rejects *niyoga* on the basis of the earlier argument that it is permissible only for women who have merely been betrothed, the much more common argument against it in the first half of the second millennium is simply that while *niyoga* was a permissible practice in past ages, it is forbidden in

92 On the date of the *Mitākṣarā*, see Kane (1962, 1:607–10).
93 *Mitākṣarā* on YDh 1.68–69: *etac ca vāgdattāviṣayam ity ācāryāḥ* |.
94 This position is also noted and rejected by Viśvarūpa.

the current one, the degenerate Kali Yuga. Such practices that are prohibited exclusively in the current age are often given the technical designation *kalivarjya* ("to be avoided during the Kali Yuga") in Dharmaśāstra writings. The argument against *niyoga* on the grounds that it is a *kalivarjya* has the distinct advantage of elegantly explaining both how revered figures of the past, such as Vyāsa, engaged in the practice and how it is, nevertheless, forbidden today.

Among Dharmaśāstra writers, Devaṇa Bhaṭṭa, who likely wrote his multivolume digest, the *Smṛticandrikā*, somewhere in South India between the years 1175 and 1225 (Kane 1962, 1:740–41), perhaps articulates this argument most clearly. He begins his discussion of *niyoga*[95] by citing several Smṛti passages (e.g., MDh 9.59, YDh 1.68) that lay down the procedure for carrying out the practice. This gives the initial impression that Devaṇa himself supports *niyoga*. However, he concludes his treatment of the topic (*Ācārakāṇḍa* p. 226) with the following statement:

> However, Manu (9.64) states:
>
> > Twice-born men should not appoint a widowed woman to another man. Those who appoint such a woman to another man kill the eternal law.
>
> And it is also said in a certain Smṛti (MDh 5.162):
>
> > A second husband is nowhere taught for virtuous women.
>
> But these statements are intended as prohibitions in the Kali Yuga. Thus, there is no conflict with them. It is precisely for this reason that Kratu states:
>
> > In the Kali Yuga, a woman should not beget a son from her husband's brother; a girl who has been given in marriage should not be given again; one should not perform sacrifices involving the slaughter of cows; and ascetics need not carry gourd-pots.
>
> *yat punar manunoktam—*
>
> > *nānyasmin vidhavā nārī niyoktavyā dvijātibhiḥ |*
> > *anyasmin viniyuñjānā dharmaṃ hanyuḥ sanātanam iti ||* (MDh 9.64)
>
> *yad api smṛtyantare—*
>
> > *na dvitīyaś ca sādhvīnāṃ kvacid bhartopadiśyata iti |* (MDh 5.162)
>
> *tat kalau niṣedhaparam ity avirodhaḥ | ata eva kratuḥ—*
>
> > *devarān na sutotpattir dattā kanyā na dīyate |*
> > *na yajño govadhaḥ kāryaḥ kalau na ca kamaṇḍaluḥ ||*

[95] This occupies pp. 224–26 of the *Ācārakāṇḍa*.

Thus, Devaṇa harmonizes those Smṛti passages that prescribe *niyoga* with those that prohibit it by arguing that the former apply to past ages, whereas the latter apply specifically to the current one. From this it is clear that he regards *niyoga* as effectively forbidden.

Moreover, it is evident from the verse of Kratu with which Devaṇa ends his discussion of *niyoga* that he also considers widow remarriage to be prohibited. Indeed, slightly earlier in his work (*Ācārakāṇḍa*, p. 202), he directly argues against the position that even a woman who is merely betrothed can legitimately remarry:

> A betrothed girl becomes a remarried woman if she undergoes the rite of marriage again. Hence, by taking her, i.e., marrying her, a man finds, that is, enjoys, neither offspring nor religious merit.
>
> *vāgdattā punaḥsaṃskārakarmaṇi punarbhūr bhavati | atas tāṃ gṛhītvā pariṇīya prajāṃ dharmaṃ ca na vinden na bhajed ity arthaḥ |*

Therefore, the South Indian jurist Devaṇa Bhaṭṭa is an unambiguous opponent of both *niyoga* and widow remarriage, including the remarriage even of girls who were never ritually married, but merely verbally promised.

As mentioned earlier, Devaṇa is hardly alone among Dharmaśāstra writers in rejecting *niyoga* and widow remarriage on the grounds that they are *kalivarjya* practices. For instance, Mādhava, another South Indian author, who wrote a voluminous commentary on the *Parāśara Smṛti* in the fourteenth century,[96] uses the *kalivarjya* argument to explain why Parāśara (4.30) seemingly enjoins widow remarriage.[97] Moreover, even earlier than Devaṇa, two twelfth-century authors, the commentator Aparārka and the digest writer Lakṣmīdhara,[98] appear to reject *niyoga* as a practice forbidden during the Kali Yuga. Unfortunately, neither of these authors explicitly makes this argument in his own words the way that Devaṇa does. Like Devaṇa, however, both begin their discussions of *niyoga* by citing Smṛti passages that prescribe the practice and conclude by quoting Smṛti passages that prohibit

[96] On Mādhava's date, see Kane (1962, 1:782–91).

[97] On PSm 4.30, the *Parāśaramādhava* simply states: "And this practice of remarriage applies to another Yuga." (*ayaṃ ca punarudvāho yugāntaraviṣayaḥ |*)

[98] On the provenance of Aparārka, see Kane (1962, 1:721–23). On that of Lakṣmīdhara, see Brick (2015, 5–11).

it.[99] And, importantly, these prohibitive Smṛti passages include several that forbid *niyoga* specifically during the present Yuga, such as the following verse ascribed to Bṛhaspati,[100] which both Lakṣmīdhara (*Vyavahārakāṇḍa*, p. 643) and Aparārka (on YDh 1.68–69) cite:

> After prescribing *niyoga*, Manu himself prohibits it. According to scriptural rules, all men are unable to observe this practice due to the shortening of the Yugas.
>
> *uktvā niyogo manunā niṣiddhaḥ svayam eva tu |*
> *yugahrāsād aśakyo 'yaṃ kartuṃ sarvair vidhānataḥ ||*

Thus, Aparārka and Lakṣmīdhara seem to hold the same position on *niyoga* as Devaṇa Bhaṭṭa, who differs from these earlier authors only in that he articulates their position more clearly.

Finally, it is worth examining the *Smṛtyarthasāra* of Śrīdhara, a work dating to the second half of the twelfth century that is neither a digest nor a commentary, but instead belongs to a rarer class of Dharmaśāstra work that may be thought of as the versified doxography.[101] Kane (1962, 2:611) notes that, despite its comparatively late date, the *Smṛtyarthasāra* (p. 12) mentions a number of views on widow remarriage that are, for their time, surprisingly tolerant of the practice:

> A girl may be given to another man, if her fiancée dies prior to the seven steps at their wedding. According to some, she may be given to another man, if he dies prior to sexual intercourse. According to some, a girl may be given again, if she has never yet menstruated. And according to others, a girl may be given again until she conceives a child. A wise man should follow the above laws in accordance with place and time. One should take away a girl who has married a man belonging to the same patrilineal clan or who has been given in marriage to a man without a family or good

[99] Aparārka discusses *niyoga* in his commentary on YDh 1.68–69, a pair of verses that together prescribe the practice. There, after giving a brief gloss of these verses, he cites exclusively Smṛti texts that prohibit *niyoga*. Lakṣmīdhara's section on *niyoga* comprises *Kṛtyakalpataru*, *Vyavahārakāṇḍa*, pp. 639–44. The first three and a half pages of this section consist of Smṛti texts that speak positively of the practice, while the remaining pages contain only Smṛtis that condemn it.

[100] In Aiyangar's attempted reconstruction of the *Bṛhaspati Smṛti*, this is BSm 25.16.

[101] On the date of the *Smṛtyarthasāra*, see Kane (1962, 1:337).

character; to a eunuch or the like; to an outcaste; to a man with epilepsy; to a man who lives by an unlawful occupation; to a man afflicted with disease; or to a renunciant. A girl should be given to another husband in a ceremony without the recitation of mantras; and a man should avoid a girl who has been deflowered. A girl must be given to another husband. A man who takes her in any other way should be punished and must pay a fine with interest.

mṛte 'nyasmai tathā deyā vare saptapadāt purā |
purā puruṣasaṃyogān mṛte deyeti ke cana ||
ṛtāv adṛṣṭe kanyaiva punar deyeti ke cana |
ā garbhadhāraṇāt kanyā punar deyeti cāpare |
deśakālād ime dharmā anuṣṭheyā vijānatā ||
kulaśīlavihīnasya ṣaṇḍhādeḥ patitasya ca |
apasmārivikarmastharogiṇāṃ veṣadhāriṇām ||
dattām apaharet kanyāṃ sagotroḍhāṃ tathaiva ca |
mantrasaṃskārarahitā deyānyasmai varāya ca ||
kanyā ca dūṣitā varjyā deyānyasmai varāya sā |
anyathā tu haran daṇḍyo vyayaṃ dadyāc ca sodayam ||

From this passage Śrīdhara appears to be rather tolerant of widow remarriage, ceding substantial authority on the matter to "time and place" (*deśakāla*), which here may effectively mean local custom. However, he does not seem to imagine that even local custom will allow a woman to be remarried after conceiving a child. Moreover, after listing certain flaws in a man that allow one to take away his bride and to give her to a more suitable husband, the text states that women's remarriages should be performed without the recitation of mantras—a clear indication of the inferior social and religious status of such marriages. It also says that a man should avoid a deflowered girl (*kanyā ca dūṣitā varjyā*), presumably as a bride. Taking all of this together, the impression one gets from the *Smṛtyarthasāra* is that while limited forms of widow remarriage are, indeed, permissible in certain communities, a man should personally avoid marrying a woman who has already been married, at least if she is not a virgin. Thus, in the final analysis, Śrīdhara's tolerance of widow remarriage seems to be only slightly greater than that of other Dharmaśāstra commentators. It is certainly a far cry from a general acceptance of such marriages.

Conclusion

As we have seen, the Smṛtis or foundational works of the Hindu legal tradition largely prohibit widows from remarrying, but allow them to engage in *niyoga*. The major exception to this general opposition to widow remarriage within Dharmaśāstra is Nārada (12.97–102), whose work consistently approves of the practice. In addition, Parāśara (4.30) also arguably regards it as a permissible option, although one that is inferior to both lifelong celibacy and sati. Moreover, we have seen passages in Gautama (18.15–17), Vasiṣṭha (17.75–80), and Manu (9.76) that prescribe periods of waiting for women whose husbands have gone abroad and such passages imply support for widow remarriage. Nevertheless, with the exception of Nārada and perhaps Parāśara, the surviving Smṛtis of the Dharmaśāstra tradition all contain passages that either explicitly condemn widow remarriage or strongly imply opposition to it. Therefore, while widows appear to have remarried with some frequency during the period of the Smṛtis (c. 300 BCE–600 CE) and there is some support for the practice among Hindu jurists, Brahmanical society, as reflected in the Dharmaśāstras, largely opposed it. This is especially true of Manu, whose work contains a lengthy screed against widow remarriage (5.157–62).

When it comes to *niyoga*, the only opposition expressed in the surviving Smṛtis comes from Āpastamba (2.27.4–7) and Manu (9.64–68). However, Viṣṇu also likely opposes the practice, although he nowhere explicitly condemns it. Furthermore, several Smṛtis that no longer survive as independent treatises, such as that of Bṛhaspati (25.16), unambiguously oppose *niyoga*. Hence, for the most part the Smṛtis of the Dharmaśāstra tradition support the practice. Opposition to it, however, goes back to the very beginning of the Hindu legal tradition and persisted as an important minority viewpoint over the following centuries.

Turning to the commentaries and legal digests, one finds no support in this entire vast literature for widow remarriage. In this, of course, there is no great change in opinion, only the eventual disappearance of what was always a minority position. On the issue of *niyoga*, however, there clearly was a major historical shift in opinion, for the author of every Dharmaśāstra commentary and digest to address the practice opposes it with the exception of Bhāruci (on MDh 9.68), who is the earliest Dharmaśāstra exegete to discuss the topic. Therefore, the closing centuries of the first millennium CE are apparently the period of time during which the Dharmaśāstra tradition came to decisively oppose *niyoga* and to require strict celibacy of all Brahmin and other high-caste widows.

The extent to which this historical turn against *niyoga* within Dharmaśāstra literature manifested itself in actual social practice is uncertain due to the general dearth of direct evidence of social life in ancient and medieval South Asia. Certainly by at least the late eighteenth century, however, Brahmins and members of other high-caste Hindu communities throughout the subcontinent more or less uniformly barred widows from remarrying and did not engage in any form of levirate. Hence, the opinions of Dharmaśāstra commentators and digest writers on these issues undoubtedly correspond to actual social practice at some point in time. And I see no reason to doubt that on these issues, although not necessarily all others, the opinions of Dharmaśāstra authors reflect the prevailing opinions within contemporaneous Brahmanical society and, thus, provide a rough approximation of historical social practice.

Furthermore, in this regard it bears noting that, according to early Dharmaśāstra literature, *niyoga* is the sole means by which a sonless widow can acquire a son. Therefore, the historical prohibition of the practice would have been of considerable consequence. A married man who was unable to beget sons, by contrast, had two methods in addition to *niyoga* of continuing his patriline according to the Smṛtis. The first of these is that he might appoint his daughter to be his legal son. That is, he might make his daughter into what Dharmaśāstra sources term a *putrikā* or "female son." The second method available to a sonless man is that he might adopt a son. However, these two methods of continuing a patriline do not appear to have been available to widows in the early period of Dharmaśāstra. To begin with, several Smṛtis explicitly state that it is a father who appoints his daughter as a *putrikā*, implying that women had no right to do so.[102] Moreover, Dharmaśāstra sources do not even consider the possibility that a widow might adopt a son until the fifteenth century. And this strongly suggest that widows within Brahmanical society did not adopt sons much prior to then.[103] Consequently, the prohibition of *niyoga* would have had a significant impact in that it would have ruled out the possibility of childless widows acquiring offspring.

[102] See, e.g., ViDh 15.5: "When a father gives his daughter in marriage with the stipulation that any son she bears will be his, she is a *putrikā*." (*yas tv asyāḥ putraḥ sa me putro bhaved iti yā pitrā dattā sā putrikā* |) See also GDh 28.18–19 and MDh 9.127–29.

[103] On the issue of a widow's right to adopt, see the Appendix.

Bearing this in mind, it is necessary to consider why Brahmanical society came to oppose first widow remarriage and then *niyoga*, particularly during the latter half of the first millennium CE. For this it seems to me useful to draw upon Sherry Ortner's (1996, 12–16) influential notion of "serious games," that is, her view that actors in a given society regularly engage in a high-stakes game of life, the precise rules of which are set by their society, and that historical change is sometimes best understood as the result of the skillful playing of this game by social actors. More concretely, I propose that, like people in many times and places, Brahmin men in premodern India frequently competed with one another and with members of other social classes for prestige and social status and that one way in which they strove to succeed in this competition was by altering their behaviors—and, in this case, the behaviors of their women as well—to be in better accord with certain values widely shared within society. That is, I hold that the phenomenon of Sanskritization incentivized not only non-Brahmins to act in greater conformity with Brahmanical norms, but Brahmins as well.[104] Hence, I propose that Brahmanical communities came to reject widow remarriage and then *niyoga*, because by rejecting these practices despite their functional value, Brahmin men could persuasively claim that their families more faithfully adhered to Brahmanical values than other families did and, thus, were more virtuous and prestigious. Of course, this explanation lacks historical specificity of a type that one might hope for, but the available evidence sadly does not allow us to pin down with much specificity the dates, places, and social contexts in which surviving Dharmaśāstra works were composed. Moreover, I would argue that large-scale shifts in opinion, such as those explored in this chapter, require equally large-scale explanations. Hence, in this regard a high level of historical specificity is not necessarily even desirable.

So what are the widely shared Brahmanical values with which widow remarriage and *niyoga* can be seen to conflict? I believe that there are two: the indissolubility of marriage and hypergamy. Regarding the former, it is noteworthy that, with the possible exceptions of Nārada (12.97) and Parāśara

[104] An excellent example of Sanskritization cited by M. N. Srinivas ([1952] 1965, 34–35), who coined the term, is the Amma Coorgs, a subgroup of the Coorg caste, who historically sought to elevate themselves above other Coorgs and claim Brahmin status by becoming vegetarians, abstaining from alcohol, donning sacred threads, and the like. As Srinivas ([1952] 1965, 35) observes: "Amma Coorgs exemplify a tendency which has always been present in the caste system: a small group of people break off from a larger whole of which they are a part, Sanskritize their customs and ritual, and achieve a higher status than their parent body in the course of a few decades."

(4.30), Dharmaśāstra texts nowhere lay down rules for divorce.[105] Instead, they simply assume that once a man and woman are married, they are always married. Therefore, they attest to an incredibly strong belief in the indissolubility of marriage within Brahmanical society. And it is easy to understand how people might deem widow remarriage to be a violation of this belief or at least how they might consider the rejection of widow remarriage to indicate a stricter adherence to the indissolubility of marriage. Furthermore, *niyoga* appears to have historically developed out of a certain form of widow remarriage, usually termed "widow inheritance," where a man's brother or other co-heir would inherit—that is, marry—his widow (and not merely procreate with her, as in the case of levirate). Therefore, given this historical origin of *niyoga*, it is easy to understand both why Dharmaśāstra authors devised strategies to dissociate the practice from remarriage and why they ultimately denied its legitimacy.

Let us turn now to hypergamy, the other Brahmanical value with which widow remarriage and *niyoga* can be said to conflict. In order to appreciate this, it is first necessary to be aware that, as portrayed in Dharmaśāstra texts as well as other sources, classical Indian society was predominantly hypergamous in nature, not endogamous as Indian society largely later became. That is, a man was permitted to marry a woman of equal or lower status, but not higher. Therefore, if the men of family A were allowed to marry the women of family B, but the men of family B were not allowed to marry the woman of family A, the superiority of family A over family B was established. Furthermore, the higher the social status that a family sought to claim, the fewer were the potential husbands for its women. Hence, it is a fact of hypergamous societies that the status of a caste or kinship group closely relates to the level of sexual restrictions that it places upon its female members. In other words, a group is deemed to be of the highest social status, precisely because its female members do not engage—or more accurately are not believed to engage—in sexual intercourse with members of any other group. Moreover, the closer a social group approximates this ideal the higher its theoretical standing becomes within the broader social hierarchy. Bearing this in mind, one might imagine that the society reflected in Dharmaśāstra literature created a rather strong incentive—namely, higher social status—for men to further restrict the women to whom they

[105] On this, see Kane (1962, 2:619–23) and Lariviere (1991). Under certain conditions, however, the *Arthaśāstra* (3.3.15–19) permits divorce, for which the Sanskrit term is *mokṣa*.

were related (i.e., their wives, daughters, mothers, etc.). Hence, a belief in hypergamy generally encourages the sexual restriction of women through the promise of increased social standing.[106] The hypergamous premise that sexual access to another man's female relatives marks him as inferior logically incentivizes female sexual restriction. As a result, one can understand why Brahmanical communities historically came to prohibit both widow remarriage and *niyoga*, despite the fact that these practices served important economic, social, and religious ends.

Of course, hypergamy would likely have had a rather different impact in cases where the social status of one family relative to another was beyond dispute and, thus, could not be contested by increasing sexual restrictions upon female members. In such cases, one would imagine that members of the socially inferior family had a general incentive to marry their daughters off to the sons of the indisputably superior family, as this might increase their social standing. This is seen, for instance, among the Kulīn Brahmins of Bengal (Inden 1976). Moreover, hypergamy has the inadvertent effect of placing increasing limitations on the possible sexual partners for men, not only women, but these limitations increase as one moves down—rather than up—the social hierarchy. However, Dharmaśāstra literature undeniably reflects the perspectives and interests of elite Brahmin men who held themselves to occupy the very highest place within society. Therefore, it is fairly safe to assume that Dharmaśāstra texts would reflect neither of the above perspectives (i.e., that of men facing the prospect of marrying their daughters into higher-ranking families and that of low-caste men).

Writing about the male guardianship prescribed for nuns in postcanonical Jain texts, Mari Jyväsjärvi Stuart (2013, 37) has eloquently articulated a related thesis:

> The reason why male authorities in various sectarian communities place such emphasis on men's guardianship of women . . . is that they share a notion of collective honor in which women's bodies function as an index of the purity and status of their community. In many hierarchical, patriarchal societies, such as would have characterized much of premodern India, the honor of a community is dependent on the honor of its female members—understood specifically as demonstrable curtailment of sexuality on the one hand, and lack of displays of independent agency on the other. Men cannot

[106] For an elaboration of this point, see Ortner (1996, 55–58).

> remain indifferent about how women conduct themselves, as the perceived virtue of those women is inseparably bound up with their own esteem: the fact that women with whom one is associated are "well-guarded" is what marks a man as authoritative, honorable, and manly.

I believe that this thesis—that the sexual and nonsexual control of women served in traditional India as a prominent index of community and family status—is not only correct but may also plausibly be connected at least in part to the hypergamous character of early Indian society. In any case, it would seem to help explain not only the widespread theme of male guardianship in premodern Indian literature but also why Brahmins and other high-caste Hindus came to oppose both widow remarriage and *niyoga*.

2
Widows' Rights of Inheritance

This chapter focuses on one particular legal issue involving widows over which there was much disagreement in Dharmaśāstra works of the ancient and medieval periods. This issue is a widow's right to inherit her deceased husband's property. In particular, this chapter outlines how views on this issue within the Dharmaśāstra tradition evolved over time, from the earliest Dharmaśāstra writings in roughly the third century BCE until around the twelfth century CE, when there was a decisive turn in favor of a widow's right to inherit, as will be shown.

This chapter builds upon conclusions made by A. S. Altekar over eighty years ago in a short, but illuminating article (1938) and then reiterated by him several decades later in a more widely known monograph ([1959] 1989, 250–68). Most importantly, Altekar accurately identifies the major ways in which Brahmanical attitudes toward a widow's right to inherit changed historically. Specifically, he recognizes that the earliest Dharmaśāstra literature almost uniformly denies a widow any right to inherit her husband's property; that the second half of the first millennium was a period of especially intense debate about a widow's right to inherit; and that, starting around the twelfth century, Dharmaśāstra literature more or less unanimously grants the wife of a sonless man the right to inherit his entire estate. Useful as Altekar's writings are, however, they are far from exhaustive in their treatment of Dharmaśāstra sources and effectively provide little more than an outline of historical developments within the Hindu legal tradition. As a result, they fail to give a detailed picture of the relevant Dharmaśāstra sources and omit a number of points that are crucial to a complete diachronic account of Brahmanical views on a widow's right to inherit. The present chapter will hopefully serve to remedy this situation. Moreover, eighty years of Indological scholarship has produced a much revised—and I believe much improved—dating of the surviving early Dharmaśāstra works. Of special importance in this regard is Olivelle's (2007) dating of the *Vaiṣṇava Dharmaśāstra*—an extremely consequential text for present purposes—to

Widows Under Hindu Law. David Brick, Oxford University Press. © Oxford University Press 2023.
DOI: 10.1093/oso/9780197664544.003.0003

the sixth or seventh century CE, rather than to many centuries earlier, as was the accepted view in Altekar's day.[1]

All evidence suggests that premodern Indian society made no use of wills. Therefore, when dealing with the topic of inheritance, Dharmaśāstra literature assumes a situation of intestate succession.[2] At the most fundamental level, it answers the question of who should inherit a person's property by prescribing sequences of heirs, such that there is theoretically no ambiguity about the person or persons to whom a particular property should devolve. Throughout its long history, the universal view of the Hindu legal tradition is that a man's sons are his first and primary heirs. It is only in the absence of sons, which Dharmaśāstra categorizes into a number of discrete types,[3] that a man's other relatives, such as his brothers, parents, daughters, wives, and patrilineal cousins, become possible heirs.[4] Consequently, when attempting to understand how various Dharmaśāstra works view the inheritance rights of widows, the essential passages to examine are those that discuss the heirs of a sonless man, which fortunately most Dharmaśāstra works contain. Therefore, the bulk of this chapter will comprise a detailed and systematic examination of such passages and the classical commentaries thereon.

The Dharmasūtras

The *Āpastamba Dharmasūtra* (2.14.2–5), probably the oldest surviving Dharmaśāstra work, explains who should inherit a sonless man's property as follows:

> In the absence of sons, a man's closest *sapiṇḍa* relative inherits his estate. In the absence of such relatives, his teacher or, failing him, his student should take his inheritance and use it to perform meritorious rites on his behalf; or

[1] Altekar (1938, 7) seems to date Viṣṇu to the first century CE, whereas Kane (1962, 1:125) dates the core of his text to the period 300 BCE–100 CE with some additions made between 400 and 600 CE.

[2] Certain Dharmaśāstra texts (e.g., YDh 2.118), however, grant a man the right to partition his estate among his sons during his lifetime however he sees fit.

[3] On this, see Kane (1962, 3:641–61).

[4] A notable exception to this is Yājñavalkya (2.119, 127), who grants even the wives of men with sons considerable, if limited, rights of inheritance.

instead his daughter may do this. In the absence of all these, the king should receive his estate.

putrābhāve yaḥ pratyāsannaḥ sapiṇḍaḥ | tadabhāva ācārya ācāryābhave 'ntevāsī hṛtvā tadartheṣu dharmakṛtyeṣu vopayojayet | duhitā vā | sarvābhāve rājā dāyaṃ hareta |

As one can see from this passage, Āpastamba holds that in the absence of sons, the person who should inherit a man's estate is his closest *sapiṇḍa*—a major Brahmanical kinship term whose precise meaning varies considerably, depending upon textual and historical context. In origin, the term undoubtedly draws upon the vocabulary of Brahmanical ancestor worship or Śrāddha ritual and, within this ritual context, denotes a person with whom one somehow has ancestral offerings (*piṇḍa*) in common. Thus, since Brahmanical ancestral offerings are fundamentally patrilineal in character, *sapiṇḍa*, in its ritual sense, is a term of patrilineal or agnatic relationship. Moreover, since in Śrāddha ritual a person makes offerings to his three immediate ancestors (father, grandfather, and great grandfather) and his three ancestors beyond them receive the remnants (*lepa*) of these offerings, the term *sapiṇḍa* refers to a relationship spanning seven generations, including the person performing the Śrāddha rite. Consequently, in the ritual sense of the term, a man's *sapiṇḍas* are as follows: (a) his six direct patrilineal ancestors to whom he makes offerings; (b) his direct patrilineal descendants for six generations who will someday make offerings to him; and (c) anyone who makes ancestral offerings to any of the same people that he does. However, although *sapiṇḍa* begins as a term of ritual kinship and continues on as such in certain contexts, at the same time it also develops into a term of biological kinship. And as such, *sapiṇḍa* covers anyone that a person is related to within seven generations on his father's side.[5] And, importantly, early sources that explicitly define the term never list a man's wife among his *sapiṇḍas*.[6] Therefore, it is highly unlikely that Āpastamba considers a man's

[5] For certain purposes, the term *sapiṇḍa* is also expanded to include those related to a person through matrilineal descent over a span of five generations. In addition, it bears noting that certain texts (e.g., BDh 1.5.11.9–10, MDh 9.186, *Dāyabhāga* 11.1.32–42) consider the *sapiṇḍa* relationship to span only three, rather than six, generations with respect to inheritance. For a comprehensive discussion of the term, see Kane (1962, 2:452–78) and especially Trautmann (1981, 246–71). For a Dharmaśāstra work that nicely explains the term in its various senses, see *Parāśara-Mādhava* vol. 1, pp. 465–67.

[6] See BDh 1.11.9 and MDh 5.60.

wife to be one of the *sapiṇḍas* who are to inherit his property in the absence of sons. Furthermore, Āpastamba clearly lays down in the above passage that in the absence of *sapiṇḍas*, a man's teacher, student, or daughter is supposed to take his property and use it to perform meritorious rites on his behalf; and failing such persons, the local king should assume possession of his property. Hence, the earliest extant Dharmaśāstra work appears to exclude a man's wife completely from his list of heirs.

Moreover, Vasiṣṭha, the author of probably the youngest surviving Dharmasūtra, holds a strikingly similar view to that of Āpastamba, as one can see from the following passage of his work (17.81–83):

> If a man has no heir among the first six types of sons,[7] his *sapiṇḍa* relatives or those standing in place of his sons should divide his estate. In the absence of these, his teacher or student should inherit his estate. In the absence of these, the king should inherit it.
>
> *yasya pūrveṣāṃ ṣaṇṇāṃ na kaścid dāyādaḥ syāt sapiṇḍāḥ putrasthānīyā vā tasya dhanaṃ vibhajeran | teṣām alābha ācāryāntevāsinau hareyātām | tayor alābhe rājā haret |*

Here Vasiṣṭha specifically lays down that in the absence of a son of one of the six prestigious types, either a man's *sapiṇḍas* or those standing in for his sons—probably referring to less prestigious types of sons, such as adoptive ones[8]—should inherit his property; that in the absence of such relatives, his teacher or student should inherit his property; and that in the absence of these, the king should inherit it.

Baudhāyana likewise considers a sonless man's heirs to be, in order, his *sapiṇḍas*, his *sakulyas* or more distant patrilineal relatives, his teacher, his pupil, and his sacrificial priest. And, failing all these, he holds that the king should donate a man's property to Brahmins versed in the three Vedas. The following passage of his work (1.11.11–15) states this in no uncertain terms:

[7] As explained at VaDh 17.13–25, these are as follows: an *aurasa*, that is, a son begotten by a man upon his lawfully wedded wife; a *kṣetraja*, that is, a son begotten through *niyoga*; a *putrikā*, or daughter appointed as a legal son; a *paunarbhava*, or son of a remarried woman; a *kānīna*, or son of an unmarried girl (regarded as the son of his maternal grandfather); and a *gūḍhotpanna*, or son born secretly in one's home.

[8] Although Vasiṣṭha (17.26–29) apparently views adopted sons (*dattaka*) as sons of a markedly inferior type, other authors, such as Manu (9.159), seem to regard them quite highly, as second in status only to the natural son (*aurasa*) and the "female son" (*putrikā*).

When there are no other heirs, a man's wealth goes to his *sapiṇḍas*. In the absence of these, it goes to a more distant patrilineal relative. In the absence of such a person, his teacher, who is like a father, his pupil, or his sacrificial priest should inherit his wealth. And in the absence of these, the king should donate his property to men versed in the three Vedas.

asatsv anyeṣu tadgāmī hy artho bhavati | sapiṇḍābhāve sakulyaḥ | tadabhāve pitācāryo 'ntevāsy ṛtvig vā haret | tadabhāve rājā tatsvaṃ traividyavṛddhebhyaḥ saṃprayacchet |

Beyond this, Baudhāyana (2.3.45–46) also quotes a line of verse, which, paraphrasing the much earlier *Taittirīya Saṃhitā*,[9] explains that the Veda regards women as inherently weak and, thus, unfit to receive inheritance:

"Women are considered devoid of strength and without inheritance," so states the Veda.

nirindriyā hy adāyāś ca striyo matā iti śrutiḥ ||

Hence, it seems that, in keeping with the earlier Vedic literature, the Dharmasūtras of Āpastamba, Baudhāyana, and Vasiṣṭha all completely deny widows the right to inherit the property of their deceased husbands.

Gautama, however, the author of the sole remaining Dharmasūtra and Baudhāyana's approximate contemporary, differs from all other early authors within the Dharmaśāstra tradition in that he recognizes a widow's right to inherit at least some portion of her husband's estate. The relevant passage of his work (28.21–22) reads as follows:

Those related through ancestral offerings (*piṇḍa*), patrilineal clan, or common ancestral seer should receive a share of a childless man's estate, as should his wife. Or instead, she may seek to become impregnated.

piṇḍagotrarṣisaṃbandhā rikthaṃ bhajeran strī cānapatyasya | bījaṃ vā lipseta |

[9] TS 6.5.8.2: "Therefore, women, being devoid of strength, receive no inheritance." (*tásmāt stríyo nírindriyā ádāyādīḥ |*)

Here, as one can see, Gautama states that the following people should share in the estate of a childless man: (a) those related to him through *piṇḍas* or ancestral offerings, which is another way of saying his *sapiṇḍas*; (b) those belonging to his same *gotra* or patrilineal clan; (c) those who share with him a common ancestral seer or *ṛṣi*; and (d) his wife, who here tellingly is not included among a man's *sapiṇḍas*. Unfortunately, it is not apparent precisely how, according to Gautama, a man's estate is to be divided among all these relatives. However, it is clear that in Gautama's view, a widow is to receive at least some portion of her husband's estate, although seemingly a relatively small portion. Moreover, Gautama goes on to state at the end of the passage that instead of inheriting a share of her husband's property, a childless widow might alternatively seek to become impregnated. That is, she might seek to bear a child through *niyoga*, in which case presumably this child would inherit the entire estate of the widow's deceased husband as his lawful son. And here it is important to note that one possible type of son generally recognized within Dharmaśāstra is the *putrikā* or "female son," which is a daughter appointed to act as a man's son for ritual and inheritance purposes.[10] Thus, even if the child begotten through *niyoga* turns out to be female, this girl could still theoretically become a man's legal son and heir, strange as that may sound.

Later Smṛtis

The *Mānava Dharmaśāstra* (9.185, 187–88), the next oldest Dharmaśāstra work after the four early Dharmasūtras, explains the heirs of a sonless man as follows:

> Neither brothers nor fathers, but sons inherit their father's property. The father of a sonless man should inherit his property or else his brothers should. . . . Whoever is next closest to a *sapiṇḍa* relative should inherit his property. Beyond these, a more distant patrilineal relative, his teacher, or his student should. In the absence of all, Brahmins who are learned in the three Vedas, pure, and self-restrained should divide his inheritance—in this way, the law is not diminished.

[10] On the *putrikā* ("female son"), see Kane (1962, 3:647, 657–59).

na bhrātaro na pitaraḥ putrā rikthaharāḥ pituḥ |
pitā hared aputrasya riktham bhrātara eva vā ||
...
anantaraḥ sapiṇḍād yas tasya tasya dhanaṃ bhavet |
ata ūrdhvaṃ sakulyaḥ syād ācāryaḥ śiṣya eva vā ||
sarveṣām apy abhāve tu brāhmaṇā rikthabhāginaḥ |
traividyāḥ śucayo dāntās tathā dharmo no hīyate ||

As one can see, Manu considers a sonless man's father or brothers to be his primary heirs. Failing these, he holds that a man's nearest *sapiṇḍa* relative should inherit his property, followed by a more distant patrilineal relative (*sakulya*), his teacher, or his pupil. Lastly, in the absence of all such persons, Manu states that learned and virtuous Brahmins should receive a sonless man's estate. Thus, in agreement with Āpastamba, Baudhāyana, and Vasiṣṭha and in disagreement with Gautama, Manu apparently denies widows any right to inherit their husbands' estates.

Following Manu, Nārada likewise denies widows the right to inherit, as one can see from the following passage of his work (13.47–48):

> In the absence of sons, a man's daughter inherits his estate, for she is seen to equally continue his line. Indeed, both a son and a daughter are said to continue their father's line. But in the absence of daughters, a man's patrilineal relatives, then his non-patrilineal relatives, and then other members of his caste inherit his estate. In the absence of all these, it goes to the king.

putrābhāve tu duhitā tulyasaṃtānadarśanāt |
putraś ca duhitā coktau pituḥ saṃtānakārakau ||
abhāve tu duhitṝṇāṃ sakulyā bāndhavās tataḥ |
tataḥ sajātyāḥ sarveṣām abhāve rājagāmi tat ||

Here, instead, Nārada lists a man's daughter as his primary heir in the absence of sons, perhaps with the understanding that this daughter will act as a *putrikā* or "female son." Whatever the case may be, Nārada then goes on to provide an exhaustive list of men who are to inherit a man's property in the absence of both sons and daughters. Hence, although he apparently has no substantial objection to women inheriting property (at least women who are or are going to be married), he does not grant widows any rights of inheritance.

Consequently, with the sole exception of Gautama (28.21–22), who allows widows at least some limited right to inherit, the entire Brahmanical tradition from the Vedas up through to Nārada in perhaps the fifth or sixth century CE completely denies widows the right to inherit. And it is in this textual and historical context that one must appreciate the full significance of the following passage of Yājñavalkya (2.139–40), whose work is roughly contemporaneous with that of Nārada:

> Wife, daughters, parents, brothers, brothers' sons, a member of one's patrilineal clan, a non-patrilineal relative, a pupil, and a fellow-student—in the absence of each prior member of this list, the following member inherits the wealth of a sonless man who has gone to heaven. This is the rule for all social classes.
>
> *patnī duhitaraś caiva pitarau bhrātaras tathā |*
> *tatsutā gotrajo bandhuḥ śiṣyaḥ sabrahmacāriṇaḥ ||*
> *eṣām abhāve pūrvasya dhanabhāg uttarottaraḥ |*
> *svaryātasya hy aputrasya sarvavarṇeṣv ayaṃ vidhiḥ ||*

As one can see from this passage, Yājñavalkya unambiguously holds the startling view that the first and primary heir of a sonless man is his wife rather than his brothers or other male patrilineal relations. Moreover, he seemingly enjoins that such a woman should inherit the entire estate of her deceased husband. At least the text gives us no reason to imagine otherwise. And, even beyond this, Yājñavalkya explicitly states that the rule of inheritance he has laid down applies to every social class, in other words, to the whole of society. Consequently, in regards to widows' rights of inheritance, Yājñavalkya's work represents a quite radical departure from tradition, far more radical than the earlier *Gautama Dharmasūtra*.

Moreover, it is noteworthy that, according to the above passage of Yājñavalkya, a man's daughters are to inherit his estate in the absence of both sons and wives. Hence, there is the implication that, after a woman's death, any property that she inherited from her sonless husband should devolve to her surviving daughters, if she has any. As a result, the property would seemingly remain in the possession of women for an extended period of time before eventually devolving either to male patrilineal relatives of the original owner (e.g., his brothers' sons) or to the sons of his daughters, if applicable.[11] This further demonstrates the extent to which Yājñavalkya differs in his views on inheritance from earlier Dharmaśāstra authors, such as Manu and Baudhāyana.

In addition, two verses of Yājñavalkya even go so far as to grant the wives of men with sons notable rights of inheritance. The first of these verses (YDh 2.119) addresses cases where a man chooses to partition his estate among his sons during his lifetime:

> If a man gives his sons equal shares, then he should also grant his wives equal shares, provided neither their husband nor father-in-law has given them any women's property.
>
> *yadi dadyāt samān aṃśān kāryāḥ patnyaḥ samāṃśikāḥ* |
> *na dattaṃ strīdhanaṃ yāsāṃ bhartrā vā śvaśureṇa vā* ||

Here Yājñavalkya essentially states that a woman must receive either special property termed *strīdhana* ("women's property")[12] from her husband's family or a share of inheritance equal to those of her sons. The second verse of Yājñavalkya (2.127) concerns cases where a man's estate is partitioned after his death:

> When sons partition their father's estate after his passing, their mother also receives a share.
>
> *pitur ūrdhvaṃ vibhajatāṃ mātāpy aṃśaṃ samāpnuyāt* ||

Here Yājñavalkya flatly states that even when a man has sons, his widow should receive a share of his estate. Thus, he clearly seeks to ensure that even the widows of men with sons receive at least some wealth of their own from their husbands' families. It is noteworthy, however, that when it comes to the wives of men deemed lowly, specifically the outcasted, impotent, lame, insane, and mentally incompetent, Yājñavalkya is markedly less generous, for he grants the sonless wives of such men the right only to maintenance (i.e.,

[11] The son of a man's daughter might then posthumously become a man's legal son as a *putrikāsuta* or "son of a female son." Such a boy would then belong to the patriline of his maternal grandfather. Yājñavalkya (2.132) clearly thinks highly of the *putrikāsuta*, listing him second among the twelve possible types of sons.

[12] For a discussion of *strīdhana*, see Kane (1962, 3:770–802).

food and shelter) and stipulates that even this can be withdrawn if they fail to observe good conduct.[13]

Let us turn now to the *Vaiṣṇava Dharmaśāstra*, the only surviving Smṛti composed after Yājñavalkya that addresses the issue of inheritance. It is clear from the following passage of Viṣṇu's work (17.4–13) that he essentially adopts Yājñavalkya's earlier position on a widow's right to inherit:

> The wealth of a sonless man goes to his wife; in her absence, to his daughters; in their absence, to his father; in his absence, to his mother; in her absence, to his brothers; in their absence, to his brothers' sons; in their absence, to his close relatives; in their absence, to his more distant relatives; in their absence, to a fellow-student; and in his absence, to the king, except for the case of Brahmins' wealth.
>
> *aputrasya dhanaṃ patnyabhigāmi | tadabhāve duhitṛgāmi | tadabhāve pitṛgāmi | tadabhāve mātṛgāmi | tadabhāve bhrātṛgāmi | tadabhāve bhrātṛputragāmi | tadabhāve bandhugāmi | tadabhāve sakulyagāmi | tadabhāve sahādhyāyigāmi | tadabhāve brāhmaṇadhanavarjaṃ rājagāmi |*

Like Yājñavalkya before him, Viṣṇu here lists a wife first and daughter second among a sonless man's heirs. Indeed, Viṣṇu's overall sequence of heirs in the above passage closely matches that of Yājñavalkya (2.139–40) and betrays a dependence upon his work. Moreover, like Yājñavalkya (2.119, 127), he states that a woman is entitled to a share of inheritance equal to those of her sons.[14] Hence, Yājñavalkya's text appears to have been quite influential with regard to a widow's right to inherit and to have inaugurated a line of Brahmanical thought that, for the first time, recognized as socially respectable a class of unmarried women of considerable independent means.

However, as one might guess, the new position on widows' property rights championed by Yājñavalkya and Viṣṇu did not go unchallenged. One clear and rather disturbing indication of this comes from the Smṛti of

[13] YDh 2.146: "The sonless wives of such men should be maintained, if they observe good conduct, but expelled, if they are adulterous or cantankerous." (*aputrā yoṣitaś caiṣāṃ bhartavyāḥ sādhuvṛttayaḥ | nirvāsyā vyabhicāriṇyaḥ pratikūlās tathaiva ca ||*)

[14] ViDh 18.34: "Mothers receive shares corresponding to the shares of their sons." (*mātaraḥ putrabhāgānusārabhāgāpahāriṇyaḥ |*)

Bṛhaspati—a work that no longer survives as an independent treatise, but can be known to a certain degree from citations of it found in later exegetical works. An oft-quoted passage of this text advocates for a widow's right to inherit, arguing that a wife constitutes half of her husband's body and, as such, can be his only legitimate heir in the absence of sons.[15] Significantly, this passage concludes with a verse that instructs a king to punish as thieves any of a man's relatives who hinder his widow from enjoying his former property[16]:

> If any of her husband's *sapiṇḍas* or other kinsmen stand in her way or damage her property, the king should punish them with the punishment for thieves.
>
> *sapiṇḍā bāndhavā ye tu tasyāḥ syuḥ paripanthinaḥ* |
> *hiṃsyur dhanāni tān rājā cauradaṇḍena śāsayet* ||

The most natural way to interpret the above verse is as a response to the actions actually taken or at least threatened by certain men in Bṛhaspati's time. It, therefore, serves as an indication of the intense controversy over a widow's right to inherit that was taking place in South Asia during the second half of the first millennium.

The Early Commentaries

Now let us turn from the Smṛtis to the commentaries, specifically to those Dharmaśāstra commentaries that were composed prior to the late eleventh century. A review of these commentaries—both those that survive as independent treatises and those that are known only from citations found in later texts—confirms that between roughly the seventh and eleventh centuries, a widow's right to inherit was a hotly debated issue within orthodox Brahmanical circles. For while three early commentators seem to

[15] BSm 26.93 (in Aiyangar's reconstruction of the text): "When a man's wife has not died, half of his body still lives. So when half of his body still lives, how can another man take his wealth?" (*yasya noparatā bhāryā dehārdhaṃ tasya jīvati* | *jīvaty ardhaśarīre 'rthaṃ katham anyaḥ samāpnuyāt* ||) This verse is cited by Aparārka (on YDh 2.136) and in the *Kṛtyakalpataru* (*Vyavahārakāṇḍa*, p. 746).

[16] This is BSm 26.105 in Aiyangar's attempted reconstruction of the text. For citations of it, see Aparārka on YDh 2.136 and *Kṛtyakalpataru, Vyavahārakāṇḍa*, p. 746.

allow widows at least some right to inherit their husbands' estates, several others are staunchly opposed to any such right.

That Bhāruci, Manu's earliest surviving commentator, acknowledges a widow's right to inherit to at least some extent becomes apparent from his commentary on the verses of Manu that list a sonless man's heirs (9.185–88). The relevant passage of Bhāruci (on MDh 9.187) reads as follows:

> From the phrase "in the absence of all" it is understood that in the absence of a man's womenfolk as well, a Brahmin endowed with the stated virtues inherits his estate.
>
> *sarveṣām apy abhāva ity etasmād gamyate tatstrīṇām apy abhāve yathoktaguṇasaṃbandha iti* |

Here, as one can see, Bhāruci explains that when Manu speaks of unrelated Brahmins inheriting a man's property "in the absence of all" (*sarveṣām apy abhāve*), the word "all" includes a man's women (*tatstrīṇām api*), presumably meaning his wives and maybe also his daughters. That is, Bhāruci clearly inserts at least some of a man's female relatives into the list of heirs given by Manu. However, he is rather ambiguous as to where exactly these women are supposed to fit within Manu's list. The vague impression one gets from Bhāruci's terse comment is that they come last among a man's relatives. Hence, although Bhāruci seemingly acknowledges a widow's right to inherit to some degree, he appears not to be a particularly strong advocate of this right.

Similar to Bhāruci is Maskarin, the earliest surviving commentator on the *Gautama Dharmasūtra*.[17] Maskarin interprets Gautama's statement on the heirs of a sonless man (28.21–22), which has been discussed above, in a more or less natural way, explaining that "when those related through ancestral offerings or the like receive a share of a man's estate, his wife also receives a share."[18] The fact that Maskarin does not attempt to explain away Gautama's apparent approval of a childless widow receiving inheritance suggests that he personally did not object to this position. It is worth emphasizing, however, that Gautama and, by extension, Maskarin hold that a sonless man's

[17] Olivelle (2000, 116) suggests that Maskarin wrote during the tenth century.

[18] Maskarin on GDh 28.22: *te yadaiva piṇḍādisaṃbandhā rikthaṃ bhajeran tadā stry api bhāgaṃ labheta* |

estate should be divided among numerous relatives, specifically his surviving *sapiṇḍas* and his wife. Hence, unlike Yājñavalkya and Viṣṇu, they limit a widow's inheritance to what would likely have been in most cases a fairly small portion of her husband's property.

Finally, Manu's other early commentator, Medhātithi, also seems to accept a widow's right to inherit her husband's estate in at least some fashion. Regrettably, however, because Medhātithi's work had to be reconstructed under the aegis of the fourteenth-century king Madanapāla on the basis of incomplete manuscripts and quotations found in other works, the portion of his commentary that would presumably have dealt directly with a widow's right to inherit has not survived.

Nevertheless, both Altekar (1938, 6) and Kane (1962, 3:706) are of the opinion that Medhātithi opposed a widow's right to inherit, for Kullūka, an influential later commentator on Manu, explicitly criticizes Medhātithi for holding such a view:

> Hence, it is nonsensical when Medhātithi claims that wives are prohibited from receiving a share of inheritance. Indeed, authorities, such as Bṛhaspati, approve of wives receiving a share of inheritance. Thus, in rejecting this, Medhātithi does not delight the minds of learned men.
>
> *ato yan medhātithinā patnīnām aṃśabhāgitvaṃ niṣiddham uktaṃ tad asaṃbaddham | patnīnām aṃśabhāgitvaṃ bṛhaspatyādisaṃmatam | medhātithir nirākurvan na prīṇāti satāṃ manaḥ* | (Kullūka on MDh 9.187)

From this statement it would appear that Medhātithi denies widows the right to inherit even a portion of their husbands' estates.

However, there is good reason to doubt the basic accuracy of Kullūka's statement about Medhātithi, for a passage from Medhātithi's commentary itself indicates that he considered a widow's right to inherit to be fully compatible with Brahmanical scriptures. This passage comprises part of his explanation of what Manu means, when he states (at MDh 8.3) that a king should adjudicate lawsuits in accordance with the "reasons" (*hetubhiḥ*) prescribed in different regions and in scripture. Commenting on the word "reason" (*hetu*) in Manu's text, Medhātithi states:

> The term "reason", here denotes a means of arriving at a judicial verdict. And such reasons are twofold, taking the form of evidence and of legal

conventions. Regarding these, a reason for deciding a lawsuit in the form of evidence is a witness or the like. A reason in the form of a legal convention is that on account of which a lawsuit successfully concludes even when there is no way to decide the case....

Legal conventions are twofold: general and specific due to a difference in regions. And the latter type is also twofold due to a difference in basis. That is, such regional conventions can be either uncontradicted or contradicted. An uncontradicted convention is, for instance, when, among certain Southerners, a sonless woman, after her husband's death, takes the stand in court; upon that stand is interrogated by appointed officials; and when her good character is ascertained, immediately thereafter receives her inheritance in the presence of her husband's *sapiṇḍas*.... And contradicted legal conventions are such as when, in a certain country, grain is loaned in the spring and twice as much is repaid in the fall or when a lender receives collateral with permission to use it, but still continues to use it until the principal is repaid, even after the borrower has made interest payments equal to twice the money lent for the collateral. For these conventions are contradicted by the scriptural statements "A lender shall charge 1.25% interest each month" (MDh 8.140) and "Interest on a loan shall not exceed twice the principal" (MDh 8.151).

hetur nirṇayasādhanam | sa ca dvividhaḥ pramāṇarūpo vyavasthārūpaś ca | tatra pramāṇarūpo 'rthanirṇayahetuḥ sākṣyādiḥ | vyavasthārūpo yato 'saty evārthaniścaye vyavahāraḥ saṃtiṣṭhate | . . . sā vyavasthā dvividhā sādhāraṇy asādhāraṇī ca deśabhedāt | āśrayabhedāt sāpi dvividhā aviruddhā viruddhā ca | aviruddhā yathā keṣāṃcid dakṣiṇātyānām aputrā strī bhartary uparate sabhāsthāṇum upārohati tam upārūḍhādhikṛtaiḥ parīkṣitā kṛtalakṣaṇā tatkṣaṇānantaraṃ sapiṇḍeṣu ṛkthaṃ labhate |... viruddhā ca | kvacid deśe vasante dhānyaṃ prayujyate śaradi dviguṇaṃ pratyādīyate | tathānujñātabhoga ādhir dviguṇe 'pi tadutthadhane praviṣṭa ā mūlahiraṇyadānād bhujyata eva | eṣā hi aśītibhāgaṃ gṛhṇīyāt (MDh 8.140) *kusīdavṛddhir dvaiguṇyaṃ nātyetīti* (MDh 8.151) *viruddhā* |

Here Medhātithi explains that, as Manu uses the term, a "reason" (*hetu*) is a means of reaching a verdict in a court case. He then divides such reasons into two types: evidence, such as witnesses and written documents, and what he calls *vyavasthā* ("legal convention"). This rather ambiguous term he explains as essentially a means whereby a judge can rule on a lawsuit even when other means, such as evidence, fail. That is, in Medhātithi's usage, a *vyavasthā* is a legalistic custom or convention. Elaborating upon the term, he furthers explains that a *vyavasthā* or legal convention can be either universal or regional in character and that a regional *vyavasthā* can be either "uncontradicted" (*aviruddha*) or "contradicted" (*viruddha*). And precisely what Medhātithi intends by this distinction becomes apparent at the end of the passage, when he cites two specific regional legal conventions or *vyavasthās* and explains that these are contradicted, because scriptural statements explicitly contradict them. Hence, it is clear that for Medhātithi an uncontradicted convention is one that is compatible with scripture. Therefore, it is quite informative for present purposes that Medhātithi cites as an uncontradicted convention a peculiar legal practice among certain Southerners, whereby a sonless widow would receive inheritance in a court of law. For this detail tells us that Medhātithi considers this practice to be in conformity with scripture. Unfortunately, however, it is not clear from Medhātithi's commentary whether the Southern custom he imagines would grant a widow her husband's entire estate or merely a portion thereof. Hence, it is impossible to know for certain whether or not he fully agrees with Yājñavalkya and Viṣṇu on a widow's right to inherit.

Beyond this, one might also be tempted to infer from Medhātithi's statement that certain South Indians in his day accepted a widow's right to inherit her sonless husband's property under the condition that she was a woman of certified good character. It is unlikely, however, that the source of Medhātithi's information here is his actual knowledge of contemporaneous South Indian customs. Instead, his information is quite likely based upon a strikingly similar passage of Yāska's *Nirukta*, a work of perhaps the fifth-century BCE dedicated to explaining difficult Vedic terms and phrases.[19]

Now, let us turn to those early commentators within the Dharmaśāstra tradition who strongly oppose the inheritance rights of widows. Of these, quite likely the earliest is Viśvarūpa, whose commentary on the *Yājñavalkya Dharmaśāstra* can be dated with some confidence to the early ninth century. The first indication of Viśvarūpa's opposition to widows inheriting property comes from his commentary on the previously cited verse of Yājñavalkya (2.119), where he effectively states that a man should give his wife a share of

[19] Explaining the second *pāda* of ṚV 1.124.7, *Nirukta* 3.5 states: "Just like a Southern woman ascends a high seat to gain wealth. A 'high seat' is a stand in court. . . . It is a place where oaths are true. A woman who is without sons or a husband ascends that there. . . . She then gains inheritance." (*gartārohiṇīva dhanalābhāya dākṣiṇājī | gartaḥ sabhāsthāṇuḥ | . . . satyasaṃgaro bhavati | taṃ tatra yāputrā yāpatikā sārohati | . . . sā rikthaṃ labhate |*)

his estate equal to those of his sons, if his family never gave her any special women's property. After briefly explaining the literal meaning of this verse, Viśvarūpa comments:

> Because a certain Smṛti states that "a woman's inheritance should be at most two thousand *paṇas*,"[20] a man's wife should be given only that much, even if there is an abundance of wealth. And if there is little wealth, she should be given only so much that she gets an equal share. Some hold, however, that the practice of childless widows receiving an equal share applies only to those intending to engage in *niyoga*, but this is improper, since *niyoga* is impossible (for twice-born women). For women who can engage in *niyoga*, however, it is proper that their share of inheritance should depend upon *niyoga*.
>
> *dvisahasraparo dāyaḥ striyā iti smṛtyantarāt tāvanmātraṃ prabhūtadhanatve 'pi deyam | svalpe 'pi samāṃśatvenaiva | anye tv anapatyānāṃ niyogābhimukhatvena samāṃśatām āhuḥ | tat tu niyogāsaṃbhavād ayuktam | saṃbhavanniyogānāṃ tu niyogāṃśatvam eva yuktam |*

Here, on the basis of a particular Smṛti text, Viśvarūpa argues that a widow's inheritance is limited to a mere two thousand *paṇas* or common copper coins, even if her husband's wealth is such that an equal share would be more than this. Moreover, later on, Viśvarūpa stipulates that Yājñavalkya's rule about a mother receiving a share of her deceased husband's estate, when her sons are partitioning it, applies only to a mother who has not been given any woman's property.[21] Hence, Viśvarūpa clearly takes pains to restrict the amount of wealth that a widow can inherit.

With this in mind, it should come as no surprise that Viśvarūpa also strives to undercut the impact of Yājñavalkya's statement (2.139–40) that a sonless man's widow is his primary heir, for commenting upon it, he states:

> The word "wife" in this verse is intended to mean a pregnant wife. And, thus, Vasiṣṭha shows that pregnant wives are fit to receive inheritance, when he (17.40–41) states:

[20] These are copper coins, which Viśvarūpa and other authors treat as the standard unit of currency.
[21] See Viśvarūpa on YDh 2.127: "A mother should also receive a share equal to those of her sons, provided that she possesses no women's property." (*avidyamānastrīdhanā mātāpi vibhāgaṃ putrasamam āpnuyāt* |)

> Now comes the partitioning of inheritance among brothers, and this should be delayed until those wives who are childless obtain sons.
>
> And the word "son" in this passage is just a synecdoche for a fetus, for Vasiṣṭha speaks of wives who are "childless," in other words, because when the child is born, even if it is female, it might become a female son. And, thus, Gautama (28.21–22), after stating that the "wife of a childless man" also shares in his estate, says: "Or she may seek to become impregnated." By this, he teaches that his mention of a wife refers to a woman already pregnant.
>
> *patnīty atra gṛhītagarbhābhipretā | tathā ca vasiṣṭhaḥ atha bhrātṝṇāṃ dāyavibhāgaḥ | yāś cānapatyā striyaḥ syus tāsāṃ cā putralābhād iti garbhiṇyo rikthārhā iti* (17.40–41) *darśayati | putraśabdaś cāyam anapatyā iti vacanād garbhopalakṣaṇam eva | utpannaṃ vā stry api putrikā yathā syāt | tathā ca gautamaḥ strī cānapatyasyety uktvāha bījaṃ vā lipseteti* (28.21–22) *| anena strīvacanaṃ garbhiṇyartham iti jñāpayati |*

As one can see from the above passage, Viśvarūpa argues that Yājñavalkya's statement is intended to apply only to a widow who is pregnant. And in support of his interpretation, he cites two passages from authoritative Smṛtis. The first of these is a passage of Vasiṣṭha (17.40–41), which Viśvarūpa takes to mean that brothers should delay partitioning their father's estate until those of his wives who are childless become pregnant, the implication of this being that these pregnant women can then inherit wealth on behalf of their future sons or "female sons" (*putrikā*), as the case may be. The second passage is the passage of Gautama (28.21–22) that I have already discussed in some detail, which seems to say that the wife of a childless man can either inherit a portion of her husband's property herself or else beget him an heir through *niyoga*. As one can see, Viśvarūpa interprets this passage rather differently to imply that the wife in it who does not engage in *niyoga*, but receives inheritance, must already be pregnant. His line of reasoning here seems to be that by conceiving a child through *niyoga*, a widow is able to acquire her husband's property, at least temporarily, on behalf of her unborn child. Therefore, according to Viśvarūpa's thinking, a widow who acquires her husband's property without *niyoga* must already be pregnant. And in order to appreciate the larger implications of this section of Viśvarūpa's commentary, it is important to recall that, as we saw in the preceding chapter, he opposes *niyoga*, regarding it as a practice permissible only for low-caste Śūdras. Hence, in his opinion, only an extremely small number of twice-born widows could inherit their husbands' estates, for such a widow must already be pregnant at the time of her husband's death in order to do so. Even beyond this, the notion underlying Viśvarūpa's interpretation would seem to be that a pregnant widow has ownership over her husband's property only until such time as the property can be transferred to her begotten son or daughter. Thus, Viśvarūpa effectively subscribes to the dominant position of the early Dharmaśāstra tradition that widows simply cannot inherit their deceased husbands' property.

In addition to Viśvarūpa, there is at least one other early Dharmaśāstra commentator who rejects a widow's right to inherit. This commentator is Dhāreśvara, an author whom scholars of Hindu law have traditionally identified with the famous patron of the arts, king Bhoja of Dhārā, a city located in modern-day Madhya Pradesh.[22] However, recent evidence from the unpublished commentary on the *Yājñavalkya Dharmaśāstra* casts serious doubt on this identification, for Bhoja is known to have reigned during the first half of the eleventh century and yet the unpublished commentary, which survives in an incomplete manuscript dated to 1002 CE, mentions Dhāreśvara several times (on YDh 1.84–85) and refutes some of his views.[23] Therefore, the Hindu jurist Dhāreśvara is unlikely to have been King Bhoja of Dhārā, contrary to received scholarly opinion, but instead was probably an earlier author who lived no later than the first half of the tenth century. In any case, Dhāreśvara's work on Hindu law is no longer extant. We can, however, get an idea of its contents from the quoted passages and opinions ascribed to Dhāreśvara by later exegetes. And as presented in surviving commentaries, Dhāreśvara is a staunch opponent of a widow's right to inherit. However, since we do not have direct access to his work, I will not discuss his views on the inheritance rights of widows here. Instead, I will discuss them within the context of another Dharmaśāstra work that is not only the first to cite them but also presents them in greatest detail. This work is the *Mitākṣarā*,

[22] For the standard argument in favor of the identification of Dhāreśvara with Bhoja, see Kane (1962, 2:585–86). For an instance of the acceptance of this view by a more recent scholar, see Rocher (2002, 11).

[23] Most scholars date Bhoja's reign to roughly 1010–1050 CE. Ganguly (1933, 80–81), however, extends it as far back as 999, which is the very earliest possible date. But even this seems too late to maintain the identification of Bhoja with Dhāreśvara, given the new manuscript evidence.

Vijñāneśvara's seminal commentary on the *Yājñavalkya Dharmaśāstra*, to which we will now turn.

Vijñāneśvara

Vijñāneśvara, who wrote his celebrated work of Hindu law between the years 1075 and 1125, is a strong advocate of a widow's right to inherit her husband's property. This first becomes apparent in his commentary on the verse of Yājñavalkya discussed above, which instructs that, when partitioning his estate, a man must either give his wives shares equal to those of his sons or have given them special women's property earlier.[24] After briefly explaining the literal meaning of this verse, Vijñāneśvara adds:

> But when a woman has been given women's property, she receives half a share. Yājñavalkya (2.152) will explain this later on, when he says, "But if she has been given women's property, he should grant her half." Moreover, when a man gives his eldest son an extra large share or the like, his wives do not receive such a share. Instead, they receive only an equal share of the total estate minus the eldest son's special share. However, wives also receive their own special share, as Āpastamba (2.14.9) states: "The household utensils and jewelry belong to the wife."
>
> *datte tu strīdhane 'rdhāṃśaṃ vakṣyati datte tv ardhaṃ prakalpayed iti* (YDh 2.152) | *yadā tu śreṣṭhabhāgādinā jyeṣṭhādīn vibhajati tadā patnyaḥ śreṣṭhādibhāgān na labhante* | *kiṃ tūddhṛtoddhārāt samudāyāt samān evāṃśāṃl labhante svoddhāraṃ ca* | *yathāhāpastambaḥ—parībhāṇḍaṃ ca gṛhe 'laṃkāro bhāryāyā iti* (2.14.9).

Thus, Vijñāneśvara not only does nothing to diminish the inheritance rights granted to wives by Yājñavalkya, unlike his predecessor Viśvarūpa, but also expands them in two significant ways. He does this first by arguing that even when a woman has received special women's property from her husband's family, she is still entitled to half a share of her husband's estate.

[24] This statement is YDh 2.119 in Viśvarūpa and Olivelle's recent critical edition of the text, but YDh 2.115 in the version commented upon in the *Mitākṣarā*.

And, tellingly, Vijñāneśvara justifies this provision on the basis of a later verse of Yājñavalkya (YDh 2.152) that has nothing to do with inheritance per se, but rather concerns the money owed to a woman, if her husband takes an additional wife. The second way in which Vijñāneśvara expands the inheritance rights of wives in the above passage is by explicitly stating that even when a man does not grant his sons strictly equal shares, but instead gives his eldest son an especially large share, his wives are still entitled to a share equal to those of junior sons. Moreover, he adds, on the basis of a statement of Āpastamba (2.14.9), which Āpastamba himself later repudiates (2.14.10–11), that a man's wife receives her own special share of his estate, namely, the household utensils and jewelry. Hence, it is clear that Vijñāneśvara is willing to read beyond the literal meaning of scriptural statements in order to increase widows' rights of inheritance.

It is noteworthy, however, that Vijñāneśvara slightly reduces widows' rights of inheritance later on, when commenting on Yājñavalkya's rule that a woman should receive an equal share of her husband's estate, if her sons partition it after his death.[25] For there Vijñāneśvara adds that this rule applies only when the woman did not receive any women's property, although Yājñavalkya makes no mention of any such restriction. As before, Vijñāneśvara holds that a woman who has received women's property from her husband's family is entitled to only half a share. Therefore, he reduces by half the amount of inheritance that, according to Yājñavalkya, a woman should receive in the event that her husband had sons and had gifted her special property. Vijñāneśvara's reason for doing this is presumably a desire to make the rules of postmortem partition more closely match those of partition during a person's lifetime. It certainly is not any fundamental opposition on his part to widows' inheritance rights.

As one might expect, the bulk of Vijñāneśvara's discussion of a widow's right to inherit occurs within the context of Yājñavalkya's statement about the heirs of a sonless man. And, indeed, in his commentary on the relevant verses,[26] Vijñāneśvara has far more to say about a widow's right to inherit than all preceding works of Dharmaśāstra combined. He begins by explaining the basic meaning of Yājñavalkya's text, noting, for instance, that the "wife"

[25] This is YDh 1.127 in Viśvarūpa and Olivelle's recent critical edition of the text, but YDh 2.123 in the version commented upon in the *Mitākṣarā*, which significantly makes explicit that "a mother receives an *equal* share" (*mātāpy aṃśaṃ samaṃ haret*).

[26] These are YDh 2.139–40 in Viśvarūpa and Olivelle's edition of the text, but YDh 2.135–36 in the version commented upon in the *Mitākṣarā*.

referred to is a woman that a man has lawfully married (*vivāhasaṃskṛtā*). He then states:

> If a man has multiple wives of the same caste or different castes, they should take his property after dividing it into proper shares. Moreover, Vṛddha Manu states that a wife receives her husband's entire estate:
>
> A sonless woman who preserves her husband's bed and adheres to her marriage vow—only such a wife should make ancestral offerings to her deceased husband and receive his entire share of inheritance.
>
> *tāś ca bahvyaś cet sajātīyā vijātīyāś ca tadā yathāṃśaṃ vibhajya dhanaṃ gṛhṇanti | vṛddhamanur api patnyāḥ samagradhanasaṃbandhaṃ vakti—*
>
> *aputrā śayanaṃ bhartuḥ pālayantī vrate sthitā |*
> *patny eva dadyāt tatpiṇḍaṃ kṛtsnam aṃśaṃ labheta ceti ||*

Hence, Vijñāneśvara addresses how a man's estate should be partitioned if he has multiple wives and wives of different castes, perhaps assuming the application of Yājñavalkya's rule concerning sons born of women of different castes, as the *Madanapārijāta* (p.672) explicitly contends.[27] Citing a verse of Vṛddha Manu, Vijñāneśvara also explicitly argues that a sonless man's widow should receive his entire estate and not merely a portion thereof.

However, the major reason why Vijñāneśvara's treatment of a widow's right to inherit extends to such length is that, as a general rule, he strives hard to propose the best and most convincing way to harmonize all of the existing Smṛtis on a given topic. And, as we have seen, the Smṛtis on inheritance law seem to be in irrefutable conflict with one another, with some denying widows the right to inherit altogether and others, such as Yājñavalkya, designating them as the primary inheritors of a sonless man's entire estate. Thus, in tackling a widow's right to inherit, Vijñāneśvara has his work cut out for him. To this end, he begins the relevant section of his commentary by citing an array of Smṛtis that grant sonless widows the status of primary heirs and juxtaposing these texts with an assortment of seemingly contradictory Smṛtis. Thereafter, having set up a daunting exegetical challenge, as

[27] According to YDh 2.129, four shares go to the son of a Brahmin man by a Brahmin woman, three to his son by a Kṣatriya woman, two to his son by a Vaiśya woman, and one to his son by a Śūdra woman; three shares go to the son of Kṣatriya man by a Kṣatriya woman, two to his son by a Vaiśya woman, and one to his son by a Śūdra woman; and two shares go to the son of a Vaiśya man by a Vaiśya woman and one to his son by a Śūdra woman.

it were, he systematically presents and refutes a number of alternative ways to harmonize the scriptures before ultimately proposing his own way to harmonize them.

And the first wrong way to harmonize the scriptures that Vijñāneśvara cites is a position he ascribes to Dhāreśvara, an author of likely the early tenth century or before, who has been briefly discussed above. The relevant passage of the *Mitākṣarā* reads as follows:

> Dhāreśvara has presented a way to harmonize scriptural statements such as those above whose meanings contradict one another:
>
> The class of statements to the effect that a wife should inherit apply only to a woman whose husband had already received his share of inheritance prior to his death and only if she is seeking to beget a child through *niyoga*. Why is this? (a) Because only a woman who intends to engage in *niyoga* can receive wealth, not an independent woman. (b) Because on account of such scriptural statements as "The father of a sonless man should inherit" (MDh 9.185), one must state some basis for harmonizing the scriptures and no other basis for such harmonizing exists. And (c) because of Gautama's statement (28.21–22): "Those related through ancestral offerings, patrilineal clan, or common ancestral seer should inherit a childless man's estate or else his wife should; or she may seek to become impregnated." The meaning of this is that those related through ancestral offerings, patrilineal clan, or common ancestral seer should inherit a childless man's estate; or else his wife should, if she seeks to become impregnated. Furthermore, Manu (9.146) states:
>
> > If a man takes care of his dead brother's wealth and wife, he should beget a child for his brother and give that wealth to him alone.
>
> By this, he shows that when a man's brother has died, even if he had received his inheritance, his wife has a claim to his wealth only through her children, not in any other way. And this is true also in the case of a man who had not received his inheritance due to the statement (MDh 9.120):
>
> > If a younger brother begets a son upon his elder brother's wife, the partition of inheritance in that case is equal—this is the settled law.
>
> Moreover, Vasiṣṭha prohibits *niyoga* out of greed for inheritance in the statement (17.65), "There is no *niyoga* out of greed for inheritance," and, thereby, shows that a wife has a claim to wealth only through *niyoga* and not in any other way. And in the absence of *niyoga*, a wife receives mere maintenance due to Nārada's statement (13.25): "And they (= a man's brothers)

should provide maintenance for his women until the end of their lives." Indeed, later on Yājñavalkya (2.146) will also state:

> The sonless wives of such men should be maintained, if they observe good conduct, but expelled, if they are adulterous or cantankerous.

Beyond this, the wealth of twice-born men is for the purpose of performing sacrifices and women are not entitled to perform sacrifices. Therefore, it is improper that they should receive wealth. And on this the author of a certain Smṛti text states:

> Wealth arose for the purpose of sacrifice. All those who are unentitled to that do not receive inheritance, but instead receive food and clothing. Property has been ordained for the purpose of sacrifice. Therefore, one should entrust it to recipients who delight in the law, not to women, fools, and the unrighteous.

ity evamādīnāṃ viruddhārthānāṃ vākyānāṃ dhāreśvareṇa vyavasthā darśitā | patnī gṛhṇīyāt ity etad vacanajātaṃ vibhaktabhrātṛstrīviṣayaṃ sā ca yadi niyogārthinī bhavati | kuta etat | niyogasavyapekṣāyāḥ patnyā dhanaharaṇaṃ na svatantrāyā iti | pitā hared aputrasya ity (MDh 9.185) *ādivacanāt tatra vyavasthākāraṇaṃ vaktavyam | nānyad vyavasthākāraṇam astīti | gautamavacanāc ca piṇḍagotrarṣisaṃbandhā rikthaṃ bhajeran strī vānapatyasya bījaṃ [vā] lipseteti* (GDh 28.21–22) | *asyārthaḥ piṇḍagotrarṣisaṃbandhā anapatyasya rikthaṃ bhajeran strī vā rikthaṃ bhajet yadi bījaṃ lipseteti | manur api—*

> *dhanaṃ yo bibhṛyād bhrātur mṛtasya striyaṃ eva ca |*
> *so 'patyaṃ bhrātur utpādya dadyāt tasyaiva tad dhanam ||* (MDh 9.146)

iti | anenaitad darśayati vibhaktadhane 'pi bhrātary uparate 'patyadvāreṇaiva patnyā dhanasaṃbandho nānyatheti | tathāvibhaktadhane 'pi—

> *kanīyāñ jyeṣṭhabhāryāyāṃ putram utpādayed yadi |*
> *samas tatra vibhāgaḥ syād iti dharmo vyavasthitaḥ ||* (MDh 9.120)

iti | tathā vasiṣṭho 'pi rikthalobhān nāsti niyoga iti rikthalobhān niyogaṃ pratiṣedhayan niyogadvāraka eva patnyāḥ dhanasaṃbandho nānyatheti darśayati | niyogābhāve 'pi patnyā bharaṇamātram eva nāradavacanād bharaṇaṃ cāsya kurvīran strīṇām ā jīvanakṣayād iti (NSm 13.25) | *yogīśvareṇāpi kila vakṣyate—*

> *aputrā yoṣitaś caiṣāṃ bhartavyāḥ sādhuvṛttayaḥ |*
> *nirvāsyā vyabhicāriṇyaḥ pratikūlās tathaiva ca ||* (YDh 2.146)

iti | api ca dvijātidhanasya yajñārthatvāt strīṇāṃ ca yajñe 'nadhikārād dhanagrahaṇam ayuktam | tathā ca kenāpi smṛtam—

yajñārthe dravyam utpannaṃ tatrānadhikṛtās tu ye |
arikthabhājas te sarve grāsācchādanabhājanāḥ ||
yajñārthaṃ vihitaṃ vittaṃ tasmāt tad viniyojayet |
sthāneṣu dharmajuṣṭeṣu na strīmūrkhavidharmiṣu || iti |

According to this passage, Dhāreśvara grants widows the right to inherit, provided that two conditions are met: (a) at the time of his death, her husband had already received his paternal inheritance and, thus, was no longer living jointly with his brothers and (b) his widow intends to beget a child through *niyoga*. However, it should be clear that this position of Dhāreśvara gives widows effectively no right to inherit for two reasons. First, similar to what we have seen in the case of Viśvarūpa, the underlying assumption here seems to be that a widow conceiving a child through *niyoga* will merely safeguard her husband's property until her child comes of age. And, second, it is extremely unlikely that Dhāreśvara actually regards *niyoga* as a viable option for widows or at least high-caste widows, considering that, as I have shown, all known Dharmaśāstra commentators after Bhāruci in the seventh century reject it as a reprehensible practice, legitimate at best only in bygone eras or for members of the lowest social class.

Dhāreśvara defends his position that only a woman who engages in *niyoga* can inherit her husband's property primarily on the basis of three arguments. The first of these is that an independent woman can never receive property, such women being widely condemned in Dharmaśāstra sources.[28] Hence, only a widow seeking to beget a child through *niyoga* could possibly be a legitimate heir, since her future son would act as her guardian. Dhāreśvara's second argument is simply that there is no other viable way to harmonize the extant Smṛtis than to construe those texts that allow widows to inherit as applying only to women intent upon *niyoga*. And his third argument is that Gautama says as much in a passage of his work (28.21–22) that we discussed earlier in this chapter, which Dhāreśvara—rather outlandishly—interprets to mean that a childless man's wife may inherit his property, if she seeks to conceive a child through *niyoga*.

[28] See, for instance, the famous verse cited (with minor variations) at BDh 2.3.45, VaDh 5.3, and MDh 9.3: "Her father protects her in her childhood. Her husband protects in her youth. Her sons protect her in old age. A woman ought never to be independent." (*pitā rakṣati kaumāre bhartā rakṣati yauvane | rakṣanti sthavire putrā na strī svātantryam arhati ||*)

Beyond these three principal arguments, Dhāreśvara also makes a number of additional remarks in support of his case against a widow's right to inherit. Specifically, he cites two verses of Manu (9.120, 146), which purportedly show that a widow's right to inherit requires her engagement in *niyoga* both in cases where her husband had received his paternal inheritance prior to his death and in cases where he had not. Thus, he rules out the possibility of harmonizing the relevant scriptures strictly on the basis of such a distinction. Dhāreśvara then cleverly points out that when the author Vasiṣṭha (17.65) prohibits *niyoga* out of greed for inheritance, he implies that *niyoga* is, in fact, a means for widows to receive inheritance, thus confirming his position. Thereafter, Dhāreśvara elaborates, on the basis of a statement by Nārada (13.25), that in the absence of *niyoga*, a widow's husband's family is to provide her only with maintenance, nothing more. And, lastly, he argues that women of the twice-born social classes can have no right to own property, because they are not entitled to perform sacrifices and the wealth of twice-born people is to be used expressly for such purposes. Thus concludes Dhāreśvara's lengthy case against a widow's right to inherit, as presented in the *Mitākṣarā*.

Now, let us look at how Vijñāneśvara responds to Dhāreśvara's position on the inheritance rights of widows. His approach is a systematic one, for as we will see, he refutes one by one each of Dhāreśvara's individual arguments against a woman's right to inherit her husband's estate. To this end, Vijñāneśvara begins by arguing the absurdity of making a widow's inheriting property contingent upon the practice of *niyoga*:

> But this position (of Dhāreśvara) is incorrect, for there is no indication of *niyoga* nor is it the topic under discussion in the statement starting "Wife, daughters . . ." (YDh 2.139). Moreover, one adhering to this position must explain whether it is *niyoga* that causes a wife to receive wealth or it is the child begotten thereby. Now, if *niyoga* itself is the cause of receiving wealth, it follows that even a wife who has not successfully begotten a son has a claim to wealth and that a son begotten in this manner does not have a claim to wealth. But suppose it is instead the woman's child itself that is the cause. If this is the case, then the son alone has a claim to his father's wealth and, consequently, Yājñavalkya should not begin his statement (2.139) with the word "wife."

tad anupapannam | patnī duhitara ity (YDh 2.139) *atra niyogasyāpratīter aprastutatvāc ca | api cedam atra vaktavyam | patnyā dhanagrahaṇe niyogo vā nimittaṃ tadutpannam apatyaṃ vā | tatra niyogasyaiva nimittatve anutpāditaputrāyā api dhanasaṃbandhaḥ prāpnoti | utpannasya ca putrasya dhanasaṃbandho na prāpnoti | atha tadapatyasyaiva nimittatvaṃ | tathā sati putrasyaiva dhanasaṃbandhāt patnīti* (YDh 2.139) *nārabdhavyam* |

Here Vijñāneśvara first observes that the passage of Yājñavalkya under discussion makes no mention of *niyoga* nor does context in any way suggest the practice. He then points out a certain logical incoherence in the position that by engaging in *niyoga* a widow is able to inherit her husband's property. For if it is *niyoga* itself that gives a widow the right to inherit, then she should inherit whether or not a child is conceived through *niyoga*. Moreover, if a child is, in fact, conceived, it should not inherit its legal father's wealth—an apparently unacceptable outcome from the viewpoint of medieval Dharmaśāstra. However, if it is not *niyoga*, but the child begotten thereby that brings about a right to inherit, then one is really not talking about a widow's right to inherit at all, but rather a son's, specifically the type of son known in Dharmaśāstra as a *kṣetraja*, who was discussed in detail in the preceding chapter. Consequently, it is puzzling why Yājñavalkya would include this sort of an heir in his discussion of a *sonless* man's estate.

Following this, Vijñāneśvara refutes Dhāreśvara's position that an independent woman cannot own property and, thus, only a woman who intends to engage in *niyoga* can inherit:

> As for the position that women have access to wealth only through their husbands or sons, never otherwise, that too is false, for it conflicts with such statements as:
>
> > Women's property is held to be of six kinds: what is attained at the nuptial fire, what is attained at the wedding procession, what is given in an act of affection, and what is received from a brother, mother, or father. (MDh 9.194)
>
> Moreover, it is with respect to the complete absence of sons of every kind that Yājñavalkya (2.139) begins his statement "Wife, daughters . . ." If he were here saying that a woman intent upon *niyoga* has a claim to her husband's wealth, he would really be saying that a *kṣetraja* son begotten through *niyoga* has a claim to his wealth. And such a son has been already discussed by Yājñavalkya (2.132). Thus, he should not begin his statement on the topic of a sonless man's inheritance by speaking of his wife.

atha strīṇāṃ patidvārako dhanasaṃbandhaḥ putradvārako vā nānyatheti matam | tad apy sat |

adhyagny adhyāvāhanikaṃ dattaṃ ca prītikarmaṇi |
bhrātṛmātṛpitṛprāptaṃ ṣaḍvidhaṃ strīdhanaṃ smṛtam || (MDh 9.194)

ity ādivirodhāt | kiṃ ca sarvathā putrābhāve patnī duhitara ity (YDh 2.139) *ārabdham | tatra niyuktāyā dhanasaṃbandhaṃ vadatā kṣetrajasyaiva dhanasaṃbandha ukto bhavati | sa ca prāg evābhihita ity aputraprakaraṇe patnīti* (YDh 2.139) *nārabdhavyam |*

Here, as readers may note, Vijñāneśvara rephrases Dhāreśvara's position slightly, so that he is opposed not merely to independent women owning property, but to women owning property independently, that is, through neither their husbands nor their sons. Vijñāneśvara's likely reason for doing this is that, like all Dharmaśāstra authors, he denies the social respectability of independent women. Thus, he simply does not accept Dhāreśvara's implication that sonless widows qualify as such. Nevertheless, Vijñāneśvara firmly believes that certain women, such as sonless widows, have the legal right to own property independently of any men. And since Dhāreśvara's position can be read as a denial of this right, he uses it as a pretext to explicitly defend it. He does this first by pointing to the established Dharmaśāstric category of property known as *strīdhana* or "women's property," which comprises largely movable wealth owned and controlled nearly exclusively by women.[29] He then argues that Yājñavalkya himself, in the passage under discussion, lays down a rule whereby women acquire property independently of their male relatives.

Next, Vijñāneśvara turns to the various scriptural passages that Dhāreśvara cites as support for his position that only a woman planning to engage in *niyoga* can inherit her husband's estate. Specifically, he begins by refuting Dhāreśvara's interpretation of a particular passage of Gautama (28.21–22), which we have already encountered several times:

Now, let us consider the position that a woman intent upon *niyoga* has a claim to her husband's wealth because of Gautama's statement (28.21–22): "Those related through ancestral offerings, patrilineal clan, or common ancestral seer should inherit a childless man's estate or else his wife should; or she may seek to become impregnated." This position is also false, for the

[29] See Kane (1962, 3:770–802).

meaning one apprehends from this statement is not that if she seeks to become impregnated, the wife of a childless man inherits his wealth. Instead, one apprehends from it the teaching of an alternative rule for such a woman, namely, that those related through ancestral offerings, patrilineal clan, or common ancestral seer should inherit a childless man's estate or else his wife should, as she may either seek to become impregnated or else remain chaste. For the word "or" expresses an alternative and, consequently, there is no reason to believe that it means "if."

Furthermore, it is proper that only a chaste woman should receive wealth, not a woman intent upon *niyoga*, who is condemned by both scripture and popular opinion. Indeed, the following scripture states that only a chaste woman can receive wealth:

> A sonless woman who preserves her husband's bed and adheres to her marriage vow—only such a wife should make ancestral offerings to her deceased husband and receive his entire share of inheritance.

And Manu likewise condemns *niyoga* in statements such as this (9.64):

> Twice-born men should never appoint a widowed woman to another man, for by appointing her to another man, they destroy the eternal law.

atha piṇḍagotrarṣisaṃbandhā rikthaṃ bhajeran strī vānapatyasya bījaṃ vā lipseteti (28.21–22) *gautamavacanān niyuktāyā dhanasaṃbandha iti | tad apy asat | na hi yadi bījaṃ lipseta tadānapatyasya strī dhanaṃ gṛhṇīyād ity ayam artho 'smāt pratīyate | kiṃ tu anapatyasya dhanaṃ piṇḍagotrarṣisaṃbandhā bhajeran strī vā sā strī bījaṃ vā lipseta saṃyatā vā bhaved iti tasyā dharmāntaropadeśaḥ | vāśabdasya pakṣāntaravacanatvena yadyarthāpratīteḥ | api ca saṃyatāyā eva dhanagrahaṇaṃ yuktaṃ na niyuktāyāḥ smṛtilokaninditāyāḥ |*

> *aputrā śayanaṃ bhartuḥ pālayantī vrate sthitā |*
> *patny eva dadyāt tatpiṇḍaṃ kṛtsnam aṃśaṃ labheta ca ||*

iti saṃyatāyā eva dhanagrahaṇam uktam | tathā niyogaś ca nindito manunā

> *nānyasmin vidhavā nārī niyoktavyā dvijātibhiḥ |*
> *anyasmin hi niyuñjānā dharmaṃ hanyuḥ sanātanam ||* (MDh 9.64)

ity ādinā |

Here Vijñāneśvara—rather humorously—refutes Dhāreśvara's interpretation of Gautama by pointing out that the word *vā* in Sanskrit means "or" and not "if." In other words, he explains that the true meaning of

Gautama's statement is not that a widow can inherit, if she pursues *niyoga*, but rather that she can either inherit or pursue *niyoga*. Beyond this, Vijñāneśvara calls attention to the fact that both authoritative Smṛtis and popular opinion condemn *niyoga*. Therefore, to make a widow's right to inherit contingent upon *niyoga* is to make it contingent upon something prohibited (although I suspect this wouldn't bother Dhāreśvara, as I have said). Moreover, Vijñāneśvara points out that a woman's acquiring inheritance through *niyoga* is impossible, because, as several Smṛtis make clear, a woman must be and remain chaste in order to acquire and maintain possession of her deceased husband's estate.

After this, Vijñāneśvara refutes the way in which Dhāreśvara interprets specific passages of Vasiṣṭha (17.65), Nārada (13.25), and Yājñavalkya (2.146):

> As for Vasiṣṭha's statement (17.65), "There is no *niyoga* out of greed for inheritance," that should be explained as indicating that a woman should not engage in *niyoga* so that a child of her own might have access to wealth with the understanding that she has no access to wealth when her husband died before receiving his paternal inheritance or after reuniting with his coparceners. Nārada (13.25) also makes the statement:
>
> > And they (= a man's brothers) should provide maintenance for his women until the end of their lives.
>
> But reunited coparceners are the subject of the preceding verse (NSm 13.23):
>
> > The shares of reunited coparceners devolve to them alone.
>
> Therefore, the purpose of Nārada's statement is to instruct that the childless wives of such men are to receive merely maintenance. And one should not suspect that Nārada's statement (13.23) that the "shares of reunited coparceners devolve to them alone" is redundant with his statement (13.24) that "if among brothers one should die without child . . . ,"[30] given that both apply to reunited coparceners. For by way of expanding upon the former statement, the latter enjoins that special women's property is not subject to partition and that the wives of reunited coparceners receive only maintenance. And as for the statement (YDh 2.146) that starts "The

[30] In its entirety, NSm 13.24 reads: "If among brothers one should die or renounce without child, the rest should divide his inheritance among themselves, excepting special women's property." (*bhrātṝṇām aprajaḥ preyāt kaścic cet pravrajet tu vā | vibhajeyur dhanaṃ tasya śeṣās tu strīdhanaṃ vinā ||*)

sonless wives of these men . . . ," this applies specifically to the wives of impotent men and the like, as will be explained later on.

yat tu vasiṣṭhavacanaṃ rikthalobhān nāsti niyoga iti (17.65) *tad avibhakte saṃsṛṣṭini vā bhartari prete tasyā dhanasaṃbandho nāstīti svāpatyasya dhanasaṃbandhārthaṃ niyogo na kartavya iti vyākhyeyam* | *yad api nāradavacanaṃ bharaṇaṃ cāsya kurvīran strīṇām ā jīvanakṣayād iti* (13.25) *tad api saṃsṛṣṭānāṃ tu yo bhāgas teṣām eva sa iṣyata iti* (NSm 13.23) *saṃsṛṣṭānāṃ prastutatvāt tatstrīṇām anapatyānāṃ bharaṇamātrapratipādanaparam* | *na ca bhrātṝṇām aprajāḥ preyād ity* (NSm 13.24) *etasya saṃsṛṣṭiviṣayatve saṃsṛṣṭānāṃ tu yo bhāga ity* (NSm 13.23) *anena paunaruktyam āśaṅkanīyam* | *yataḥ pūrvoktivivaraṇena strīdhanasyāvibhājyatvaṃ tatstrīṇāṃ ca bharaṇamātraṃ vidhīyate* | *yad api aputrā yoṣitaś caiṣām ity* (YDh 2.146) *ādivacanaṃ tat klībādistrīviṣayam iti vakṣyate* |

Vijñāneśvara starts this passage by considering the implication of Vasiṣṭha's (17.65) prohibition against performing *niyoga* out of greed for inheritance, which Dhāreśvara takes as confirmation of his position that only by engaging in *niyoga* can a widow receive inheritance. As readers can see, Vijñāneśvara interprets Vasiṣṭha's statement quite differently, as alluding to situations where a woman has no hope of inheriting any wealth herself and, thus, is tempted to engage in *niyoga* in order to gain some wealth indirectly through her son. And given that Vasiṣṭha (17.81–83) completely excludes widows from his list of heirs, this interpretation is historically plausible. Unlike Vasiṣṭha, however, Vijñāneśvara generally grants the wives of sonless men the right to inherit their entire estates. Hence, he has to restrict the scope of Vasiṣṭha's statement to the few cases where he considers such women to lack this right. And, as we will see later on, there are principally two such cases in Vijñāneśvara's view: (a) when a woman's husband had not received his inheritance from his father prior to his death and (b) when he had received his inheritance, but then resumed living jointly with his coparceners, who would typically be his brothers. In other words, Vijñāneśvara restricts a widow's right to inherit to cases where her husband was living separately from his father and coparceners at the time of his death. This is why he construes Vasiṣṭha's statement as applying to such cases. And it is for this very reason that Vijñāneśvara interprets Nārada's statement (13.25), instructing a man's brothers to provide for the maintenance of his wives, as applying only to reunited coparceners. As for the similar statement of Yājñavalkya (2.146), enjoining that maintenance be provided for the sonless wives of certain men, Vijñāneśvara rightly notes the specific men to whom Yājñavalkya (2.144) clearly intends this statement to apply: outcastes, their sons, the impotent, the lame, the mentally insane, the mentally incompetent, the blind, and those afflicted with incurable diseases.

Finally, Vijñāneśvara concludes his long refutation of Dhāreśvara by countering his argument that women are unfit to receive the property of twice-born men, since such property is intended for use in sacrifices, which women have no right to perform:

> Let us turn now to the argument that it is improper for women to receive wealth, because the wealth of twice-born people is for the purpose of sacrifice and women are unentitled to perform sacrifices. This too is false, for if every sort of wealth were only for the purpose of sacrifices, then gifts, oblations, and the like could not be accomplished. Now, one might argue that the word "sacrifice" is here merely a synecdoche for any meritorious action and, since gifts, oblations, and the like are meritorious actions, it does not conflict with scripture to use wealth for such activities. But if this is the case, it would still be impossible to carry out the pursuit of material gain and sensual pleasure, as these can be accomplished only through wealth. And this being the case, there would be a conflict with scriptural statements such as the following by Yājñavalkya, Gautama, and Manu:
>
> To the best of one's ability, one should not abandon the pursuit of religious merit, worldly gain, and sensual pleasure in their own times. (YDh 1.114)
>
> To best of one's ability, one should never make a morning, afternoon, or evening fruitless regarding the pursuit of religious merit, worldly gain, and sensual pleasure. (GDh 9.46)
>
> These (= sense-organs) can never be restrained by not indulging them. (MDh 2.96)
>
> Furthermore, if wealth were only for the purpose of sacrifice, consider the stated position that wearing gold, as enjoined in the Vedic statement (TB 2.2.4.6) "One should wear gold," is for a person's direct benefit, since one can rule out that it serves as part of a sacrifice. This would be overturned. Moreover, if the word "sacrifice" is, indeed, tantamount to a synecdoche for any meritorious action, then it would be most appropriate for women to receive wealth, given that they are entitled to engage in the meritorious

act of gift-giving. There are also statements that prescribe women's perpetual dependence such as: "A woman ought never be independent."[31] I acknowledge such dependence, but how does that conflict with a woman's acquiring wealth?

Of course, one may well ask how one should understand such statements as "Wealth arose for the purpose of sacrifice." To this the answer I give is that they express the following: when a man acquires wealth for the explicit purpose of sacrifice, it should be used only for sacrifice even by his sons and the like. For in the statement (YDh 1.126), "One who does not offer what has been obtained for the purpose of sacrifice becomes a vulture or a crow," the sin that is mentioned applies without distinction also to a man's sons and the like.

yat tu dvijātidhanasya yajñārthatvāt strīṇāṃ ca yajñe 'nadhikārād dhanagrahaṇam ayuktam iti tad asat | sarvasya dravyajātasya yajñārthatve dānahomādyasiddheḥ | atha yajñaśabdasya dharmopalakṣaṇatvād dānahomādīnām api dharmatvāt tadarthatvam aviruddham iti matam | evaṃ tarhy arthakāmayor dhanasādhyayor asiddhir eva syāt | tathā sati

dharmam arthaṃ ca kāmaṃ ca yathāśakti na hāpayet | (YDh 1.114)

tathā

na pūrvāhnamadhyaṃdināparāhnān aphalān kuryād yathāśakti dharmārthakāmebhyaḥ | (GDh 9.46)

tathā

na tathāitāni śakyante saṃniyantum asevayā | (MDh 2.96)

ity ādiyājñavalkyagautamamanuvacanavirodhaḥ | api ca dhanasya yajñārthatve hiraṇyaṃ dhāryam iti (TB 2.2.4.6) *hiraṇyadhāraṇasya kratvarthatānirākaraṇena puruṣārthatvam uktaṃ tatpratyuddhṛtaṃ syāt | kiṃ ca yajñaśabdasya dharmopalakṣaṇaparatve strīṇām api pūrtadharmādhikārād dhanagrahaṇaṃ yuktataram | yat tu pāratantryavacanaṃ na strī svātantryam arhatīty ādi tad astu pāratantryam | dhanasvīkāre tu ko virodhaḥ | kathaṃ tarhi yajñārthaṃ dravyam utpannam ity ādivacanam | ucyate | yajñārtham evārjitaṃ yad dhanaṃ tad yajña eva niyoktavyaṃ putrādibhir api ity evaṃparaṃ tat | yajñārthaṃ labdham adadad bhāsaḥ kāko 'pi vā bhaved iti* (YDh 1.126) *doṣaśravaṇasya putrādiṣv aviśeṣāt* |

[31] See note 28.

The Mīmāṃsā tradition of Brahmanical hermeneutics, which had an enormous influence on Dharmaśāstra, considers there to be three principal types of acts that constitute *dharma*: "sacrifices" (*yāga*), "oblations" (*homa*), and "gifts" (*dāna*).[32] Vijñāneśvara begins the above passage by using this Mīmāṃsaka notion to argue that clearly all wealth cannot be used only for the purpose of sacrifices, for otherwise oblations and gifts, which also constitute *dharma*, would never be performed. Moreover, Vijñāneśvara notes that even if the word "sacrifice" functions as a synecdoche in this context and, thus, includes gifts and oblations, there are still numerous Smṛti texts that instruct a person to pursue not only the goal of *dharma* or religious merit but also those of material gain (*artha*) and sensual pleasure (*kāma*). Hence, if all wealth must be used only for sacrifices, oblations, and gifts, how is one supposed to obey these scriptures?

Getting even more technical, Vijñāneśvara then refers to a particular passage of Śabara's commentary on the *Pūrvamīmāṃsāsūtra* (3.4.20), where he discusses the Vedic passage: "Therefore, one should wear bright-colored gold."[33] The pertinent question that Śabara addresses in the passage is whether this Vedic injunction to wear gold is part of a sacrifice or something done for a person's own direct benefit.[34] And his answer, deemed authoritative by the later tradition, is that wearing gold is done for a person's own direct benefit.[35] For Vijñāneśvara's purposes, the significance of this is that it furnishes an instance where wealth is used in the performance of *dharma*, yet not in connection with a sacrifice, oblation, or gift. Consequently, it constitutes yet another refutation of Dhāreśvara's argument that women cannot inherit property, since they cannot perform sacrifices and all wealth must be used only for sacrifices.

Following this, Vijñāneśvara also points out that, in any case, women are entitled to offer gifts and, thus, to use wealth in the performance of *dharma*. He also adds—almost as an aside—that, simply by acquiring property, women do not violate the well-established prohibition against their independence. Thereafter, Vijñāneśvara offers his own interpretation of those scriptures that seemingly require all wealth to be used for sacrifices: they

[32] On these, see Jha (1964, 316–17).

[33] TB 2.2.4.6: *tásmāt suvárṇaṃ híraṇyaṃ dhāryám* |

[34] Śabara on PMS 3.4.20: "About these statements there is the question: are they rules within the context of a sacrifice or rules for a person in general?" (*tatra kiṃ prakaraṇadharma uta puruṣadharma iti saṃśayaḥ* |)

[35] Śabara on PMS 3.4.20: "Therefore, statements of this type are rules for a person in general." (*tasmād evaṃjātīyakaḥ puruṣadharmaḥ* |)

only apply to property that a person has acquired for the specific purpose of performing a sacrifice.[36] And in support of his position, he cites a verse of Yājñavalkya (1.126), according to which a man who fails to offer wealth obtained for a sacrifice is reborn as a crow or a vulture.

Having thus refuted Dhāreśvara at considerable length, Vijñāneśvara then seeks to explain away two other Smṛti texts that seemingly conflict with widows being the primary heirs of sonless men:

> Kātyāyana also states:
>
> > Heirless property goes to the king, excepting women's maintenance and funerary rites, but the property of a learned Brahmin one should give to learned Brahmins.
>
> This verse should be construed as follows: "heirless property," i.e., wealth that is without heirs, "goes to the king," i.e., becomes the king's possession, "excepting women's maintenance and funerary rites," i.e., excepting or excluding what is required for the feeding and clothing of the deceased owner's women and his funerary rites, meaning whatever is required for his ancestral rites and the like. Such property goes to the king. The latter half of this verse then contains an exception to this: one should give the property of a learned Brahmin—excepting what is necessary for the maintenance of his women and his funerary rites—to a learned Brahmin. However, this verse of Kātyāyana applies only to kept women (not to wives), for it uses the word "women" (rather than "wives"). And the following statement of Nārada (13.49) likewise applies only to kept women, for it too uses the word "women":
>
> > A righteous king should provide a livelihood for a man's women—this is held to be the law of inheritance.[37]
>
> The statement being commented upon (YDh 2.139–40), however, uses the word "wife." Consequently, there is nothing that conflicts with a chaste, lawfully wedded wife receiving property.
>
> Therefore, it is established that when a sonless man who has received his inheritance and not reunited with his coparceners dies, his wife firstly inherits his wealth, for Yājñavalkya has already discussed the partitioning

[36] For a discussion of the *Mitākṣarā*'s theory of ownership and its basis in worldly practice rather than scriptural prescription, see Fleming (2020, 29–57).

[37] I have not translated the first *pāda* of this verse, because it must be construed with the final words of the preceding verse: *sarveṣām abhāve rājagāmi tat*. Taken together, the text means: "In the absence of all, property goes to the king, except in the case of a Brahmin."

of inheritance (2.118) and will only discuss reunited coparceners later on (2.142).

yad api kātyāyanenoktam—

adāyikaṃ rājagāmi yoṣidbhṛtyaurdhvadehikam |
apāsya śrotriyadravyaṃ śrotriyebhyas tad arpayet ||

iti | adāyikaṃ dāyādarahitaṃ yad dhanaṃ tad rājagāmi rājño bhavati yoṣidbhṛtyaurdhvadehikam apāsya tatstrīṇām aśanācchādanopayuktam aurdhvadehikaṃ dhaninaḥ śrāddhādyupayuktam cāpāsya parihṛtya rājagāmi bhavatīti saṃbandhaḥ | asyāpavāda uttarārdhe śrotriyadravyaṃ ca yoṣidbhṛtyaurdhvadehikam apāsya śrotriyāyopapādayed iti | tad apy avaruddhastrīviṣayaṃ yoṣidgrahaṇāt | nāradavacanaṃ ca—

anyatra brāhmaṇāt kiṃ tu rājā dharmaparāyaṇaḥ |
tatstrīṇāṃ jīvanaṃ dadyād eṣa dāyavidhiḥ smṛtaḥ || (NSm 13.49)

ity avaruddhastrīviṣayam eva strīśabdagrahaṇāt | iha tu patnīśabdād ūḍhāyāḥ saṃyatāyā dhanagrahaṇam aviruddham | tasmād vibhaktāsaṃsṛṣṭiny aputre svaryāte patnī dhanaṃ prathamaṃ gṛhṇātīty ayam arthaḥ siddho bhavati vibhāgasyoktatvāt saṃsṛṣṭināṃ tu vakṣyamāṇatvāt |

In this passage, Vijñāneśvara cites a verse ascribed to Kātyāyana and another one of Nārada (13.49), both of which instruct a king to provide for the maintenance of a man's women, apparently meaning his wives. Consequently, these verses seemingly conflict with the statements of Yājñavalkya (2.139–40), Viṣṇu (17.4), and others that make a sonless man's widow the heir to his entire estate. In order to resolve this apparent conflict, Vijñāneśvara seizes upon the convenient fact that both of the verses in question use Sanskrit words that can denote women in general (*yoṣit*, *strī*) and not necessarily wives. This enables him to argue that their statements do not, in fact, apply to lawfully wedded wives at all, but rather to "kept women" (*avaruddhastrī*), that is, to women whom a man provides for and maintains a sexual relationship with, but has never married.

Moreover, having thus thoroughly refuted Dhāreśvara's position on widows' rights of inheritance and explained away a few additional Smṛti texts, Vijñāneśvara states at the end of the passage above his own position on the matter, which is that a sonless man's faithful and lawfully wedded wife is, indeed, the primary inheritor of his entire estate on just one condition: he must have received his inheritance from his father prior to his death and not reunited with his coparceners. In other words, as mentioned earlier, in order for a widow to inherit her husband's estate, he must have been living separately from and not jointly with his father and his brothers at the time of his death. And as one can see, Vijñāneśvara's stated reason for imposing this restriction on a widow's right to inherit is the fact that Yājñavalkya prescribes this right after discussing the partitioning of paternal estates (2.118), where sons take precedence over daughters-in-law, but before addressing the rules for reunited coparceners (2.142), where brothers take precedence over wives.

Even at this point, however, Vijñāneśvara's discussion of a widow's right to inherit is not done. Instead, he goes on to refute several other possible positions on the issue that severely limit a widow's rights to property. And the first of these positions is one that we have already seen expressed in the commentary of Viśvarūpa, namely, that a widow's inheritance is restricted to only a small amount of wealth. Interestingly, however, although Vijñāneśvara certainly knew of Viśvarūpa's work,[38] he attributes this position not to Viśvarūpa, but rather to an exegete named Śrīkara, of whom no works have survived and very little is known.[39] The relevant passage of the *Mitākṣarā* reads:

> One should understand that by this the position espoused by Śrīkara and others that a widow's right to inherit is restricted to cases of little wealth is refuted. For Yājñavalkya has already stated that, even when a man has lawfully begotten sons, his wife receives a share equal to those of his sons in cases of partition both during and after his lifetime, saying:
>
> > If a man gives his sons equal shares, then he should also grant his wives equal shares. (YDh 2.119)
>
> and
>
> > When sons partition their father's estate after his passing, their mother also receives an equal share. (YDh 2.127)
>
> This being the case, it is pure idiocy to hold that when a sonless man dies, his wife receives no more of his wealth than is necessary for her maintenance. Now, one might counter that, in both Yājñavalkya's statement that a man "should grant his wives equal shares" (2.119) and his statement that "their mother also receives an equal share" (2.127), the intent is that a woman receives only wealth sufficient for her to live. But that too would be

[38] The *Mitākṣarā* mentions Viśvarūpa by name in the second of its two opening verses.
[39] On Śrīkara, see Kane (1962, 1:571–73).

incorrect, for it would result in the words "share" and "equal" being meaningless. One might then counter that a widow receives wealth sufficient for her to live when there is an abundance of wealth, but a share equal to the shares of her sons when there is little. But this cannot be right, since it results in the fault of construing a single injunction unevenly. For thus the statement that a man "should grant his wives equal shares" (YDh 2.119) and the statement that "their mother also receives an equal share" (YDh 2.119) refer to wealth merely sufficient for living in the case of a rich man on the basis of another scriptural statement, but then refer to a share equal to the share of a son in the case of a poor man.

etenālpadhanaviṣayatvaṃ śrīkarādibhir uktaṃ nirastaṃ veditavyam | *tathā hy auraseṣu putreṣu satsv api jīvadvibhāge ajīvadvibhāge ca patnyāḥ putrasamāṃśagrahaṇam uktam—*

yadi kuryāt samān aṃśān patnyaḥ kāryāḥ samāṃśikā iti | (YDh 2.119)

tathā

pitur ūrdhvaṃ vibhajatāṃ mātāpy aṃśaṃ samaṃ hared iti | (YDh 2.127)

ca | *tathā saty aputrasya svaryātasya dhanaṃ patnī bharaṇād atiriktaṃ na labhata iti vyāmohamātram* | *atha patnyaḥ kāryāḥ samāṃśikā ity* (YDh 2.119) *atra mātāpy aṃśaṃ samaṃ hared ity* (YDh 2.127) *atra ca jīvanopayuktam eva dhanaṃ strī haratīti matam* | *tad asat* | *aṃśaśabdasya samaśabdasya cānarthakyaprasaṅgāt* | *syān mataṃ bahudhane jīvanopayuktaṃ dhanaṃ gṛhṇāti alpe tu putrāṃśasamāṃśaṃ gṛhṇātīti* | *tac ca na vidhivaiṣamyaprasaṅgāt* | *tathā hi patnyaḥ kāryāḥ samāṃśikāḥ* (YDh 2.119) *mātāpy aṃśaṃ samaṃ hared iti* (YDh 2.127) *ca bahudhane jīvanamātropayuktaṃ vākyāntaram apekṣya pratipādayati alpadhane tu putrāṃśasamam aṃśaṃ pratipādayatīti* |

Here Vijñāneśvara argues that a widow's inheritance cannot be restricted to only a small amount of wealth, since Yājñāvalkya (2.119, 127) has already stated that even when a man has sons, his wife is to receive an equal share. Therefore, to hold that she should receive no more than is necessary for her maintenance is to render the phrase "equal share" (*samāṃśa*) in Yājñavalkya's text meaningless. Someone might then argue, as Viśvarūpa (on YDh 2.119) does, that a rich man's wife receives only enough so that she can survive, whereas a poor man's wife receives even less: merely a share of his estate equal to those of his sons. But Vijñāneśvara rejects this way of interpreting Yājñavalkya's statements, because it entails the hermeneutic fallacy of construing a single scriptural rule in multiple ways—what is called *vidhivaiṣamya* in Sanskrit.[40] In this way he refutes the position held by Viśvarūpa, Śrīkara, and perhaps other Dharmaśāstra commentators that a widow's inheritance is limited to only a small amount.

Following this, Vijñāneśvara addresses another *pūrvapakṣa* or opponent's view that differs only slightly from the preceding one:

> There is also this position: The fact that the property of a sonless man devolves to his brothers follows from Manu's statement (9.185):
>
> > The father of a sonless man should inherit his property or else his brothers should.
>
> This also follows from Śaṅkha's statement:
>
> > The property of a sonless man who has gone to heaven belongs to his brothers. In their absence, his parents should take it or else his senior wife should.
>
> And the fact that a man's wife receives only wealth sufficient for her maintenance is established on the basis of such statements as: "And they (= a man's brothers) should provide maintenance for his women until the end of their lives." (NSm 13.25) This being established, when a sonless man with a lot of wealth dies, his wife receives wealth sufficient for her maintenance and his brothers take the rest. But when a man only has enough wealth for his wife's maintenance, the conflict arises: Should only his wife receive his property or should his brothers as well? It is in order to communicate that the former consideration (i.e., the maintenance of the wife) overrules the latter that Yājñavalkya (2.139) begins his statement: "Wife, daughters . . ."
>
> However, the venerable teacher here has no tolerance for this position, since the following Smṛti (MDh 9.185) lays down an option:
>
> > The father of a sonless man should inherit his property or else his brothers should.
>
> Therefore, this statement is not intended to convey a sequence of heirs, but rather merely to provide examples of the right to inherit property. And that is possible, even when the group of heirs, starting with a wife, does not occur. Thus has the teacher explained. And he has also explained that the previous

[40] After the passage cited above, Vijñāneśvara refers to the classical treatment of this fallacy within the Mīmāṃsā tradition (on PMS 7.3.19–25) in a passage that would be needlessly time-consuming to discuss here and, thus, has been left out. For an explanation of this issue, see Kane (1962, 3:704–05) and L. Rocher (2002, 216–18).

statement of Śaṅkha pertains only to cases involving reunited coparceners. Moreover, one in no way gleans from the statement under discussion (YDh 2.139–40) or from its context that it applies only to cases involving little wealth. And suppose that Yājñavalkya's statement (2.140), "the following member inherits," applies only to small amounts of wealth in the case of two members of his list, namely, wives and daughters, on the basis of another scriptural statement, but applies to wealth in general in the case of parents and the rest. Then the aforementioned fault of construing a single injunction unevenly would apply. Hence, this position is easily dismissed.

yad api matam

pitā hared aputrasya rikthaṃ bhrātara eva vā | (MDh 9.185)

iti manusmaraṇāt tathā

svaryātasya hy aputrasya bhrātṛgāmi dravyam | tadabhāve pitarau hareyātāṃ jyeṣṭhā vā patnī |

iti śaṅkhasmaraṇāc cāputrasya dhanaṃ bhrātṛgāmīti prāptam | bharaṇaṃ cāsya kurvīran strīṇām ā jīvanakṣayād ity (NSm 13.25) *ādivacanāc ca bharaṇopayuktaṃ dhanaṃ patnī labhata ity api sthitam | evaṃ sthite bahudhane 'putre svaryāte bharaṇopayuktāṃ patnī gṛhṇāti śeṣaṃ ca bhrātaraḥ | yadā tu patnībharaṇamātropayuktam eva dravyam asti tato nyūnaṃ vā tadā kiṃ patny eva gṛhṇāty uta bhrātaro 'pīti virodhe pūrvabalīyastvajñāpanārthaṃ patnī duhitara ity* (YDh 2.139) *ārabdham iti | tad apy atra bhagavān ācāryo na mṛṣyati | yataḥ*

pitā hared aputrasya rikthaṃ bhrātara eva vā | (MDh 9.185)

iti vikalpasmaraṇān nedaṃ kramaparaṃ vacanam api tu dhanagrahaṇe 'dhikārapradarśanamātraparam | tac cāsaty api patnyādigaṇe ghaṭata iti vyācacakṣe | śaṅkhavacanam api saṃsṛṣṭabhrātṛviṣayam iti | api cālpaviṣayatvam asmād vacanāt prakaranād vā nāvagamyate | dhanabhāg uttarottara ity (YDh 2.140) *asya ca patnī duhitara iti* (YDh 2.139) *viṣayadvaye vākyāntaram apekṣyālpadhanaviṣayatvaṃ pitrādiṣu tu dhanamātraviṣayatvam iti pūrvoktaṃ vidhivaiṣamyaṃ tadavastham eveti yat kiṃcid etat* |

As one can see, the *pūrvapakṣa* in this passage first establishes, on the basis of statements by Manu (9.185) and Śaṅkha, that the brothers of a sonless man are his first and primary heirs. It then establishes, on the basis of a statement by Nārada (13.25), that a man's brothers are merely supposed to maintain his widow. These two facts, it argues, raise an unanswered question: If a man's estate is sufficient only to maintain his widow or even less extensive than that, should his brothers' right to his estate or his widow's right to maintenance take precedence? The *pūrvapakṣa* argues that the statement of Yājñavalkya under discussion (2.139–40) serves simply to answer this question by affirming a widow's right to maintenance. Thus, in effect, like the previous position ascribed to Śrīkara, it holds that a widow's inheritance is restricted to only a small amount of wealth.

Vijñāneśvara begins his refutation of this *pūrvapakṣa* by citing the opinion of an unidentified "venerable teacher" (*bhagavān ācāryaḥ*), perhaps referring to his own teacher.[41] This teacher—whoever he was—argues that the *pūrvapakṣa* has misinterpreted the statements of Manu and Śaṅkha, which it cites as evidence that a sonless man's brothers are his primary heirs. He explains that, contrary to the *pūrvapakṣa*'s claim, the statement of Manu in question (9.185) does not lay down a sequence of heirs at all, but instead merely serves to illustrate possible heirs to a sonless man's property. And the statement of Śaṅkha, the teacher argues, applies not to inheritance in general, but only to the estates of reunited coparceners. To this Vijñāneśvara then adds two points of his own. First, he notes that nothing in Yājñavalkya's text itself indicates that it applies only to small amounts of wealth. Second, he argues that if one were to construe it as applying to small amounts of wealth in the case of wives and daughters, but wealth in general in all other cases, it would result in the previously discussed fallacy of *vidhivaiṣamya*, that is, construing a single injunction in multiple ways.

Finally, Vijñāneśvara's lengthy discussion of a widow's right to inherit her husband's property comes to an end. However, before restating his overall position on the matter, he first explains the meaning of a rather problematic verse ascribed to Hārīta:

> The following statement of Hārīta is intended to prohibit a woman suspected of infidelity from inheriting her husband's entire estate:
>
> > If a widowed woman is young or ill-tempered, she should be given merely enough to survive on in order to diminish her vigor.
>
> From this very statement one understands that a woman not suspected of infidelity inherits her husband's entire estate. It is with precisely

[41] The *Subodhinī*, a fourteenth-century subcommentary on the *Mitākṣarā*, identifies this teacher as Viśvarūpa, but this is untenable, considering Viśvarūpa's strong opposition to widows' rights of inheritance.

this intention that Śaṅkha says that a man's senior wife might alternatively receive his property. Here a "senior wife" is one who is senior in terms of virtue, that is, one not suspected of infidelity. Such a woman receives her husband's entire estate and looks after the other wives like a mother, even though they are ill-tempered. In this way everything is unobjectionable. Therefore, the established position is that, provided that she is chaste, the lawfully wedded wife of a deceased sonless man, who had received his inheritance and not reunited with his coparceners, should receive his entire estate.

yat tu hārītavacanam—
vidhavā yauvanasthā cen nārī bhavati karkaśā |
āyuṣaḥ kṣapaṇārthaṃ tu dātavyaṃ jīvanaṃ tadeti ||
tad api śaṅkitavyabhicārāyāḥ sakaladhanagrahaṇaniṣedhaparam | asmād eva vacanād anāśaṅkitavyabhicārāyāḥ sakaladhanagrahaṇaṃ gamyate | etad evābhipretyoktaṃ śaṅkhena jyeṣṭhā vā patnīti | jyeṣṭhā guṇajyeṣṭhā anāśaṅkitavyabhicārā | sā sakalaṃ dhanaṃ gṛhītvānyāṃ karkaśām api mātṛvat pālayatīti sarvam anavadyam | tasmād aputrasya svaryātasya vibhaktasyāsaṃsṛṣṭino dhanaṃ pariṇītā strī saṃyatā sakalam eva gṛhṇātīti sthitam |

As one can see, the verse of Hārīta cited here plainly states that a young or ill-tempered widow should receive only enough to subsist on for the purpose of crushing her spirit. Vijñāneśvara, however, takes the verse to mean that even a widow who is merely suspected of infidelity should receive only maintenance. In this his apparent intention is to make explicit the underlying logic of Hārīta's statement. That is, Vijñāneśvara apparently considers youth and an ill temper by themselves to be legitimate grounds for suspecting a woman of being unfaithful to her deceased husband and, thus, for annulling her right to inherit his property. At the same time, however, Vijñāneśvara clearly does not wish for a young or ill-tempered widow to receive the harsh punishment prescribed for a woman who is actually guilty of marital infidelity.[42] Instead, she is to receive simply a reduction to subsistence-level food. And this position of Vijñāneśvara is notably consistent with a position that he takes later on, when commenting on a verse of Yājñavalkya (2.146) that prescribes

[42] MDh 8.371, for instance, instructs a king to have dogs publicly devour a woman who commits adultery.

banishment for the cantankerous widows of impotent men and the like, for there he similarly argues that such widows are still entitled to maintenance, if they have not committed adultery.[43] Beyond this, Vijñāneśvara notes an important implication of Hārīta's statement, as he interprets it: a woman whose chastity is beyond doubt should inherit her husband's entire estate, if he died without sons. And he also interprets the statement of Śaṅkha cited by the previous *pūrvapakṣa* so that it includes a man's faithful wife among his heirs, even when he had reunited with his coparceners.[44]

Thereafter, at the end of the above passage, which concludes Vijñāneśvara's lengthy treatment of a widow's right to inherit, he restates his personal position on the matter, which he first articulated earlier after his refutation of Dhāreśvara. This position, as readers may recall and as they can clearly see from the above passage, is that a woman inherits her husband's entire estate under the following conditions: (a) she is lawfully and ritually wedded to her husband; (b) she remains celibate; (c) her husband left no surviving sons; (d) he had received his inheritance from his father prior to his death; and (e) he had not reunited with his coparceners to form a joint household. Therefore, when viewed within his historical context, Vijñāneśvara looks like a particularly strong advocate for a widow's right to inherit, certainly a far stronger advocate than all preceding Dharmaśāstra commentators of which we have certain knowledge. Substantively, however, Vijñāneśvara's position on widows' rights of inheritance is nothing new, for it is virtually identical to that of Yājñavalkya himself, only argued at much greater length and in rigorous detail. Indeed, even Vijñāneśvara's explicit restriction of a widow's right to inherit to cases where her husband had received his paternal estate prior to his death and had not reunited with his coparceners seems to be implicit in Yājñavalkya's text, for if a woman's husband died before receiving his paternal estate, that estate would still be in the possession of her father-in-law. Thus, in order for her to inherit it, it would have to devolve from a man to his

[43] *Mitākṣarā* on YDh 2.142 (= 2.146): "Cantankerous widows are likewise to be banished, but must also be maintained, if they have not committed adultery. It is not the case that one should not provide a widow with maintenance, simply because she is cantankerous." (*pratikūlās tathaiva ca nirvāsyā bhavanti bharaṇīyāś cāvyabhicāriṇyaś cet* | *na punaḥ prātikūlyamātreṇa bharaṇam api na kartavyam* |)

[44] Based upon Śaṅkha's statement, Mādhava (*Vyavahārakāṇḍa*, p. 540) explicitly lists the heirs of a reunited coparcener in the absence of sons and uterine and reunited brothers as follows: "When neither a reunited father nor a reunited paternal uncle survives, then a non-reunited brother of a different mother should inherit. Failing such a brother, a non-reunited father should inherit; failing him, a mother; and failing her, a wife." (*yadā pitā pitṛvyo vā saṃsṛṣṭo na vidyate tadā tv asaṃsṛṣṭabhinnodaro bhrātā gṛhṇīyāt* | *tadabhāve tv asaṃsṛṣṭapitā* | *tadabhāve mātā* | *tadabhāve patnī* |)

daughter-in-law, yet as we have seen, Yājñavalkya (2.118, 139–40) clearly puts forth a very different sequence of heirs: son, wife, parent, brother, brother's son, more distant patrilineal relative, nonpatrilineal relative, student, teacher's student. Furthermore, Yājñavalkya (2.142) elsewhere puts forth a separate rule of inheritance for reunited coparceners, according to which a man's uterine brothers are his primary heirs. Therefore, in placing these restrictions on a widow's right to inherit her husband's estate, Vijñāneśvara seems merely to be articulating implicit assumptions in Yājñavalkya's work.

As for the motives for placing these restrictions on a widow's right to inherit, they are not entirely clear. One important implication of the former restriction, however, is that younger widows would have been markedly less likely to inherit significant wealth than older ones, even withstanding the verse of Hārīta just examined. The reason for this is that their husbands would have been less likely to have received their paternal estates prior to their deaths, as their fathers are more likely to have still been alive and active. And it certainly makes sense that Dharmaśāstra authors would have favored a rule that decreased the likelihood of younger women acquiring independent wealth, given the apparent importance of assuring the sexual control of women in premodern Brahmanical culture. It bears noting, however, that the *Mitākṣarā* famously considers a man to have a sort of ownership in his paternal estate simply by virtue of his birth and grants him considerable rights to compel the partition of this estate during his father's lifetime.[45] Hence, if implemented in actual practice, this doctrine of the *Mitākṣarā* would obviously increase the likelihood at least somewhat that a young widow's husband had received his paternal inheritance.

Later Digests and Commentaries

Although Vijñāneśvara's position on a widow's right to inherit differs little in substance from that of Yājñavalkya centuries earlier, his work seems to have coincided with a massive shift in the prevailing views on this issue both within the Dharmaśāstra tradition and within South Asian society at large. Indeed, as it did in many matters, the *Mitākṣarā* appears to have exerted

[45] On this, see Kane (1962, 3:544–74). For a translation of the relevant section of the *Mitākṣarā* (on YDh 2.114), see L. Rocher and R. Rocher (2001).

enormous influence on how the Dharmaśāstra tradition as a whole viewed a widow's right to inherit, for as P. V. Kane (1962, 3:706)—the undisputed doyen of Dharmaśāstra studies—notes, "Almost all Dharmaśāstra writers since the time of the *Mitākṣarā* accept the widow's right to succeed to her husband's wealth."[46] Many texts confirming this observation could be cited. For the sake of space, however, we will examine only three in the present section, all of which broadly agree with the *Mitākṣarā* on a widow's right to inherit, although they come from diverse areas of the subcontinent and were likely composed within a century of it. Thus, when read in their historical contexts, these works show the apparent speed with which Brahmanical communities throughout South Asia came to accept a widow's right to inherit during the course of the twelfth century. The three specific texts that we will look at are the *Kṛtyakalpataru* of Lakṣmīdhara (c. 1110–1150, Kannauj), Aparārka's commentary on the *Yājñavalkya Dharmaśāstra* (c. 1125–1175, North Konkan), and the *Smṛticandrikā* of Devaṇa Bhaṭṭa (c. 1150–1225, South India).

In his *Kṛtyakalpataru* (*Vyavahārakāṇḍa*, pp. 748–49), a massive topical digest of Smṛtis likely composed within living memory of Vijñāneśvara, Lakṣmīdhara briefly explains his position on a widow's right to inherit as follows:

> The statement of Viṣṇu (17.4), which starts, "The wealth of a sonless man goes to his wife," teaches that, even when a sonless man has brothers, his wealth goes to his wife. This applies to a wife who engages in such virtuous practices as preserving her husband's bed and performing his ancestral rites, as one can discern from the statement of Vṛddha Manu that starts, "A sonless woman who preserves her husband's bed. . . ."[47] When his wife is not of this type, however, his wealth goes strictly to his brothers, even though she still lives. Śaṅkha further states that a wife receives mere maintenance:
>
> > They should provide maintenance for his wives until the end of their lives, if they preserve their husband's bed. They should cease to do so in the case of others.
>
> But this statement applies merely to women who, while not unfaithful to their husbands, fail to observe the vows of widowhood.

[46] In this regard, see also Altekar (1938, 15).

[47] For the complete citation of this verse of Vṛddha Manu, see the section "Vijñāneśvara" in this chapter.

yac cāputradhanaṃ patnyabhigāmīty ādiviṣṇuvacanena bhrātṛsadbhāve 'py aputradhanasya patnyabhigāmitvaṃ pratipāditaṃ tad aputrā śayanaṃ bhartur ity ādivṛddhamanuvākyaparyālocanayā bhartṛśayana-paripālanaśrāddhakaraṇādiguṇopetā yā patnī tadviṣayam | yā caivaṃ-vidhā na bhavati tasyāṃ vidyamānāyām api bhrātṛgāmy eva taddhanam | yac ca—

bharaṇaṃ cāsya kurvīran strīṇām ājīvanakṣayāt |
rakṣanti śayyāṃ bhartuś ced ācchindyur itarāsu tat ||

iti bharaṇamātraṃ śaṅkhenoktaṃ tad vaidhavyavratarahitāvyabhicāriṇīm ātraviṣayam |

As one can see here, the *Kṛtyakalpataru* interprets those Smṛtis that deny widows the right to inherit as applying only to those women who are either unfaithful to their husbands or otherwise fail to perform the duties incumbent upon a widow. Consequently, like the *Mitākṣarā*, it grants the widows of sonless men the right to inherit their entire estates, provided that they remain faithful and chaste. Moreover, given that the *Kṛtyakalpataru* (*Vyavahārakāṇḍa*, pp. 754–57) treats cases of inheritance involving reunited coparceners in a separate section and there cites no statements that list a man's wife as a possible heir, Lakṣmīdhara appears to have shared Vijñāneśvara's opinion that a widow's right to inherit her husband's entire property applied only to cases where he had received his inheritance prior to his death and not reunited with his coparceners.

Writing at roughly the same time as Lakṣmīdhara, Aparārka similarly grants the wives of sonless men the right to inherit their estates. Like Vijñāneśvara, he begins his discussion of the topic (on YDh 2.135–36)[48] by citing an array of seemingly contradictory Smṛtis, only some of which make a sonless man's wife his primary heir. Having done this, Aparārka then presents his own preferred way of harmonizing these scriptures:

> How then is one to remove the apparent contradiction between scriptures? I say that even when a man's father and brothers still live, his wife by herself inherits his entire estate and performs ancestral offerings and the like for him, provided that she has the qualities mentioned in such statements as the one of Manu that starts, "A sonless woman who

[48] This is YDh 2.139–40 in Olivelle's edition.

preserves her husband's bed. . . ."[49] It is with precisely this intention that Bṛhaspati states:

> A son should make ancestral offerings of food and water for his father. If a man has no sons, his wife should do it; and if he has no wife, his uterine brother.

Moreover, if a woman has properly served her husband, who acquired wealth on his own without diminishing his father's, and keeps her sense-organs restrained, then she inherits all of her husband's property, although his brothers still live. However, if she is deemed to be possibly adulterous on account of her youth or the like, then her dead husband's property goes to his brothers, not his wife, although she still lives.

kathaṃ tarhi virodhaparihāraḥ | ucyate—aputrā śayanaṃ bhartur ity ādimanuvākyoktaguṇā patnī pitṛbhrātṛsadbhāve 'pi svayam eva patidhanaṃ samagraṃ gṛhṇāti patyuś ca śrāddhādi karoti | anenaivābhiprāyeṇa bṛhaspatināpy uktam—

> *pituḥ putreṇa kartavyā piṇḍadānodakakriyā |*
> *putrābhāve tu patnī syāt tadabhāve sahodara iti ||*

tathā yā pitṛdhanānupaghātena svayam arjayitur bhartuḥ paricaryāṃ yathāvat kṛtavatī saṃyatendriyā ca sā bhartuḥ sakalam eva dhanaṃ devareṣu vidyamāneṣv api gṛhṇāti | yā tu tāruṇyādinā saṃbhāvitavyabhicārā tasyāṃ vidyamānāyām api mṛtakasya bhartur bhrātṛgāmy eva vittaṃ na tu patnīgāmi |

Here, like Vijñāneśvara and Lakṣmīdhara, Aparārka clearly harmonizes the scriptures in such a way that a sonless man's widow inherits all of his property, if she has been and remains faithful to her husband and observes the various duties incumbent upon a widow, such as the performance of ancestral offerings. Moreover, there is nothing anywhere in Aparārka's commentary to suggest that he thinks the wives of men who died prior to receiving their paternal estates or after reuniting with their coparceners are entitled to inherit their husbands' estates. Hence, his position appears to be fundamentally the same as that of Vijñāneśvara and Lakṣmīdhara.

However, one seemingly insignificant detail in the above passage of Aparārka deserves special comment: the fact that the husband of the inheriting widow is explicitly described as a man who "acquired wealth on his own without

[49] For the full verse, see the section "Vijñāneśvara" in this chapter.

diminishing his father's" (*pitṛdhanānupaghātena svayam arjayituḥ*). For the inclusion of this detail implies that, in Aparārka's view, a man must be economically productive in order for his wife to inherit his property. His basis for making such a restriction, which is unlike anything seen in the *Mitākṣarā* or *Kṛtyakalpataru*, is unclear. Perhaps the restriction is simply Aparārka's own extrapolation from the later statement of Yājñavalkya (2.146), where he grants the sonless wives of men who are impotent, blind, lame, and so on merely the right to maintenance. In any case, given that Aparārka explicitly speaks of a widow inheriting all of her husband's property (*bhartuḥ sakalam eva dhanam*), there is good reason to believe that he does not intend to restrict a widow's inheritance only to wealth that her husband earned on his own. Hence, like Vijñāneśvara and Lakṣmīdhara, he is a fairly strong advocate of a widow's right to inherit.

Consistently with this, Aparārka also interprets in a natural fashion Yājñavalkya's statement (2.119)[50] instructing a man who partitions his estate equally among his sons to give equal shares to his wives as well, if he or his father had never given them any women's property. That is, unlike Viśvarūpa, he makes no attempt to place a cap on the amount of wealth that a woman can inherit in this way. However, unlike Vijñāneśvara, he also does not add that even a woman who has received women's property still gets half a share. Similarly, Aparārka also interprets in a fairly natural fashion Yājñavalkya's statement (2.127)[51] that a woman is entitled to an equal share when her sons divide her husband's estate after his passing. However, he does stipulate—without obvious textual basis—that this rule applies only to a woman who has not received any women's property.[52] Aparārka's interpretation of these two verses of Yājñavalkya is consistent with his general advocacy of widows' rights of inheritance. Nevertheless, it also suggests that he was not quite so strong an advocate of these rights as his predecessor Vijñāneśvara was.

Beyond this, Aparārka also refutes several of the same objections to a widow's right to inherit that we have already seen Vijñāneśvara refute in his *Mitākṣarā*. The first such objection that Aparārka rebuts is Dhāreśvara's argument that only a woman who intends to engage in *niyoga* can inherit her husband's estate, although Aparārka never mentions Dhāreśvara specifically by name. The second is the argument that since all wealth was created for the purpose of sacrifice and widows lack the right to perform sacrifices, they also have no right to own property. And the final objection to a widow's right to

[50] This is YDh 2.115 in Aparārka.
[51] This is YDh 2.123 in Aparārka.
[52] Aparārka on YDh 2.123: *adattastrīdhanaviṣayam etat* |

inherit refuted by Aparārka is the argument, based upon certain Smṛti texts (e.g., NSm 13.25), that widows have a right to no more property than is required for their maintenance. Consequently, much of Aparārka's commentary on the relevant verses of Yājñavalkya (2.139–40) comprises a repetition of ideas and arguments already encountered in the *Mitākṣarā*.

However, at the very end of his commentary on these verses, Aparārka addresses a new and interesting objection to a widow's right to inherit:

> Regarding the mention of a wife and daughters in the statement under discussion (YDh 2.139), some object that a woman only has a right to perform sacrifices and give gifts together with her husband, not by herself. Moreover, because the wife referred to is one separated from her husband, she is not allowed to pursue her own sensual pleasure, but must instead perform harsh austerities. And when wealth is not used in the pursuit of religious merit or sensual pleasure, it is of no benefit to a person. Therefore, a woman should not inherit her husband's property, when his father and the like still live, as they are fit to receive wealth and use it in the pursuit of religious merit and sensual pleasure. Hence, when a man dies without sons, his wife should take only enough of his wealth to survive on, no more. Yājñavalkya's statement about a wife inheriting property applies to such limited wealth. And, therefore, his statement about daughters inheriting property is held to apply to cases where a man died without a wife and left only enough wealth for his daughters to get married. Hence, one should understand that even when a man's wife and daughters survive, his *sapiṇḍa* relatives, such as his father, should inherit any of his property that exceeds these purposes, as the statements of Śaṅkha and others are surely meaningful.

patnī duhitara ity (YDh 2.139) *atra vākye ke cit paryanuyuñjate yathā striyāḥ sabhartṛkāyā eveṣṭāpūrtayor adhikāro na tu kevalāyāḥ | tasyā bhartṛrahitatvād eva ca tayā na kāmaḥ sevanīyaḥ kiṃ tu tapas tīvram | na ca dharmakāmayor anupayujyamāno 'rtho bhavati puruṣārthaḥ | tasmāt pitrādiṣu dharmakāmopayogidhanabhājaneṣu satsu na patnyā dhanabhāktvam | tasmād aputrasya mṛtakasya dhanaṃ patnī nirvāhamātrasamartham ādadyān nādhikam | tadviṣayaṃ patnyā dhanabhāktvavacanam | yasya tu patnīrahitasya dhanaṃ duhitṛvivāhamātraparyāptaṃ tadviṣayaṃ duhitṝṇāṃ dhanagrāhitvam anenocyate | ato 'dhikasya mṛtakadhanasya patnīduhitṛsadbhāve 'pi sapiṇḍāḥ pitrādaya eva grāhakāḥ śaṅkhādivākyasārthyād bhavantīti mantavyam iti |*

As readers may note, this *pūrvapakṣa* or opponent's view against a widow's right to inherit resembles others that we have seen, but at the same time it is also notably different from them. It begins by arguing that a widow cannot use any of her wealth to pursue *dharma* or religious merit as a woman has no right to give gifts or perform sacrifices on her own, only in conjunction with her husband. And in this respect, the *pūrvapakṣa* looks very much like the argument against a widow's right to inherit on the grounds that women cannot perform sacrifices. However, the above *pūrvapakṣa* goes beyond this, as one can see, for it proceeds to argue that a woman also cannot pursue her own sensual pleasure or *kāma*, but must instead practice harsh asceticism. This incidentally shows that the *pūrvapakṣa* assumes some version of widow asceticism—the topic of the next chapter—to be mandatory for all women who outlive their husbands. Furthermore, the fact that Aparārka nowhere objects to this point suggests that he, too, shares this assumption. From the fact that a widow cannot use wealth for the purposes of religious merit (*dharma*) and sensual pleasure (*kāma*), the *pūrvapakṣa* concludes that she has no use for it beyond what is necessary for her survival and, as a result, should receive no more than that. And it also extends this same argument to a man's daughters, but instead of holding that they should receive only what is necessary for their maintenance, it argues that they should receive no more than is needed to pay for their marriages. Therefore, this *pūrvapakṣa* is fundamentally different from anything found in the preceding literature. Moreover, it is especially interesting in that it asks a question that modern readers themselves are apt to ask, but that the Dharmaśāstra tradition largely ignores, namely, what good is wealth to a widow, if she can't use it to make her life better?

Having presented the above *pūrvapakṣa*, Aparārka immediately commences to refute it:

> This position is incorrect, given that the arising of another person's ownership in a property can be enjoined only upon the death of that property's owner, as the venerable one explains: "The ownership of a man's wife and daughters in his property has already arisen; it need not be produced. The rite of marriage itself establishes a wife's ownership in her husband's property. Āpastamba's statement (2.14.17) that starts, 'From marriage a husband and wife function jointly,' enjoins this. And one should understand that a daughter's ownership in her father's property is established simply by birth, just like a son's ownership. Therefore, the statement under discussion (YDh

2.139–40) cannot overrule the ownership of a man's wife and daughter, when they exist, and enjoin the ownership of his parents and the rest. Instead, it enjoins the ownership of his parents, etc. when he has no wife or daughter, without overruling their ownership."

Moreover, this position entails construing a single injunction unevenly. Therefore, in order to avoid this, one must understand that a man's parents, etc. only inherit his property in the absence of a wife and so forth. As for the statements of Śaṅkha and others that a man's wife inherits his proper in the absence of his parents, etc., one must recognize that they apply to cases where a woman's ownership in her husband's property, which is the basis of words such as "right," has been taken away for a particular reason. And Yājñavalkya already explained this particular reason for a wife's loss of ownership in her husband's property, when he (1.70) said that a man should force an adulterous wife to live "stripped of rights, filthy . . ." Therefore, the position that I have already stated is the proper one. Furthermore, it is also incorrect to claim that any wealth owned by women beyond what is necessary for their maintenance is useless, for it has been explained that women without husbands have a right to perform acts of religious merit, such as gifts, except for those that require the use of mantras and sacred fires. Therefore, they do have a use for wealth that must be used independently.

tad ayuktaṃ dhanasvāminaḥ pramaye sati taddhane 'nyasya svāmitvotpattau vidheyāyāṃ yathāha bhagavān—patnyā duhitṝṇāṃ svāmitotpannaiva na tūtpādyā | pāṇigrahaṇād dhi sahatvam ity (2.14.17) *ādināpastambavākyena bhartṛdhane strīṇāṃ svāmitvaṃ pāṇigrahaṇam eva sādhayatīti vidhīyate | duhitṝṇāṃ putravaj janmanaiva pitṛdhane svāmibhāvasiddhir iti veditavyam | tataś ca patnyāṃ duhitari satyāṃ tayoḥ svāmitvaṃ bādhitvā pitrādisvāmitvavidhir anena vākyena na kāryaḥ | abhāve tu patnīduhitror bādhanirapekṣaṃ vidhāyakatvam asyeti | vairūpyam āpadyate | tatas tatparihārārthaṃ patnyādyabhāva eva pitrādīnāṃ dhanabhāktvam iha prameyam | yat tu śaṅkhādibhiḥ pitrādyabhāve patnyā dhanagrāhakatvam ucyate tat kāraṇāntareṇa bhartṛdhane yasyā adhikārādipadāspadaṃ svāmitvam apetaṃ tadviṣayaṃ draṣṭavyam | uktaṃ ca kāraṇāntaraṃ hṛtādhikārāṃ malinām ity* (YDh 1.70) *atra bhartṛdhane patnyāḥ svāmitvabhraṃśaṃ prati | tasmād uktaiva vyavasthā yuktā | yad uktaṃ strīṇāṃ svanirvāhasamarthād adhiko 'rtho nirarthaka iti tad api naiva yuktam | uktaṃ hi strīṇām abhartṛkāṇāṃ mantrāgnisādhyadharmād anyatra dharme dānādāv asty adhikāra iti | tena svatantropayujyamāne 'rthe tāsām upayogaḥ |*

As one can see, Aparārka begins his refutation of the previous *pūrvapakṣa* by noting that, at least within the context of inheritance, a person can only become the owner of a property, when the previous owner of that property has died. He then quotes the opinion of an unspecified "venerable one" (*bhagavān*)[53] that he believes clarifies the implications of this. According to this venerable one, whoever he may have been, a man's wife and daughter already have some ownership in his property, even prior to his death. Specifically, he holds that, through marriage, a husband and wife function jointly in all things, including the ownership of property, and that a daughter acquires ownership in her father's property merely through birth, just as a son does.[54] From this the venerable one concludes that the statement of Yājñavalkya under discussion (2.139–40) is not intended to overrule the already established ownership in a man's property of his wife and daughters, but instead to enjoin that a man's parents and so on inherit his property in the absence of wives and daughters.

To this argument Aparārka then adds that the *pūrvapakṣa* in question also entails the hermeneutic fallacy of construing a single scriptural injunction in multiple different ways, namely, as applying to only small amounts of wealth in the case of wives and daughters, but to wealth in general in the case of all other heirs. That is, Aparārka rebuts this particular *pūrvapakṣa* in the same way that we have seen Vijñāneśvara rebut another similar one. He then goes on to explain that the previously cited statement of Śaṅkha,[55] which allows a man's wife to inherit only in the absence of brothers and parents, really only applies to women who have been stripped of their normal ownership in their husbands' estates due to marital infidelity. And, lastly, he points out that, contrary to the *pūrvapakṣa*'s contention, women without husbands can, in fact, use wealth in the pursuit of *dharma* or religious merit; they are simply prohibited from performing religious rites that require the recitation of Vedic mantras or the use of sacred fires. In this way, Aparārka defends a widow's right to inherit from an interesting objection not found in the *Mitākṣarā*.

Now, let us turn to the *Smṛticandrikā* of Devaṇa Bhaṭṭa, which was composed somewhere in South India roughly between the years 1175 and

[53] The identity of this person is unclear. Perhaps he was Aparārka's own teacher.
[54] See Kane (1962, 3:544–74).
[55] See the section "Vijñāneśvara."

1225. Like Vijñāneśvara, Lakṣmīdhara, and Aparārka before him, Devaṇa fundamentally accepts a widow's right to inherit. Unlike Aparārka and Vijñāneśvara, however, he barely refutes any objections against his own position. Thus, for example, while Vijñāneśvara and Aparārka refute at length Dhāreśvara's position that only a woman who engages in *niyoga* can inherit her husband's property, Devaṇa simply notes that this position has already been rebutted by other authors and, as a result, can be ignored.[56] Indeed, the only notable exception to Devaṇa's general pattern of ignoring objections to a widow's right to inherit is his brief refutation of the *pūrvapakṣa* found in Aparārka, which holds that wealth beyond what is needed for survival is useless for widows and, consequently, should not devolve to them.[57]

Nevertheless, although Devaṇa does not defend widows' rights of inheritance against possible objectors in the same exhaustive way that Vijñāneśvara and Aparārka do, statements in his *Smṛticandrikā* make clear that he fundamentally agrees with them on the issue. Specifically, like them, Devaṇa holds that a sonless man's widow should inherit all of his property, provided that he had received his paternal inheritance prior to his death and had not reunited with his coparceners. The following passage of the *Smṛticandrikā* (*Vyavahārakāṇḍa*, p. 681) states this in no uncertain terms:

> And, thus, one should understand that when scripture states that a wife alone receives her husband's entire estate, it applies only to cases where her husband had received his paternal inheritance prior to his death and not reunited with his coparceners.
>
> *evaṃ ca patny eva samastam aṃśaṃ labheteti vibhaktāsaṃsṛṣṭaviṣayam iti mantavyam |*

Hence, Devaṇa's basic position on a widow's right to inherit is the same as that of Vijñāneśvara, Lakṣmīdhara, and Aparārka. Despite his lack of originality on this crucial point, however, his treatment of the inheritance rights of widows is innovative in a number of other ways that bear mentioning.

One major innovation of the *Smṛticandrikā* in this regard is its explicit statement that the principle underlying the sequence of heirs to a person's

[56] *Smṛticandrikā, Vyavahārakāṇḍa*, p. 681: "The opinion of Dhāreśvara can be ignored, as it has been properly refuted by Viśvarūpa and others." (*dhāreśvaramataṃ viśvarūpādibhiḥ samyag dūṣitatvād upekṣaṇiyam |*) Contrary to what is stated here, however, Viśvarūpa nowhere refutes Dhāreśvara's position on a widow's right to inherit.

[57] See *Smṛticandrikā, Vyavahārakāṇḍa*, p. 676.

property is closeness (*āsannatva*), specifically closeness as determined by the amount of worldly and otherworldly help (*dṛṣṭādṛṣṭopakāra*) that one has and will render the property's owner. That is, Devaṇa Bhaṭṭa holds that the strength of one's claim to a person's property is proportionate to the degree to which one has helped that person in this world and, most importantly, will help that person in the next one. The following passage of the *Smṛticandrikā* (*Vyavahārakāṇḍa*, pp. 672–73) spells this out fairly clearly:

> Manu (9.185) states:
>
> > The father of a sonless man should inherit his property or else his brothers should.
>
> The author of the *Saṃgraha* has shown that while the meaning of each word here is clear, the purport of this statement is not:
>
> > When the owner of a property dies without sons of any type, who now should inherit his property? It is in order to answer this that this now is said.
>
> The meaning of this verse is as follows: When the owner of a property dies without a son of a primary or secondary type, there is the desire to know what person should now inherit the man's property after his death. To answer this Manu now says that his father, etc. should inherit it. And this statement applies when a man has no one closer to him, who will help him in numerous ways, than his father and the like. Hence, knowing that even sons of a secondary type are closer to a man than his father, etc., the author of the *Saṃgraha* explains the purport of Manu's statement (9.185) that the "father of a sonless man should inherit" by describing the man as one "without sons *of any type*." There is absolutely nothing wrong with this. However, just as a son of a secondary type takes precedence over a man's father, etc. in that he renders him worldly and otherworldly assistance and, thus, is closer to him than they are, so a wife also takes precedence over a father, etc. in rendering a man worldly and otherworldly assistance based upon a careful consideration of the Vedas and Smṛtis and, thus, is closer to him than they are. Therefore, it is also in the absence of a wife that Manu (9.185) says that the "father of a sonless man should inherit." In this way, the purport of his statement is inferred.

tatra manuḥ—

> *pitā hared aputrasya rikthaṃ bhrātara eva veti* | (MDh 9.185)

akṣarārtho vyaktas tātparyārthas tv avyaktaḥ saṃgrahakāreṇa darśitaḥ—

aśeṣātmajahīnasya mṛtasya dhanino dhanam |
kenedānīṃ grahītavyam ity etad adhunocyate ||

asyāyam arthaḥ—mukhyagauṇaputravihīnasya dhanavato mṛtasya dhanam idānīṃ tanmaraṇānantaraṃ kena janena hartavyam ity ākāṅkṣāyāṃ pitrādinā hartavyam ity etad adhunā pitrādyapekṣayeha bahuvidhopakārakāsannajanābhāve manunocyata iti | ata eva pitrādibhyo gauṇaputrāṇām āsannataratvaṃ jñātvā saṃgrahakāreṇa pitā hared aputrasyety asya aśeṣātmajahīnasyeti tātparyam uktam | tad anavadyam eva | kiṃ tu yathā gauṇaputrāṇāṃ dṛṣṭādṛṣṭopakārakatvena pitrādyapekṣayāgresaratvāt tadapekṣayāsannataratvaṃ tathā patnyā api dṛṣṭādṛṣṭopakārakaraṇe śrutismṛtyādiparyālocanayā pitrādyapekṣayāgresaratvāt tadapekṣayāsannataratvam astīti patnyā apy abhāve pitā hared aputrasyety etan manunocyata ity evaṃ tātparyam ūhyate |

This passage begins Devaṇa's lengthy discussion of the inheritance of a sonless man's estate and, as one can see, he starts it by citing a verse of Manu (9.185), according to which a sonless man's father or brothers should inherit his property. In order to clarify the meaning of Manu's verse, Devaṇa then quotes another verse, this one attributed to the author of the *Saṃgraha*, a work of uncertain identity, but apparently a versified doxography of some sort. As Devaṇa explains it, the author of the *Saṃgraha* recognizes that closeness to a person determines the sequence of heirs to his property and, thus, clarifies that when Manu speaks of a "sonless man" (*aputra*), he means a "man without sons of any type" (*aśeṣātmajahīna*), for even sons of a secondary type or figurative sons, such as adoptive ones, are closer to a man than his father and brothers are. Applying this principle of closeness further, Devaṇa proceeds to argue that a man's wife is also closer to him than his father and so on in that she helps him to a greater degree both in this world and the next, as the scriptures make clear. From this he concludes that Manu's statement about a sonless man's father or brothers inheriting his property applies only when he has no surviving wife. That is, he holds that a sonless man's wife is his primary heir due to her closeness, as determined by the amount of worldly and otherworldly help that she renders.

Another notable innovation of the *Smṛticandrikā* is that it (*Vyavahārakāṇḍa*, p. 674) defines the term "wife" (*patnī*) within the context of inheritance more strictly or at least more precisely than do all preceding Dharmaśāstra works:

> A "wife" (*patnī*) is a woman who has been consecrated through a marriage of one of the praiseworthy types, such as the Brāhma marriage, which result in a woman's right to participate in sacrifices, for Pāṇini (4.1.33) prescribes the use of the word "wife" specifically for a woman involved in the performance of sacrifices. No other woman is a wife, as it is inappropriate that a woman excluded from the term "wife" should be referred to as a wife. And, thus, there is a Smṛti that states:
>
> > A woman who is bought through a sale is not called a "wife." She cannot participate in rites to the gods or to the ancestors. Sages know her as a slave.
>
> Here it is said that the sages "know her as a slave" in order to show that if a woman does not qualify as a wife, she can render her husband only worldly assistance. And, thus, use of the word "wife"[58] communicates that fitness to participate in rites to the ancestors, etc. is required for inheriting a husband's estate.
>
> *patnī yajñādhikārāpādakapraśastabrāhmādivivāhasaṃskṛtā patyur no yajñasaṃyoga iti* (4.1.33) *pāṇinismaraṇāt | netarā patnīpadena vyāvartitāyās tasyāḥ patnītvāyogāt | tathā ca smṛtyantaram—*
>
> > *krayakrītā tu yā nārī na sā patny abhidhīyate |*
> > *na sā daive na sā pitrye dāsīṃ tāṃ kavayo viduḥ ||*
>
> *patnītvābhāve kevaladṛṣṭopakāratvaṃ striyā iti darśayituṃ dāsīṃ vidur ity uktam | evaṃ ca pitryādikarmaṇy arhatāpi patibhāgahāritve prayojiketi patnīgrahaṇena jñāpitam |*

Whereas Vijñāneśvara (on YDh 2.139–40) explains merely that a *patnī* ("wife") is a woman who has been consecrated through marriage (*vivāhasaṃskṛtā*), Devaṇa adds to this that in order to qualify as a *patnī*, a woman's marriage must have been specifically a marriage of one of the prestigious types that grant her the right to participate in sacrificial rituals.[59] And

[58] This refers to the use of the word "wife" in BSm 26.94: "When a man dies without sons, his wife inherits his estate." (*asutasya pramītasya patnī tadbhāgahāriṇī |*)

[59] These types of marriage are as follows: the Brāhma marriage, where a father simply summons a learned and virtuous man and offers him his daughter; the Daiva marriage, where a father gives his daughter to the officiating priest after a sacrifice; the Ārṣa marriage, where a father receives a bull and cow from the groom and then gives him his daughter; and the Prājāpatya marriage, where a father gives his daughter to a man and exhorts them both to jointly follow the law. For these and

he justifies this restriction on the basis of a statement of the Sanskrit grammarian Pāṇini (4.1.33), which prescribes the form *patnī* ("wife") as the feminine equivalent of *pati* ("husband, lord") with the unusual *n* infix, only when there is a connection with sacrifice (*yajñasaṃyoge*). In this way, Devaṇa makes a woman's ability to perform ancestral rites and, thus, offer otherworldly help to her deceased husband a requirement for her inheriting his estate. Hence, he apparently considers a widow's right to inherit somewhat more limited than certain other authors, such as Vijñāneśvara, do.

A similar, but even more significant restriction on widows' rights of inheritance within the *Smṛticandrikā* concerns immovable property. The passage where Devaṇa articulates and defends this restriction (*Vyavahārakāṇḍa*, pp. 676–77) reads:

> And one must recognize that a wife becomes owner of her deceased husband's property only when he had received his paternal inheritance prior to his death, as Bṛhaspati states:
>
> > If her husband had received his paternal inheritance, then upon his death his spouse inherits whatever wealth of various sorts, including that offered as collateral, that is held to belong to him, excepting immovable property.
>
> The meaning of this is that whatever wealth of various sorts, be it movable or immovable, is held to belong to a woman's husband, she inherits it all in cases where he had received his paternal inheritance. One understands from the fact that the verse speaks of a husband who "had received his paternal inheritance" that, in cases where a man has not received his paternal inheritance, only his father, brothers, or the like who lived jointly with him should inherit his property, if he died without sons. The word "spouse" means wife. The stipulation "excepting immovable property" applies to wives without daughters. If it applied to wives in general instead, it would conflict with the previously cited statement that a man's wife "should take his movable property, immovable property, gold, base metal, grain, spices, and clothing."[60] And, in order to avoid conflict with this, one should not respond that Bṛhaspati's stipulation, excluding immovable property, must apply either to the estate of a man who had not received his paternal

the four nonprestigious forms of marriage, see MDh 3.20–34. For an insightful analysis of them, see Trautmann (1981, 288–93).

[60] *Smṛticandrikā*, *Vyavahārakāṇḍa*, p. 675.

inheritance prior to death or to a wife who acts improperly, for in order to rule out such a position, Bṛhaspati himself states:

> Even if she adheres to proper conduct and her husband had received his share of inheritance, a woman is unworthy to receive immovable wealth.

Worthiness to receive immovable wealth, which is a means of livelihood for one's children, requires that one has children. Therefore, a woman without them, even if she adheres to proper conduct and even in cases where her husband had received his paternal inheritance, is unworthy to receive immovable wealth. This is the meaning of this verse.

etac ca patnīsvāmitvaṃ vibhakte patyau draṣṭavyaṃ yad āha bṛhaspatiḥ—

> *yad vibhakte dhanaṃ kiṃcid ādhyādi vividhaṃ smṛtam |*
> *taj jāyā sthāvaraṃ muktvā labheta mṛtabhartṛkā ||*

yat kiṃcid ādhyādi vividhaṃ dhanaṃ sthāvarajaṅgamātmakaṃ bhartṛsvāmikātmakaṃ smṛtaṃ tat sarvaṃ vibhaktaviṣaye labhetety arthaḥ | vibhaktagrahaṇād avibhaktaviṣaye tu sahavāsina eva pitṛbhrātrādayo mṛtāputradhanaṃ labherann iti gamyate | jāyā patnī | sthāvaraṃ muktvety etad duhitṛrahitapatnīviṣayam | patnīmātraviṣayatve tu jaṅgamaṃ sthāvaraṃ hema kupyaṃ dhānyarasāmbaram ādāyeti pūrvoktavacanavirodhaḥ syāt | na ca tadvirodhaparihārāyāvibhaktapatyaṃśaviṣayaṃ vṛttahīnapatnīviṣayaṃ vedaṃ vacanam astv iti vācyam | yata evaṃprakārāṃ vyavasthāṃ nirākartum āha sa eva—

> *vṛttasthāpi kṛte 'py aṃśe na strī sthāvaram arhatīti |*

saṃtānavṛttibhūtasthāvaralabdhyarhatā tu saṃtānaśālitāyatteti tacchūnyā strī vṛttasthāpi vibhaktaviṣaye 'pi sthāvaraṃ nārhatīty arthaḥ |

Devaṇa begins this passage by stating his position that a widow only inherits her husband's estate if he had received his paternal inheritance prior to his death and by citing a verse of Bṛhaspati in a support of this view. As one can see, however, this verse also excludes immovable property from the wealth that a widow can inherit; and this constitutes an extremely significant exclusion, as land was almost certainly the single most important form of wealth in premodern South Asian society. Instead of accepting Bṛhaspati's exclusion of immovable property at face value, however, Devaṇa limits its application to only daughterless widows. And he justifies this interpretive move by pointing out that if the exclusion of immovable property applied to all widows, it would directly conflict with another Smṛti that allows widows to inherit specifically immovable property. Devaṇa then proceeds to rule out some alternative ways of harmonizing the relevant scriptures before explaining why daughterless widows should be excluded from inheriting immovable property: such property functions primarily as a means of providing a livelihood for one's progeny. Hence, by denying daughterless women the right to inherit immovable property, Devaṇa severely limits the wealth that a widow can receive.

In addition to placing restrictions on the kinds of wealth that widows can inherit, the *Smṛticandrikā* (*Vyavahārakāṇḍa*, p. 677) also limits the ways in which widows can use the wealth that they inherit from their husbands:

> That same author (i.e., Bṛhaspati) also says the following:
>
> > After her husband's death, a woman who preserves his family should inherit his estate, but without any power to give it away, offer it as collateral, or sell it so long as she lives.
>
> A "woman who preserves his family" is one who preserves her husband's lineage, in other words, a woman who adheres to proper conduct. Because scripture enjoins a widow to give for otherworldly purposes by providing a livelihood for the old, indigent, and the like,[61] one should understand that the purpose of this statement of Bṛhaspati is to teach that a woman lacks independence to give away her husband's estate, etc. in any other way than that, i.e., for worldly purposes. And, thus, a woman certainly has independence to give away her husband's estate for the purpose of religious merit. Therefore, with the thought that a widow should constantly practice giving for the purpose of religious merit, Bṛhaspati himself says:
>
> > Even a sonless woman goes to heaven, if she delights in performing vows and fasts, remains strictly celibate, and constantly rejoices in giving gifts for religious merit.
>
> For if a woman were dependent upon others, it makes no sense that she could constantly practice giving. And, thus, one should understand that a widow's independence to offer her husband's estate as collateral and to sell it is also not prohibited, provided that these things are done in order to acquire property that will achieve otherworldly ends.

yad aparam uktaṃ tenaiva—
mṛte bhartari bhartraṃśaṃ labheta kulapālikā |
yāvajjīvaṃ hīnasvāmyaṃ dānādhamanavikraya iti ||

[61] See *Smṛticandrikā*, *Vyavahārakāṇḍa*, p. 675: "One should honor the old, the indigent, and guests with ancestral offerings and gifts." (*pūjayet kavyapūrtābhyāṃ vṛddhānāthātithīṃs tathā |*)

kulapālikā vaṃśapālikā vṛttastheti yāvat | tad vṛddhānāthādyupajīvanāyādṛṣṭārthadānavidhānāt taditaradṛṣṭārthadānādāv asvātantryapratipādanārtham iti mantavyam | evaṃ ca dharmārthadāne svātantryam asty eva | ata eva dharmārthadānaṃ aniśam āvartanīyam ity āha sa eva—

vratopavāsaniratā brahmacarye vyavasthitā |
dharmadānaratā nityam aputrāpi divaṃ vrajet ||

na hi pāratantrye nityadānakriyā yujyate | evaṃ cādṛṣṭasādhakadravyasaṃpādanārthayor ādhivikrayayor api svātantryam apratiṣiddham iti mantavyam |

Here Devaṇa cites another verse of Bṛhaspati, this time one that denies widows the right to give away, sell, or offer as collateral any wealth that they have received from their husbands. And, as one can see, Devaṇa generally accepts Bṛhaspati's limitations on a widow's ability to alienate inherited property. However, he does make the exception that a widow can freely alienate such property for purposes of *dharma*, that is, in order to finance the performance of pious acts and, thereby, acquire religious merit, perhaps with the understanding that this merit will also provide otherworldly benefits for her husband.

Beyond this, another major innovation of the *Smṛticandrikā* is that it spells out with markedly greater clarity than all preceding Dharmaśāstra works what exactly comprises maintenance for the widow of a sonless man and precisely which wives of a man are entitled to it. Just as Vijñāneśvara considers a man's heirs obligated to provide maintenance for his "kept women" (*avaruddhastrī*), so Devaṇa considers a man's heirs obligated to provide maintenance for his wives of lesser status, that is, his wives who are not entitled to participate in sacrifices, bear the designation *patnī*, and receive inheritance. Moreover, like Vijñāneśvara and other early commentators, he considers all of a man's wives entitled to maintenance, if he had not received his paternal inheritance prior to his death. Devaṇa lays out the particulars of this situation in the following passage (*Vyavahārakāṇḍa*, p. 678):

> Kātyāyana explains the details of this (i.e., widows' maintenance) as follows:
> When her husband dies without receiving his paternal inheritance, his wife receives food and clothing. Instead, she might receive a share of money until her death.

The phrase "share of money" means however much money is sufficient for her to live untroubled and perform obligatory rites—whether routine or occasioned by certain events—and optional rites, such as vows, which women have a right to perform and which require the spending of money. The word "instead" in this verse means "or." Thus, the meaning is: "Or alternatively she might receive a share of money." Moreover, she might instead receive a portion of a field that will yield the equivalent amount of money, for the word "money" here functions as a synecdoche for any means of attaining a livelihood and the like. The first option in the above verse (i.e., receiving just food and clothing) applies to wives who do not qualify as *patnīs*, for it is said that they receive only a very small amount of wealth sufficient for their mere livelihood. And Nārada explains what constitutes the very small amount of wealth sufficient for a woman's mere livelihood as follows:

> Each year a virtuous woman whose husband has died should receive twenty-four *āḍhakas* and forty *paṇas*.

An *āḍhaka* is a unit of grain equal to 192 handfuls.

atra viśeṣam āha kātyāyanaḥ—

> *svaryāte svāmini strī tu grāsācchādanabhāginī |*
> *avibhakte dhanāṃśaṃ tu prāpnoty ā maraṇāntikam ||*

dhanāṃśaṃ yāvatā dhanenākliṣṭajīvanaṃ dhanasādhyaṃ ca nityanaimittikaṃ karma stryadhikārakaṃ kāmyavratādikaṃ ca sidhyati tāvantam ity arthaḥ | tuśabdo vāśabdārthe dhanāṃśaṃ vā prāpnotīty arthaḥ | etāvaddhanasaṃpādakaṃ kṣetrāṃśaṃ vā prāpnoti dhanagrahaṇasya vartanādyupāyopalakṣaṇārthatvāt | atrādyapakṣaḥ patnīvyatiriktabhāryāviṣayo jīvanamātrasādhanasvalpārthabhāgitvābhidhānāt | jīvanamātrasādhanasya svalpām iyattām āha nāradaḥ—

> *āḍhakāṃs tu caturviṃśat catvāriṃśat paṇāṃs tathā |*
> *pratisaṃvatsaraṃ sādhvī labheta mṛtabhartṛkā ||*

āḍhako 'ṣṭonadviśataprasṛtiparimito dhānyacayaḥ |

Here Devaṇa explains that, if a man had not received his paternal inheritance, his *patnī*—that is, his wife of the prestigious type entitled to participate in sacrificial rites—should receive a share of money or land sufficient for her both to live comfortably and to carry out assorted pious activities. Thus, Devaṇa's position somewhat resembles Yājñavalkya's position (2.119, 127) that, even in cases where a man had sons, his wives are entitled to equal shares of his estate. As one can see, however, Devaṇa holds that wives who do not qualify as *patnīs* should receive as their yearly maintenance only forty *paṇas*, or common copper coins, and just under 185 pounds of grain.[62] This would almost certainly have been tantamount to a life of considerable material deprivation and have amounted to far less than the wealth given as maintenance to a *patnī*.

When it comes to cases where a man died after receiving his paternal inheritance, however, Devaṇa somewhat reduces the plight of his less prestigious wives, for he (*Vyavahārakāṇḍa*, p. 679) adds that, in such cases, a man's heir might at his own discretion give the man's lesser wives not merely food and clothing, but instead a share of wealth similar to that given to *patnīs*:

> Continuing his discussion of a widow whose husband had received his paternal inheritance, Bṛhaspati states:
>
> > One should certainly give to her either food or a portion of a field as one feels inclined.
>
> The word "food" here functions as a synecdoche for food and clothing. And, thus, the verse means this: "In cases where a man had received his paternal inheritance, one should give according to one's own desire either food and clothing of the aforementioned amounts or a portion of a field that will yield the aforementioned share of money for a livelihood to his widow, if she is not a *patnī* and, thus, not entitled to her husband's estate." The word "certainly" in the verse serves to indicate that giving one or the other thing to a widow is mandatory. The first of the two options (i.e., giving only food and clothing) applies to women who do not faithfully serve their mothers-in-law, etc.

kṛte 'py aṃśa ity anuvṛttau bṛhaspatiḥ—

pradadyāt tv eva piṇḍaṃ vā kṣetrāṃśaṃ vā yadṛcchayeti |

piṇḍagrahaṇam aśanācchādanopalakṣaṇārtham | evaṃ cāyam arthaḥ—aśanācchādanaṃ pūrvoktaparimāṇakaṃ pūrvoktadhanāṃśasaṃpādakakṣetrāṃśaṃ vā svarucyā bhartraṃśārhapatnīvyatiriktavidhavāyai

[62] This calculation is based upon Monier-Williams's ([1899] 2002, 134) estimation that an *āḍhaka* is equal to 7 lbs., 11 oz. If instead the term *prasṛti* ("handful") in Devaṇa's commentary is taken to denote a precise unit of volume equal to 165 cc or 250 cc (Srinivasan 1979, 71), this results in the untenable conclusion that a widow should receive for her maintenance either 760 liters or 1,267 liters of grains per year, that is, more than two liters of grain per day!

> *vibhaktaviṣaye jīvanārthaṃ pradadyād iti | evakāraḥ pradānasyāvaśyakatvajñāpanārthaḥ | śvaśrvādyaśuśrūṣakastrīviṣayo 'trādyaḥ pakṣaḥ |*

Thus, Devaṇa's view of maintenance in cases where a man had received his paternal inheritance prior to his death is this: a widow who does not qualify as a *patnī* and fails to serve the elders with whom she lives, such as her mother-in-law, is entitled only to the barest necessities of grain and a few copper coins to pay for clothes. However, if she faithfully serves her elders and the inheritor of her husband's estate sees fit, she may receive a larger share of money or a portion of a field in order to make her life more comfortable. From this it should be clear that the *Smṛticandrikā* treats the important issue of widows' maintenance in considerably greater detail than all earlier Dharmaśāstra works.

Lastly, unlike earlier commentators within the Dharmaśāstra tradition, Devaṇa bothers to explain away a passage of the Vedic *Taittirīya Saṃhitā* (6.5.8.2), which flatly declares women ineligible to receive inheritance. And, from a theoretical perspective at least, such an explanation is important, since it is an accepted principle of Brahmanical hermeneutics that the Veda is of greater authority than Smṛti. Consequently, if the Veda prohibits women from inheriting property, it is unclear how widows can inherit their husbands' estates on the basis of statements found only in Smṛti texts. The passage of the *Smṛticandrikā* (*Vyavahārakāṇḍa*, p. 681) where Devaṇa presents a solution to this problem reads:

> It is said in the Veda (TS 6.5.8.2): "Therefore, women, being devoid of strength, receive no inheritance." But this does not overrule the statements of Vṛddha Manu and others that permit widows to inherit, for one should understand that this Vedic passage applies to women who are a man's children (i.e., daughters), as they are associated with sons devoid of strength. Or instead, one might understand it to apply to all women. Nevertheless, this Vedic passage is merely an exhortatory statement that applies to women other than wives and the like, who are straightforwardly said to be heirs. In this way, all is well.

> *yat tu śrutāv uktaṃ tasmāt striyo nirindriyā adāyādīr iti* (TS 6.5.8.2.) *tad api na vṛddhamanvādivacanabādhakaṃ nirindriyaputrasāhacaryād apatyabhūtastrīviṣayatvāvagateḥ | bhavatu vā sarvastrīviṣayatvāvagatiḥ |*

tathāpi dāyādatayā śṛṅgagrāhikoktapatnyādistrīvyatiriktaviṣayārthavāda-śrutir iti sarvaṃ sustham |

Here Devaṇa proposes two different ways to account for the passage of the *Taittirīya Saṃhitā* (6.5.8.2) that declares women unfit to inherit. His first proposal is that the passage applies not to wives, but to daughters; and as support for this, he notes the association of daughters with weakling sons, perhaps alluding to a popular male chauvinist belief. The second interpretation of the passage proposed by Devaṇa is that it is simply an *arthavāda* or "exhortatory expression" and, thus, devoid of injunctive force.[63] Specifically, Devaṇa suggests that the passage could be an exhortatory statement intended to apply to women other than wives and the like, which Smṛti texts unambiguously declare to be heirs.

Thus, as one can see, Devaṇa agrees with Vijñāneśvara, Lakṣmīdhara, and Aparārka that, in the absence of sons, a man's widow should inherit his entire estate, if he had received his paternal inheritance prior to his death and not reunited with his coparceners. Unlike these authors, however, Devaṇa places three noteworthy limitations on widows' rights of inheritance. First, he holds that, in order to inherit her husband's estate, a woman must have been married specifically via a prestigious form of marriage rite, which entitles her to participate in the hallowed sacrifices of Vedic religion. Second, Devaṇa holds that unless a man's wife has daughters, she cannot inherit his immovable property. And, finally, he prohibits a widow from alienating property inherited from her husband except in the service of performing pious acts.

Before moving on, however, it is worth noting that although, from the twelfth century onward, most authors within the Dharmaśāstra tradition accept a widow's right to inherit her husband's estate, there are a few exceptions to this salient trend. For instance, the prolific commentator Haradatta, whom Kane (1962, 1:744–47) dates to the period 1100–1300, is strongly opposed to widows inheriting any property. That Haradatta holds such a view is evident from his commentary on the *Gautama Dharmasūtra*, specifically on Gautama's statement (28.21) that a sonless man's *sapiṇḍas*, other male agnates, and wife should inherit his property, for there Haradatta states:

[63] For a more detailed discussion of the concept of *arthavāda*, see the section "The *Madanaparijāta*" in Chapter 4.

A man's wife is here grouped together with all of his kinsmen, such as the members of his patrilineal clan. When his *sapiṇḍa* relatives or the like inherit his property, his wife also inherits a single share of it together with them. Thus, it is said:

> When sons partition their father's estate after his passing, their mother also receives an equal share. (YDh 2.127)

It is for this reason that a wife is listed separately, but *sapiṇḍa* relatives, etc. collectively. In the teacher's preferred view, however, a wife does not receive a share of inheritance. And Manu concurs:

> Women are always devoid of strength and receive no inheritance—this is the fixed rule.[64]

In the event that a man has no *sapiṇḍas* or the like, Bṛhaspati states:

> A righteous king should provide a livelihood for a man's women—this is held to be the law of inheritance.[65] Each afternoon he should give to them a *prastha* (= 600 grams) of rice for food as well as firewood; and every three months he should give to them a single garment worth three *paṇas*. The law enjoins only this much food for virtuous women.

Thus, both Manu and Bṛhaspati prescribe the complete absence of inheritance for wives. Yājñavalkya (2.139–40), however, proclaims that a man's wife should inherit his property in his statement that starts, "Wife, daughters . . ." But regarding this, Vyāsa states:

> One should give a man's wife a share of his property equal to two thousand *paṇas*. If one desires, she may also receive what her husband has given to her.

The teacher, by contrast, prescribes that a man's wife should receive a share of his estate equal to the shares of his *sapiṇḍas* or the like. On this issue, the best option is for a sonless man's *sapiṇḍas* or the like to receive his entire property and maintain his wives so long as they live. But if this is impossible, they should set aside as the wives' share money, fields, etc. sufficient for their food and clothing and take the rest.

strī tu sarvaiḥ sagotrādibhiḥ samuccīyate | yadā sapiṇḍādayo gṛhṇanti tadā taiḥ saha patny apy ekam aṃśaṃ haret | tathā—

pitur ūrdhvaṃ vibhajatāṃ mātāpy aṃśaṃ samaṃ hared iti | (YDh 2.127)

[64] This verse is not found in Manu, although it is similar to MDh 9.18.
[65] See note 37.

ata eva strī pṛthaṅ nirdiṣṭā | sapiṇḍādayaḥ samānena | patnīdāyas tv ācāryasya pakṣe na bhavati | manur api—

nirindriyā adāyādāḥ striyo nityam iti sthitir iti |

atra sapiṇḍādyabhave bṛhaspatiḥ—

anyatra brāhmaṇāt kiṃ tu rājā dharmaparāyaṇaḥ |
tatstrīṇāṃ jīvanaṃ dadyād eṣa dāyavidhiḥ smṛtaḥ ||
annārthaṃ taṇḍulaprastham aparāhṇe tu sendhanam |
vasanaṃ tripaṇakrītaṃ deyam ekaṃ trimāsataḥ |
etāvad eva sādhvīnāṃ coditaṃ vidhināśanam iti ||

tad evaṃ manubṛhaspatibhyāṃ patnīdāyasyātyantābhāva uktaḥ | yājñavalkyena tu patnīdāyaḥ sa uktaḥ patnī duhitaraś cety (YDh 2.139) *ādi | atra vyāsaḥ—*

dvisahasrapaṇo dāyaḥ patnyai deyo dhanasya tu |
yac ca bhartrā dhanaṃ dattaṃ sā yathākāmam āpnuyād iti ||

ācāryeṇa tu sapiṇḍādisamāṃśagrahaṇam uktam | tatra sarvam eva dhanaṃ sapiṇḍādyā gṛhītvā striyo yāvajjīvaṃ rakṣeyur iti mukhyaḥ kalpaḥ | tadasaṃbhave 'śanavasanayoḥ paryāptaṃ dhanakṣetrādikam aṃśatvena vyapohya śeṣaṃ gṛhṇīyuḥ |

Here Haradatta interprets Gautama's statement to mean that a childless man's wife receives a single share of his estate equal to those shares received by his various *sapiṇḍa* relatives or, failing them, more distant male agnates. Thus, he seemingly interprets Gautama's text in a natural and plausible way. As one can see, however, Haradatta then goes on to claim that in the view actually preferred by Gautama, whom he here and elsewhere refers to simply as the "teacher" (*ācārya*), a wife should inherit nothing. And in support of this position, he cites a verse of Manu that flatly prohibits women from inheriting and one of Bṛhaspati that details the precise amount of maintenance to which widows are entitled. Nevertheless, it is unclear on what basis Haradatta considers Gautama to hold the same views on a widow's right to inherit as Manu and Bṛhaspati. Perhaps he imagines that Gautama expresses his preferred view in the following *sūtra* (28.22), where he says that a childless man's widow might alternatively engage in *niyoga*. But Haradatta gives no obvious indication of this in his commentary, and it is also unlikely that he personally approves of *niyoga*, given his late date.

In any case, Haradatta proceeds to note that Yājñavalkya (2.139–40) makes a sonless man's widow his primary heir, but then limits the amount of inheritance that she can receive to two thousand *paṇas*, or standard copper coins, on the basis of a statement ascribed to Vyāsa. Thereafter, at the end of the above passage he presents his own position on this issue, which is that a sonless man's male agnates should inherit his entire estate and look after his wives. However, if his agnates are unable to do this, they should set aside for his wives enough property to pay for their food and clothing. And it is important to note that here Haradatta reads Gautama in a rather forced way that drastically reduces the inheritance rights granted to widows. Hence, it is clear that, unlike the vast majority of Dharmaśāstra writers belonging to the twelfth century and later, he strongly opposes a widow's right to inherit.

Jīmūtavāhana

Before concluding our examination of a widow's right to inherit in classical Hindu law, there is one final important text that needs to be discussed: the *Dāyabhāga* of Jīmūtavāhana, a legal digest devoted exclusively to the topic of inheritance. Given the work's topical focus, it is unsurprising that it contains a lengthy discussion of a widow's rights of inheritance. Jīmūtavāhana's date has been the subject of significant scholarly debate. After a careful and thorough examination of the relevant evidence and scholarly arguments, Ludo Rocher (2002, 9–24) concludes that he is likely an approximate contemporary of Vijñāneśvara (c. 1075–1125 CE). This seems to be a prudent position to adopt. Judging solely from the perspective of a widow's right to inherit, however, the *Dāyabhāga* appears to be decidedly younger than the *Mitākṣarā*, for it argues directly and at considerable length against a position not attested earlier than Vijñāneśvara's work, namely, that those Smṛtis that make a sonless man's wife his primary heir apply only to cases where a man had received his inheritance prior to his death and not reunited with his coparceners. Beyond this, the *Dāyabhāga* also makes no argument against a number of positions rejected by the *Mitākṣarā*, such as that ascribed to Dhāreśvara; and this arguably suggests that these positions had fallen thoroughly out of favor in Jīmūtavāhana's day, unlike Vijñāneśvara's.

Jīmūtavāhana begins his discussion of a widow's right to inherit by noting that authoritative scriptures are in apparent disagreement on the topic and, as a result, commentators are in disagreement as well (11.1.1). Thereafter, he cites a number of Smṛtis that make a sonless man's wife the primary heir to his wealth (11.1.2–5) and refutes the argument that such Smṛtis apply only to wealth sufficient for a woman's maintenance (11.1.6–14). This argument, which we have already encountered several times, Jīmūtavāhana refutes on essentially two grounds. First, it entails the hermeneutic fallacy of construing the word "wealth" in certain key Smṛti passages (YDh 2.139–40, ViDh 17.4–13) in two different ways, namely, as denoting wealth merely sufficient for maintenance in the case of wives and daughters, but as denoting wealth in general in the case of all other heirs.[66] Second, there is a passage ascribed to Vṛddha Manu, which explicitly states that a man's wife should inherit his entire share of inheritance.[67]

After citing a selection of Smṛtis that make a sonless man's wife his primary heir and refuting the argument that these apply only to a limited amount of wealth, Jīmūtavāhana (11.1.15–18) then cites two seemingly contradictory Smṛti texts that make a sonless man's brothers his primary heirs. The first of these is the following passage, which Jīmūtavāhana attributes to the sages Śaṅkha, Likhita, Paiṭhīnasi, and Yama[68]:

> The property of a sonless man who has gone to heaven belongs to his brothers. In their absence, his parents should take it or else his senior wife should.
>
> *svaryātasya hy aputrasya bhrātṛgāmi dravyam | tadabhāve pitarau hareyātāṃ jyeṣṭhā vā patnī |*

The second passage supporting a brother's right to inherit, which is ascribed to Devala, reads:

> The uterine brothers of a sonless man should inherit his estate; or else his daughters of equal status should; or else his father, if he stills lives, his

[66] *Dāyabhāga* 11.1.6: "And one should not argue that those statements that make a sonless man's wife his heir grant her the right only to enough wealth as is necessary for her maintenance, for it is illogical to construe the word 'wealth,' which occurs only once in these statements, to have two different senses, that is, as denoting less than all of a man's wealth in the case of his wife, but as denoting all of his wealth in the case of his brothers and the rest." (*na ca vartanopayukta-dhanamātrādhikārārthaṃ patnīvacanaṃ vācyam | sakṛcchrutadhanapadasya patnyapekṣam akṛtsnaparatvaṃ kṛtsnaparatvaṃ ca bhrātrādyapekṣam iti tātparyabhe[da]syānyāyyatvāt* |) Note that this is essentially the same as Vijñāneśvara's refutation of this argument on the grounds that it entails *vidhivaiṣamya*.

[67] See *Dāyabhāga* 11.1.7. For a citation of the full passage of Vṛddha Manu, see the section "Vijñāneśvara" in this chapter. Beyond this, Jīmūtavāhana (11.1.8–14) argues that the word "share" (*aṃśa*) in Vṛddha Manu must refer to the husband's share of inheritance (i.e., his estate), not the wife's.

[68] The *Mitākṣarā* cites this same passage, but ascribes it only to Śaṅkha.

brothers of the same caste, his mother, and his wife, in order. In the absence of such relatives, those who live with him should inherit his estate.

tato dāyam aputrasya vibhajeran sahodarāḥ |
tulyā duhitaro vāpi dhriyamāṇaḥ pitāpi vā ||
savarṇā bhrātaro mātā bhāryā ceti yathākramam |
teṣām abhāve gṛhṇīyuḥ kulyānāṃ sahavāsinaḥ ||

Thus, by juxtaposing those Smṛtis that make a sonless man's wife his primary heir with those that make his brothers his primary heirs, Jīmūtavāhana illustrates the serious exegetical challenge faced by Hindu jurists, trying to determine the proper rules of inheritance for a sonless man's estate.

In typical Brahmanical fashion, Jīmūtavāhana then presents and refutes a wrong way to harmonize the scriptures regarding a widow's right to inherit before presenting his own preferred way of harmonizing them. And the primary wrong way to harmonize the scriptures that he presents is as follows:

Some people harmonize the scriptures by arguing that a brother's right to inherit first applies to cases where the deceased either had not received his inheritance or had reunited with his coparceners, whereas a wife's right to inherit first applies to cases where the deceased had received his inheritance and had not reunited with his coparceners.

atra kecid avibhaktasaṃsṛṣṭagocaro bhrātradhikāraḥ prathamaṃ vibhaktāsaṃsṛṣṭagocaraś ca patnyadhikāra iti samādadhati | (*Dāyabhāga* 11.1.19)

As one can see, this way of harmonizing the scriptures is precisely the position first articulated among extant commentators by Vijñāneśvara—a position to which a large number of later commentators, such as Aparārka, Lakṣmīdhara, and Devaṇa Bhaṭṭa, subscribe. Crucially, however, Jīmūtavāhana never mentions Vijñāneśvara or his work by name; nor does he mention the name of any demonstrably later author. Therefore, it is possible that this section of the *Dāyabhāga* does not reflect a familiarity with Vijñāneśvara per se, but rather with a juridical position that predates him, although it is not mentioned in any earlier surviving work. If this is not the case, Jīmūtavāhana must be younger than Vijñāneśvara. In any event, he is clearly familiar with the position that the wife of a sonless man should inherit his entire estate, but only if he died after receiving his inheritance and had not reunited with his coparceners.

Furthermore, Jīmūtavāhana manifestly disagrees with this way of harmonizing the scriptures and, in fact, argues against it at great length. His refutation begins:

> This position conflicts with Bṛhasapti, when he states:
>
> > If brothers who have received their inheritances resume living jointly out of mutual affection, then no one among them has the status of eldest if they partition their property again. If one of them dies or in any way becomes a renunciant, his share is not lost, but rather assigned to a uterine brother. And if he has a sister, she should receive a portion of that. This is the law for a man without children, wife, or father. However, if among reunited brothers one in particular acquires wealth through his knowledge, bravery, or the like, then he should be granted a double share and the rest should get equal shares.
>
> Because both the beginning and end of this passage speak of brothers who have reunited, one must admit that the statement, "his share is not lost, but rather assigned to a uterine brother," which occurs in the middle, pertains to reunited coparceners. But the author also makes clear that a reunited uterine brother has a right to a man's property only in the absence of a son, daughter, wife, and father, as he states in the passage: "This is the law for a man without children, wife, or father." So how can such a brother bar a man's wife from inheriting his estate? Moreover, consider the statement that a man's share "is not lost." It only makes sense to say that a man's share "is not lost," when there is reason to worry that it will be lost, because it is not separately recognized, as it mixed together with his other brothers' property, this being the case when a man either had not received his inheritance prior to his death or had reunited with his coparceners. By contrast, what reason is there to worry that the property of a man who received his inheritance and not reunited with his coparceners will be lost, given that it is easily recognized due to its having undergone partition? Therefore, the above statement must pertain to reunited coparceners.

> *tad bṛhaspativiruddhaṃ yad āha—*
>
> > *vibhaktā bhrātaro ye ca saṃprītyaikatra saṃsthitāḥ |*
> > *punar vibhāgakaraṇe teṣāṃ jyaiṣṭhyaṃ na vidyate ||*
> > *yadā kaścit pramīyeta pravrajed vā kathaṃcana |*

> *na lupyate tasya bhāgaḥ sodarasya vidhīyate* ||
> *yā tasya bhaginī sā tu tato 'ṃśaṃ labdhum arhati* |
> *anapatyasya dharmo 'yam abhāryāpitṛkasya ca* ||
> *saṃsṛṣṭānāṃ tu yaḥ kaścid vidyāśauryādinā dhanam* |
> *prāpnoti tasya dātavyo dvaṃśaḥ śeṣāḥ samāṃśinaḥ* ||
>
> *atr[a] prakramopasaṃhārayoḥ saṃsṛṣṭatvakīrtanāt tatsaṃdaṃśapaṭhitaṃ na lupyate tasya bhāgaḥ sodarasya vidhīyata iti vacanaṃ saṃsṛṣṭaviṣayaṃ vācyam* | *tatra anapatyasya dharmo 'yam abhāryāpitṛkasya ceti putraduhitṛpatnīpitṝṇām abhāve saṃsṛṣṭasya sodarabhrātur adhikāraṃ bodhayatīti kathaṃ tasya patnībādhakatvam* | *kiṃ ca na lupyata iti* | *avibhaktatve saṃsṛṣṭatve ca bhrātrantarīyadravyamiśrībhūtasya pṛthagapratītau lopāśaṅkāyāṃ na lupyata iti vacanam upapadyate* | *vibhaktasyāsaṃsṛṣṭasya tu dhane vibhaktatvapratītau kā lopāśaṅkā* | *tasmāt saṃsṛṣṭaviṣayatvam evāmīṣāṃ vacanānām* | (*Dāyabhāga* 11.1.20–23)

As Jīmūtavāhana explains, the statement of Bṛhaspati quoted above concerns inheritance in the case of brothers who have resumed living jointly after receiving their paternal inheritances, that is, reunited coparceners. And it makes uterine brothers heirs only in the absence of sons, daughters, wives, and parents, thereby implying that the estate of a reunited coparcener should devolve to these relatives before his brothers. Hence, Jīmūtavāhana argues, it is impossible to hold—as Vijñāneśvara and others do—that when a man dies after reuniting with his coparceners, his wealth should go to his brothers rather than his wife.

Having thus explained how Bṛhaspati rules out the possibility that a man's brothers should inherit before his wife in cases where he had resumed living jointly with them, Jīmūtavāhana turns to the statements of Śaṅkha and others that seemingly makes a sonless man's brothers his primary heirs:

> Moreover, the position that the statements of Śaṅkha and others, which indicate that a man's brother has a right to his property before his wife, etc., apply specifically to reunited brothers must be justified on the basis of either scripture or reason. Now, this cannot be done on the basis of scripture, because there is no scripture that specifically says this. Furthermore, statements such as Yājñavalkya's (2.142) that a reunited brother inherits the property of a reunited brother are intended to convey the particular details in the event that a man's brothers have a right to his property. Therefore, it is improper to construe them as

intended to convey the general right of a man's brothers to his property. Furthermore, the statement of Bṛhaspati quoted above, which pertains to reunited coparceners, indicates that a man's uterine brother has a right to his property only in the absence of a son, daughter, wife, and father. Hence, given that the statements of Śaṅkha, etc. would conflict with this, it is reasonable to conclude that they apply only to brothers who have not reunited, not to reunited brothers.

kiṃ ca patnyādeḥ pūrvaṃ bhrātradhikārajñāpakaśaṅkhādivacanānāṃ saṃsṛṣṭabhrātṛviṣayatvaṃ vacanād vā nyāyād vā | tatra na tāvad vacanād viśeṣavacanābhāvāt | saṃsṛṣṭinas tu saṃsṛṣṭīty (YDh 2.142) *ādivacanānāṃ tu bhrātradhikārāvasare viśeṣajñāpanaparatvena bhrātradhikāramātrapara-tvānupapatteḥ | anantaropanyastabṛhaspativacanānāṃ ca saṃsṛṣṭaviṣayatve putraduhitṛpatnīpitṛparyantābhāve sodarabhrātradhikārajñāpakatvāt tadvi-ruddhatvād asaṃsṛṣṭaviṣayatvam eva tāvad yuktaṃ na tu saṃsṛṣṭa-viṣayatvam* | (*Dāyabhāga* 11.1.23–24)

Here Jīmūtavāhana first notes that if one wishes to construe scriptural statements, such as that of Śaṅkha, as applying specifically to reunited coparceners, then one must do so on the basis of either scripture itself or logical reasoning. And regarding scripture, he observes that none of the scriptural passages that make a sonless man's brothers his primary heirs give any explicit indication that they apply specifically to reunited coparceners. Of course, there is a verse of Yājñavalkya (2.142), which explicitly states that one reunited brother should inherit the property of another reunited brother. Jīmūtavāhana, however, explains this away by arguing that it is intended to specify merely that if a man has reunited with some of his brothers, then those brothers are entitled to inherit his property before his other brothers, not that they are entitled to inherit his property before all other relatives. Furthermore, he adds that the passage of Bṛhaspati discussed earlier (11.1.20–22) applies specifically to reunited coparceners and explicitly makes a man's brother his heir only if he has no surviving son, daughter, wife, or father. Therefore, it would directly conflict with this authoritative scripture to construe those statements that make a sonless man's brothers his primary heirs as applying to cases involving reunited coparceners.

After showing that scripture cannot justify restricting a widow's right to inherit to cases where her husband had not reunited with his coparceners,

Jīmūtavāhana then presents one reason-based argument that might conceivably justify such a restriction:

> Suppose instead that the position in question is justified on the basis of reason as follows: In the case of reunited brothers, whatever property belongs to one of them belongs to the other as well. Thus, even if one brother dies and his ownership in a property ceases, his living brother's ownership in that property continues. Consequently, that property belongs only to him and not to his deceased brother's widow, for her ownership in the property also ceases due to her husband's death, just as a man's wife does not acquire his property, if he has sons, etc. (i.e., sons' sons or sons' sons' sons).
>
> *atha nyāyād idam abhidhīyate | tathā hi saṃsṛṣṭatve yad ekasya bhrātur dhanaṃ tad aparasyāpi | tatraikasya maraṇena svatvanāśe 'pi jīvatas tatra svāmitvānapāyāt tasyaiva tad bhavati na tu patnyā bhartṛmaraṇena patnīsvatvasyāpi nāśāt | yathā satsu putrādiṣu na taddhanaṃ patnyā iti |* (*Dāyabhāga* 11.1.25)

As one can see, this argument starts with the premise that reunited brothers own all of their property jointly and proceeds by pointing out that if one such brother were to die, his surviving brothers' ownership of his property would continue. Therefore, they should logically be entitled to own or, more precisely, to continue to own their deceased brother's property. As for their dead brother's widow, this argument holds that her ownership in husband's property ends with his death, just as it would if he had left surviving sons.

Unsurprisingly, Jīmūtavāhana does not accept the preceding argument. He refutes it as follows:

> This is a dim-witted argument, for it is not the case that when brothers have reunited, whatever belongs to one of them belongs to the other as well. To the contrary, as I explained at the beginning of this treatise (1.8), each brother owns a part of the property in question, but the precise part is unknown. The entire property does not belong to both brothers, for there is no grounds for imagining that they own the entire property. This argument is also dim-witted, because there is no grounds for holding that a woman's ownership in her husband's property, which originates in their marriage, ceases when her husband dies. Instead, a woman's ownership in her husband's property is understood to cease when her husband has a son

> on account of the scripture prescribing a son's right to his father's property. One might counter that a wife's ownership is understood to cease on account of the scripture prescribing a reunited brother's right to a man's property, but this does not work, for it still has not been established that the scriptures in question apply to reunited brothers. Indeed, this argument entails the following circular reasoning: the scriptures prescribing a brother's right to inherit must apply to reunited brothers, since we know that a wife's ownership in her husband's property ceases if he dies while reunited with his brothers; and we know that a wife's ownership in such cases ceases, because the scriptures prescribing a brother's right to inherit apply to reunited brothers!
>
> *tan mandam | na hi saṃsṛṣṭatve 'pi yad evaikasya tad aparasyāpi | kiṃ tv avijñātaikadeśaviṣayam | tad dvayor na tu samagram eva | samagrasvatvakalpanāpramāṇābhāvād ity uktam ādāv eva | pariṇayanotpannaṃ bhartṛdhane patnyāḥ svāmitvaṃ bhartṛmaraṇān naśyatīty atra ca pramāṇābhāvāt | sati tu putre tadadhikāraśāstrād eva patnīsvatvanāśo 'vagamyate | atrāpi saṃsṛṣṭabhrātradhikāraśāstrāt tadvināśo 'vagamyata iti cen na saṃsṛṣṭabhrātṛgocaratvasyādyāpy asiddheḥ | siddhe hi bhrātṛsaṃsṛṣṭabhartṛmaraṇena patnīsvāmitvanāśe bhrātradhikāraśāstrasya saṃsṛṣṭaviṣayatvam | sati ca tadviṣayatve śāstrasya patnīsvāmitvanāśa itītaretarāśrayatvam |* (*Dāyabhāga* 11.1.26–27)

As one can see, Jīmūtavāhana begins the above passage by flatly denying that reunited coparceners jointly own the entirety of their property. Instead, as explained in the opening chapter of the *Dāyabhāga* (1.8), he holds that each reunited coparcener owns merely a portion of their total joint property, but the precise identity of that portion remains unknown until the property is repartitioned. As a result, Jīmūtavāhana rejects the proposed reason-based argument justifying a reunited brother's status as the primary heir to his reunited brother's property. Moreover, he similarly rejects as baseless the notion that a wife's ownership in her husband's estate, which originates with marriage, ends with her husband's death. He then ends by pointing out the circularity in a certain way of interpreting the relevant texts that might be used to justify the position that he has just refuted.

Following this, Jīmūtavāhana focuses on the fact that, according to the statement of Śaṅkha and others, a sonless man's parents are apparently supposed to inherit his property in the absence of any brothers. In particular, he points out the serious interpretive difficulty that results from this fact, if one construes Śaṅkha's statement as applicable specifically to cases involving reunited coparceners:

> Moreover, if the statements of Śaṅkha, Likhita, and the rest pertain to cases where the deceased either had not received his inheritance or had reunited with his coparceners, then one must construe them to mean that the wealth of a man who had not received his inheritance or had reunited with his coparceners goes to his brothers of the same sort, but when he has no such brother, his parents should take it. This then leads one to wonder whether the parents who take the property are ones who have partitioned their estate and not reunited with their heirs or ones who either have not partitioned their estate or have reunited with their heirs. It cannot be the first option, for parents that have partitioned their estates and not reunited with their heirs are barred from inheriting a man's property by his wife on account of Yājñavalkya's statement (2.139) that starts, "Wife, daughters . . ." So how can they have a right to his property before his wife? Nor is the second option viable, for no one disputes that even when a man has brothers who either have not received their inheritance or have reunited with their coparceners, his father who has not partitioned his estate or has reunited with his heirs inherits his wealth.
>
> Furthermore, when a man has received his inheritance and not reunited with his father or his brother, his father has a right to his wealth before his brothers do for the following reasons: (a) the Veda speaks of the oneness of father and son in that a father furnishes his son with a body, "One's self is, indeed, born as one's son,"[69] and, therefore, a father is master over his son's wealth and body; (b) when a son dies, he enjoys through the rite of joining the ancestors the pair of ancestral offerings that his father offers to his grandfather and great grandfather; and (c) so long as his father lives, his sons (i.e., the deceased's brothers) do not give him monthly ancestral offerings. And just as a man's father has a right to his property before his brothers in this scenario, it is fitting that he should have this right in the opposite scenario as well (i.e., when he had not received his inheritance or had reunited with his father or brother). Alternatively, since there is no difference between a father and a brother when an estate has not undergone

[69] This appears to be a paraphrase of a statement such as AiB 33.1: "(The father) himself is born from himself." (*ātmā hi jajña ātmanaḥ*)

partition or the coparceners have reunited, it is fitting that their right to a man's property should be virtually identical. It is not fitting that his father should receive it only in the absence of a brother.

In addition, if the text means that parents who either have not partitioned their estate or have reunited with their heirs should inherit a sonless man's property, it makes no sense to speak of parents as opposed to just a father, for there can be no question of an estate being partitioned or not partitioned with one's mother. Hence, there can also be no reuniting with her, as Bṛhaspati explains:

> If after receiving his inheritance a man dwells in one place again with his father, brother, or paternal uncle out of affection, he is said to be reunited with them.

By this statement he shows the following about those people, such as fathers, brothers, and paternal uncles, who are by birth undivided heirs to the property acquired by their fathers, grandfathers, etc.: they become reunited, if after receiving their inheritances they nullify their previous partition and out of mutual affection dwell in a single home as members of a single joint household, declaring, "What is yours is mine and what is mine is yours." It is not the case, however, that merchants who do not fit this description, but have merely engaged in a joint venture by combining their wealth are considered reunited. Nor is it the case that divided heirs become reunited by simply combining their properties without making the aforementioned declaration out of mutual affection. Therefore, since it is impossible for one to be reunited with one's mother or an undivided heir together with her, how can one resolve the conflict over who has the right to a sonless man's property when he has brothers as it pertains to his mother?

kiṃ ca śaṅkhalikhitādivacanānām avibhaktasaṃsṛṣṭagocaratve 'vibhaktasya saṃsṛṣṭasya ca dhanaṃ tadvidhabhrātṛgāmi | tasya tu tathāvidhasyābhāve pitarau haretām ity anvayo vācyaḥ | tadā ca vikalpanīyam | kiṃ vibhaktāsaṃsṛṣṭau pitarau gṛhṇīyātām utāvibhaktasaṃsṛṣṭau | na tatra prathamaḥ kalpaḥ | patnī duhitaraś cety (YDh 2.139) *ādinā vibhaktāsaṃsṛṣṭayoḥ pitroḥ patnībādhyatvāt kathaṃ patnītaḥ pūrvaṃ tayor adhikāraḥ | nāpi dvitīyaḥ | avibhaktasaṃsṛṣṭabhrātṛsadbhāve 'py avibhaktasaṃsṛṣṭapitṛgrāhyatvasya sarveṣām avivādāt |*

kiṃ ca yathā pitrā bhrātrā ca vibhaktāsaṃsṛṣṭadhane śarīradātṛtayā ātmā vai jāyate putra ity ekatvaśruter dhanaśarīrayoś ca prabhutvāt tatpitṛdeyapitāmahaprapitāmahapiṇḍadvaye ca sapiṇḍanena mṛtasya bhoktṛtvāj jīvati ca pitari putrāṇāṃ pārvaṇapiṇḍadānābhāvāt bhrātṛbhyo pūrvaṃ pitur adhikāraḥ | tathetaratrāpi yuktaḥ | avibhāgasaṃsargayor vāviśeṣāt pitṛbhrātros tulyavad adhikāro yuktaḥ | na tu bhrātur abhāve pitur iti yuktam |

kiṃ cāvibhaktasaṃsṛṣṭau pitarau gṛhṇīyātām iti dvivacanam anupapannam | mātrā saha vibhāgāvibhāgayor abhāvāt | ata eva saṃsargābhāvo 'pi | yad āha bṛhaspatiḥ—

vibhakto yaḥ punaḥ pitrā bhrātrā caikatra saṃsthitaḥ |
pitṛvyeṇātha vā prītyā sa tu saṃsṛṣṭa ucyate ||

anenaitad darśayati—yeṣām eva hi pitṛbhrātṛpitṛvyādīnāṃ pitṛpitāmahārjitadravyeṇāvibhaktatvam utpattitaḥ saṃbhavati ta eva vibhaktāḥ santaḥ parasparaprītyā yadi pūrvakṛtavibhāgadhvaṃsena yat tava dhanaṃ tan mama yan mama dhanaṃ tat taveti ekagṛha ekagṛhirūpatayā saṃsthitāḥ saṃsṛjyante | na punar anevaṃrūpāṇāṃ dravyasaṃsargamātreṇa saṃbhūya vaṇijām api saṃsargitvam | nāpi vibhaktānāṃ dravyasaṃsargamātreṇa pūrvoktaprītipūrvakābhisaṃdhānaṃ vinā | ataḥ saṃsargitvāvibhaktatvayor mātrā sahāsaṃbhavāt kathaṃ mātṛgato bhrātṛsadbhāvādhikāravirodhaḥ samādheyaḥ | (*Dāyabhāga* 11.1.28–30)

Jīmūtavāhana begins the above passage by asking a question of those who imagine Śaṅkha's statement to apply to the estate of a man who either had not received his inheritance prior to his death or had reunited with his coparceners. Specifically, he asks: are the parents who are supposed to inherit such a man's estate in the absence of brothers understood to be (a) ones who have given the deceased his inheritance and not reunited with him or (b) ones who either have not given the deceased his inheritance or have reunited with him? Jīmūtavāhana then proceeds to demonstrate that both options are untenable and, consequently, that Śaṅkha's statement and other similar ones cannot apply strictly to cases where a man either had not received his inheritance prior to his death or had reunited with his coparceners.

Regarding the first option, Jīmūtavāhana argues that it is untenable, because Yājñavalkya's statement about the heirs of a sonless man (2.139–40) grants a man's wife the right to inherit before his parents. Therefore, since this statement is by all accounts applicable to cases where a man died after receiving his inheritance and had not reunited with his coparceners, he holds that it—not Śaṅkha's statement—must lay down the applicable rule in cases where a man's parents had partitioned their estate prior to his death and not reunited with him.

Regarding the second option, Jīmūtavāhana argues that it is also untenable and this time on the basis of three separate arguments. The first argument is that, at least according to Jīmūtavāhana, it is obvious to all that a sonless man's father should inherit his property before his brothers, if the father's estate had not yet been partitioned or it had been and they had all reunited into a single joint household.[70] The second argument is that there are discernible reasons why a man's father is his heir before his brothers in cases where he had received his inheritance and not reunited with his coparceners; and these same reasons hold equally well in cases where a man had not received his inheritance or had reunited with his coparceners. As readers can see, Jīmūtavāhana cites three such reasons: (a) scriptures considers a father to be master over his son and his property; (b) a father helps his son in the hereafter if he dies before him by feeding him through ancestral Śrāddha offerings; and (c) his brothers do not help him in this way through Śrāddha rites so long as his father lives. Here it is worth noting that, in the second and third reasons, Jīmūtavāhana invokes what for him is the guiding principle underlying the entire Dharmaśāstra system of inheritance: the sequence of heirs to a person's property corresponds to the amount of assistance that various people will render to him in the hereafter.[71] Jīmūtavāhana's third and final argument against construing Śaṅkha's statement as involved with considerations of partition and reuniting concerns the fact that it lists a man's parents, rather than only his father, as heirs. The problem with this, as Jīmūtavāhana points out, is that mothers play no part in partition and, thus, can be neither financially separated from nor reunited with their sons.

In this way, Jīmūtavāhana refutes the position of Vijñāneśvara and other authors that a widow's right to inherit is restricted only to cases where her husband had received his inheritance prior to his death and not reunited with his coparceners. One should note, however, that Jīmūtavāhana's refutation focuses largely on showing that a widow is a sonless man's primary heir even when he had reunited with his coparceners.[72] It makes relatively little effort

[70] If a father has not yet partitioned his estate, then his son will not yet be in possession of his inheritance. So it is possible to understand why, in such a situation, a son's property would devolve to his father: the bulk of his property (i.e., anything that he did not acquire on his own) would still belong to his father. However, it is not so obvious—at least to a modern reader—why a son's property would devolve first to his father in cases where he had reunited with both his father and his brothers.

[71] For a discussion of this aspect of Jīmūtavāhana's thought, see Dutta (2016, 134–78; 2018).

[72] Note that most of the *Dāyabhāga*'s refutation of the position held by Vijñāneśvara (11.1.20–27) concerns only cases where the deceased was *saṃsṛṣṭin* ("reunited with his coparceners"), not with cases where he was *avibhakta* ("one who had not yet received his inheritance").

to establish that a widow should inherit her husband's estate when he had not yet received his inheritance from his father, although Jīmūtavāhana seems to support this right.[73] And this makes sense, for the estate of a man who had not received his paternal inheritance would likely have been fairly small in most cases. As for the share of his father's estate that the deceased would have received had he not died prematurely, the position of Jīmūtavāhana, like other Dharmaśāstra authors, appears to be that it should devolve to the brothers of the deceased rather than to his wife, for Dharmaśāstra literature makes no allowance for a woman to inherit her father-in-law's property. Nevertheless, in eliminating significant restrictions on a widow's right to inherit, Jīmūṭavāhana grants women uniquely strong rights of inheritance among authors within the Hindu legal tradition, as scholars have long noted.[74]

Immediately after rebutting the widely held restriction on a widow's right to inherit only to cases where her husband had received his inheritance and not reunited with his coparceners, Jīmūtavāhana states his own preferred way of harmonizing the relevant Smṛtis:

> Now, wise men harmonize the scriptures as follows: a wife's right to a man's property merely in the absence of sons, etc. (i.e., sons' sons and sons' sons' sons) is clearly understood from statements such as Viṣṇu's (17.4).
>
> *saṃprati dhīmadbhiḥ samādhīyate | tatra viṣṇvādivacanebhyaḥ putrādyabhāvamātreṇa patnyadhikāraḥ spaṣṭam avagamyate |* (*Dāyabhāga* 11.1.31)

Following this, Jīmūtavāhana engages in a rather long digression (11.1.31–42) where he explains why a man's sons, sons' sons, and sons' sons' sons all inherit his property before his wife. In short, he argues that a man's direct patrilineal descendants—at least for three generations—render him uniquely strong assistance in the hereafter in that they will provide him with sustenance through Śrāddha offerings after his death.

[73] This is perhaps most clearly expressed at *Dāyabhāga* 11.1.46, where Jīmūtavāhana declares the wife of a sonless man to have an unqualified right to her husband's entire estate.

[74] It is noteworthy that later Bengali authors, such as Raghunandana (*Dāyatattva* pp. 188–93), grant widows similarly strong rights of inheritance, although Hindu jurists outside of Bengal never seem to have done so.

Jīmūtavāhana then explains why a man's wife is entitled to inherit his property in the absence of sons and other direct male descendants:

> Because she helps her husband in the next world in the absence of male offspring down to great grandsons by keeping her marital vow and the like since becoming a widow, a man's wife is next in order after his sons and other direct male descendants. Thus, in their absence, she is entitled to his wealth. Vyāsa says as much:
>
> > When her husband has died, a virtuous woman should adhere to a vow of celibacy and each day, having bathed, offer him handfuls of water. She should daily worship the gods with devotion and regularly propitiate Viṣṇu and fast. She should give gifts to the greatest of Brahmins in order to increase her merit and perform assorted fasts prescribed in the scriptures, O good lady. A woman who is constantly devoted to the law, O fair-faced lady, rescues both her husband residing in another world and herself.
>
> One learns from statements such as this that a wife also rescues her husband from hell. Conversely, by doing things she should not do on account of poverty, she also casts her husband into hell, as they share together in the rewards of their good and bad actions. Hence, when his wealth benefits her, it in fact benefits him, its previous owner. Thus, it is fitting that a man's wife becomes the owner of his property.

prapautraparyantābhāve tu vaidhavyāt prabhṛti vratādinā bhartuḥ paralokahitācaraṇena putrādibhyo jaghanyeti teṣām abhāve dhanādhikāriṇī patnī | tad āha vyāsaḥ—

mṛte bhartari sādhvī strī brahmacaryavrate sthitā |
snātā pratidinaṃ dadyāt svabhartre salilāñjalīn ||
kuryāc cānudinaṃ bhaktyā devatānāṃ ca pūjanam |
viṣṇor ārādhanaṃ caiva kuryān nityam upoṣitā ||
dānāni vipramukhyebhyo dadyāt puṇyavivṛddhaye |
upavāsāṃś ca vividhān kuryāc chāstroditān śubhe ||
lokāntarasthaṃ bhartāram ātmānaṃ ca varānane |
tārayaty ubhayaṃ nārī nityaṃ dharmaparāyaṇā ||

tad evamādibhir vacanaiḥ patnyā api narakanistārakatvaśruteḥ dhanahīnatayā vākāryaṃ kurvatī puṇyāpuṇyaphalasamatvena bhartāram api pātayatīti tadarthaṃ taddhanaṃ pūrvasvāmyartham eva bhavatīti yuktaṃ patnyāḥ svāmyam | (*Dāyabhāga* 11.1.43–44)

Here, citing a statement of Vyāsa as support, Jīmūtavāhana argues that a man's widow is able to help him in the next world by remaining celibate and engaging in an array of pious activities, such as fasting, giving gifts to Brahmins, and venerating the gods. Thus, although a widow cannot make Śrāddha offerings to her deceased husband as his sons, grandsons, and great grandsons are required to do, she can nevertheless provide him with enormous soteriological benefits and is, therefore, a worthy heir. Moreover, as Jīmūtavāhana points out, since a husband and wife are held to share equally in the karmic results of all their actions, whether good or bad, a woman who out of poverty is driven to engage in prohibited behaviors will bring her husband considerable harm in the hereafter. Hence, by making her the heir to his estate a man may be able to avoid such potential calamity.

Having established and justified a widow's right to her husband's property in the absence of direct male descendants, Jīmūtavāhana then explains how to properly interpret the troubling statement ascribed to Śaṅkha, Likhita, Paiṭhīnasi, and Yama (p. 141) that seemingly makes a man's brothers his primary heirs:

> Therefore, in the statement of Śaṅkha and the others, one must construe together words that are separated from each other so that the passage means: "The property of a sonless man who has gone to heaven his senior wife should take. In her absence, his parents should take it. And in their absence, it belongs to his brothers." The phrase "in their/her absence," which occurs in the middle of the passage, is connected with the previous statement that a sonless man's property "belongs to his brothers" and with the subsequent statement that "his parents should take it," for this avoids conflict with other scriptures and the logic has been stated. One should not construe Śaṅkha's statement as applying to cases where the deceased either had not received his inheritance prior to his death or had reunited with his coparceners, as the wording of the text contains no indication of this. Hence, as advocated by Jitendriya, one should respect a widow's right to inherit her sonless husband's entire estate without qualification, irrespective of whether he had received his inheritance prior to his death and so forth.

ataḥ śaṅkhādivacaneṣu vyavahitayojanā kāryā | aputrasya svaryātasya dhanaṃ jyeṣṭhā patnī haret | tadabhāve pitarau haretām | tadabhāve bhrātṛgāmīti | tadabhāva iti madhyapaṭhitaṃ pūrveṇa bhrātṛgāmity anena pareṇa ca pitarau haretām ity anena saṃbadhyate avirodhān nyāyasya coktatvāt | na tv aśrutāvibhaktasaṃsṛṣṭagocaratvakalpanā | ato 'viśeṣeṇaiva vibhaktatvādyanapekṣayaivāputrasya bhartuḥ kṛtsnadhane patnyadhikāro jitendriyanigadita ādaraṇīyaḥ | (*Dāyabhāga* 11.1.45–46)

Here Jīmūtavāhana proposes an extremely forced reading of Śaṅkha's text, which requires among other things that one construe the phrase "senior wife" (*jyeṣṭhā patnī*) first in the list of heirs, although it occurs last in the passage. Clearly he does this with the sole aim of eliminating the text's obvious conflict with those Smṛtis that make a sonless man's wife his primary heir—works with which Jīmūtavāhana personally agrees. Incidentally, we also learn from this passage the interesting detail that, even before Jīmūtavāhana, a jurist named Jitendriya, about whom virtually nothing is known,[75] had already opposed restricting a widow's right to inherit to cases where her husband had received his inheritance prior to his death and had not reunited with his coparceners.

After this, Jīmūtavāhana engages in a digression where he explains—on the basis of Śaṅkha's stipulation that a man's "senior wife" should inherit—that, in order to inherit her husband's property, a woman must be of the same social class as her husband or, failing that, of just one social class lower.[76] Beyond this, he argues that the Śūdra wife of a twice-born man can never inherit his property (11.1.47) and explains those statements of Nārada and others that prescribe mere maintenance for a sonless man's women to be applicable only to his wives of lower status, who do not qualify as fully entitled wives or *patnīs*.[77]

Having thus explained how to properly interpret the problematic statement of Śaṅkha and others, Jīmūtavāhana then turns to the other passage that he cited earlier in the *Dāyabhāga* (11.1.17) as an example of a text that seemingly grants a man's brothers and other relatives the right to inherit

[75] See Kane (1962, 1:593–95).

[76] See, e.g., *Dāyabhāga* 11.1.47: "And the status of 'wife' (*patnī*) belongs firstly to a spouse of the highest social class, for the right to inherit is granted to a man's 'senior wife' and seniority here corresponds to the order of the social classes." (*patnītvaṃ ca prathamam uttamavarṇāyāḥ | jyeṣṭhā patnīty abhidhānād varṇakrameṇa jyeṣṭhatvāt* |)

[77] *Dāyabhāga* 11.1.48: "Hence, because some women, although properly married, do not qualify as 'wives' (*patnī*), Nārada's statement (13.24–25) applies to them." (*ataḥ pariṇītastrīṇām apy apatnītvāt tadabhiprāyeṇa nāradavacanam* |) On the term *patnī* and its requirement that a woman be qualified to participate in sacrificial rites, see the section "Viśvarūpa" in Chapter 1. It is noteworthy that later on Jīmūtavāhana (11.1.52) rejects the position, endorsed by Vijñāneśvara, that statements prescribing maintenance apply only to "kept women" (*avaruddhastrī*): "The interpretation that those statements that prescribe maintenance apply only to kept women whom a man has not married ought to be rejected as a favor to his lawfully wedded wives." (*yad apy anūḍhāvaruddhābhiprāyaṃ vartanavacanaṃ varṇitaṃ tad api dharmapatnīnām anugrahārtham iti heyam eva* |)

before his wives.[78] This passage, which is ascribed to Devala, he explains away as follows:

> In that statement, the order in which the group of relatives, starting with uterine brother and ending with wife, is written down is not intended to convey the order in which a man's relatives acquire a right to his estate, for that would conflict with the statements of Viṣṇu (17.4–13) and others. To the contrary, the meaning of the statement is that these relatives should inherit a sonless man's property in the order laid down by Viṣṇu and others. In order to make clear that there is no importance to the order in which he lists the various relatives, Devala uses the phrase "or else" in two places, saying "or else his daughters" and "or else his father." And this phrase should be carried over to the other relatives he lists as well. In this way, by saying "either his uterine brothers, or else his daughters, or else his father," Devala shows that he places no importance on the order in which he lists the various relatives.
>
> *tatrāpi sahodarādibhāryāntasya likhanakramo nādhikārakramārthaḥ viṣṇvādivirodhāt | kiṃ tu viṣṇvādyuktakrameṇa gṛhṇīyur ity etadarthaḥ | likhanakrame 'nāsthāvyañjanārtham eva duhitaro vāpi pitāpi vety api vāśabdam ubhayatra prayuktavān | tac cānyatrāpy anuṣajyate | tena sahodarā vā duhitaro vā pitā vety anāsthā kīrtanakramasya devalena darśitā* | (*Dāyabhāga* 11.1.50)

Here Jīmūtavāhana argues that Devala's statement is not intended to lay down the sequence of heirs to a sonless man's property, but instead simply to provide examples of possible heirs. And as support for this interpretation, he points to Devala's repeated use of the word "or" (*vā*) in the passage.

Finally, let us turn to the issue of the limitations placed upon a widow's right to alienate and otherwise use the property that she inherits from her husband. Like the *Smṛticandrikā* (*Vyavahārakāṇḍa*, p. 677), the *Dāyabhāga* broadly denies a widow the legal authority to alienate any wealth that she has inherited from her husband. However, Jīmūtavāhana's text elaborates upon this issue in markedly greater detail than Devaṇa Bhaṭṭa's and also places significant restrictions on the ways in which a widow can simply enjoy the use of—not only alienate—property that she inherited from her husband. Hence, although Jīmūtavāhana grants widows uniquely strong rights of inheritance,

[78] For the full citation of this passage, see above.

he severely limits their ability to use and alienate their inherited wealth. His discussion of the topic begins:

> A wife can merely enjoy the use of her husband's wealth. She can not give it away, offer it as collateral, or sell it. Kātyāyāna explains this:
>
> > If she preserves her husband's bed, resides with an elder, and is forbearing, a sonless woman may enjoy her husband's property until her death. After that, other heirs receive it.
>
> Thus, residing with an elder, such as her father-in-law, in other words, with her husband's family, a woman can enjoy the use of her husband's property for as long as she lives, but she cannot give it away, offer it as collateral, or sell it as she wants, as she could women's property. And after her death, those who have a right to a man's property in the absence of a wife, such as his daughters, should receive it. Other relatives, however, do not receive it, for they come after a man's daughters, etc. and, thus, it is improper that they could bar them, as it is the wife alone who bars a man's daughters and so forth. And it is also improper that they could bar daughters, etc., given that their inability to bar applies equally to cases where a widow's right to a property never came into effect and to cases where it has come to end. Moreover, those entitled to inherit women's property do not receive the property in question, since such heirs pertain only to women's property and the above statement of Kātyāyana would become redundant, given that he himself lays down in other statements those persons entitled to inherit women's property. Hence, just as statements, such as "Wife, daughters, . . ." (YDh 2.139), designate each subsequent member of this list as entitled to inherit in the absence of all prior members and these people inherit in cases where a wife's right to a property never came into effect, so they also inherit whatever is left over after being used by a wife whose right to a property has come into effect, when her right has come to an end.
>
> *patnī ca bhartṛdhanaṃ bhuñjītaiva paraṃ na tu tasya dānādhānavikrayān kartum arhati | tad āha kātyāyanaḥ—*
>
> > *aputrā śayanaṃ bhartuḥ pālayantī gurau sthitā |*
> > *bhuñjītā maraṇāt kṣāntā dāyādā ūrdhvam āpnuyuḥ ||*
>
> *gurau śvaśurādau bhartṛkule sthitā yāvajjīvaṃ bhartṛdhanaṃ bhuñjīta | na tu strīdhanavat svacchandaṃ dānādhānavikrayān api kurvīta | tasyāṃ tu mṛtāyāṃ patnyabhāve ye duhitrādayo dāyādhikāriṇas*

te gṛhṇīyuḥ | na punar jñātayaḥ | teṣāṃ duhitrādibhyo jaghanyatvāt tadbādhakatvānupapatteḥ | patnī hi teṣāṃ bādhikā | tadadhikārasya prāgabhāve pradhvaṃse ca bādhakābhāvasyāviśeṣād bādhānupapatteḥ | nāpi strīdhanādhikāriṇo gṛhṇīyuḥ | teṣāṃ strīdhanaviṣayatvāt | kātyāyanenaiva ca strīdhanādhikāriṇāṃ vacanāntarair uktatvāt punaruktatvāpatteḥ | ataḥ patnī duhitaraś cety (YDh 2.139) *ādinā ye pūrvapūrvasyābhāve parabhūtādhikāriṇo nirdiṣṭās te yathā patnyadhikāraprāgabhāve gṛhṇīyus tathā jātādhikārāyāḥ patnyā adhikārapradhvaṃse 'pi bhogāvaśiṣṭaṃ gṛhṇīyuḥ* | (*Dāyabhāga* 11.1.56–59)

Here, like Devaṇa Bhaṭṭa, Jīmūtavāhana argues that widows can only enjoy the use of—not give away, mortgage, or sell—their husbands' estates. In this regard he notes that wealth which a woman has inherited from her husband differs considerably from so-called women's property or *strīdhana*, which a woman has much greater freedom to use and to alienate. While on the topic of this distinction, Jīmūtavāhana also makes the important point that the sequence of heirs to *strīdhana* is completely different from that to property that a woman has inherited from her husband—property that does not transform into *strīdhana* simply by virtue of a woman taking possession of it. Specifically, according to Jīmūtavāhana, a widow's right to her husband's estate that has come to an end (e.g., due to death) is no different from a widow's right to her husband's property that never came into effect (e.g., because she died before her husband). Therefore, if one wishes to understand who should inherit the property of a sonless man that has devolved to his wife upon his wife's death, one should simply consult once more Yājñavalkya's list of heirs to a sonless man's estate (2.139–40) and proceed as though his wife's right to his estate had never come into effect.[79]

After the above passage, Jīmūtavāhana proceeds to further explain how a widow can enjoy the use of her husband's property:

Even when it comes to using her husband's property, a widow is permitted only to use as much as is appropriate for her bodily sustenance, for she helps her husband simply by sustaining her body, not by dressing in fine clothes

[79] Like the wealth of a sonless man, *strīdhana* devolves from wife to daughter. In the absence of daughters, however, it devolves along markedly different lines than a sonless man's estate. For Jīmūtavāhana's understanding of this, see *Dāyabhāga* 4.3.1–42.

and the like. And, thus, she is even permitted to give away her husband's property or otherwise alienate it in order to pay for his funerary rites and so forth. This is why it is said (MBh 13.47.24) that "women should not take away" from the wealth of their husbands. "Taking away" here refers to not using the wealth for its (prior) owner's benefit. Hence, a widow is permitted even to offer her husband's wealth as collateral if she is unable to sustain herself. And she is also able to sell it if she is similarly unable, for the underlying logic is no different.

upabhoge 'pi na sūkṣmavastraparidhānādinā kiṃ tu svaśarīradhāraṇena patyur upakārakatvād dehadhāraṇocitopabhogānujñānam | evaṃ ca patyur aurdhvadehikakriyādyarthaṃ dānādikam apy anumatam | ata eva nāpahāraṃ striyaḥ kuryur ity (MBh 13.47.24) *āha | apahāraś ca dhanasvāmyanupayoge bhavati | ata eva vartanāśaktāv ādhānam apy anumatam | tatrāpy aśaktau vikrayaṇam api nyāyasyāviśeṣāt* | (*Dāyabhāga* 11.1.61–62)

Thus, according to Jīmūtavāhana, a widow can use wealth that she inherited from her husband only to provide for her mere sustenance, not to purchase fancy clothes or other luxuries. And he justifies this restriction on the basis of his position that a man's heirs must use his wealth to benefit him in the hereafter. Therefore, since a man's widow only needs to be alive, not pampered or even too comfortable, to perform the activities that will help him in his next life, she may not spend his wealth on material comforts. And this restriction also makes sense, given that the institution of the classical Hindu widow ascetic had likely developed by Jīmūtavāhana's time, as I will explain in the following chapter. Despite this restriction on a widow's ability to enjoy the use of her husband's estate, however, Jīmūtavāhana allows a woman to give, mortgage, or even sell her husband's estate in order maintain herself, if necessary. Moreover, in keeping with his principles, he allows a widow to use her husband's estate to pay for the performance of his funerary rites and presumably other pious activities that will benefit him soteriologically. To this Jīmūtavāhana subsequently adds that a widow can also give wealth to her husband's kinsmen as part of the performance of his funerary rites, but should not give to members of her natal family without the permission of her affines (11.1.63–64). In addition, he states that a widow may use a quarter of her husband's estate to pay for the wedding of an unmarried daughter (11.1.66).

Conclusion

Thus, to summarize how opinions on a widow's right to inherit evolved over time within the Hindu legal tradition from the third century BCE to the twelfth century CE and beyond, it is useful to group the relevant texts into three periods. In the first period, all authors within the Dharmaśāstra tradition, with the minor exception of Gautama (28.21), are in broad agreement that a widow has no right whatsoever to inherit her husband's property. Following this, the second period begins in the fourth or fifth century CE with the *Yājñavalkya Dharmaśāstra* (2.139–40), a text that unambiguously makes a widow her husband's primary heir if he dies without sons. This is a period that covers largely the second half of the first millennium and is characterized by intense debate and disagreement with a number of Smṛtis, such as those ascribed to Viṣṇu (17.4) and Bṛhaspati (26.93–94), strongly advocating for a widow's right to inherit, but several commentators, such as Viśvarūpa and Dhāreśvara, denying this right by greatly diminishing the scope and impact of these Smṛtis. The third and final period begins with the *Mitākṣarā* of Vijñāneśvara, a work composed around the turn of the twelfth century. As I have shown, this is a text that grants a sonless man's wife the right to inherit the entirety of his estate, provided only that he has received his paternal inheritance and is not living jointly with his brothers at the time of his death. Thus, the *Mitākṣarā* grants fairly strong inheritance rights to widows. And, importantly, almost all Dharmaśāstra works composed after it acknowledge similarly strong rights for such women. Indeed, the *Dāyabhāga* of Jīmūtavāhana even goes so far as to eliminate the widespread requirement that, in order for a woman to inherit her husband's estate, he must have received his inheritance and not reunited with coparceners, although the *Dāyabhāga* appears to be rather unique in this regard and still places significant restrictions on a widow's ability to use her husband's wealth. Therefore, in short, the history of a widow's right to inherit in classical Hindu law is—from our modern perspective—a happy tale of increasing rights and financial independence for women (albeit still well within confines of a deep-rooted patriarchy).

Moreover, certain evidence strongly suggests that the twelfth century was a turning point for widows' rights of inheritance not only within the Dharmaśāstra tradition but also within South Asian society at large. For instance, there is an inscription in the Kannada language dated to 1178, which records a command of the king Saṅkamadeva that "if anyone should die without sons, his wife, female children, divided parents and brothers and their children . . . , and any kinsmen and relatives of the same *gotra*, who might survive, should take possession of all his property, such as bipeds, quadrupeds, coins, grain, house, and fields."[80] Hence, this inscription not only makes the wives of sonless men their primary heirs but also lays down exactly the same sequence of heirs to a man's estate as Yājñavalkya (2.139–40) and all of the many commentators that follow him do. Therefore, it suggests the direct influence of Dharmaśāstra on the actual practice of inheritance law in twelfth-century Karnataka. And such influence is made even more likely by the fact that the inscription under discussion was composed specifically in the Bijapur district, which is only about 100 miles from the city of Kalyāṇa, where the *Mitākṣarā* was composed less than a century earlier. Beyond this, the very composition of such an inscription also implies that, prior to it, locally a man's property did not devolve to his wives in the absence of sons. Thus, this inscription supports the position that Dharmaśāstra literature on a widow's right to inherit is not wholly divorced from social reality, but rather reflects actual historical changes in cultural norms and legal practices.

Another piece of evidence that widows' rights of inheritance increased dramatically during the twelfth century comes from Jain hagiographies of King Kumārapāla of Gujarat, who lived between the years 1143 and 1172. Specifically, the *Dvyāśrayakāvya* (20.38–102) of the famed Jain polymath Hemacandra, an advisor of Kumārapāla, describes how the king radically broke from tradition and began granting sonless widows the right to inherit their husbands' estates. Moreover, several later Jain works recount this same episode, only in much more concise and straightforward language. Note, for example, the following passage of Merutuṅga's *Prabandhacintāmaṇi* (p. 86), written in 1304:

> As King Kumārapāla was accepting the twelve lay vows rooted in righteousness and the third of these vows, i.e., abstaining from taking what is not given, was being explained to him, he was made aware that the misdeed of taking widows' property was his only cause of sin in this regard. So he summoned the group of administrators charged with this; tore up their ledgers, which recorded widows' property to the sum of seventy-two

[80] *Epigraphia Indica*, vol. 5, pp. 26–28. The translation given is that of J. F. Fleet, the inscription's editor.

lakhs; and released that property. Then, when he had released it, wise men praised him:

> Even past kings like Raghu, Nahuṣa, Nābhāga, and Bharata, who were born during the righteous Kṛta Yuga, never released widows' property. By releasing it today out of compassion, O King Kumārapāla, you have become the crest jewel of great men.

And even Lord Hemacandra congratulated the king:

> By taking the wealth of sonless men, a king becomes a son. By happily releasing it instead, you have truly become a grandfather among kings.

saṃyaktvamūlāni dvādaśavratāny aṅgīkurvan adattādānaparihārarūpe tṛtīyavrate vyākhyāyamāne rudatīvittadoṣān pāpaikanibandhanān jñāpito nṛpas tadadhikṛtaṃ pañcakulam ākārya dvāsaptatilakṣapramāṇaṃ tadīyapaṭṭakaṃ vipāṭya mumoca | tasmin mukte

na yan muktaṃ pūrvai raghunahuṣanābhāgabharata-
prabhṛtyurvīnāthaiḥ kṛtayugakṛtotpattibhir api |
vimuñcan kāruṇyāt tad api rudatīvittam adhunā
kumārakṣmāpāla tvam asi mahatāṃ mastakamaṇiḥ ||

iti vidvadbhiḥ stūyamāne

aputrāṇāṃ dhanaṃ gṛhṇan putro bhavati pārthivaḥ |
tvaṃ tu saṃtoṣato muñcan satyaṃ rājapitāmahaḥ ||

iti prabhur api sa nṛpatim anumodayāṃcakre |

Passages such as this one provide strong evidence that, during the twelfth century, the widows of sonless men gained the right to inherit their husbands' estates in Gujarat, much as appears to have happened elsewhere in South Asia. Of course, Jain authors like Hemacandra and Merutuṅga attribute this change in inheritance rights to the influence of Jain doctrine and present it as a unique legal innovation of the devout Jain, King Kumārapāla. However, there is good reason to doubt the historical accuracy of both of these points and instead to view them as a reflection of sectarian Jain interests, for as we have seen, numerous Brahmanical authors of the twelfth century likewise support a widow's right to inherit her husband's estate, such as Aparārka, a contemporary of Kumārapāla, who ruled the North Konkan just south of modern-day Gujarat.

Nevertheless, evidence from Jain sources should make us hesitant to attribute widows' increasing rights of inheritance during the twelfth and later centuries specifically to the influence of Dharmaśāstra. Perhaps a more prudent position would be to hypothesize a more nebulous and wide-ranging change in the moral and legal zeitgeist throughout much of the subcontinent—a change that is reflected equally in Jain hagiographies and Dharmaśāstra literature, but that is reducible to neither one. This hypothetical change in the zeitgeist would begin in roughly the middle of the first millennium CE, as reflected in the *Yājñavalkya Dharmaśāstra*, but gain special momentum in the twelfth century. It would fundamentally be a change in male attitudes toward women's ownership of sizeable independent wealth and in particular constitute a greater tolerance for it.

In any case, it seems highly unlikely that the increase in widows' inheritance rights in medieval South Asia was actually the result of either the Jain doctrine of not taking what has not been given or the simple conviction that certain new ways of harmonizing Brahmanical scriptures on inheritance were intellectually more convincing than earlier ones. Instead, it would seem that broader social forces must underlay this gradual, yet monumental shift in opinion regarding widows. Therefore, it is worth speculating about what these social forces might have been, even if solid evidence upon which to ground such speculation remains elusive.

Over eighty years ago, A. S. Altekar (1938, 6–7) argued that the prohibiting of *niyoga* and widow remarriage historically led to a marked increase in the number of sonless and, therefore, indigent widows in Indian society and that widows' rights of inheritance increased in order to remedy this situation. That is, he proposed that the societal prohibition against *niyoga* and widow remarriage was the primary cause of widows' increasing rights of inheritance in Dharmaśāstra literature. And it certainly makes sense that the disappearance of remarriage as an option for widows would have made them more viable heirs in the minds of many men, since without widow remarriage there would be little fear of a man's wealth passing to another man outside of his patriline. Moreover, if remarriage was at one time the standard way of ensuring that widowed women were looked after in Brahmanical society, it makes sense that, once widow remarriage became widely condemned, certain Hindu jurists would have devised a new legal strategy to ensure widows' well-being.

Nevertheless, Altekar's argument suffers from the major flaw that widow remarriage appears never to have been widely accepted within Brahmanical society, as demonstrated in Chapter 1. And certainly there is no evidence to suggest that it became markedly less popular in Brahmanical communities shortly before the fifth and twelfth centuries, when belief in a widow's right to inherit became more widespread. Hence, in order for Altekar's argument to be viable, one has to assume without clear evidence that widow remarriage was much more common in medieval Brahmanical society than our textual sources indicate. As for *niyoga*, it is rather doubtful that, prior to its being generally prohibited, the custom resulted in so many children that its disappearance would have led to a significant increase in the number of sonless widows. And, in any case, *niyoga* still appears to have been fairly widely accepted within Brahmanical circles in the fifth century, when Yājñavalkya first grants widows dramatically increased rights of inheritance. In fact, as shown in Chapter 1, Yājñavalkya (1.68–69), like his approximate contemporary Nārada (12.79–88), clearly permits the practice of *niyoga* despite Manu's (9.64–68) earlier opposition to it. Therefore, I remain unconvinced by Altekar's argument that the widespread prohibition against widow remarriage and *niyoga* led to the increasing inheritance rights of widows under classical Hindu law. Unfortunately, however, I do not have a more satisfactory explanation of this development to offer. Nonetheless, there is considerable value, I would argue, in simply tracing the trend toward increasing inheritance rights for widows within Dharmaśāstra, so that we can at least recognize it and consider its underlying causes with as much historical precision as our sources allow.

3
Widow Asceticism

The first chapter of this book presented a largely diachronic account of the treatment of widow remarriage and *niyoga* within Dharmaśāstra. That is, it effectively examined the restrictions that the Hindu legal tradition historically placed upon the sexual behavior of widows—restrictions that increased over time, as we saw, particularly between the seventh and tenth centuries. The second chapter then explored in detail the single most important and controversial aspect of widows' property rights within Dharmaśāstra: their right to inherit their husbands' estates. And there we saw that widows' rights of inheritance markedly increased over time with the fifth-century *Yājñavalkya Dharmaśāstra* and the late eleventh-century *Mitākṣarā* being watershed texts in this historical shift. In this chapter, we now turn to the various restrictions that the Dharmaśāstra tradition placed upon the nonsexual behavior of widows.

In their classical formulation, which we will examine in detail later on, these nonsexual restrictions amount to an extremely austere lifestyle required of widows, according to which all women who outlive their husbands must keep their heads shaved, sleep only on the ground, eat just one meal a day, emaciate their bodies, eschew ornamentation, and perform a rigorous regimen of vows and fasts. Sanskrit authors of the medieval period seem to have widely assumed that widows would adopt such an austere lifestyle. For instance, the twelfth-century author Rāmacandra in his *Kumāravihāraśataka* (verse 45) poetically describes the splendor of one famous Jain temple as follows:

> Myriad rays from the red stones there give the beauty of lac to the tops of lotus-like feet, streaks of vermillion to the middles of foreheads, powders of smooth saffron to sections of the body, a safflower sheen to silken clothes, and delectable betel leaf to petal-like lips—there the women of the city, even those who are widowed, wear the ornaments of married ladies.

śoṇagrāvāṃśujālaiḥ kramakamalatale yāvakaśrīr lalāṭa-
prānte sindūrarekhā masṛṇaghusṛṇabhūr aṅgabhāge 'ṅgarāgaḥ |

Widows Under Hindu Law. David Brick, Oxford University Press. © Oxford University Press 2023.
DOI: 10.1093/oso/9780197664544.003.0004

kausumbhī cīnapaṭṭe dyutir adharadale hāri tāmbūlam itthaṃ
yasmin vaidhavyabhājo 'py avidhavavanitāmaṇḍanāḥ pauranāryaḥ ||

Here the poet clearly assumes that, unlike married women, widows did not adorn themselves in any way or engage in the pleasurable pastime of chewing betel leaf, for he imagines that the glow of the red stones at the Jain temple he describes give usually unadorned widows the sumptuous appearance of married women dressed up in their full attire.

Because austere restrictions of the type alluded to here by Rāmacandra bear so many obvious similarities to those placed on male ascetics, scholars (e.g., Leslie 1991) often conveniently refer to a woman who lives in accordance with them as a "widow ascetic"—a useful practice that I will here adopt. This chapter will trace the historical development of the widow ascetic within Dharmaśāstra from the tradition's inception in roughly the third century BCE until the fourteenth century CE, when the archetypal figure of the classical Hindu widow ascetic becomes established. Unlike in other chapters, however, there will also be a sizable digression where I examine an array of non-Dharmaśāstra sources written in Sanskrit. My reason for doing this is that these sources provide important insights into the practice of widow asceticism within Brahmanical society during the first millennium CE—insights that cannot be gained by examining strictly Dharmaśāstra works. An examination of non-Dharmaśāstra texts, therefore, provides crucial context for understanding developments within the Dharmaśāstra tradition itself.

The Dharmasūtras

An exhaustive search of the four Dharmasūtras, the earliest surviving works of the Dharmaśāstra tradition, reveals that they contain just a single passage that places special lifelong restrictions on the nonsexual behavior of widows. This passage, which comes from quite likely the very youngest of the Dharmasūtras, namely, that of Vasiṣṭha (19.33–34), reads:

> The (deceased) king's wives should receive food and clothing; or if they do not want that, they may go forth.

rājapatnyo grāsācchādanaṃ labheran | anicchantyo vā pravrajeran |

Brahmanical texts frequently use the verb "to go forth" (*pra* + √*vraj*) to denote becoming a world renouncer; and Vasiṣṭha almost certainly uses it in this sense elsewhere in his text.[1] Consequently, the above passage apparently prescribes the lifestyle of a wandering ascetic as an option for widowed queens, when it states that they "may go forth" (*pravrajeran*). This raises the interesting possibility that, like the custom of sati or widow self-immolation, the practice of widow asceticism originated in royal circles and only gradually gained popularity within Brahmanical communities.[2] Nevertheless, it must be stressed that the above passage of Vasiṣṭha clearly does not lay down a mandatory undertaking. Furthermore, it does not express a rule intended for widows in general. Thus, given that it is the only passage in the Dharmasūtras that in any way expresses a lifelong restriction on the nonsexual aspects of a widow's life, it is obvious that the earliest legal literature hardly recognizes the institution of the widow ascetic at all.

Of course, there are several statements in these texts that lay down the well-known Dharmaśāstric prohibition against a woman ever being free from male supervision. Note, for instance, the following verse, which is found in the Dharmasūtras of both Baudhāyana (2.3.45) and Vasiṣṭha (5.3):

> Her father guards her in her childhood, her husband in her youth, and her son in her old age—a woman is never fit for independence.
>
> *pitā rakṣati kaumāre bhartā rakṣati yauvane |*
> *putraś ca sthavire bhāve na strī svātantryam arhati ||*

However, revealing as they are about general Brahmanical attitudes towards women, statements such as this provide no evidence whatsoever of asceticism, much less of the more specific nonsexual restrictions for widows that are the focus of this chapter. They simply state that a widow should live under her sons' supervision, since she is a woman and, like all women, ought never to be independent of male control.

[1] See VaDh 19.23 and 19.37, both of which list a *pravrajita* (lit. "one who has gone forth") as a type of tax-exempt person. The term *pravrajita* there can hardly denote any sort of person other than a renunciant of some type.

[2] On the origin of sati as a royal custom, see Kane (1962, 2:624–29) and Brick (2018, 164–68) as well as Chapter 4 of this book.

Perhaps more revealing than Vasiṣṭha's previously discussed statement about widowed queens are the following statements of Baudhāyana and Vasiṣṭha:

> For a year a woman whose husband has died should avoid honey, meat, liquor, and salt and sleep only on the ground. According to Maudgalya, she should do this for six months.
>
> *saṃvatsaraṃ pretapatnī madhumāṃsamadyalavaṇāni varjayed adhaḥ śayīta | ṣaṇ māsān iti maudgalyaḥ |* (BDh 2.4.7–8)
>
> For six months a woman whose husband has died, performing her vow, should eat only food without added salt and sleep only on the ground.
>
> *pretapatnī ṣaṇ māsān vratacariṇy akṣāralavaṇaṃ bhuñjānādhaḥ śayīta |* (VaDh 17.55–56)

In these passages the authors of the two youngest Dharmasūtras prescribe what amounts to a special period of mourning for all widows, lasting either one year or six months according to various authorities. Baudhāyana, who is in all probability the older of these authors, states that for one year or, according to Maudgalya, six months after her husband's death, a woman should avoid eating meat, honey, and salt, drinking liquor, and sleeping in a bed, whereas Vasiṣṭha holds that for six months, a widow should, as a religious vow, similarly avoid eating salt and sleeping in a bed. As one can see, these passages indicate that at the time of the two youngest surviving Dharmasūtras, there was a customary period of mourning, during which widows were supposed to avoid certain pleasurable activities in which they could thereafter presumably indulge. Nevertheless, there is no indication whatsoever that any of these restrictions placed upon widows were considered lifelong. Indeed, the time limit of either one year or six months set upon them indicates quite unambiguously that they were not.

The Dharmaśāstras

Following Baudhāyana and Vasiṣṭha, rather surprisingly, one finds no evidence within the Dharmaśāstra tradition of a customary period of mourning for widows similar to what these authors prescribe. And, in fact, even more surprisingly, the later Dharmaśāstras of Manu, Yājñavalka, Nārada, Viṣṇu, and Parāśara contain almost no specific restrictions on the non-sexual behavior of widows at all. Regarding the general freedom of widowed women, however, Manu (9.3) and Nārada (13.31) contain the very same verse as Baudhāyana (2.3.45) and Vasiṣṭha (5.3), which was cited earlier and prescribes that widows remain under constant male supervision, specifically under the supervision of their sons. In addition, both Yājñavalkya (1.84) and Viṣṇu (25.12–13) effectively paraphrase this verse. Hence, there appears to have been a continuing consensus within the Dharmaśāstra tradition that widows, like all women, must be carefully watched over by the men in their families. Significantly, there is also nothing to suggest that any later Dharmaśāstra author seriously challenged this consensus.

Beyond this, Nārada (13.27–29) gives a more exhaustive account of the men responsible for supervising a widow's conduct:

> If the husband of a sonless woman dies, his side of the family has control over her. It has the power to appoint her (for leviratic union), watch over her, and maintain her. If her husband's family has died out, has no men left, or can offer her no refuge and her husband has no *sapiṇḍa* relatives, her father's side of the family has control over her. However, if both sides of her family have died out, the king is held to be her supporter. He should provide for her maintenance and restrain her, if she strays from the right path.
>
> *mṛte bhartary aputrāyāḥ patipakṣaḥ prabhuḥ striyāḥ |*
> *viniyogātmarakṣāsu bharaṇe ca sa īśvaraḥ ||*
> *parikṣiṇe patikule nirmanuṣye nirāśraye |*
> *tatsapiṇḍeṣu vāsatsu pitṛpakṣaḥ prabhuḥ striyāḥ ||*
> *pakṣadvayāvasāne tu rājā bhartā smṛtaḥ striyāḥ |*
> *sa tasyā bharaṇaṃ kuryān nigṛhṇīyāt pathaś cyutām ||*

Thus, according to Nārada, a sonless widow should ideally remain under the control of her husband's family. However, if it is unable to provide for her, her father's family is responsible for supervising her; and if neither her husband's nor her father's family is capable of this, the king should assume the responsibility. In this way, a widow is assured of a male guardian no matter her family's surviving members and financial resources. In addition, one can see clearly from the above passage that there are two basic aspects to the duty of supervising a widow, as conceived within Dharmaśāstra. First, her male supervisors or guardians must provide for her material sustenance. And, second, they must ensure that she conducts herself appropriately, presumably because the disreputable behavior of a woman or even the suspicion thereof would impugn her family's honor.[3]

Thus, the surviving Smṛtis of the Dharmaśāstra tradition give us some impression of the prescribed living situation of Brahmanical widows and betray a deep concern that they observe proper conduct. These texts do not, however, offer many specifics as to what the proper conduct of widows looked like beyond the issue of sexual intercourse. Of course, Manu dedicates a sizable passage of six consecutive verses (5.157–62) to the topic of widows, which I cited and discussed in Chapter 1. But despite the length of this passage, a careful consideration of its actual contents reveals that there Manu strives almost entirely to make just one point, namely, that a widow should remain perpetually celibate and absolutely never remarry. The following verse from this passage (MDh 5.158), for instance, conveys precisely this:

> Until death, she should remain forbearing, self-restrained, and celibate, pursuing the unsurpassable law of women devoted to a single husband.
>
> *āsītā maraṇāt kṣāntā niyatā brahmacāriṇī |*
> *yo dharma ekapatnīnāṃ kāṅkṣantī tam anuttamam ||*

Although this verse technically lays down not only that a widow should be celibate until her death but also that she should be forbearing and self-restrained, these latter two qualities are by no means uniquely prescribed for widows. They are rather general virtues that all women—indeed, all people—should strive to cultivate throughout their lives according to the basic Brahmanical worldview. Hence, the real thrust of this verse is simply perpetual celibacy. And this it has in common with the four subsequent verses that Manu devotes to discussing widows (5.159–62).

In fact, it is only in the first of his verses on widows that Manu prescribes what may possibly be interpreted as a special lifelong restriction on the

[3] This is spelled out in straightforward terms at MDh 5.149: "A woman should never seek to be separated from her father, husband, or sons, for by being separated from them she makes both her families (i.e., her natal and affinal families) dishonorable." (*pitrā bhartrā sutair vāpi necched viraham ātmanaḥ | eṣāṃ hi viraheṇa strī garhye kuryād ubhe kule ||*) See also MDh 9.5.

nonsexual behavior of widows, a restriction of a distinctly ascetic nature. This verse (MDh 5.157) reads:

> A woman may emaciate her body as she desires by living on auspicious flowers, roots, and fruits, but she should never even mention the name of another man, when her husband has died.
>
> *kāmaṃ tu kṣapayed dehaṃ puṣpamūlaphalaiḥ śubhaiḥ |*
> *na tu nāmāpi gṛhṇīyāt patyau prete parasya tu ||*

I have here given my earlier translation of this verse from Chapter 1. According to the textual interpretation underlying it, the adverb *kāmam* denotes optionality, as it frequently does. In order to reflect this in English, I have translated it as "as she desires." Hence, according to this interpretation, the above verse conveys the following: a widow should emaciate her body as she wishes by subsisting on only auspicious fruits and vegetables, but she should have absolutely nothing to do with another man. In other words, the verse lays down a sort of optional asceticism for widows, the performance of which was presumably deemed supererogatory or especially meritorious.

Although this interpretation of the verse of Manu given earlier is entirely plausible, a careful reading of it reveals another plausible interpretation, based upon a different construal of the adverb *kāmam*. This interpretation takes *kāmam* not as expressing an option, but instead as expressing a concession, that is, in the well-established sense of "granted" or "admittedly." Thus, according to this interpretation, the verse essentially means the following: granted a widow might have to emaciate her body, being forced to live on auspicious fruits and vegetables, but even in a dire situation like this, she should never take another man. That is, this interpretation does not regard this verse as expressing a restriction on the nonsexual behavior of widows at all. Instead, it takes it as a condemnation of the emaciation of widows, but an even stronger condemnation of widow remarriage.

Furthermore, it is noteworthy that Manu himself seems to use the word *kāmam* to express both optionality and concession at various other places in his text. Most frequently, he uses *kāmam* to indicate that a given statement lays down an optional rule or behavior.[4] However, there are two passages in which *kāmam* seems to have a distinctly concessive meaning:

> A king might admittedly (*kāmam*) have to have someone who lives merely off his birth or a Brahmin in name only expound the law, but he should never have a Śūdra do so.
>
> *jātimātropajīvī vā kāmaṃ syād brāhmaṇabruvaḥ* |
> *dharmapravaktā nṛpater na tu śūdraḥ kathaṃcana* || (MDh 8.20)
>
> His daughter might admittedly (*kāmam*) have to remain in his house until death, though she has reached puberty, but a father should never give her in marriage to a man bereft of virtue.
>
> *kāmam ā maraṇāt tiṣṭhed gṛhe kanyartumaty api* |
> *na caivaināṃ prayacchet tu guṇahīnāya karhicit* || (MDh 9.89)

As one can see, both of the above verses share broadly the same structure. Specifically, each consists fundamentally of two distinct statements. The first statement in each verse lays out an undesirable scenario and contains the adverb *kāmam*, while the second absolutely prohibits an even worse scenario and contains the particle *tu* ("but"). Therefore, the adverb *kāmam* in both of these verses would appear to express a concession, unless one makes the dubious assumption that, in Manu's opinion, a marriageable woman is perfectly entitled not to marry or that a king is likewise entitled to appoint an ignorant Brahmin as expounder of *dharma*. And this makes a similar interpretation of *kāmam* as concessive in the verse of Manu in question (5.157) distinctly plausible, if by no means certain.[5]

Beyond this, both of the aforementioned, radically different interpretations of the verse are attested in the extant commentaries on Manu. For instance, Medhātithi, the earliest surviving commentator to

[4] See MDh 2.189, 2.216, 3.111, 3.144, 3.222, 10.90, 10.117, and 11.13.

[5] Curiously, however, despite the roughly equal grammatical and contextual plausibility of both interpretations, the better-known English translators of Manu (Bühler [1886] 1970; Doniger and Smith 1991; Olivelle 2005) all make no mention whatsoever of the interpretation that takes MDh 5.157 as condemning the emaciation of widows.

discuss this verse in detail,[6] adopts the second interpretation, according to which *kāmam* has a concessive meaning:

> Hence, if a childless widow receives no money or the like from her husband or a share of inheritance, she would have to live by some means such as yarn-spinning. Given that life would still be very dear to her and that it would be forbidden for her to forsake it as that would be in violation of the scriptures, one might imagine that she could live off sinful activities, since all sins are permitted in a calamity due to such examples as Viśvāmitra's eating the dog's thigh.[7] It is with this in mind that Manu (5.157) says: In such a state, *a woman may admittedly emaciate*—i.e., cause to waste away—*her body by living on flowers, fruits, and roots*. In other words, she may arrange a livelihood for herself however she happens to. *But she should never even mention the name of another man*, saying, "Today you are my husband." Nevertheless, there is the following statement (NSm 12.97, PSm 4.30):
>
> > When her husband is lost, dead, a renunciant, impotent, or an outcaste—
> > in these five calamities another lord (*pati*) is enjoined for a woman.
>
> But this merely means that a woman might resort to another lord, in the sense of protector, in order to secure a livelihood for herself by working as his maid or the like. And this will be explained in detail in the ninth chapter (MDh 9.76). This is also the rule for a woman whose husband has gone abroad. The word *admittedly* (*kāmam*) is used here in order to indicate displeasure as follows: emaciating her body is also a bad thing for a woman to do, but this other thing that is union with another man is an even worse thing for her to do.

ato mṛtapatikāyā anapatyāyā asati bhartṛdhanādau dāyike ca kartanādinā ca kenacid upāyena jīvantyā jīvitasyātipriyatvāt tadupekṣaṇasyāśāstratvāt pratiṣiddhatvād āpadi sarvavyabhicārāṇāṃ viśvāmitrajāghanīm ity ādinānujñātatvād vyabhicāropajīvitāprāptāv idam ucyate | kāmam asyām avasthāyāṃ śarīraṃ kṣapayet kṣayaṃ nayet puṣpamūlaphalair yathopapādaṃ vṛttiṃ vidadhīta | na tu nāmāpi gṛhṇīyāt patir me tvam evādyety anyasya | yat tu—

[6] The commentary of Bhāruci on this verse, which certainly predates Medhātithi and has recently been made available thanks to the editorial work of S. Jagannātha, is very short. It consists only of the words *vṛttyasaṃbhave 'pi ca* ("And even in the absence of a livelihood").

[7] This refers to the story told at MBh 12.139.12–94, in which the sage Viśvāmitra eats the haunch of a dog in order to survive during a prolonged famine and is regarded as faultless in this act.

naṣṭe mṛte pravrajite klībe 'tha patite patau |
pañcasv āpatsu nārīṇāṃ patir anyo vidhīyate || (NSm 12.97, PSm 4.30)
iti tatra pālanāt patim anyam āśrayet sairandhrakarmādinātmavṛtty-artham | *navame ca nipuṇaṃ nirneṣyate* | *proṣitabhartṛkāyāś ca sa vidhiḥ* | *kāmaśabdaprayogo 'rucisaṃsūcanārtham* | *dehakṣapaṇam apy akāryam idaṃ tv anyad akāryataraṃ yad anyena puruṣeṇa saṃprayogaḥ* |

In this passage, which comes immediately after his rather tangential argument against sati,[8] Medhātithi turns to the meaning of Manu's verse (5.157) itself, which he interprets as opposed to widow asceticism, but even more vehemently opposed to widow remarriage. To this end, he argues that Manu has composed the verse to rule out a conclusion that one might otherwise reasonably draw. This conclusion is that an indigent widow might lawfully take another husband based upon the established principle that one may violate normal rules of conduct in order to survive in a time of calamity. According to Medhātithi, Manu's verse exists to block the use of this principle to justify widow remarriage. Furthermore, Medhātithi goes on to argue that there is, in fact, no true conflict between Manu's position here and that expressed in a famous verse found in both Nārada (12.97) and Parāśara (4.30), which was examined in Chapter 1. In Medhātithi's view, contrary to appearances, this verse does not permit widow remarriage, for the word *pati* in it really means "lord" or "protector" rather than "husband." Hence, it simply permits a widow to take another employer or benefactor and not another husband. From all of this, it should be clear that Medhātithi opposes not only widow remarriage, as we saw earlier, but also widow asceticism, which was likely a recognized social institution in at least parts of India during his time.

Moreover, writing several centuries later,[9] the commentators Nandana and Sarvajñanārāyaṇa fundamentally adopt Medhātithi's interpretation of Manu:

Thinking that even in the event of a calamity, a woman should not partake of another man, Manu says, "Admittedly . . ." (MDh 1.157).

āpady api nānyaṃ bhajed ity āha kāmam iti | (Nandana)

[8] On this, see the section "Medhātithi" in Chapter 4.
[9] Kane (1962, 1:347–48) assigns a date of 1100–1300 to Sarvajñanārāyaṇa and regards Nandana as a "late writer," but offers no guess as to his precise date.

> The meaning of the verse is this: even if her husband died without arranging a way for her to live, she should not be unfaithful to him in order to acquire wealth and the like suitable for a living.
>
> *yady asyā jīvanopāyam avidhāyaiva bhartā mṛtas tadāpi jīvanocita-dhanādyarthaṃ na vyabhicared ity arthaḥ* | (Sarvajñanārāyaṇa)

As one can see from the above statements, both of these commentators are here clearly indebted to Medhātithi and accept his exegesis on this particular verse. It is important to be cautious, however, about concluding from this that either one of them actually opposes the institution of the widow ascetic per se, as Medhātithi appears to. Instead, they may simply interpret Manu's verse as a hyperbolic statement to the effect that a woman should never take another husband, even if it means nearly starving to death. In other words, they may interpret *kāmam* in Manu (5.157) as concessive, simply because their revered predecessor Medhātithi has done so, but not fully share Medhātithi's view that the emaciation of widows is something that should not be done (*akāryam*). Given the brevity of their commentaries, this is apparently impossible to tell.

Kullūka, however, who probably wrote his famous commentary on Manu in thirteenth-century Benares,[10] explicitly rejects the interpretation favored by Medhātithi, Sarvajñanārāyaṇa, and Nandana and unambiguously endorses the practice of widow asceticism:

> Even when a livelihood is possible, she should emaciate her body by living on purifying flowers, roots, and fruits, i.e., make her body emaciated by eating little. And when her husband has died, she should not even utter the name of another man with the thought of infidelity.
>
> *vṛttisaṃbhave 'pi puṣpamūlaphalaiḥ pavitraiś ca dehaṃ kṣapayed alpāhāreṇa kṣīṇaṃ kuryāt | na ca bhartari mṛte vyabhicāradhiyā parapuruṣasya nāmāpy uccārayet* |

As one can see from the above citation, Kullūka construes Manu as laying down an ascetic-like rule for the nonsexual behavior of widows. Moreover, in his short commentary, he curiously makes no mention of

[10] See Kane (1962, 1:758–59).

the optionality of this rule, neglecting entirely to gloss the word *kāmam*. Hence, his commentary appears to reflect a stage of historical development at which certain Brahmanical thinkers had come to look upon certain special ascetic practices as mandatory for any woman who outlived her husband.

Thus, to summarize what has been established up to this point, from at least the time of Baudhāyana (c. second century BCE), authors within the Dharmaśāstra tradition held that widows, like all women, should remain under the constant supervision of their male relatives. Furthermore, two Dharmasūtras (BDh 2.4.7-8, VaDh 17.55-56) give evidence of a customary period of mourning for widows, during which certain ascetic practices were enjoined; and one of these texts (VaDh 19.33-34) prescribes optional asceticism for the wives of a deceased king. Beyond this, however, a single verse of Manu (5.157) is the only possible indication within the extant Smṛtis of the Dharmaśāstra tradition that the nonsexual behavior of widows was subject to specific lifelong restrictions; and there is no indication whatsoever in any of these texts that it was subject to mandatory restrictions of this sort.

Nevertheless, although one finds very little evidence within the surviving Dharmaśāstras of special nonsexual restrictions for women whose husbands have died, this is decidedly not the case when it comes to women whose husbands have gone abroad. For instance, we have already seen in Chapter 1 that Manu (9.75) enjoins a woman whose husband has gone abroad to stay at home unless her husband has failed to provide for her, in which case she may take up a respectable occupation. But such a rule, restrictive though it may be, can hardly be characterized as ascetic.

The later Dharmaśāstras of Yājñavalkya and Viṣṇu, however, borrow from Manu his theme of "rules for women whose husbands have gone abroad"—what the commentators call *proṣitabhartṛkādharma*—and explicitly impose a number of specific ascetic-type restrictions upon such women:

> A woman whose husband has gone abroad should avoid playing, adorning her body, attending gatherings and festivals, gaiety, and going to another man's home.

krīḍāśarīrasaṃskārasamājotsavadarśanam |
hāsaṃ paragṛhe yānaṃ tyajet proṣitabhartṛkā || (YDh 1.83)

When her husband has gone abroad, a woman should not adorn herself, go to other men's homes, or linger in doorways or windows.

bhartari pravasite 'pratikarmakriyā | *paragṛheṣv anabhigamanam* | *dvāradeśagavākṣeṣv anavasthānam* | (ViDh 25.9-11)

Here we find for the first time sets of mandatory restrictive rules very much like those known to have been applied to orthodox Hindu widows in later periods.[11] It must be stressed, however, that the authors of the above statements do not explicitly prescribe these rules for widows, but rather for women who are geographically separated from their husbands. Moreover, whether or not they implicitly intend them for widows as well is uncertain. Although it is distinctly possible that they do, the medieval commentaries certainly do not interpret them this way. Whatever the case may be, given the similarities between these early rules for women whose husbands have gone abroad and the later rules for widows, it is reasonable to connect them historically in at least some loose fashion. In order to find Dharmaśāstra works directly advocating mandatory lifelong widow asceticism, however, one must turn to a markedly later period, to that of the *nibandhas* or legal digests. But before doing that, we will look at some evidence of early Brahmanical widow asceticism from outside of the Dharmaśāstra tradition.

Early Hints of Widow Asceticism

Interestingly, the earliest clear evidence of mandatory lifelong widow asceticism in India comes not from a Dharmaśāstra work, a Sanskrit work, or even a Brahmanical work, but rather from the *Puṟanāṉūṟu*, a Tamil work composed in South India likely between 100 and 250 CE (Hart and Heifetz 1999, xvi). Specifically, the *Puṟanāṉūṟu* is a collection of four hundred short poems on kingship composed in the old Tamil language, the precursor of modern Tamil and Malayalam. Importantly, several poems within it depict women who outlive their husbands as required to obey at least four of their classic restrictions: tonsure, self-emaciation, the avoidance of beds, and the avoidance of ornaments.[12] Thus, based upon this evidence and the comparatively

[11] See, e.g., Julia Leslie (1989, 298–304; 1991) for detailed discussions of the lifelong ascetic rules prescribed for a widow in the *Strīdharmapaddhati*, an eighteenth-century legal digest.

[12] See *Puṟanāṉūṟu* 224, 246, 253, 261, and 280.

early date of the *Puṟanāṉūṟu*, George Hart (1973) has argued that the widow asceticism practiced within orthodox Brahmanical communities during the medieval and later periods is to a substantial degree the result of cultural influence from the Dravidian South.

Alongside this fairly clear evidence from Tamil sources, however, one also finds in Sanskrit texts of the first millennium CE occasional hints of widow asceticism of a rather unique type. This type of widow asceticism seems to be distinctly Hindu or more precisely Brahmanical in religious orientation, as opposed to Buddhist or Jain. It also appears to be open exclusively to women whose husbands have died. That is, it apparently does not belong to a broader tradition of female asceticism in which an array of women, including widows, could participate, such as one finds in early Indian Buddhism and Jainism. Instead, it seems to be an ascetic tradition comprised entirely of widows. For these reasons, a discussion of it is germane to a general treatment of widow asceticism under classical Hindu law.

An excellent way to begin to recognize the form of early Brahmanical widow asceticism to which I have been referring is to carefully consider the meaning and usage of the little known Sanskrit common noun *kātyāyanī*. The *Amarakośa* (2.6.17), the preeminent work of classical Indian lexicography, likely dating to around the sixth century CE, defines a *kātyāyanī* as follows:

A *kātyāyanī* is a middle-aged widow who wears an ochre robe (*kāṣāya*).

kātyāyany ardhavṛddhā yā kāṣāyavasanādhavā |

Hence, according to the *Amarakośa*, a *kātyāyanī* is a woman of middle age whose husband has died and who has donned an "ochre robe" or *kāṣāya*. Given that this term is widely used to denote the distinctive garment worn by renunciants in both Buddhist and Brahmanical traditions,[13] there can be no doubt that, as defined in the *Amarakośa*, a *kātyāyanī* is a widow ascetic of some kind.

[13] For use of the term to denote a Buddhist monk's robe, see, e.g., *Mattavilāsa* 16, which are the words of a Śaiva mendicant to a Buddhist monk, suspected of stealing his skull-bowl: "You're covered inside and out with unfading ochre (*kaṣāya*). So how could a skull-bowl that has fallen into your clutches remain unsullied?" (*āvṛtaṃ bahir antaś ca kaṣāyeṇānapāyinā* | *tvāṃ prāptaṃ syāt kathaṃ nāma kapālam akaṣāyitam* ||) For a case where *kāṣāya* is used to denote a Brahmanical ascetic's robe, see *Yatidharmasamuccaya* 3.17: "Devala states: 'Ochre robe (*kāṣāya*), bald head, triple-staff, water-pot, begging bowl, water-strainer, sandals, stool, and ragged shawl—these are the insignia of an ascetic.'" (*āha devalaḥ—kāṣāyamuṇḍatridaṇḍakamaṇḍalupātrapavitrapādukāsanakanthā mātrā iti* |)

Moreover, importantly, such a woman would seem to be an ascetic of a type much more closely akin to male renunciants than the later classical Hindu widow ascetic, which we will examine in the next section. For as we will see, the classical Hindu widow ascetic is not supposed to wear the ochre robe of a typical male ascetic, but rather undyed cloth; nor is she supposed to depart from her home, as renunciants do, but rather live under the direct supervision of her sons. By contrast, the fact that a *kātyāyanī* wears an ochre robe or *kāṣāya* strongly suggests that, like other people in classical India who wore such a garment, she was a person who had freely chosen to go forth from her home and adopt a more typically renunciant lifestyle. Beyond this, the very existence of a special term for a female renunciant who was middle-aged and widowed implies that women fitting this description constituted a notably distinct type of renunciant in premodern India for at least some period of time. Thus, it is worth making some effort to flesh out the character of the *kātyāyanī* alluded to in the *Amarakośa*'s intriguing definition.

Sadly, however, the evidence upon which to do this is extremely scant, for so far as I have been able to determine, only a single Sanskrit text actually uses the word *kātyāyanī* to denote anything other than a proper name. This text is the *Harṣacarita*, an incomplete biography of the historical emperor Harṣa written by Bāṇa in the seventh century CE. Specifically, the *Harṣacarita* uses the diminutive form of the Sanskrit word *kātyāyanī*, *kātyāyanikā*, twice in the sense given in the *Amarakośa*. The first instance of the term occurs in a strikingly candid, autobiographical passage, where Bāṇa explains how he was orphaned around age fourteen and how, being a young man of means and free from normal parental control, he subsequently engaged in all sorts of unruly behavior that led him into disrepute. The significant part of this passage for present purposes reads as follows:

> And he (i.e., Bāṇa) had friends of equal age and companions such as: the brothers Candrasena and Mātṛṣeṇa, born of a Brahmin father and Śūdra mother; the vernacular poet Īśāna, his great friend; the hangers-on Rudra and Nārāyaṇa; the scholars Vārabāṇa and Vāsabāṇa; the descriptive poet Veṇībhārata; the well-born Prakrit author Vāyuvikāra; the panegyrists Anaṅgabāṇa and Sūcībāṇa; the middle-aged widow-ascetic (*kātyāyanikā*) Cakravākikā; . . . .

abhavaṃś cāsya vayasā samānāḥ suhṛdaḥ sahāyāś ca | tathā ca bhrātarau pāraśavau candrasenamātṛṣeṇau bhāṣākavir īśānaḥ paraṃ mitraṃ praṇayinau rudranārāyaṇau vidvāṃsau vārabāṇavāsabāṇau varṇakavir veṇībhārataḥ prākṛtakṛt kulaputraḥ vāyuvikāraḥ bandināv anaṅgabāṇasūcībāṇau kātyāyanikā cakravākikā . . . | (*Harṣacarita*, p. 19)

Here Bāṇa lists the various people with whom he associated during his wild years before he settled down, came to Harṣa's court, and wrote the *Harṣacarita*. And as one can see, one of Bāṇa's companions in his youth was a *kātyāyanikā* named Cakravākikā. It is hard to explain the meaning of the term *kātyāyanikā* here without reference to the *Amarakośa*'s aforementioned definition of *kātyāyanī*; and, indeed, this is precisely how the editor P. V. Kane (1986, 231) and the translators E. B. Cowell and F. W. Thomas (1968, 33) have interpreted the term. Thus, this reference to a *kātyāyanikā* named Cakravākikā in Bāṇa's work usefully informs us that the definition of *kātyāyanī* given in the *Amarakośa* is not a pure fabrication on the part of the lexicographer Amarasiṃha, for a least one nonlexicographical Sanskrit text attests to it. Moreover, given the unusually realistic and candidly autobiographical character of the passage in which the term occurs, it is likely, in my estimation, that *kātyāyanīs*—in the sense of middle-aged widow ascetics—actually existed in seventh-century North India, where Bāṇa spent his youth.

The second occurrence of the word *kātyāyanikā* in the *Harṣacarita* is part of a passage, where Harṣa's father, King Prabhākara Vardhana, lies dying and Harṣa goes to comfort his mother. As he approaches the women's quarters, he hears the king's various wives, who have decided to take their own lives, speak their parting words to their beloved plants, pets, and human attendants. Significantly, these words include the following, where one queen respectfully addresses a *kātyāyanikā* and effectively urges her not to grieve her passing:

O noble widow-ascetic (*kātyāyanikā*), why are you crying? Fate compels me!

ārye kātyāyanike kiṃ rodiṣi | *nītāsmi daivena* | (*Harṣacarita*, p. 83)

From this, we learn two important details: first, that a *kātyāyanī* was the kind of person that might typically be part of a queen's retinue and, second, that they were persons of notable respect, given how the queen in the *Harṣacarita* is depicted as addressing one.

Aside from these two passages from the *Harṣacarita* and the definitions given in the *Amarakośa* and a few other lexicographical works,[14] the term *kātyāyanī* seems only to be used as a proper name in Sanskrit and Prakrit literature.[15] Nevertheless, I believe that we can gain important insights into the figure of the *kātyāyanī* from a text that never actually uses the word as a common or proper noun, namely, the *Mālavikāgnimitra*, one of the three surviving plays of Kālidāsa, an author generally dated to the fourth or fifth century CE. The play's basic plot concerns a princess Mālavikā who travels with her brother Mādhavasena to Vidiśā, the capital city of King Agnimitra, with whom he has promised to establish a marital alliance. But on their way, Mādhavasena is captured by his rival cousin, the king of Vidarbha. Mālavikā, for her part, alludes capture and, under the protection of the minister Sumati and his younger sister Kauśikī, joins a caravan headed for Vidiśā. But as fate would have it, this caravan is also attacked, this time by menacing forest tribesmen. And although Mālavikā manages to escape, her protector Sumati is slain and his sister Kauśikī knocked unconscious. Thereafter, bereft and alone, Mālavikā finds her way to Vidiśā, where she joins the retinue of King Agnimitra's senior wife Dhāriṇī, but still keeps her royal identity secret due to a prophecy that she would spend a year as a servant before finding her husband.

For present purposes, it is not the play's heroine Mālivikā who is of interest, but rather the character Kauśikī, for her behavior and social status within the play exactly match what we would expect of a *kātyāyanī*. To

[14] In a lengthy lexicographical section, the *Agni Purāṇa* (364.3) defines a *kātyāyanī* simply as a middle-aged woman (*ardhavṛddhā*) and does not include that she is also a widow and an ascetic. However, the text often seems to provide only abbreviated definitions of words. For instance, immediately after its definition of a *kātyāyanī*, it defines a maid (*sairindhrī*) simply as a woman who goes to others' homes (*paraveśmagā*)—hardly a sufficient definition of such a woman. Thus, it is unlikely that the author of this passage truly understands the term *kātyāyanī* to denote nothing more than a middle-aged woman. Similar to the *Agni Purāṇa*, Halāyudha's eleventh-century lexicon, the *Abhidhānaratnamālā* (2.33) defines a *kātyāyanikā* simply as a middle-aged woman (*ardhavṛddhā tu yā nārī sā kātyāyanikā smṛtā*).

[15] For instance, Kātyāyanī is the name of one of Yājñavalkya's two wives in the *Bṛhadāraṇyaka Upaniṣad* (2.4.1, 4.5.1–2), where she is explicitly described as less erudite than her co-wife Maitreyī. In Pali literature, there are also two women named Kātyāyanī (Pali: *kaccānī*, *kātiyānī*), one in the *Aṅguttara Nikāya* (vol. 1, p. 26) and the other in the *Jātakatthavaṇṇanā* (vol. 3, pp. 422–28). Significantly, neither of these women is a renunciant, although the latter is a widow and likely middle-aged. Beyond this, Kātyāyanī is a fairly common epithet of the Goddess/Devī (see, e.g., *Harivaṃśa* app. 1.8.1, 1.24.90, 1.30.361–62, *Amarakośa* 1.1.36, and *Harṣacarita*, p. 26). And, finally, there is a female ascetic (*pravrājikā*, *tāpasī*) named Kātyāyanī in the *Kathāsaritsāgara* (12.34.54–100), who closely matches the definition of the common noun *kātyāyanī* given in the *Amarakośa* (2.6.17). Especially telling is the fact that she is explicitly introduced as middle-aged (KSS 12.34.54: *prauḍhā*).

begin with, consider how Kauśikī recounts to King Agnimitra her actions following the attack by the forest-dwelling tribesmen:

> Female ascetic (i.e., Kauśikī): Then I consigned my brother's body to the fire and, feeling the pain of widowhood made new again, arrived at your country and donned these ochre robes (*kāṣāya*).
>
> *parivrājikā—tato bhrātuḥ śarīram agnisāt kṛtvā punar navīkṛtavaidhavyaduḥkhayā mayā tvadīyaṃ deśam avatīrya ime kāṣāye gṛhīte* | (*Mālavikāgnimitra* 5.11)

Here, as one can see, Kauśikī explains that after cremating her brother's body, she donned a pair of ochre robes (*kāṣāya*), while experiencing literally "the pain of widowhood made new again." From this we learn not only that Kauśikī, who is identified as a female mendicant (*parivrājikā*) in the play, wore specifically ochre robes, but also that she was a widow prior to her brother's death. In addition, there is also the suggestion here that her decision to don ochre robes and become a renunciant was associated with the pain of widowhood. And it is also fairly safe to assume that Kauśikī was understood to be broadly middle-aged in the play, given that even senior male characters treat her with considerable respect and yet she was physically fit enough to undertake a long journey. Therefore, the character Kauśikī in the *Mālavikāgnimitra* perfectly fits the definition of a *kātyāyanī* given in the *Amarakośa*.

Moreover, as readers familiar with Kālidāsa's play may recall, after taking on a renunciant lifestyle, Kauśikī joins the retinue of Queen Dhāriṇī and, in this regard, her behavior notably matches that of one of the two *kātyāyanikās* mentioned in the *Harṣacarita*. Furthermore, one might reasonably imagine that the other *kātyāyanikā* in Bāṇa's text—his companion Cakravākikā—was an especially learned woman, considering that many of the other companions that Bāṇa kept during his youth are identified as poets and men of learning. And if this is the case, Kauśikī once again matches our image of a *kātyāyanī*, for she stands out in Kālidāsa's plays as the only female character who speaks Sanskrit, the language of educated men, rather than Prakrit. Consequently, Kauśikī looks to be precisely the sort of woman that both Bāṇa and Amarasiṃha would have referred to as a *kātyāyanī*.

Of course, there is the issue that Kālidāsa himself never identifies Kauśikī as such, but this can easily be explained by the fact that there is no evidence for the existence of the common noun *kātyāyanī* prior to the sixth or seventh century, several centuries after Kālidāsa's likely date. Thus, although certain middle-aged widows may have donned the ochre robes and adopted the ascetic lifestyles of male renunciants during Kālidāsa's time, the word *kātyāyanī* may not yet have been used to denote them.

In any case, despite the absence of the word *kātyāyanī* in Kālidāsa's works, it seems that the very coinage of the term—perhaps in a later century—adds significantly to our understanding of the character Kauśikī, for it indicates that her behavior, rather than being anomalous or idiosyncratic, conformed to an established and respected social practice, even if our textual sources barely allow us to discern it. Conversely, the character Kauśikī in the *Mālavikāgnimitra* allows us to much more fully understand the social figure of the *kātyāyanī*. For example, one learns from her that *kātyāyanīs* were probably high-caste women, for Kauśikī's brother was a high-ranking royal official and, thus, almost certainly a Brahmin or Kṣatriya by birth. One also gets the distinct impression from the character Kauśikī that *kātyāyanīs* were typically widows who renounced in middle age, as that was deemed the proper time for women to renounce, rather than widows who renounced at any age and just happened to have reached middle age. And this makes good sense, for as mentioned earlier, the very existence of a special term for female renunciants who are widows and middle-aged suggests that women with these qualities comprised a distinct class of renunciant. Yet if widows of any age could renounce, why would specifically middle-aged widows comprise a distinct class of renunciants and why don't we find a generic Sanskrit word for a widow renunciant of any age? Moreover, if women who had never married were allowed to renounce, what would be distinctive in a good way about being a middle-aged widow renunciant? Hence, it seems easiest to imagine that the common noun *kātyāyanī* was coined, because certain people considered middle-aged widows to be the only women properly entitled to renounce and sought a term to distinguish renunciants of this type from other female renunciants of less reputable types.

This in turn implies that *kātyāyanīs* were not Buddhist in religious orientation, but rather Hindu or, more accurately, Brahmanical. And the religious orientation of Kauśikī confirms this, for although a number of noteworthy scholars have understood her to be a Buddhist nun,[16] the evidence clearly points toward her being a Brahmanical renunciant. To begin

[16] See, for instance, Böthlingk and Roth (1855, 2:468) and Jamison (2006, 209n).

with, nowhere in the *Mālavikāgnimitra* is Kauśikī said to be a Buddhist nor is she ever associated with any distinctively Buddhist terms or paraphernalia. And, in this regard, she contrasts sharply with the similar character Kāmandakī in the *Mālatīmādhava*, who is explicitly introduced as an "old Buddhist nun" (*saugatajaratparivrājikā*).[17] The frequently encountered view that Kauśikī is a Buddhist nun then seems to stem entirely from the fact that she is obviously not a Jain and the assumption that there were essentially no female Brahmanical renunciants in early India. However, there is good reason to believe that this assumption is wrong, such as the passage of Vasiṣṭha (19.33–34) discussed earlier in this chapter, according to which the wives of a deceased king can either receive maintenance or become renunciants.

Furthermore, within the *Mālavikāgnimitra* (1.14) itself, when King Agnimitra sees his wife Dhāriṇī enter his court accompanied by Kauśikī, he likens her to the triple Veda accompanied by "knowledge of the Supreme Self incarnate":

> Adorned with ornaments herself and accompanied by Kauśikī in her ascetics' garb, she looks like the triple Veda accompanied by knowledge of the Supreme Self incarnate.
>
> *maṅgalālaṃkṛtā bhāti kauśikyā yativeṣayā |*
> *trayī vigrahavatyeva samam adhyātmavidyayā ||*

Thus, here the play's protagonist compares Kauśikī to knowledge of the Supreme Self (*adhyātma*), which he regards as an austere complement to the Vedas with their lavish rites. Obviously, this is not how one would describe a Buddhist nun! Hence, Kālidāsa must intend his character Kauśikī to be a Brahmanical renunciant. And since she so strikingly conforms to the image of a *kātyāyanī* gleaned from the *Amarakośa* and *Harṣacarita*, it would seem that the term also denotes a female Brahmanical renunciant rather than a Buddhist nun.

Thus, whether or not everything suggested here about the elusive figure of the *kātyāyanī* is correct, this much at least is highly probable: during at least part of the first millennium and within at least segments of Brahmanical society, it was an established and accepted practice for high-caste widows of

[17] See *Mālatīmādhava*, p. 10.

middle age to become renunciants, if they so chose, and for elite members of society to treat them with roughly the same sort of respect and deference afforded to male renunciants. Certainly such venerated widow ascetics are a far cry from the classical Hindu widow ascetic known from later times, who is always deemed an inauspicious figure and required to engage in varied and extreme forms of self-mortification simply to mitigate the stigma of her widowhood. Within Dharmaśāstra literature, it is the *nibandhas* or legal digests that first recognize and prescribe widow asceticism of this classical variety. And it is these texts to which we will turn shortly.

Before turning to the legal digests, however, it is worthy briefly considering the etymology of the common noun *kātyāyanī*, that is, how the word, which was undoubtedly originally a proper name, came to denote generically a type of a middle-aged widow ascetic. Probably the best explanation of this puzzling semantic development is to connect the common noun *kātyāyanī* with the use of *kātyāyanī* as an epithet of the grand Hindu goddess, generally referred to by scholars as either "the Goddess" or "Devī" and variously identified in primary sources with such major Hindu goddesses as Pārvatī, Durgā, and Kālī. Both the *Amarakośa* (1.1.36) and *Harṣacarita* (p. 26)—the earliest texts to use the common noun *kātyāyanī*—use *kātyāyanī* as an epithet of the Goddess. Therefore, it is clear that those who employed *kātyāyanī* as a common noun also knew the word as a name of the Goddess. Hence, certain people might have come to refer to middle-aged widow ascetics of a particular type as *kātyāyanīs*, because, like the Goddess, they were rare independent females deemed worthy of considerable veneration within Brahmanical society.[18] As to why *kātyāyanī* was chosen among the various available epithets of the Goddess, a plausible answer is that it had the added advantage of connoting sageliness and profound learning, for masculine *kātyāyana* had long been the name of a celebrated Brahmanical sage. And here it is interesting to note that, in addition to being the name of an erudite widow ascetic in Kālidāsa's play, the word *kauśikī* is also used as an epithet of the Goddess and one that particularly sounds like the name of a female sage, given that masculine *kauśika* is a common patronym of the Vedic seer Viśvāmitra. Indeed, a passage of the *Harivaṃśa* (app. 1.8.1)—albeit one not included in the critically reconstructed text—lists *kātyāyanī* and *kauśikī* alongside one another as

[18] Note that it does not necessarily follow from this that *kātyāyanīs* were Śāktas or devotees of the Goddess, only that the Goddess served as a model for understanding them.

epithets of the Goddess. Thus, it may have been a practice for middle-aged widow ascetics to take names that both connoted sageliness and connected them with the Goddess. That one of these names came to be used as a common noun for the entire class of such women seems a plausible explanation of the common noun *kātyāyanī*.

The Legal Digests

The *Kṛtyakalpataru* (*Vyavahārakāṇḍa*, pp. 635–38), a *nibandha* or legal digest composed during the first half of the twelfth century, appears to be the earliest Dharmaśāstra work to contain rules placing specific obligatory, lifelong restraints on the nonsexual conduct of widows. And the *Smṛticandrikā* (*Vyavahārakāṇḍa*, pp. 594–97), which was probably composed less than a century later, also advocates more or less the same rules in this regard as those found in the *Kṛtyakalpataru*. In particular, both of these texts begin their discussions of the rules applicable to the nonsexual behavior of widows by quoting the same Smṛti passage, which they ascribe to Hārīta. As it is quoted and commented upon in the *Smṛticandrikā* (*Vyavahārakāṇḍa*, pp. 594–95), this passage reads:

> Now are explained the laws for a woman whose husband has died. Regarding these, Hārīta states the following for the wife of an Āhitāgni ("man who has established the sacred Śrauta fires"):
>
> > If an Āhitāgni dies, his widow should take the fire lying in the coals of his domestic fire and live, kindling it morning, noon, and evening, while reciting the Sarparājñī verses (TS 1.5.4).
>
> In cases where the Śrauta fires were established with half of the domestic fire, a dead Āhitāgni should be cremated with his three Śrauta fires. His domestic fire, however, should be kept for his widow to kindle. The pieces of kindling lying among the embers are called the "coals." And, thus, this is the meaning of Hārīta's statement: his widow should take his domestic fire residing in the embers and live in the house of her father-in-law or the like, kindling that fire morning, noon, and evening, while reciting the four verses that start, "The earth with plenty . . ." (TS 1.5.4). The wife of a dead non-Āhitāgni should also live in exactly this way, but there is this difference: she should either perform the re-establishment of the domestic fire following the procedure laid down in her family's

Gṛhyasūtra or take a mundane fire. And, thus, Hārīta himself goes on to state:

> If a non-Āhitāgni (dies), his widow should establish another fire or, having taken a common fire, (kindle it as before).

The verb "dies" needs to be carried over after the phrase "If a non-Āhitāgni." The phrase "kindle it as before" needs to be supplied after the phrase "having taken a common fire." In the cremation rite of a non-Āhitāgni, it is understood that there is a previously existing domestic fire. Therefore, for the reproduction of that, Hārīta says that the widow "should establish another fire."

[Objection:] But in cases where the fires were established with the entire domestic fire,[19] how does a woman whose husband has died worship his fires? And it cannot be that what was said with respect to the wife of a non-Āhitāgni should be inferred to apply to her as well, since a woman whose husband has died can bring about a non-mundane fire only through the force of a scriptural statement.

[Reply:] Such a widow should kindle the fire as before, having taken a churned fire, for in cases such as this Āpastamba enjoins that the funerary rite of a wife should be performed with a churned fire, when he says, "With a churned fire (they should cremate) a wife" (*Hiraṇyakeśi Pitṛmedhasūtra* 3.12.12).[20]

Having thus explained the particular fires that particular women should kindle, Hārīta also states the laws common to all women whose husbands have died:

> She should reside in the house of her husband's father or of her own people; restrain her tongue, hands, feet, and sense-organs; practice good conduct; lament her husband day and night; and emaciate herself with vows and fasts. At the end of her life, she will then win her husband's world and never again be separated from her husband.

atha mṛtabhartṛkāyāḥ striyā dharmāḥ | tatrāhitāgner bhāryāṃ praty āha hārītaḥ—

> *āhitāgniś cet pramīyeta aupāsanāvakṣāṇāgniṃ parigṛhya sarparājñībhir anusavanam indhānā vased iti* |

[19] In such cases, unlike in cases where only half the domestic fire is used in establishing the Śrauta fires, there is no longer a separate domestic fire. For a brief discussion of the difference between *ardhādhāna* and *sarvādhāna*, see Kane (1962, 2:919n).

[20] The "churned fire" (*nirmathitāgni*) referred to here is presumably a fire separately produced using the fire-drill (*araṇi*) of the woman's husband.

ardhādhānapakṣe mṛtasyāhitāgnes tretāgninā dahanam | aupāsanāgnis tu pa[tny]artham indhane dhriyate | ulmukāvasthendhanāny avakṣāṇāny ucyante | evaṃ cāyam arthaḥ—ulmukāvastham aupāsanāgniṃ parigṛhya bhūmir bhūmneti catasṛbhir anusavanam indhānā śvaśurādigṛhe vased iti | evam evānāhitāgner mṛtasya bhāryā vaset | iyāṃs tu viśeṣaḥ—aupāsanāgneḥ svagṛhyoktavidhinā punaḥ saṃdhānaṃ laukikāgner vā parigrahaṃ kuryāt | tathā ca sa eva—

anāhitāgniś ced anyam ādadhyāj janāgniṃ vā parigṛhyeti |

anāhitāgniś cet pramī[ye]tety anuṣajyate | parigṛhya pūrvavat samindhanam ācared iti śeṣaḥ | anāhitāgner dahanakarmaṇi pūrvasthitasyaupāsanasya pratipattir jāteti punar utpattyartham anyam ādadhyād ity uktam |

kathaṃ punaḥ sarvādhānapakṣe mṛtabhartṛkāyā agniparicaryā na cānāhitāgner bhāryāyām uktam apy ūhyaṃ vacanabalenaiva mṛtabhartṛkāyā alaukikāgniniṣpatteḥ | ucyate—nirmathitāgniṃ parigṛhya pūrvavat samindhanam ācaret | nirmanthyena patnīm ity āpastambenaitasmin pakṣe nirmanthyena patnyāḥ pitṛmedhavidhānāt |

evaṃ strīviśeṣe 'gniviśeṣasamindhanam uktvā sarvapramītabhartṛkāyāḥ sādhāraṇadharmam apy āha sa eva—

bhartuḥ pituḥ svajanasya vā gṛham āśritya saṃyatajihvāhastapādendriyā svācāravatī divārātraṃ bhartāram anuśocantī vratopavāsaiḥ kṛśātmā āyuṣo 'nte patilokaṃ jayati na bhūyaḥ pativiyogam āpnotīti |

As one can see, the end of this passage lays down what the *Smṛticandrikā* regards as the general rules for all widows and these are clearly mandatory, lifelong, and, broadly speaking, ascetic in nature. Specifically, they require a widow to live in a house belonging to either her husband's or her father's kin; act with verbal and physical restraint; practice virtuous conduct; lament her deceased husband day and night; and emaciate herself by performing a regimen of vows and fasts.

Furthermore, it is noteworthy that while other Smṛti passages cited in the *Kṛtyakalpataru* and *Smṛticandrikā* prescribe some of the same ascetic practices as those enjoined by Hārīta, none adds anything substantial beyond them. Note, for example, the following verse ascribed to Bṛhaspati,[21] which is quoted in both the *Kṛtyakalpataru* (*Vyavahārakāṇḍa*, p. 636) and the *Smṛticandrikā* (*Vyavahārakāṇḍa*, p. 595):

[21] In Aiyangar's attempted reconstruction of the *Bṛhaspati Smṛti*, this is BSm 25.15.

Even a sonless woman goes to heaven, if she delights in performing vows and fasts, remains strictly celibate, and constantly rejoices in practicing self-restraint and giving gifts.

vratopavāsaniratā brahmacarye vyavasthitā |
damadānaratā nityam aputrāpi divaṃ vrajet ||

Aside from the minor detail that a widow should give pious gifts, this passage adds nothing to what Hārīta has already expressed. And one can rightly say this about all of the other Smṛtis pertaining to lifelong widows that are cited in either the *Kṛtyakalpataru* or the *Smṛticandrikā*.

The first part of Hārīta's statement, however, is unique among the Smṛtis cited in these early *nibandhas* in that is unconcerned with any activities that one might consider ascetic within the Brahmanical context. Instead, it deals with a particular ritual duty incumbent upon an orthodox Brahmanical widow, namely, the maintenance of a sacred fire associated with her deceased husband. The *Smṛticandrikā* explains the details of this duty as follows: if a man had maintained both the single domestic fire, originating from his nuptial fire, and the three solemn Śrauta fires used in Vedic ritual, his widow should faithfully kindle his domestic fire thrice a day, while reciting the Vedic Sarparājñī verses. If, however, he had maintained only the three Śrauta fires, she should take up a freshly produced fire and kindle it in this same way. And if he had not maintained any sacred fires at all or simply maintained the single domestic fire, she should either take up an ordinary fire or ritually reestablish the domestic fire used in his cremation and faithfully kindle that in the aforementioned manner. Hence, following Hārīta, both the *Smṛticandrikā* and the *Kṛtyakalpataru* imagine that a widow should engage not only in a set of austere practices but also in a certain form of continuous domestic fire ritual. And given the well-established connections between domestic ritual and domesticity in general within the classical Indian context, this suggests that, according to these texts, widows were not wholly marginalized from ongoing social life.[22]

Therefore, it is quite revealing that all of the later commentaries and *nibandhas* within the Dharmaśāstra tradition omit Hārīta's statement

[22] For an excellent treatment of a somewhat related phenomenon, see Olivelle's (1995, 12–26) discussion of the "domestication of asceticism" within the Śrī-Vaiṣṇava tradition.

altogether and, indeed, make no mention whatsoever of a widow's right or obligation to engage in domestic fire ritual. Instead, in the period following the *Kṛtyakalpataru* and *Smṛticandrikā*, a new, rather lengthy, and markedly different Smṛti passage becomes the dominant expression of the orthodox Brahmanical attitude toward widows or at least toward those widows that did not perform sati. The earliest firmly datable occurrence of this passage is in the fourteenth-century digest, *Madanapārijāta* (pp. 202–3). However, it is also found in the *Kāśīkhaṇḍa* of the *Skanda Purāṇa* (4.73–105), which likewise may date to the fourteenth century,[23] and in the *Nirṇayasindhu* (p. 440) and *Saṃskāramayūkha* (p. 119), both of which date to the seventeenth century.[24] Significantly, in all of these texts the passage in question constitutes virtually the only passage that lays down rules for the nonsexual behavior of widows.[25]

This passage, as cited in the *Madanapārijāta* (pp. 202–3),[26] reads:

> Even for remaining a lifelong widow, special rewards, such as heaven, are laid down in a particular Smṛti:
>
> If a woman remains a lifelong widow after her husband has died, she will reunite with her husband and attain the pleasures of heaven. However, when a widow binds her hair into a braid, it puts her husband in bondage. Therefore, a widow should always shave her head. She should always eat just one meal a day, never a second. She should perform vows for three nights, five nights, or fortnights; fast for a month or perform

[23] See Adriaensen, Bakker, and Isaacson (1998, 15–16).

[24] On the provenance of these two texts, see Kane (1962, 1:932–33, 940).

[25] The *Madanapārijāta* (pp. 202-3) cites absolutely no other passages dealing with lifelong widows. The *Saṃskāramayūkha* (p. 119), however, also quotes MDh 1.157-58 (cited above) and the *Nirṇayasindhu* (p. 440) quotes a Smṛti ascribed to Pracetas that prohibits renunciants, students, and widows from chewing betel leaf, using unguents, and eating out of copper bowls. In addition to this, the *Nirṇayasindhu* troubles to account for BDh 2.4.7–8 (cited above) by explaining that it applies only to wives of different social classes and attributing this position to Aparārka (*yat tu baudhāyanaḥ . . . tad asavarṇāparam ity aparārkaḥ*). It is noteworthy, however, that Aparārka himself does not appear to express this position in his twelfth-century commentary on Yājñavalkya.

[26] This passage is virtually identical to verses 4.73–83, 102–5 of the *Kāśīkhaṇḍa* of the so-called *Skanda Purāṇa*, compiled and printed by Nag Publishers. The *Nirṇayasindhu* (p. 440) and *Saṃskāramayūkha* (p. 119) also cite this same passage, but in a significantly abridged form. Neither the *Madanapārijāta* nor the *Saṃskāramayūkhā* ascribes the passage to a specific text. The *Nirṇayasindhu*, however, explicitly ascribes it to the "*Skanda Purāṇa* as cited in the *Madanaratna*" (*madanaratne skānde*). The *Madanaratna* (also called *Madanaratnapradīpa*) is an apparently vast *nibandha*, likely dating to the fifteenth century. For a discussion of it, see Kane (1962, 1:804–9). Unfortunately, only two sections of the text (on gifting and judicial procedure) have been published, neither of which contains a discussion of widows.

a lunar penance; and perform Kṛcchra, Parāka, or Tapta-Kṛcchra penances. She should subsist by eating food comprised of only barley, fruits, or vegetables or by performing vows to consume only milk, until life departs on its own. If a widowed woman lies on a bed, it casts her husband into hell. Therefore, a widow who desires her husband's happiness should sleep on the ground. A widowed woman should never decorate her body; she should never use fragrant substances; and she should each day offer a libation of water mixed with *kuśa* grass and sesame seeds to her husband.

This libation applies only in the absence of sons and grandsons.

She should worship Viṣṇu only with the thought of her husband, never otherwise. She should always meditate upon her husband as supreme and bearing the form of Viṣṇu. Whatever her husband most desired in the world and whatever he strove after she should give to virtuous men with the desire to please her husband. In the months of Vaiśākha, Kārttika, and Māgha, she should perform special vows, bathe, give gifts, travel to sacred sites, and constantly recite the names of Viṣṇu. By performing such scripturally sanctioned vows and observances in accordance with the prescribed rules, she should pass the days of Vaiśākha, Kārttika, and Māgha. She should never mount an ox even if she's near death; don a cloak; or wear altered clothes. Devoted to her husband, she should never do anything without first seeing his sons. Even a widow who observes these laws is a faithful wife. She will reach the worlds of her husband and never be sad.

vaidhavyapālane 'pi svargādiphalaviśeṣaḥ smṛtyantare smaryate |
patyau mṛte ca yā yoṣid vaidhavyaṃ pālayet kvacit |
sā punaḥ prāpya bhartāraṃ svargabhogān samaśnute ||
vidhavākabarībandho bhartṛbandhāya jāyate |
śiraso vapanaṃ tasmāt kāryaṃ vidhavayā sadā ||
ekāhāraḥ sadā kāryo na dvitīyaḥ kadācana |
trirātraṃ pañcarātraṃ vā pakṣavratam athāpi vā ||
māsopavāsaṃ vā kuryāc cāndrāyaṇam athāpi vā |
kṛcchraṃ parākaṃ vā kuryāt taptakṛcchram athāpi vā ||
yavānnena phalāhāraiḥ śākāhāraiḥ payovrataiḥ |
prāṇayātrāṃ prakurvīta yāvat prāṇaḥ svayaṃ vrajet ||
paryaṅkaśāyinī nārī vidhavā pātayet patim |

tasmād bhūśayanaṃ kāryaṃ patisau[khya]samī[hayā][27] ||
naivāṅgodvartanaṃ kāryaṃ striyā vidhavayā kvacit |
gandhadravyasya saṃbhogo naiva kārya[s][28] *tayā punaḥ* |
tarpaṇaṃ pratyahaṃ kāryaṃ bhartuḥ kuśatilodakaiḥ ||
tarpaṇaṃ putrapautrābhāvaviṣayam |
viṣṇos tu pūjanaṃ kāryaṃ patibuddhyā na cānyathā |
patim eva sadā dhyāyed viṣṇurūpadharaṃ param ||
yad yad iṣṭatamaṃ loke yad yat patyuḥ samīhitam |
tat tad guṇavate deyaṃ patiprīṇanakāmyayā ||
vaiśākhe kārttike māghe viśeṣaniyamaṃ caret |
snānaṃ dānaṃ tīrthayātrāṃ viṣṇor nāmagrahaṃ muhuḥ ||
evaṃvidhaiś ca vidhivad vidhisthair niyamair vrataiḥ |
vaiśākhān kārttikān māghān evam evātivāhayet ||
nādhirohed anaḍvāhaṃ prāṇaiḥ kaṇṭhagatair api |
kañcūkaṃ na parīdadhyād vāso na vikṛtaṃ vaset ||
adṛṣṭvā [tu sutān][29] *kiṃcin na kuryād bhartṛtatparā* |
evaṃdharmasamāyuktā vidhavāpi pativratā |
patilokān avāpnoti na bhavet kvāpi duḥkhitā ||

As one can see, the above passage explicitly requires a widow to keep her head perpetually shaved; eat just one meal a day; regularly perform vows, fasts, and penances; sleep only on the ground; eschew bodily ornamentation; worship Viṣṇu only as an aspect of her husband; avoid wearing cloaks or altered garments; and refrain from doing anything without first consulting her sons. Hence, it contains a large number of discrete nonsexual restrictions that are conspicuously absent from the earlier Dharmaśāstra literature, but many of which are well-known from the early colonial and later periods.[30] Therefore, Kane (1962, 2:587–93) appears quite right in his claim that this passage is probably the earliest literary attestation of the well-known Brahmanical custom of shaving a widow's head, a ritual act which Olivelle (1998) persuasively interprets as symbolic of profound ritual and social separation. Kane seems to miss, however, that the passage under discussion

[27] This is the reading of the printed *Kāśīkhaṇḍa*. The *Madanapārijāta* reads as *patisaukhyaṃ samīhitā*.
[28] This is the reading of the printed *Kāśīkhaṇḍa*. The *Madanapārijāta* reads as *kāryaṃ*.
[29] This is the reading of the printed *Kāśīkhaṇḍa*. The *Madanapārijāta* reads as *ca tāsu na*.
[30] See, e.g., the description of the lives of Brahmin widows in modern rural Bengal in Lamb (2000, 213–38).

also constitutes the first evidence within the Dharmaśāstra tradition of a sizable array of other harsh restrictions placed upon widows. Therefore, when viewed diachronically, the content and tone of this passage suggest a major shift in Brahmanical attitudes toward widows, specifically a shift in favor of notably increased social marginalization and material deprivation.

Furthermore, when compared with the earlier passage of Hārīta, the above passage ritually marginalizes widows from ongoing domestic and familial life in a markedly increased way. For whereas Hārīta requires a widow to engage in what is essentially a special form of domestic fire ritual, this passage makes no mention of any such ritual activity. Instead, it requires a widow to engage in a number of ritual actions that are by no means unique to domestic existence, but rather generally allowable for any person to perform. Specifically, it enjoins a widow to carry out a grueling regimen of meritorious vows, fasts, penances, pilgrimages, baths, and gifts and to regularly worship Viṣṇu, but only with her husband in mind. Indeed, the only truly domestic ritual activity prescribed here for a widow is the daily offering of libations to her deceased husband—a part of the well-known Brahmanical system of ancestor worship known as Śrāddha. But far from indicating nuptial or domestic well-being, which are the obvious Brahmanical connotations of sacred fire, this ritual activity is morosely associated only with the death of the widow's husband—something it is clear that a widowed woman is supposed to keep constantly in mind, according to the orthodox Brahmanical thought of this time. Moreover, it must be noted that the *Madanapārijāta* limits even this ritual allowance to cases where a man has no surviving sons or grandsons. And the *Nirṇayasindhu* (p. 440) and *Saṃskāramayūkha* (p. 119) both endorse this same restriction. Hence, the ritual marginalization of widows within these Dharmaśāstra texts is especially severe.

Finally, given that the Smṛti passage quoted in the *Madanapārijāta* and other later *nibandhas* describes what one may think of as the classical Hindu widow ascetic (i.e., the traditional high-caste widow as described in most broad surveys of Hinduism[31]), it is useful to consider how this widow ascetic differs from the standard male ascetic or world renouncer described in Brahmanical literature. Three major points of difference in particular stand out. First, as Julia Leslie (1989, 58–59) points out, the widow ascetic differs from the male world renouncer in that she does not voluntarily opt out of domestic life. Instead, domestic life is—according to the normative Brahmanical

[31] See, e.g., A. L. Basham (1968, 187–88).

view at least—simply out of reach for her, as she has no socially respectable choice other than celibate asceticism or suicide by self-immolation. Second, unlike the male world renouncer, the widow ascetic does not leave her home, but rather must emphatically stay put, dwelling in the home and under the supervision of either her affinal or her natal relatives. In this regard, the previously discussed figure of the *kātyāyanī* and Vasiṣṭha's statement (19.34) allowing widowed queens to become renunciants differ notably from later descriptions of the classical Hindu widow ascetic. Lastly, although she must perform an array of religious vows, fasts, and the like, which in ordinary life would be regarded as supererogatory, the widow ascetic is not generally depicted as engaged in the single-minded pursuit of the highest religious goal, namely, liberation from the cycle of rebirth, as the male ascetic is. Instead, the Smṛti first quoted in the *Madanapārijāta* that most clearly prescribes classical widow asceticism says that a widowed woman should follow the prescribed rules in order to "reunite with her husband and attain the pleasures of heaven."[32] Moreover, this same passage explains that a widow is prohibited from both braiding her hair and sleeping on a bed because of the immense otherworldly harm these acts would cause her deceased husband. Hence, according to this passage, the goal of widow asceticism is not the typical ascetic goal of liberation from the cycle of rebirth altogether, but rather the joyful reunion in heaven of husband and wife.

There is, however, one noteworthy piece of evidence from the Dharmaśāstra tradition that some Brahmanical thinkers understood widows as at least potentially engaged in the pursuit of liberation. This piece of evidence comprises one of the arguments that two medieval opponents of sati, Vijñāneśvara and Devaṇa Bhaṭṭa, raise against the practice. The essence of this argument, which we will examine in detail in the following chapter, is that widow asceticism is superior to sati, because sati results merely in rebirth in heaven, whereas a living celibate widow may possibly attain liberation from the cycle of rebirth itself. Moreover, from the way he uses the technical terminology of renunciate Vedānta philosophy in articulating this argument,[33] Vijñāneśvara

[32] *Madanapārijāta*, p. 202: *sā punaḥ prāpya bhartāraṃ svargabhogān samaśnute*

[33] See *Mitākṣarā* on YDh 1.86: "So long as life remains, it is possible that, through knowledge of the Self, a person who has destroyed his mind's blemishes by performing regular and occasional rites and succeeded at learning, reflecting, and meditating will attain liberation, which is defined as the attainment of *brahman*, which is eternal and unsurpassed bliss." (*āyuṣaḥ śeṣe sati nityanaimittikakarmānuṣṭhānakṣapitāntaḥkaraṇakalaṅkasya śravaṇamanananididhyāsanasaṃpattau satyām ātmajñānena nityaniratiśayānandabrahmaprālakṣaṇamokṣasaṃbhavaḥ*) Note, in particular, the explicit mention here of the threefold Vedāntic process of *śravana* ("learning"), *manana* ("reflecting"), and *nididhyāsana* ("meditating"), whereby one fully internalizes the liberating message of the Upaniṣads.

apparently understands the liberation attained by a celibate widow to be fully the same as that attained by a male ascetic. Hence, for him the goal of widow asceticism is complete liberation, at least for those widows who aspire to it. And in this regard, his understanding of widow asceticism is reminiscent of the earlier figure of the *kātyāyanī*. Furthermore, it appears that other Brahmanical thinkers, including opponents and proponents of sati, by and large accepted the position that widowed women might attain liberation. For although Devaṇa Bhaṭṭa is the only other Dharmaśāstra author to endorse Vijñāneśvara's argument against sati,[34] it is striking that proponents of the practice nowhere reject the claim that by living, celibate widows can attain liberation. Instead, as will be shown in the next chapter, authors in favor of sati eventually overcome Vijñāneśvara's argument by citing a new Smṛti that explicitly lists liberation as one of the rewards of the practice.

Conclusion

To summarize, although the evidence is admittedly scant, it appears that restrictions on the nonsexual behavior of widows are by and large a relatively late innovation within the Dharmaśāstra tradition. Early on, the two youngest Dharmasūtras (BDh 2.4.7–8, VaDh 17.55–56) give evidence of a period of ascetic mourning for widows, and the younger of these texts (VaDh 19.33-34) also prescribes optional lifelong asceticism for widowed queens. Moreover, a verse of the *Mānava Dharmaśāstra* (5.157) may be interpreted as prescribing perpetual asceticism as a supererogatory option for all widows. Beyond this, however, there is essentially no textual evidence of special nonsexual restraints for widows within the Dharmaśāstra tradition prior to the twelfth century, when *nibandha* literature begins to appear.

Nevertheless, as I have shown, there is evidence of Brahmanical widow asceticism in a few non-Dharmaśāstra works dating to roughly the middle of the first millennium CE. Participation in the type of early Brahmanical widow asceticism alluded to in these texts seems to have been restricted to middle-aged women. And the common noun *kātyāyanī* was apparently coined to designate such middle-aged widow ascetics, who seem to have been much more akin to typical male renunciants in their attire, basic lifestyle, and social status than to later Hindu widow ascetics. Particularly important in

[34] See *Smṛticandrikā*, *Vyavahārakāṇḍa*, pp. 596–97.

this regard is the element of choice, for the earlier and more esteemed form of Brahmanical widow asceticism, unlike later classical Hindu widow asceticism, appears to have been a strictly optional undertaking.

The *Puṟanāṉūṟu*, a collection of classical Tamil poems likely dating to the second or third century CE, is the earliest text where one finds a depiction of a widow ascetic of the classical Hindu type (i.e., a widow required to shave her head, eschew ornamentation, sleep on the ground, etc.). Within the Dharmaśāstra tradition, one has to wait roughly a millennium for the *nibandha* literature to find a similar sort of widow ascetic, for it is in this literature that one encounters, for the first time, sets of lifelong, mandatory restrictive rules directed specifically at the nonsexual aspects of a widow's life. Furthermore, when one compares the *nibandhas* of the twelfth and thirteenth centuries with those of the fourteenth and later centuries, there is a discernible trend toward increasingly harsh and visible restrictions for widows. Indeed, it is only in the fourteenth-century *Madanapārijāta* that all of the various restrictive rules associated with the classical Hindu widow ascetic become established within the Dharmaśāstra tradition.

Thus, Dharmaśāstra rules governing the nonsexual behavior of widows change considerably over time from the third century BCE to the fourteenth century CE and beyond. Specifically, although widows are always supposed to live under male control and supervision, they enjoy markedly greater freedom early on with regard to diet, dress, and general lifestyle. In later times, by contrast, particularly between the twelfth and fourteenth centuries, the freedom of Brahmanical widows is sharply curtailed and a new set of harsh ascetic restrictions is imposed upon all women who outlive their husbands. It is interesting to note, however, that although Dharmaśāstra literature testifies to this major shift in Brahmanical opinion regarding widows, it contains little evidence of a real juridical debate on widow asceticism, for the literature expresses changes in opinion on the topic simply by citing new scriptural passages rather than by arguing about the correct interpretations of established scriptures. And in this regard, the issue of widow asceticism differs notably from the three other widow-related issues that are the subjects of chapters in this book.

The preceding summary of this chapter's major findings naturally invites the question: Why did Brahmanical communities come to regard and to treat widows as unfit for ongoing social life and why does this feeling appear to have intensified specifically between the twelfth and fourteenth centuries? This is an interesting question that requires the detailed and careful consideration of diverse historical developments in the subcontinent between 200 BCE and 1400 CE. It is also a question that is unlikely to have a simple monocausal solution. Hence, rather than attempting to provide a definitive answer to it, I will here merely propose and consider a number of separate possible explanations that may help account for the major shift in Brahmanical opinion regarding widows that has been outlined in this chapter.

The first possible explanation is that widow asceticism was initially popular primarily within elite martial communities and that Brahmanical groups gradually adopted the custom in emulation of members of such communities. The key piece of evidence supporting this explanation is that by far the earliest Dharmaśāstra passage to mention lifelong asceticism for widows (VaDh 19.33–34) prescribes it specifically only for the wives of deceased kings. However, as explained earlier, the kind of asceticism prescribed in this passage appears to differ markedly from the more famous and influential form of widow asceticism prescribed in the later *nibandhas*, which I have been referring to as classical Hindu widow asceticism. Furthermore, even if one were to accept the royal origin of classical Hindu widow asceticism, it is unclear precisely why Brahmanical groups would seek to emulate elite warrior communities in their treatment of widows and also why their emulation would intensify between the twelfth and fourteenth centuries. Consequently, this explanation is not a very persuasive one.

A considerably more persuasive explanation is the influence of Dravidian custom, for as mentioned earlier, a work of classical Tamil poetry, the *Puṟanāṉūṟu*, is by far the earliest text to depict widows as obeying at least four of their classic restrictions. Thus, based upon this evidence and the comparatively early date of the *Puṟanāṉūṟu*, Hart (1973, 241–42) argues that the widow asceticism practiced within orthodox Brahmanical communities throughout India during the medieval and later periods is to a substantial degree the result of cultural influence from the Dravidian South. Buttressing his case, he also argues that it is "only in early Tamil literature that the real reason for suttee and widow asceticism is stated: that the widow is full of sacred forces which might endanger herself and others unless they are suppressed" (1973, 250). Hence, according to Hart, widow asceticism evinces a distinctly Dravidian cultural logic. However, even if one accepts that the dangerous sacred forces believed to reside in widows in early South India are the original reason for widow asceticism, it is rather doubtful that they constitute the primary reason for these practices within orthodox Brahmanical communities, given—as Hart himself implies—that the voluminous literature of these communities provides little or no evidence of a belief in such forces. Moreover, although the evidence from the *Puṟanāṉūṟu* constitutes a plausible case for Dravidian influence, it does nothing to explain why Brahmanical attitudes toward widows changed specifically during the first four centuries of the second millennium.

In order to account for this, it is useful to consider the influence of Islamicate culture and especially Islamicate political power as a third possible explanation. The crucial fact to note here is that during the period 1100–1400 CE, when Brahmanical advocacy of widow asceticism dramatically increases, Islamicate power in South Asia also dramatically and famously increases. Furthermore, evidence suggests that the more extreme form of widow asceticism, involving perpetual tonsure, sleeping only on the ground, and so on, which I have called classical Hindu widow asceticism, may have first become a Brahmanical custom specifically in the Benares area, a region that was especially threatened by and eventually fell under the sway of Islamicate military power.[35] It, therefore, seems distinctly possible that the shift in attitude toward widows reflected in Dharmaśāstric discourse is somehow a reaction to the Muslim military conquests of the twelfth to the fourteenth centuries.

There are, however, two apparent shortcomings to this explanation. First, one of the earliest Dharmaśāstra texts to prescribe widow asceticism, the *Smṛticandrikā*, was composed in an area—early thirteenth-century South India—that was seemingly free from the threat of Islamicate political power. Thus, although the historically momentous encounter with Islamic civilization during the period 1100–1400 may have greatly impacted Brahmanical attitudes toward widows, it can only account for part of the historical developments outlined in this chapter. Second, even if one accepts significant Islamic influence, it remains to be explained precisely why contact with Islamicate culture or the threat of Islamicate power inspired orthodox Brahmanical communities to change their treatment of widows in the way they did.

Another way to account for the development of mandatory widow asceticism within Dharmaśāstra specifically between the twelfth and fourteenth

[35] Note that although the *Madanapārijāta* was composed in fourteenth-century Kath near Delhi (Kane 1962, 1:798–84), the *Kāśīkhaṇḍa* of the *Skanda Purāṇa* was likely composed in fourteenth-century Benares (Adriaensen, Bakker, and Isaacson 1998, 15–16); the *Nirṇayasindhu* was composed in sixteenth-century Benares (Kane 1962, 1:932–33); and the *Saṃskāramayūkha* was composed in sixteenth-century Bhareha just outside of Benares (Kane 1962, 1:938–40).

centuries is to connect it with widows' markedly increased inheritance rights beginning around the turn of the twelfth century. For as readers may recall from the preceding chapter, the *Mitākṣarā*, a work dating to c. 1075–1125, seemingly ushers in a new period of Hindu law, wherein it was unanimously agreed for the first time that the wife of a sonless man was the primary heir to his entire estate. Moreover, it is crucial to recall that a man's wife supplanted specifically his brothers as his primary heir. Hence, it may not be a coincidence that the first Dharmaśāstra texts to advocate widow asceticism—the *Kṛtyakalpataru* and *Smṛticandrikā*—were composed shortly after the *Mitākṣarā* and that the form of widow asceticism prescribed in Dharmaśāstra texts becomes notably harsher around the fourteenth century. For it is easy to interpret these developments as a reaction against the significantly increased inheritance rights of widows, that is, as a juridical attempt to prevent women from properly enjoying their wealth in a context where their lawful right to it was deemed undisputable.

As to why men would seek to prevent widows from enjoying the use of their lawfully owned property, two reasons present themselves. On the one hand, there is the possibility of simple resentment on the part of a man's brothers and other male relatives, as they watched his widow receive property that would otherwise have been theirs. And on the other, there is the great value placed upon the control of women in early South Asia as an index of family honor and social status—a value that, drawing upon the work of Sherry Ortner (1996, 55–58), I have tentatively connected to the hypergamous nature of classical Indian society. Bearing this in mind, one can readily understand how threatening men living in traditional Brahmanical communities would have found female relatives who were independently wealthy, such as many sonless widows would have been according to the *Mitākṣarā* and all subsequent Dharmaśāstra texts. Hence, unpleasant as it may be to contemplate, it is plausible to interpret the development of widow asceticism within Dharmaśāstra, in part or in full, as a reaction to the increasing inheritance rights of widows. Furthermore, as we will see in the next chapter, it is even more plausible to interpret the adoption of sati within Brahmanical communities as precisely such a reaction.

4
Sati

This chapter deals with what is undoubtedly the most widely discussed and hotly debated aspect of traditional Hindu widowhood: the practice of widow self-immolation, or more precisely the practice of a Hindu widow committing suicide by ritually ascending the funeral pyre of her deceased husband. A number of terms both in English and in Indian languages have been used to denote this practice. Although English sources often refer to it simply as "widow burning," they perhaps more frequently use the term "sati" to denote it—a practice that I will here adopt both for the sake of convenience and because it has become rather standard usage in scholarly works. Given its currency in modern English, one might regard the term "sati," which is often given the alternative spelling "suttee" in older sources, as an English loan-word rather than a properly foreign word. In any case, its derivation from Sanskrit *satī* during the British colonial period is clear. Importantly, however, the shift from Sanskrit *satī* to English sati involves more than simply the loss of italics and a diacritical mark. It involves a significant semantic shift, too, for the word *satī* in Sanskrit sources never refers to the practice of widow self-immolation. Instead, it denotes a good and virtuous woman. The explanation for the semantic shift from woman to practice in the process of English borrowing is almost certainly that some Hindus came to regard a good, virtuous woman—a *satī*—as one who, among other things, ascends her husband's funeral pyre. Hence, what was at first a term associated with a self-immolating widow became in English the standard term for widow self-immolation itself. Contrary to English usage, however, Sanskrit sources use several different—typically euphemistic—terms to denote the Hindu practice of widow self-immolation, specifically: *sahagamana* ("going with"), *anugamana* ("going after"), *sahamaraṇa* ("dying with"), *anumaraṇa* ("dying after"), and *anvārohaṇa* ("ascending after").

As I have already alluded, sati has often been discussed in an array of modern sources, including newspaper articles, colonial administrative

Widows Under Hindu Law. David Brick, Oxford University Press. © Oxford University Press 2023.
DOI: 10.1093/oso/9780197664544.003.0005

reports, Christian missionary accounts, and scholarly publications.[1] Despite the enormous amount of attention that it has received, however, a large number of other cultures have historically observed practices strikingly similar to sati—practices that we may collectively describe as ritualized forms of widow suicide or "following into death" (German: Totenfolge). Such practices are attested, for instance, in premodern Japan and China, in an array of colonial and precolonial African societies, and among the medieval Rus and at least a few native tribes of North America.[2] Hence, from a certain perspective, one might say that sati is hardly a uniquely Indian cultural practice and sympathize with those who resent the Western fascination with it as part of the Orientalist legacy, committed to showing the inherent backwardness of traditional Indian society.

Nevertheless, sati must be a subject of sustained discussion in this book, for it was the subject of a lengthy and complex debate within medieval Dharmaśāstra, a debate with important echoes in the later colonial debate on the same topic. Beyond this, there are at least three salient features of sati that seem to set it apart from most other forms of ritual widow suicide and, therefore, make it arguably an object worthy of special scholarly attention. The first of these is that while most cultures that have had institutionalized forms of widow suicide or following into death abandoned the practice altogether by the early twentieth century at the latest, sati is a notable exception. Indeed, as Joerg Fisch (2006, 345) notes in his masterful study of ritual widow suicide as a global phenomenon, "India is the only region in the world in which following into death can be proved to exist even today."[3] The second rather distinctive feature of sati—and one that is likely related to the first—is its historical spread beyond royal circles to larger segments of Indian society. For while ritual widow suicide in most societies seems to have been effectively restricted to select members of the ruling class, sati in India eventually came

[1] In terms of scholarly writings, H. T. Colebrooke (1795) very early on wrote an article in which he translates and briefly discusses an array of Dharmaśāstra texts on sati. Since then, a number of later Indologists (e.g., Hall 1868; Kane 1962, 2:624–36; Garzilli 1997) have also cited and analyzed these and a handful of other Sanskrit texts on the topic. Most scholarship on sati, however, has dealt with non-Sanskrit sources and especially with the colonial and modern periods (e.g., Mani 1998; Narasimhan 1992; Nandy 1994).

[2] For an extensive discussion of ritualized widow suicide outside of India, see Fisch (2006, 23–209).

[3] For scholarly discussions of the most recent known act of sati, that performed by the Rajput widow Roop Kanwar on September 4, 1987, see Narasimhan (1992, 1–10), Oldenburg (1994, 101–30), and Nandy (1994, 131–59).

to be an established custom among Hindu widows of virtually every social class, although members of the higher castes do seem to have engaged in the practice more frequently.[4] The final unique feature of sati is that it is much better documented and, thus, known than any other form of ritual widow suicide (Fisch 2006, 9).

Earliest Sources

There is absolutely no mention of sati in the Dharmasūtras, Manu, Yājñavalkya, or Nārada. It is only in the two youngest surviving Smṛtis of the Dharmaśāstra tradition—those ascribed to Viṣṇu and Parāśara—that one encounters any reference to the practice. Thus, sati first appears in Dharmaśāstra literature at a relatively late date, specifically around the seventh century CE. Far earlier than this, however, we find references to sati in non-Dharmaśāstra sources. Therefore, it is worth giving a brief account of these sources in order to provide relevant context for understanding later Dharmaśāstric treatments of the topic.

Much like the early Dharmaśāstra literature, the Vedas do not contain any clear references to sati. Nevertheless, as I will show later on, several Dharmaśāstra commentators interpret the following verse of the *Ṛgveda* (10.18.7), the earliest surviving South Asian text, as an oblique reference to the practice:

> Let these women, who are not widows, but rather have good husbands, enter together with fresh butter as ointment! Without tears or afflictions and possessed of fine jewels, let the wives ascend the womb first!
>
> *imâ nârīr avidhavâḥ supátnīr âñjanena sarpíṣā sáṃ viśantu |*
> *anaśrávo 'namīvâḥ surátnā â rohantu jânayo yónim ágre ||*

I will explain how and why certain Dharmaśāstra commentators find in this cryptic verse a reference to sati, when analyzing their general treatments of the practice. For now, however, it is sufficient to note that the verse almost certainly does not refer to any form of widow self-immolation. In order to

4 See Fisch (2006, 258–59) and Mani (1998, 22).

understand its likely meaning, one must read it in connection with the immediately following verse (ṚV 10.18.8):

> "Arise, woman, to the world of the living. You lie beside him whose life is gone. Come here! You have come into existence now as wife of a husband who has grasped your hand and desires to have you."[5]
>
> *úd īrṣva nary abhí jīvalokáṃ gatâsum etám úpa śeṣa éhi |*
> *hastagrābhásya didhiṣós távedáṃ pátyur janitvám abhí sáṃ babhūtha ||*

As Jamison and Brereton (2014, 1399) explain, these two verses apparently refer to an old Vedic funerary practice: "From verse 8 it appears that the widow lies down, temporarily, beside her dead husband, but is summoned back to life and indeed symbolically reborn to become the wife of a new husband (quite possibly her brother-in-law, in levirate marriage). The happy women in verse 7 apparently approach the funeral pyre to adorn the widow for her return to life."[6] Hence, *Ṛgveda* 10.18.7 provides an extremely dubious basis upon which to establish the custom of sati in the early Vedic period (c. 1200–1000 BCE), especially when one considers the absence of references to the practice in the subsequent Vedic literature, which significantly includes numerous detailed descriptions of late Vedic funerals.[7]

Perhaps the earliest surviving references to sati come not from the Indian subcontinent itself, but rather from several Western Greek sources, specifically from the *Geographica* of Strabo and the *Bibliotheca historica* of Diodorus Siculus, both authors belonging to the first century BCE who apparently rely upon earlier historians connected with Alexander the Great for their descriptions of sati.[8] Hence, Greek sources indicate that the practice of sati was current in at least Northwestern India as early as the fourth century BCE. Moreover, the specific content of these sources suggests that it was practiced largely or perhaps even exclusively by members of the ruling class, specifically the widows of kings.[9]

[5] Translation by Jamison and Brereton (2014).

[6] Basham (1968, 188–89), however, concludes from this passage that while widow burning had become obsolete by the time of the *Ṛgveda*, it was practiced in earlier times.

[7] It bears noting, however, that a hymn of the *Atharvaveda* (17.50.1–3) seemingly speaks of a husband and wife traveling together to the next world and, thus, perhaps alludes to some form of sati. I thank Timothy Lubin for drawing my attention to this passage.

[8] For a detailed discussion of Greek and Latin sources on sati, see Garzilli (1997).

[9] If Garzilli (1997, 221) is correct in her suggestion that the Kathaioi mentioned in Strabo should be identified with Brahmins of the Kāṭhaka Vedic school, this would constitute an important exception to the above statement.

Probably the earliest references to sati in Indian literature come from the *Mahābhārata*, the longer of the two great Sanskrit epics. In keeping with its narrative focus on kingly culture and warfare, the *Mahābhārata* contains numerous literary descriptions of how royal women would conduct themselves after the deaths of their husbands. In fact, the eleventh book of the epic, the *Strī Parvan* or "Book of Women" centers on such descriptions. Tellingly, however, the *Strī Parvan* makes no mention whatsoever of sati, and occurrences of sati throughout the entire epic are rather rare and restricted almost exclusively to the widows of kings and princes.[10] This suggests that sati was a rather exceptional practice in North India, during the period in which the epic as we have it took shape (c. 300 BCE–300 CE). It, furthermore, confirms the general impression gathered from early Greek sources that it was observed mainly or perhaps exclusively by members of royal families.

To give just one concrete example of sati from the *Mahābhārata* that is fairly representative of its treatment throughout the epic, one might point to the story of the death of Pāṇḍu, the father of the epic's five chief protagonists, the Pāṇḍava brothers. Prior to his death, Pāṇḍu has renounced his role as king of the city of Hastināpura and taken up a life of ascetic celibacy, because a Brahmin sage has fatefully cursed him to an immediate death should he ever again have sex. Despite his sworn celibacy, however, Pāṇḍu's two young wives, Kuntī and Mādrī, accompany him to the forest. Then, on a beautiful day in spring—the season most associated with sexual love in India as in the West—Pāṇḍu takes a stroll through the forest accompanied only by his younger wife Mādrī (MBh 1.116.2–5); becomes smitten by her beauty (6–7); forces himself upon her despite her attempts to resist him and, thereby, save his life (8–10); and dies at once (11–12). Kuntī then hears Mādrī's piteous lament (13); comes quickly with their five young sons to investigate (14); learns what has happened and grieves her husband's passing (15–21); and thereafter decides to perform sati as his eldest lawful wife (23–24). Mādrī, however, asks Kuntī's permission to perform sati in her stead for two basic reasons (25–30). First, Pāṇḍu has died out of a sexual desire for her and only by following him in death can she carry out in the hereafter her wifely duty of fulfilling her husband's desire. Second, she claims that she is incapable of

[10] References to sati in the *Mahābhārata* include the following: 4.22.5–25, where the kinsmen of Kīcaka, King Virāṭa's brother-in-law, unsuccessfully try to burn Draupadī on Kīcaka's pyre (here the wicked character of the perpetrators would seem to account for the element of overt coercion); 12.144.1–12, where a grief-stricken dove performs sati; 16.8.18, where several wives of King Vasudeva resolve to perform sati; and 16.8.71, where several wives of Kṛṣṇa perform sati.

treating Kuntī's sons as lovingly as her own should she have to act as their mother. Mādrī's arguments immediately persuade Kuntī, who lives on as the Pāṇḍavas' sole surviving mother throughout the epic, while Mādrī ritually ascends her husband's funeral pyre (31). As readers can see, this narrative reveals two crucial features of sati as it is presented in the *Mahābhārata* and many other works of Sanskrit literature. The first of these is that it is a strictly voluntary undertaking. It is not presented as a mandatory practice nor does physical coercion constitute a motivating factor in its lawful execution. The second feature of sati is its special goal, which is the unbroken continuation in the next life of a wife's faithful and devoted service to her husband—the very reason for her existence, according to many classical Hindu texts.

Another early description of sati comes from a work that we have already encountered in the preceding chapter on widow asceticism, namely, the *Puṟanāṉūṟu*, a collection of classical Tamil poetry that has been dated to the second or third century CE. In particular, poems 246 and 247 of the *Puṟanāṉūṟu* deal with sati. The former is ascribed to Peruṅkōpeṇṭu, the wife of a recently deceased Tamil king, who conveys her ardent desire to ascend her husband's pyre despite the plans to the contrary of her male guardians. The essential reason given in the poem for her decision to perform sati is a profound aversion to the ascetic hardships of South Indian widowhood, which include the consumption of only bland food and sleeping on the bare ground.[11] The latter poem is ascribed to a male witness to Peruṅkōpeṇṭu's self-immolation, who expresses his wonder at her act. Together these poems confirm the exceptional nature of sati, its voluntary character at least in the literary imagination, and its restriction to the ruling classes in early South Asia. Their rather realistic tone—in contrast, for instance, to the Sanskrit epics—also supports the impression that sati was an actual cultural practice at the time, rather than a mere literary trope. And the general provenance of the *Puṟanāṉūṟu* shows that even fairly early on, sati was practiced in South India as well as the North.

Following these early literary references to sati, there also begin to appear around the sixth century CE an increasingly large number of inscriptions that record specific instances of sati, as well as uninscribed stones that clearly memorialize acts of sati.[12] These objects and inscriptions attest both to the actual practice of sati throughout much of the Indian subcontinent and to its

[11] For more on widow asceticism in early India, see Chapter 3 and Hart (1973).
[12] On these, see Kane (1962, 2:629), Seṭṭar and Sontheimer (1982), and Fisch (2006, 226–28).

gradual spread to new segments of society beyond high-caste ruling families. For example, an inscription in the Kannada language dated to the year 1057 records in laudatory words how the daughter of a provincial governor of explicitly low-caste origin performed sati against her parents' objections.[13] Unfortunately, not enough research has been done to map the spread of sati geographically and socially with any real precision on the basis of inscriptional sources. Relying on both inscriptional and literary evidence, however, one can say with some confidence that it spread historically from royal circles to the rest of Hindu society[14] and that this spread began in the second half of the first millennium CE and gained special momentum in the first half of the second millennium.

The Smṛtis

As mentioned earlier, of all the extant Smṛtis of the Dharmaśāstra tradition, only the two youngest, namely, the *Vaiṣṇava Dharmaśāstra* and the *Parāśara Smṛti*, make any mention of sati. The relevant passages of these works read as follows[15]:

> When a woman's husband has died, she should either practice lifelong celibacy or ascend the funeral pyre after him.
>
> *mṛte bhartari brahmacaryaṃ tadanvārohaṇaṃ vā* | (ViDh 25.14)
>
> If a woman adheres to a vow of celibacy after her husband has died, then when she dies, she obtains heaven, just like those who were celibate. Further, three and a half crores or however many hairs are on a human body—for that long a time in years a woman who follows her husband in death shall dwell in heaven. And just as a snake-catcher forcefully lifts up

[13] See *Epigraphia Indica*, vol. 6, pp. 213–19.

[14] Fisch (2006, 12–15, 248–54) refers to this as a shift from institutionalized following into death to individual following into death—the latter form being a distinguishing feature of sati throughout much of its history.

[15] Like ViDh 25.14, ViDh 20.39 also apparently refers to a form of following into death: "Even when he has died, relatives cannot follow a dead man, for the path of Yama is cut off for all save his wife." (*mṛte 'pi bāndhavaiḥ śakyaṃ nānugantuṃ naraṃ mṛtam | jāyāvarjaṃ hi sarvasya yāmyaḥ panthā vibhidyate* ||) However, the later commentarial literature of the Dharmaśāstra tradition never cites this passage in connection with sati.

a snake out of its hole, so does this woman lift up her husband and then rejoices together with him.

mṛte bhartari yā nārī brahmacaryavrate sthitā |
sā mṛtā labhate svargaṃ yathā te brahmacāriṇaḥ ||
tisraḥ koṭyo 'rdhakoṭī ca yāni romāṇi mānuṣe |
tāvatkālaṃ vaset svarge bhartāraṃ yānugacchati ||
vyālagrāhī yathā vyālaṃ balād uddharate bilāt |
evaṃ strī patim uddhṛtya tenaiva saha modate || (PSm 4.31–33)

From these passages it is clear that the authors of these two late Dharmaśāstras regarded sati as a meritorious alternative to lifelong celibacy for at least some widows. Moreover, both passages provide some slight evidence that their authors regarded sati as the superior of these two alternatives. In the case of Parāśara, this evidence consists of the fact that the otherworldly rewards of sati are elaborated in far greater detail than those of lifelong celibacy, which would seem to imply that sati is the more meritorious of the two options.[16] In the case of Viṣṇu, this evidence consists of the fact that the text (25.14) lists sati second as an alternative marked by the particle *vā* ("or"). At first glance, this by itself might appear to tell us nothing. However, Kiparski (1979) has convincingly demonstrated that, in his *Aṣṭādhyāyī*, the famed Sanskrit grammarian Pāṇini uses the word *vā* to mark the more preferable of two alternatives. In other words, *vā* does not simply mean "or" for Pāṇini; it means "or preferably." Hence, if Viṣṇu is here following Pāṇini's particular usage of *vā*, then he must consider sati to be preferable to lifelong celibacy as an option for widows. Unfortunately, however, it is unclear whether or not he is in fact following Pāṇini's precise usage here and, as a result, the issue must remain unresolved.

In any case, it is clear from the above passage of Parāśara that sati is held to possess two special soteriological powers. First, it ensures the continuation in the hereafter of the marital union and close personal bond between husband and wife and, second, it brings about a rebirth in heaven for a widow's husband, even if his past actions would ordinarily have resulted in a less desirable rebirth. Hence, the vision of the hereafter and the soteriology underlying sati differ markedly from the standard classical Hindu view on these matters,

[16] The commentator Mādhava reaches precisely this conclusion, for he introduces PSm 4.32 with the statement: "Now the author shows that the reward for sati is even greater than that just stated for celibacy." (*uktabrahmacaryād apy adhikaphalam anugamane darśayati* |) This shows that Mādhava regards sati as the superior of the two alternatives, although certainly not mandatory.

for according to this view, one's future rebirths depend solely upon one's own past actions, not upon the actions of any others, including one's wife. As such, a person's journey through various rebirths can be regarded as highly individualistic in that his/her social position and personal relationships in one life do not carry over to subsequent ones. In its special otherworldly effects, therefore, sati reflects a notable departure from classical Hindu soteriology. And this is unlikely to be a coincidence, for Joerg Fisch (2006, 10–11) has argued that a major precondition for the practice of following into death to develop and endure in a given society is a belief that the social order of this life is part of the next life as well. And yet, as he readily acknowledges and as is generally well-known, classical Indian religions, including Hinduism, espouse a markedly different soteriology from this, one based fundamentally upon laws of *karma*. Thus, the preservation of sati within Hinduism seems to require it to be exceptional from a soteriological point of view. And, indeed, in its special telos, sati appears to contain a combination of older and newer soteriological elements. The practice reflects an older soteriology in that a woman who performs it and her husband continue on as a married couple in the hereafter. Yet it reflects a newer soteriology based on *karma* in that the union of husband and wife in the next life is not simply assumed. Instead, it is only through the extraordinary and highly meritorious act of sati that this, as well as an especially long stay in heaven, becomes possible. Fisch (2006, 463) aptly characterizes this development as the "moralization" of sati.

In addition to the above passages of Viṣṇu (25.14) and Parāśara (4.31–33), an examination of the commentarial literature reveals a number of passages advocating sati ascribed to authors of Dharmaśāstras that are no longer extant. Such authors include Aṅgiras, Uśanas, Paiṭhīnasi, Vyāsa, Hārīta, and Bṛhaspati.[17] Taken together with the previous textual citations, these passages constitute the entirety of the Dharmaśāstras' injunctions regarding sati. However, a complete account of the scriptural injunctions related to sati must also include several passages from Smṛti works of other genres, specifically the Purāṇas and Sanskrit epics.[18]

[17] See Medhātithi on MDh 1.157; *Mitākṣarā* on YDh 1.86; Aparārka on YDh 1.87; Mādhava on PSm 4.32–33; *Madanapārijāta*, pp. 196–200; *Smṛticandrikā*, *Vyavahārakāṇḍa*, p. 596; *Śuddhimayūkha*, pp. 68–69; and *Nirṇayasindhu*, pp. 438–39.

[18] For instance, Aparārka (on YDh 1.87), the *Kṛtyakalpataru* (*Vyavahārakāṇḍa*, p. 634), and the *Nirṇayasindhu* (p. 438) all cite an identical passage that they ascribe to the *Brahma Purāṇa*; the *Nirṇayasindhu* (pp. 438–40) cites passages ascribed to the *Skanda*, *Vāyu*, *Bṛhannārada*, and *Brahmavaivarta Purāṇas*; Aparārka (on YDh 1.87) mentions but does not cite a story from the *Rāmāyaṇa*, which purportedly approves of Brahmin widows performing sati; the *Mitākṣarā* (on

Considering the complete absence of any mention of sati in both Vedic literature and the earliest works of the Dharmaśāstra tradition, it is reasonable to conclude that this practice first gained enough popularity within Brahmanical culture to warrant mention at approximately the time when Viṣṇu, Parāśara, Aṅgiras, Uśanas, and others composed their works on Hindu law. Consequently, sati appears to have first become a recognized custom within orthodox Brahmanical communities around the seventh century CE, to which Viṣṇu and Parāśara have been plausibly dated (Olivelle 2010, 46–48). Beyond this, it is clear from citations found in later digests and commentaries that by the twelfth century, these works and the practice of sati were widely known to orthodox Brahmins throughout India.[19]

Importantly, however, not all Smṛti passages that mention sati endorse the practice, for beginning with Vijñāneśvara (c. 1075–1125), authors working within the Dharmaśāstra tradition cite a number of authoritative scriptures that explicitly prohibit Brahmin widows from performing sati. The two most frequently cited of these are ascribed to Paiṭhīnasi and Aṅgiras.[20] They read as follows:

> Due to Vedic injunction, a Brahmin woman should not follow her husband in death, but for the other social classes, tradition holds this to be the supreme law of women.
>
> *mṛtānugamanaṃ nāsti brāhmaṇyā brahmaśāsanāt* |
> *itareṣāṃ tu varṇānāṃ strīdharmo 'yaṃ paraḥ smṛtaḥ* ||

YDh 1.86) cites MBh 12.144.9–10 and 12, which refers to the story of a female dove performing sati; and the *Madanapārijāta* (pp. 197, 199) and *Nirṇayasindhu* (p. 439) also cite MBh 12.144.9–10, as well as another passage ascribed to the *Mahābhārata*, but not found in the critical edition of that text.

[19] The following Dharmaśāstra works/authors all discuss sati at some length: Medhātithi on MDh 5.157 (c. 825–1000, Kashmir); the *Mitākṣarā* on YDh 1.86 (c. 1075–1125, Karnataka); Aparārka on YDh 1.87 (c. 1125–1175, North Konkan); the *Kṛtyakalpataru, Vyavahārakāṇḍa*, pp. 632–36 (c. 1110–1150, Kannauj); the *Smṛticandrikā, Vyavahārakāṇḍa*, pp. 596–97 (c. 1150–1225, South India); Mādhava on PSm 4.32–33 (c. 1330–1360, Vijayanagara); the *Madanapārijāta*, pp. 196–201 (c. 1350–1400, U. P.); the *Śuddhitattva*, pp. 234–43 (c. 1510–1580, Bengal); the *Śuddhimayūkha*, pp. 68–71 (c. 1610–1650, eastern U. P.); the *Nirṇayasindhu*, pp. 438–40 (1612, Benares); and the *Dharmasindhu*, pp. 384–86 (1790–1791, Maharashtra). On the provenances of these works, see Kane (1962, vol. 1).

[20] See Aparārka on YDh 1.87; *Mitākṣarā* on YDh 1.86; *Madanapārijāta*, p. 197; *Śuddhimayūkha*, p. 69; and *Nirṇayasindhu*, p. 438.

> When a woman of Brahmin caste follows her husband in death, by killing herself she leads neither herself nor her husband to heaven.
>
> *yā strī brāhmaṇajātīyā mṛtaṃ patim anuvrajet |*
> *sā svargam ātmaghātena nātmānaṃ na patiṃ nayet ||*

Although all medieval exegetes who cite these passages and others like them manage to greatly reduce their proscriptive scope, to a neutral reader their intention is clear: they issue a general prohibition against sati in the case of Brahmin widows. Hence, they inform us that while their authors, who were undoubtedly Brahmins themselves, had no specific objection against non-Brahmin widows performing sati, they strongly objected to this practice among widows of their own social class. This, in turn, suggests that, at the time these scriptures were composed, sati was an established custom among the ruling elites and perhaps certain other social groups as well, but still relatively new and, therefore, controversial among orthodox Brahmins. At the very least, these scriptures tell us that some authoritative Brahmin men felt deeply apprehensive about widows within their own families performing sati.

Medhātithi

Let us turn now from the Smṛtis to the Dharmaśāstra commentaries. The earliest commentator to discuss the issue of sati is Medhātithi, who probably wrote his influential commentary on Manu in ninth-century Kashmir. Bearing in mind the general Brahmanical apprehension about sati detectable in certain Smṛtis and Medhātithi's personal opposition to widow asceticism, it should not come as a major surprise that he staunchly opposes the practice of sati. The relevant passage of his work (on MDh 5.157)[21] reads as follows:

> Suicide is prohibited for women just as it is for men. There is the following statement from the Dharmaśāstra of Aṅgiras: "Women should follow their husbands in death." But one should certainly not carry this out like a mandatory duty, for this statement praises the reward of performing this act. And since it makes a woman's desire for that reward a qualification for her to perform it, the case is analogous to the *śyena* rite. Indeed, even when a

[21] In Jha's edition of Medhātithi, this is MDh 1.155.

person who is qualified to "kill living beings by means of the *śyena* rite" actually engages in that rite when blinded by excessive hatred, it is not in accordance with the law. It is just so here as well. When a woman who has an excessive desire for the result kills herself despite the fact that there is a prohibition against this and she is acting in violation of it, her reason for doing so is not based upon the scriptures. Hence, a woman is certainly prohibited also from following her husband in death. Moreover, since it is in contradiction with the express Vedic scripture, "Therefore, one should not die before one's natural lifespan" (ŚPB 10.2.6.7), one can construe this Smṛti text to have a different meaning. In this regard, it is just like the Smṛti, "Having recited the Veda, one should bathe," which indicates that a person who has not learned the Veda's meaning should bathe after simply reciting it.[22]

puṃvat strīṇām api pratiṣiddha ātmatyāgaḥ | yad apy āṅgirase patim anumriyeran ity uktaṃ tad api na nityavad avaśyaṃ kartavyam | phalastutis tatrāsti | phalakāmāyāś cādhikāre śyenatulyatā | tathaiva śyenena hiṃsyād bhūtānīty adhikārasyātipravṛddhataradveṣāndhatayā satyām api pravṛttau na dharmatvam | evam ihāpy atipravṛddhaphalābhilāṣāyāḥ saty api pratiṣedhe tadatikrameṇa maraṇe pravṛttyupapatter na śāstrīyatvam | ato 'sty eva patim anumaraṇe 'pi striyāḥ pratiṣedhaḥ | kiṃ ca tasmād u ha na purāyuṣaḥ preyād iti pratyakṣaśrutivirodhe smṛtir apy eṣā anyārthā śakyate kalpayitum yathā vedam adhītya snāyād ity adhyayanānantaram akṛtārthāvabodhasya snānasmaraṇam |

Here Medhātithi puts forth two different arguments against sati. First, he argues that the practice is contrary to *dharma*, because it is analogous to the *śyena* sacrifice, a Vedic ritual already encountered in Chapter 1, whose explicit result is the death of the sacrificer's enemies. As readers may recall, the

[22] I have been unable to identify the text to which this Smṛti passage belongs. However, here Medhātithi is likely referring to Śabara's commentary on PMS 1.1.1: "Next, therefore, is the inquiry into the law." (*athāto dharmajijñāsā* |) Śabara interprets the word *atha* ("next") in this *sūtra* as indicating that the inquiry into *dharma* (*dharmajiñāsā*) should occur after one has learned to recite the Veda. The hypothetical objection to this interpretation is raised that the scripture cited by Medhātithi enjoins a person to take a bath—presumably the graduation bath marking the end of Vedic study—after reciting the Veda, not to then seek to understand its meaning. In response to this objection, Śabara construes this scripture in the following manner, which is compatible with his position: "This scripture does not enjoin bathing that has an otherworldly purpose (i.e., the graduation bath). Instead, by implication, it simply states that the restrictions placed upon a Vedic student, such as that he should not bathe, cease to apply at the same time that he recites the Veda." (*na vā idaṃ snānam adṛṣṭārthaṃ vidhīyate | kiṃ tu lakṣaṇayāsnānādiniyamasya paryavasānaṃ vedādhyāyanasamakālam āhuḥ* |)

accepted interpretation of this rite is that it is unlawful to perform it, since there is a general scriptural prohibition against violence. The Veda simply states that if a person wants to kill his enemies, the *śyena* sacrifice is one means of accomplishing his goal. It does not, however, enjoin the killing of one's enemies. Consequently, there is no specific injunction that would override the general prohibition against violence. Using the analogy of this rite, Medhātithi argues that Smṛtis like that of Aṅgiras do not actually enjoin sati, because they explicitly mention its result, namely, heaven. They only state that if a widow wants to be reborn in heaven, sati is one possible means. Thus, as in the case of the *śyena* sacrifice, the general prohibition against violence still applies. Medhātithi's second argument against sati is considerably simpler: those Smṛtis that evidently prescribe sati as a means of attaining heaven are in direct contradiction with those statements in the extant Veda that prohibit suicide. And since it is an accepted exegetical principle that the Veda is of greater authority than Smṛti, the various Smṛti statements that appear to advocate sati can be construed to have a different meaning. On these two grounds, the earliest commentarial work within the Dharmaśāstra tradition to address the topic of sati takes a position that is completely opposed to the practice.

Unpublished Commentary on the *Yājñavalkya Dharmaśāstra*

After Medhātithi, the next Dharmaśāstra work to discuss sati is the unpublished commentary on Yājñavalkya that was discussed in Chapter 1 on *niyoga* and widow remarriage. Unlike Medhātithi, this commentary, which Olivelle (2019, xxx) has tentatively dated to the tenth century, fully supports the practice of sati. The relevant passage of it (on YDh 1.87) reads:

> If a woman follows her husband in death, they both attain great prosperity, as Vyāsa has shown via the pretext of a story about a female dove. For he (MBh 12.144.9–10) first states:
>
> > Devoted to her husband, she (= female dove) entered the blazing fire.
> > Then she saw her husband adorned with glittering armbands.
>
> And after this Vyāsa (MBh 12.144.12) states:
>
> > Then that bird went to heaven, united with his wife. There he was honored due to her act and rejoiced together with his wife.

Moreover, Aṅgiras (PSm 4.32) first teaches:

> Three and a half crores or however many hairs are on a human body—for that long a time a woman who follows her husband in death shall dwell in heaven.

Then he (PSm 4.33) teaches that through sati a husband and wife are never separated:

> And just as a snake-catcher forcefully lifts up a snake out of its hole, so this woman lifts up her husband and then rejoices together with him.

Even if her husband went to hell as a result of his actions, because she performed a very difficult deed for the express reward of not being separated from him, she lifts him out of hell. And she does this through the power of her miraculous deed, even if he was a great sinner, just as one draws a snake or the like out of its hole in the earth through the power of spells and herbs. Moreover, she is honored in heaven once more with her husband, all of his sins washed away by the strength of her austerities. The unit of time in the statement about "three and a half crores" is years. And this comprises the universal law for all women right down to Cāṇḍālas,[23] for the scriptural passage speaks generically of "a woman who follows her husband in death" (PSm 4.32). However, she must not be pregnant, as it is a grievous sin for a woman to kill her fetus or husband. Hārīta also speaks the same two verses that start "Three and a half crores . . ." (PSm 4.32–33) and, thereafter, states:

> Her mother's family, her father's family, and the family into which she was given—these three families a woman purifies, if she follows her husband in death.

anugamane ca mahān abhyudayo dvayor api yathā vyāsena kapoti-kākhyānavyājena darśitam—

> *pativratā saṃpradīptaṃ praviveśa hutāśanam |*
> *tataś citrāṅgadadharaṃ bhartāraṃ sānvapaśyateti* || (MBh 12.144.9–10)

uktvā

> *tataḥ sva[r]gaṃ gataḥ pakṣī bhāryayā saha saṃgataḥ |*
> *karmaṇā pūjitas tatra reme tu saha bhāryayeti*[24] || (MBh 12.144.12)

tathāṅgirāḥ[25]

[23] A Cāṇḍāla (sometimes spelled Caṇḍāla) is a member of what is deemed to be the lowliest of all castes in classical Brahmanical literature. For a description of their purported origins and prescribed treatment, see MDh 10.12, 16, 51–56.

[24] Ms. *bhāryāyeti*

[25] Ms. *tathāśāṅgirasoḥ* (cf. *śaṅkhāṅgirasau* in the *Mitākṣarā*)

tisraḥ koṭyo 'rdhakoṭī ca yāni [romāṇi] mānuṣe |
tāvatkālaṃ vaset s[v]arge bhartāraṃ yānugacchatīti || (PSm 4.32)

pratipādya tayor aviyogaṃ pratipādayati—

vyālagrāhī yathā sarpaṃ balāḍ uddharate bilāt |
tadvad uddhṛtya sā nārī saha tenaiva modata iti || (PSm 4.33)

yady api svakarmavipākena narakam asau gatas tathāpi tadaviyoga-phaloddeśenātiduṣkare karmaṇi pravṛtteti yadvan mantrauṣadhibalāt pātālāt[26] *sarpādy ākṛṣyate tadvad asāv apy acintyakarmasāmarthyān narakād uddhṛtyātyantapāpakāriṇam api punas tenaiva svatapaḥprabhāvanirdhauta-sakalakalmaṣeṇa saha svarge mahīyate | tisraḥ koṭyo 'rdhakoṭī ca varṣāṇām | ayaṃ ca sarvāsām ā caṇḍālastrīṇāṃ sādhāraṇo bhartāraṃ yānugacchatīty* (PSm 4.32) *aviśeṣāt | agarbhiṇī garbhabhartṛvadhe mahāpātakatvāt | hārīte[nā]pi tisraḥ koṭyo 'rdhakoṭītyādi ślokadvayam adhidhāyoktam—*

mātṛkaṃ pitṛkaṃ caiva yatra caiva pradīyate |
kulatrayaṃ punāty eṣā bhartāraṃ yānugacchatīti ||

As one can see, this passage does not address any possible objections to the practice of sati and, thus, does not engage in a real juridical debate on the topic in the way that Medhātithi does. Instead, its author is largely content simply to cite a number of Smṛti texts that effectively enjoin widows to follow their husbands in death. The first such text is a section of the *Mahābhārata* (12.144.9–10, 12), recounting the tale of a female dove who ascends the funeral pyre of her deceased husband and is subsequently reunited with him in heaven. The second comprises a pair of verses ascribed to Aṅgiras but also found in Parāśara's work (4.32–33). These verses essentially state that any woman who follows her husband in death will reside with him in heaven for an unfathomably long period of time, even if her husband's actions in life would ordinary have resulted in his rebirth in hell. The commentary on these verses largely just reiterates their evident meaning. However, it does add that sati is a permissible course of action for all women from the highest to the very lowest with the exception of those who are pregnant due to the established prohibition against killing a fetus.[27] The final Smṛti text cited in the commentary is ascribed to Hārīta and proclaims that by performing sati, a woman rescues not only herself but also the families of her mother, father, and husband. Hence, when read alongside Medhātithi, this early

[26] Ms. *pātālatālatāt*
[27] See, e.g., ĀpDh 1.24.6–9.

unpublished commentary on Yājñavalkya reveals significant divergence of opinion on the topic of sati within Brahmanical society during the closing centuries of the first millennium.

Vijñāneśvara

Following Medhātithi and the early unpublished commentary on the *Yājñavalkya Dharmaśāstra*, the next work of Hindu law to discuss the issue of sati is the *Mitākṣarā*, Vijñāneśvara's watershed commentary on Yājñavalkya, which was composed around the turn of the twelfth century. Vijñāneśvara's discussion of the legitimacy of sati is the fullest and most nuanced such discussion in the entire Dharmaśāstra tradition; and, as we will see, its impact on the later literature was considerable. In short, although Vijñāneśvara himself held serious reservations about sati, his work reflects the gradual weakening of opposition to the practice among Dharmaśāstra authors and intellectually sets the stage for the eventual disappearance of all such opposition.

Vijñāneśvara starts his discussion of sati (on YDh 1.86) by citing all of the same Smṛti passages prescribing the practice as the earlier unpublished commentary on Yājñavalkya as well as several more. In language strikingly similar to this earlier commentary, he also goes on to specify that sati is a permissible course of action for all women from the highest to the very lowest with the exception of those who are pregnant or have small children:

> And all of this constitutes the universal law for all women right down to Cāṇḍālas, provided that they are not pregnant and do not have young children, for the scriptural passage speaks generically of "a woman who follows her husband in death." (PSm 4.32)

> *ayaṃ ca sakala eva sarvāsāṃ strīṇām agarbhiṇīnām abālāpatyānām ācāṇḍālaṃ sādhāraṇo dharmaḥ bhartāraṃ yānugacchatīty* (PSm 4.32) *aviśeṣopādānāt* |

After this, however, Vijñāneśvara's work diverges significantly from that of his predecessor in that it explicitly addresses and refutes numerous objections to the practice of sati.

To begin with, Vijñāneśvara attempts to reconcile those Smṛtis that generally enjoin sati with those that apparently prohibit the practice in the case of Brahmin widows. And, importantly, he does this in a way that allows Brahmin women to perform sati with little restriction. His statement on this matter reads as follows:

> Those passages, such as the following, which prohibit Brahmin women from performing sati, apply only to the ascending of separate funeral pyres:
>
> > Due to Vedic injunction, a Brahmin woman should not follow her husband in death, but among the other social classes, this is said to be the highest austerity. Living, she should do what is beneficial to her husband. By dying she commits suicide. When a woman of Brahmin caste follows her husband in death, by killing herself she leads neither herself nor her husband to heaven.
>
> This is so due to the following specific rule given in this Smṛti:
>
> > A Brahmin woman ought not to depart by ascending a separate pyre.

yāni ca brāhmaṇyanugamananiṣedhaparāṇi vākyāni
mṛtānugamanaṃ nāsti brāhmaṇyā brahmaśāsanāt |
itareṣu tu varṇeṣu tapaḥ paramam ucyate |
jīvantī taddhitaṃ kuryān maraṇād ātmaghātinī ||
yā strī brāhmaṇajātīyā mṛtaṃ patim anuvrajet |
sā svargam ātmaghātena nātmānaṃ na patiṃ nayet ||
ityevamādīni tāni pṛthakcityadhirohaṇaviṣayāṇi
pṛthakcitiṃ samāruhya na viprā gantum arhati |
iti viśeṣasmaraṇāt |

Here Vijñāneśvara argues that those Smṛtis that apparently prohibit Brahmin women from performing sati really only prohibit them from performing it on different funeral pyres than those of their husbands. And in support of this interpretation, he cites another scriptural passage that appears to express precisely this idea. Via this argument, essentially based upon a technicality, Vijñāneśvara effectively does away with any objections aimed specifically at the right of Brahmin widows to perform sati.

Moreover, it is noteworthy that Vijnāneśvara's line of argumentation on this point appears to have exerted considerable influence on a large number of later exegetes. For instance, consider the following statements of Aparārka and the *Madanapārijāta* of Madanapāla[28]:

> [Objection:] Isn't it the case that certain Smṛtis prohibit a Brahmin woman from performing sati? For instance, Paiṭhīnasi states:
>
> > Due to Vedic injunction, a Brahmin woman should not follow her husband in death, but for the other social classes, tradition holds this to be the supreme law of women. A virtuous Brahmin woman stricken by grief cannot help her husband when she's dead the way she does when she's alive.
>
> Virāj also states:
>
> > A woman should follow her husband when he's alive, but not follow him into death. She should live on and do what is beneficial to her husband. By dying she is guilty of suicide.
>
> Further, Aṅgiras states:
>
> > When a woman of Brahmin caste follows her husband in death, by killing herself she leads neither herself nor her husband to heaven.
>
> And Vyāghrapad states:
>
> > A Brahmin woman befuddled by grief should not die alongside her husband. She should instead take up a life of renunciation. By dying she is guilty of suicide.
>
> "Renunciation" here denotes the abandonment of such pleasures as sexual intercourse.
>
> [Author:] It is true. Certain Smṛtis say this. However, their actual sphere of applicability is established by another Smṛti, as Uśanas states:
>
> > A Brahmin woman ought not to depart by ascending a separate pyre, yet for other women, tradition holds this to be the supreme law of women.
>
> Therefore, the prohibition against Brahmin women performing sati refers only to ascending separate funeral pyres.

nanu ca brāhmaṇyā anvārohaṇapratiṣedhaṃ smaranti yathā tāvat paiṭhīnasiḥ—

> *mṛtānugamanaṃ nāsti brāhmaṇyā brahmaśāsanāt |*
> *itareṣāṃ varṇānāṃ strīdharmo 'yaṃ paraḥ smṛtaḥ ||*
> *upakāraṃ yathā bhartur jīvantī na tathā mṛtā |*
> *karoti brāhmaṇī śreyo bhartuḥ śokavatī satī ||*

[28] Also see *Śuddhimayūkha*, p. 69 and *Nirṇayasindhu*, p. 438.

virāṭ—

anuvarteta jīvantaṃ na tu yāyān mṛtaṃ patim |
jīved bhartur hitaṃ kuryān maraṇād ātmaghātinī ||

aṅgirāḥ—

yā strī brāhmaṇajātīyā mṛtaṃ patim anuvrajet |
sā svargam ātmaghātena nātmānaṃ na patiṃ nayet ||

vyāghrapāt—

na mriyeta samaṃ bhartrā brāhmaṇī śokamohitā |
pravrajyāgatim āpnoti maraṇād ātmaghātinī ||

pravrajyā maithunādibhogatyāgaḥ | satyam evaṃ smaranti kiṃ tu smaraṇāntareṇaiteṣāṃ viṣayo vyavasthāpyate yathośanāḥ—

pṛthakcitiṃ samāruhya na viprā gantum arhati |
anyāsāṃ caiva nārīṇāṃ strīdharmo 'yaṃ paraḥ smṛtaḥ ||

tataś ca brāhmaṇyanugamananiṣedhaḥ pṛthakcitisamārohaṇaviṣayaḥ |
(Aparārka on YDh 1.87)

As for the following statements of Paiṭhīnasi, Aṅgiras, etc., which prohibit Brahmin women from performing sati, these apply only to separate funeral pyres:

Due to Vedic injunction, a Brahmin woman should not follow her husband in death.

When a woman of Brahmin caste follows her husband in death, by killing herself she leads neither herself nor her husband to heaven.

This is so due to the following specific rule laid out in the Smṛti of Uśanas:

A Brahmin woman ought not to depart by ascending a separate pyre, yet for other women, tradition holds this to be the supreme law of women.

yāni ca brāhmaṇyanugamananiṣedhaparāṇi paiṭhīnasyaṅgiraḥprabhṛtīnāṃ vākyāni

mṛtānugamanaṃ nāsti brāhmaṇyā brahmaśāsanāt ||
yā strī brāhmaṇajātīyā mṛtaṃ patim anuvrajet |
sā svargam ātmaghātena nātmānaṃ na patiṃ nayet ||

ityevamādīni tāni pṛthakcitiviṣayāṇi |

pṛthakcitiṃ samāruhya na viprā gantum arhati |
anyāsāṃ caiva nārīṇāṃ strīdharmo 'yaṃ paraḥ smṛtaḥ ||

ity uśanaso viśeṣasmaraṇāt | (*Madanapārijāta*, pp. 197–98)

Here both Aparārka and Madanapāla adopt Vijñāneśvara's exact line of thinking. This is not only apparent in their conclusions: those Smṛtis which seemingly issue a general prohibition against Brahmin women performing sati really prohibit them merely from ascending separate funeral pyres. It is also apparent in their supporting evidence, which comprises the very same Smṛti cited by Vijñāneśvara, only here explicitly ascribed to Uśanas. From the presence of such statements and the complete absence of contrary ones, it is evident that commentators within the Dharmaśāstra tradition, starting with Vijñāneśvara, differ markedly from the authors of some earlier Smṛtis in that they feel no particular reservations about Brahmin widows performing sati.

To return to the *Mitākṣarā*, after severely limiting the prohibitive scope of those Smṛtis that seemingly proscribe sati for Brahmin widows, Vijñāneśvara then attempts to demonstrate that the practice is dissimilar to the *śyena* rite and, therefore, in full conformity with *dharma*. In other words, at this point Vijñāneśvara responds directly to Medhātithi's earlier discussion of sati, with which he was obviously familiar, and specifically tries to refute the first of Medhātithi's arguments against the practice. The relevant portion of Vijñāneśvara's discussion reads as follows:

> Some have argued the following: "Since suicide is prohibited for women as for men, this instruction that prescribes self-immolation is for women who have an excessive desire for heaven and so violate the scripture prohibiting suicide. Hence, it is like the *śyena* rite, as the instruction to perform the *śyena* rite, namely, 'One who uses black magic should perform the *śyena* sacrifice' (ṢB 3.8.1), is for a person whose mind is overcome with excessive anger and so violates the scripture prohibiting violence."
>
> This argument is not proper. Now, some explain that the *śyena* rite is detrimental to perform because of its result (i.e., the death of one's enemies), it being the case that the force brought about through the instrument of the *śyena* rite results in injury to living beings. Therefore, the general prohibition against violence still applies, because no specific injunction applies. According to this opinion, sati is quite clearly dissimilar to the *śyena* rite, but is rather like the *agnīṣomīya* rite (which involves animal sacrifice), for the scripture regarding sati enjoins violence itself for the purpose of rebirth in heaven. Consequently, no prohibition applies (i.e., there is no prohibition against rebirth in heaven).
>
> Others, however, hold the following opinion: "What is called 'violence' is any activity conducive to death; and the *śyena* rite itself is, in fact, violence, because it consists of an activity conducive to death. Furthermore, since desire constitutes a qualification for the *śyena* rite, any injunction to perform

it fails to result in a mandatory undertaking, as it is possible that one would undertake the part of the rite that is the instrument (i.e., the ritual actions of the *śyena*) out of passion. Therefore, the *śyena* rite is prohibited and detrimental to perform by its very nature, since it has the form of violence employed out a natural desire." According to this opinion as well, there is no occasion for the prohibition of sati. Instead, the practice is analogous to the statement, "One desiring prosperity should sacrifice a white animal for Vāyu" (TS 2.1.1.1). This is because the scripture regarding sati enjoins death itself as a means of attaining heaven. Thus, although one might undertake to kill oneself out of a natural desire to reach heaven, nevertheless one undertakes those activities conducive to death (i.e., violence), such as entering the fire, on account of the injunctions themselves, since such activities have the nature of necessary steps in the process. Therefore, sati's dissimilarity from the *śyena* rite is quite clear.

yat tu kaiścid uktaṃ puruṣāṇām iva strīṇām apy ātmahananasya pratiṣiddhatvād atipravṛddhasvargābhilāṣāyāḥ pratiṣedhaśāstram atikrāmantyā ayam anugamanopadeśaḥ śyenavat yathā śyenenābhicaran yajeteti tīvrakrodhākrāntasvāntasya pratiṣedhaśāstram atikrāmataḥ śyenopadeśa iti tad ayuktam | ye tāvat śyenakaraṇikāyāṃ bhāvanāyāṃ bhāvyabhūtahiṃsāyāṃ vidhisaṃsparśābhāvena pratiṣedhasaṃsparśāt phaladvāreṇa śyenasyānarthatāṃ varṇayanti teṣāṃ mate hiṃsāyā eva svargārthatayā anugamanaśāstreṇa vidhīyamānatvāt pratiṣedhasaṃsparśābhāvād agnīṣomīyavat spaṣṭam evānugamanasya śyenavaiṣamyam | yat tu mataṃ hiṃsā nāma maraṇānukūlo vyāpāraḥ śyenaś ca paramaraṇānukūlavyāpārarūpatvād dhiṃsaiva | kāmādhikāre ca karaṇāṃśe rāgataḥ pravṛttisaṃbhavena vidher apravartakatvāt rāgaprayuktahiṃsārūpatvāt śyenaḥ pratiṣiddhaḥ svarūpeṇaivānarthakara iti tatrāpy anugamanaśāstreṇa maraṇasyaiva svargasādhanatayā vidhānān maraṇe yady api rāgataḥ pravṛttis tathāpi maraṇānukūle vyāpāre 'gnipraveśādāv itikartavyatārūpe vidhita eva pravṛttir iti na niṣedhasyāvakāśaḥ vāyavyaṃ śvetam ālabheta bhūtikāma itivat | tasmāt spaṣṭam evānugamanasya śyenavaiṣamyam |

In order to refute Medhātithi's thesis that sati is analogous to the *śyena* rite, Vijñāneśvara here postulates two different arguments, both of which aim to explain why the performance of the *śyena* sacrifice violates *dharma*. He then attempts to show that these arguments do not work in the case of sati.

In outline, the first argument he presents goes as follows: (a) There is a general prohibition against violence. (b) The *śyena* sacrifice involves violence, since its outcome is the death of one's enemies. (c) Only a specific injunction stating that one should kill one's enemies could override the general prohibition, but no such injunction exists.[29] Therefore, (d) the *śyena* rite is prohibited by the scriptures. Vijñāneśvara holds that part c of this argument does not apply in the case of sati, since the practice is actually enjoined by certain Smṛtis. He points out that unlike the *śyena* rite, which results in violence, a prohibited outcome, sati results in heavenly rebirth, a permissible outcome. The *śyena* sacrifice is prohibited, because its violence is its result and its result is not enjoined. In other words, it is prohibited because the scriptures nowhere state that a person should kill his enemies and this is the violent part of the sacrifice. By contrast, the violence of the sati rite (i.e., the widow's suicide) is actually enjoined, as a means to rebirth in heaven; and although the scriptures may not specifically enjoin rebirth in heaven, they certainly do not prohibit it. Vijñāneśvara adds that sati should instead be treated like the Vedic *agnīṣomīya* rite, which both involves violence to living beings (animals) and leads to a permissible outcome. Since the *agnīṣomīya* rite is permitted, sati should be as well.

The second argument presented by Vijñāneśvara is somewhat more complex. It begins by defining violence: violence is any activity that is conducive to death. Hence, according to this definition, the *śyena* sacrifice itself, and not its outcome, is violence. Consequently, the general prohibition against violence does not apply to the result of the *śyena* sacrifice, only to the rite itself. A difficulty then arises: the Veda technically enjoins the *śyena* sacrifice (though not its result) and such an injunction would normally override a general prohibition, according to the standard exegetical principles of Dharmaśāstra. If this is the case, then how can the *śyena* sacrifice be prohibited? In order to solve this dilemma, the argument relies upon another accepted principle of interpretation that we encountered several times in Chapter 1, namely, that in order to qualify as *dharma*, a scriptural injunction must lack a visible or worldly purpose. That is to say, a scriptural statement that recommends a course of action to which people are naturally inclined does not have injunctive force. This principle is used to divest scriptural statements concerning the *śyena* sacrifice of injunctive force. It is argued that people naturally seek to injure their enemies and, therefore, those Vedic

[29] Instead, technically there is only an injunction to perform the *śyena* rite.

passages that mention the *śyena* rite are not true injunctions. This being the case, the prohibition against violence still applies.

Again, Vijñāneśvara holds that this argument does not apply to the case of sati. He concedes that a widow might seek to die out of a natural desire for heaven, but points out that, according to the proposed definition of violence, which is "activity conducive to death" (*maraṇānukūlo vyāpāraḥ*), dying itself does not constitute violence. However, the parts of the sati rite that do constitute violence, such as entering the fire, are merely necessary steps in the process (*itikartavyatā*). As such, one does not perform them out of a natural desire for heaven, but rather out a desire to complete the rite as enjoined. In this way, Vijñāneśvara refutes Medhātithi's objection to the practice of sati on the grounds that it is analogous to the *śyena* sacrifice. And, significantly, this refutation seems to have been quite effective as not a single later commentator within the Dharmaśāstra tradition takes up this line of argumentation against the custom.

Nevertheless, despite his strong refutation of the *śyena* analogy, Vijñāneśvara appears not to have wholly approved of sati, for he cites two arguments against the practice that he regards as "unobjectionable" (*anavadya*):

> However, there is this argument: "Sati is wrong, because it is opposed to the Vedic statement, 'Therefore, one who desires heaven should not die before one's natural lifespan' (ŚPB 10.2.6.7)." And there is another argument: "Since heaven is indicated as the result in the following scriptural passage, 'Thus, it is not the case that one who desires heaven should not die before one's natural lifespan,' a person who desires liberation should not relinquish his life before his natural lifespan. In other words, so long as life remains, it is possible that through knowledge of the Self, one who has destroyed his mind's blemishes through the performance of perpetual and occasional rites and succeeded at learning, reflecting, and meditating (the three stages of Vedic study) will attain liberation, which is defined as the attainment of *brahman*, which is eternal and unsurpassed bliss. Therefore, one should not relinquish one's life for the sake of heaven, which consists of only impermanent and trivial happiness. And hence, like any other undertaking aimed at fulfilling a specific desire, sati is proper only for a woman who does not desire liberation and instead seeks heaven, which consists of impermanent and trivial happiness." All of this is unobjectionable.

> *yat tu tasmād u ha na purāyuṣaḥ svaḥkāmī preyād iti śrutivirodhād anugamanam ayuktam iti yac ca tad u ha na svaḥkāmy āyuṣaḥ prāṅ na preyād iti svargaphaloddeśenāyuṣaḥ prāg āyurvyayo na kartavyo mokṣārthinā | yasmād āyuṣaḥ śeṣe sati nityanaimittakakarmānuṣṭhāna kṣapitāntaḥkaraṇakalaṅkasya śravaṇamanananididhyāsanasaṃpattau satyām ātmajñānena nityaniratiśayānandabrahmaprālakṣaṇamokṣasaṃbhavaḥ tasmād anityālpasukharūpasvargārtham āyurvyayo na kartavya ity arthaḥ | ataś ca mokṣam anicchantyā anityālpasukharūpasvargārthinyā anugamanaṃ yuktam itarakāmyānuṣṭhānavad iti sarvam anavadyam |*

The first of these arguments against sati is essentially the same as Medhātithi's second argument, namely, that Vedic statements prohibiting suicide effectively negate Smṛti statements enjoining widows to immolate themselves on their husbands' funeral pyres. The second "unobjectionable" argument against sati that is mentioned by Vijñāneśvara goes as follows: Although certain Smṛtis do enjoin sati as a means of attaining heaven, heaven itself is a vastly inferior goal to liberation from the cycle of rebirth altogether. Therefore, since a woman pursuing the alternative practice of lifelong celibacy might possibly attain liberation, this alternative is undoubtedly far superior to sati. Vijñāneśvara's judgment of these two arguments as "unobjectionable" (*anavadya*) shows that while he does not appear to share Medhātithi's strong opposition to sati, he does have considerable reservations about the practice.

Aparārka

It is noteworthy that none of the commentators or digest writers in the centuries following the *Mitākṣarā* takes up the position that Vedic statements prohibiting suicide negate those Smṛtis that apparently enjoin sati. And this—it should be noted—is the only argument accepted by Vijñāneśvara that would actually prohibit sati and not just demote it to the lesser of two alternatives. Moreover, Aparārka, who may have written only a few decades after Vijñāneśvara, explicitly refutes this line of argumentation. His refutation (on YDh 1.87) reads:

> And it should not be objected that the Smṛti passages that enjoin sati are in conflict with the following Vedic passage: "Therefore, one who desires heaven should not die before one's natural lifespan" (ŚPB 10.2.6.7). The

reason for this is that they have different spheres of applicability: the Vedic passage prohibits dying by one's own desire in general, but the Smṛtis enjoin the particular method of dying that is entering the fire when one's husband has died. Hence, there is no conflict, for they have different spheres of applicability. Likewise, there is no conflict with other Vedic passages that have general spheres of applicability, such as "Desiring heaven, one should sacrifice" and "One should perform the Agnihotra rite as long as one lives." And, thus, the *Brahma Purāṇa* states:

> There is no other recourse (than sati) for a good woman when her husband dies, for there is no other way to extinguish the burning pain of being separated from her husband. And when he dies in a distant place, a virtuous woman should place a pair of his sandals on her chest and, purified, enter fire. Due to the statement of the *Ṛgveda*, such a virtuous woman does not commit suicide. And when the three days' impurity has ceased, she obtains an everlasting ancestral offering.

The statement of the *Ṛgveda* referred to here is the set of verses that begins with the phrase "Let these women, who are not widows . . ." (ṚV 10.18.7). Therefore, the Smṛtis that enjoin sati are authoritative. Furthermore, it is not the case that sati can be prohibited by this rule: "One should not kill." For this rule prohibits killing another person who is to be killed by means of the killer. It does not, however, prohibit killing oneself. That is instead prohibited by this: "Therefore, one who desires heaven should not die before one's natural lifespan" (ŚPB 10.2.6.7). And as I have said, because this passage has a general sphere of applicability, the Smṛtis enjoining sati, which have a specific sphere of applicability, restrict it so that it prohibits suicide only in cases other than that (i.e., sati).

na cānvārohaṇasmṛtīnāṃ tasmād u ha na purāyuṣaḥ svaḥkāmī preyād iti (ŚPB 10.2.6.7) *śrutivirodho vācyaḥ bhinnaviṣayatvāt | sāmānyena śrutiḥ svecchayā maraṇaṃ niṣedhati | smṛtis tu mṛte bhartari vahnipraveśamaraṇaviśeṣaṃ vidhatte | ato bhinnaviṣayatvād avirodhaḥ | svargakāmī yajeta yāvaj jīvam agnihotraṃ juhuyād ity evamādikayā śrutyā sāmānyaviṣayayā na virodhaḥ | tathā ca brahmapurāṇam*

> *mṛte bhartari satstrīṇāṃ na cānyā vidyate gatiḥ |*
> *nānyad bhartṛviyogārtidāhapraśamanaṃ bhavet ||*
> *deśāntaramṛte tasmin sādhvī tatpādukādvayam |*
> *nidhāyorasi saṃśuddhā praviśej jātavedasam ||*
> *ṛgvedavādāt sādhvī strī na bhaved ātmaghātinī |*

tryahā[ś]auce tu nivṛtte śrāddhaṃ prāpnoti śāśvatam || imā nārīr avidhavā ityādayo vedaśrutayaḥ | tasmād etāḥ smṛtayaḥ pramāṇam | na ca na hiṃsyād ity anenānvārohaṇaṃ śakyaṃ niṣeddhum | anena hi hantuḥ sakāśād anyasya hantavyasya hiṃsā pratiṣidhyate na tu svavadharūpā | sā tu tasmād u ha na purāyuṣa ity (ŚPB 10.2.6.7) *anena niṣidhyate | idaṃ ca sāmānyaviṣayatvād viśeṣaviṣayayānvārohaṇasmṛtyā tadvyatiriktasvavadhaniṣedhakatvena saṃkocyata ity uktam |*

In this passage, Aparārka engages in the standard Dharmaśāstric practice of harmonizing apparently contradictory scriptures by ascribing to them different spheres of applicability. According to his analysis, those Vedic statements that proscribe suicide or otherwise stand opposed to ending one's life prematurely are only of a general nature, whereas those Smṛti statements that prescribe sati are of a specific nature. Therefore, since it is a standard principle of Brahmanical hermeneutics that a specific rule overrides a general one, the Smṛtis that enjoin sati are of sufficient authority in this case to overrule even extant Vedic texts. In other words, Aparārka concludes that those Vedic passages that prohibit suicide apply everywhere except for the specific case of sati, where the less general rules of the various Smṛtis apply. Significantly, a number of later authors accept the very same position on this issue as Aparārka, and none attempts to refute it.[30]

However, Aparārka appears to have been more thorough than other Dharmaśāstra commentators in his advocacy of this position. Perhaps the reason for this is that in his day many people still accepted the objection to sati on the grounds that it contradicts express Vedic statements and, thus, a more thorough refutation of this objection was necessary than in later times. Whatever the reason, unlike later authors, Aparārka explicitly justifies the reconciliation of the following generally accepted exegetical principles: (a) Vedic texts override Smṛti texts, and (b) more specific rules override more

[30] For instance, Mādhava (on PSm 4.32) writes:

[Objection:] Surely this act of sati is contrary to the perceived Veda, because suicide is prohibited in the following Vedic text, "Therefore, one who desires heaven should not die before one's natural lifespan" (ŚPB 10.2.6.7); and also due to this other Vedic text: "Those worlds are called 'Sunless' that are enveloped in pitch darkness. Those people who kill themselves go to them after death." (ĪU 3)

[Author:] This is not so, for the Smṛti enjoining sati is of greater force, as these Vedic texts do not apply here. Instead, the Vedic texts that prohibit suicide apply only to people other than women that desire heaven.

nanv idam anugamanaṃ pratyakṣaśrutiviruddhaṃ tasmād u ha na purāyuṣaḥ svargakāmī preyād iti śrutyā ātmahatyāpratiṣedhāt | asūryā nāma te lokā andhena [t]amasāvṛtāḥ | tāṃs te pr[e]tyādhigacchanti ye ke cātmahano janā iti śrutyantarāc ca | maivam anugamanasmṛter niravakāśatvena prābalyāt | ātmahatyāniṣedhaśrutis tu svargakāmiyoṣito 'nyatra sāvakāśā |

general ones. In the case of sati, these two principles clearly come into conflict, since principle b leads to the endorsement of the practice, whereas principle a leads to its prohibition. As a result, some reconciliation of these would seem to be necessary. Obviously, Aparārka holds that principle b should be of greater authority here as he supports sati. And in order to justify his position, he states:

> Furthermore, it should not be objected that when a Smṛti text is contradicted by a Vedic text that has a general sphere of applicability, it becomes unauthoritative, for there is really no contradiction between them as these texts have different spheres of applicability: one is general and the other is specific. For contradiction exists only when there is no difference between spheres of applicability, not when there is a difference between specific spheres of applicability. And, therefore, from a Smṛti text that has a specific sphere of applicability, one can infer a Vedic text that has its same specific sphere of applicability and is the basis of it. And that Vedic text carries greater weight than a Vedic text with a general sphere of applicability and, hence, causes it to be restricted.
>
> *na ca sāmānyaviṣayaśrutiviruddhā smṛtir apramāṇam iti vācyaṃ sāmānyaviśeṣarūpaviṣayabhedena virodhābhāvāt | viṣayābheda eva hi virodho na tu viśeṣaviṣayabhede | tataś ca viśeṣaviṣayayā smṛtyā svamūlabhūtā śrutir viśeṣaviṣayaivānumīyate | sā ca sāmānyaviṣayaśruter balīyasī satī tasyāḥ saṃkocahetur bhavati* | (Aparārka on YDh 1.87)

Here Aparārka argues that principle b (specific rules override general ones) is of greater force than principle a (the Veda overrides Smṛti) because of a particular form of inference that is characteristic of Brahmanical hermeneutics, namely, the inference of Vedic texts. Like the Mīmāṃsā tradition of Brahmanical hermeneutics, Dharmaśāstra holds that there are basically three sources of knowledge about *dharma*: the Veda, Smṛti, and the customs of good people. However, of these only the Veda is a direct and ultimate source of knowledge. The other two—Smṛti and the customs of good people—are authoritative only because one can infer from them the existence of other, no longer available Vedic texts that express their essential meanings.[31] In other words, there is the following belief: if a non-Vedic text enjoins and prohibits

[31] On this, see Jha (1964, 187–224).

the same actions as available Vedic texts but also enjoins and prohibits certain other actions not mentioned in available Vedic texts, we can safely infer that these additional injunctions and prohibitions must be equally Vedic, only based upon unavailable Vedic texts. In the above passage, Aparārka uses this widely held belief, which is tantamount to a legal fiction, to argue that one can infer from Smṛtis enjoining sati the existence of some no longer available Vedic text that enjoins the practice. And being specific in nature, this Vedic scripture would be of greater force than those Vedic scriptures that generally prohibit suicide. In this way, Aparārka puts forth a uniquely thorough refutation of the objection to sati on the grounds that it contradicts express Vedic injunctions.

In addition, as we saw above, Aparārka approvingly cites an interesting line of verse, which he ascribes to the *Brahma Purāṇa*[32]: "Due to the statement of the *Ṛgveda*, such a virtuous woman (who performs sati) does not commit suicide." Moreover, a roughly contemporaneous digest, the *Kṛtyakalpataru* (*Vyavahārakāṇḍa*, p. 634), also cites this same line. Both Aparārka and Lakṣmīdhara, the author of the *Kṛtyakalpataru*, identify the *Ṛgveda* passage referred to here as ṚV 10.18.7, a verse that was cited and briefly discussed at the beginning of this chapter. As explained there, it is extremely unlikely that this cryptic verse has anything originally to do with sati, given that neither Vedic literature nor the early Dharmaśāstras make any mention of the practice. Indeed, although the hymn to which it belongs apparently refers to a funerary rite of some type, the verse clearly issues a command to women who are not widows (*avidhavâḥ*), but rather have good husbands (*supátnīḥ*). Despite this, however, the *Brahma Purāṇa*, Aparārka, and Lakṣmīdhara all apparently regard it as in some way sanctioning sati, at least for a woman whose husband has died abroad.[33] The underlying reason for this highly dubious interpretation is undoubtedly their desire to find Vedic support for the practice and, thus, to overcome one of Vijñāneśvara's two arguments against it. Other facilitating factors presumably include that the verse pertains to a funerary rite; is ambiguous in parts; and contains the imperative verbs *viśantu* ("enter!") and *â rohantu* ("ascend!"), both of

[32] This passage does not occur in the version of the *Brahma Purāṇa* consulted for this book.

[33] In such an event, the *Brahma Purāṇa* instructs a widow to immolate herself with a pair of her husband's sandals in lieu of his body. If this rule is taken to apply to Brahmin women as well as others, it effectively undermines Vijñāneśvara's position that a Brahmin woman can only perform sati on her husband's pyre, not a separate one. There is no indication, however, that Aparārka or Lakṣmīdhara interprets this rule in this way.

which take feminine subjects and, therefore, fit the performance of sati. Beyond this, there is also the distinct possibility that within the context of the Dharmaśāstric debate on sati, ṚV 10.18.7 underwent certain changes to make it appear more germane to the practice. Of these the most important is the possible change of the word *agre* ("first") to *agne* ("O fire") or *agneḥ* ("of fire").[34]

Nevertheless, despite the fact that Aparārka obviously approves of sati, it is important to note that, like all Dharmaśāstra writers who approve of the practice, he does not regard it as obligatory, but rather optional. Unlike many of these authors, however, Aparārka (on YDh 1.87) explicitly mentions the optional character of sati in his treatment of the topic:

> And since it is optional, sati is not obligatory. For this very reason, Viṣṇu (25.14) states: "When a woman's husband has died, she should either practice lifelong celibacy or ascend the funeral pyre after him."
>
> *anvārohaṇaṃ ca kāmyatvād anityam | ata eva viṣṇuḥ mṛte bhartari brahmacaryaṃ tadanvārohaṇaṃ veti* |

Nonetheless, given the especially lavish praise that sati receives in many Smṛtis approvingly cited by Aparārka, it is likely that he and most other Dharmaśāstra authors who support the practice consider it to be not simply optional, but rather supererogatory.

[34] Like Aparārka, the *Nirṇayasindhu* (p. 438) and *Dharmasindhu* (p. 385) both mention ṚV 10.18.7 within the context of sati, but—in keeping with standard Brahmanical practice—cite only the first few words of the verse rather than the entire verse. The printed edition of Raghunandana's *Śuddhitattva* (p. 243), however, cites ṚV 10.18.7 in its entirety, but in markedly altered form:

> *imā nārīr avidhavāḥ sapatnīr añjanena sarpiṣā saṃ viśantu* |
> *anasvaro 'namīrā suratnā ā rohantu jalayonim agne* ||

In places, this version of ṚV 10.18.7 is clearly just corrupt (e.g., *sapatnīḥ* and *anasvaro 'namīrā*). The change from original *jánayo yónim ágre* to *jalayonim agne*, however, is arguably a deliberate change to the verse carried out with the intention of making it appear more germane to the practice of sati, for the verse then becomes addressed to the fire god Agni (*agne*). Moreover, if *jalayoni* ("one whose origin is water") is taken as an epithet of Agni on the basis of his identification with the "child of the waters" (*apāṃ napāt*) in Vedic literature, the verse essentially beseeches women to ascend a fire. Indeed, as R. Rocher and L. Rocher (2007, 25) have discussed, a number of prominent Western Indologists during the nineteenth century charged the Brahmin priesthood with unscrupulously altering ṚV 10.18.7 to make it better support the practice of sati. Kane (1962, 2:634) plausibly refutes this charge by noting that changing ṚV 10.18.7 in this way was both unnecessary and likely to be rejected in conservative Brahmanical circles, where knowledge of the exact wording of the entire *Ṛgveda* was common. Instead, he argues that the *Śuddhitattva*'s reading of ṚV 10.18.7 is better explained as a simple scribal error or typo.

Even beyond noting the optional character of sati, Aparārka also specifies a special procedure for stopping the rite, if the widow loses her resolve:

> However, they say that if the woman feels a desire for her sons or for the world of the living, her husband's brother or the like should lift her up from the pyre.
>
> *devarādinā tūtthāpanaṃ tasyāḥ putrakāmanāyāṃ vā jīvalokakāmanāyāṃ vā satyām āhuḥ* | (Aparārka on YDh1.87)

This statement shows that even after resolving to perform sati, if a woman became terrified or otherwise regretted her decision, one or another of her husband's relations was considered obligated to stop the rite. Moreover, rather unusually, Aparārka does not cite any scriptural evidence in support of this rule. Hence, it seems a distinct possibility that here a classical Hindu jurist may for once be implicitly acknowledging the harrowing nature of the sati rite and allowing a role for general compassion in what is otherwise treated as a matter of dry scriptural analysis. At the very least, it shows that Aparārka believed strongly in the voluntary nature of sati.

It is noteworthy, however, that two later digests, the *Nirṇayasindhu* (p. 438) and the *Dharmasindhu* (p. 385), prescribe an identifical procedure to that put forth earlier by Aparārka but also implicitly refer to scriptural support for it:

> However, if the woman becomes afraid after lying down to the left of her dead husband, either her husband's brother or one of his students should cause her to get up from the pyre with the two verses that begin, "Rise..." (ṚV 10.18.8–9).
>
> *kātarāṃ tu pretottarataḥ suptāṃ devaraḥ śiṣyo vā udīrṣveti dvābhyām*[35] *utthāpayet* |

The fact that these two digests explicitly include the recitation of two verses of the *Ṛgveda* (10.18.8–9) in this procedure suggests that they understand these verses to somehow sanction it, even if technically the rules of Brahmanical hermeneutics do not allow for this.[36]

[35] The *Dharmasindhu* here reads *mantrābhyām*.

[36] Mīmāṃsā classifies texts like ṚV 10.18.8–9, which are recited as part of rituals, as *mantras*. As such, they are incapable of issuing true injunctions (*vidhi*) or prohibitions (*pratiṣedha*). On this, see Jha (1964, 159–67).

In a somewhat related vein, Aparārka (on YDh 1.87) also makes the interesting stipulation that grief cannot motivate a Brahmin woman to perform sati or else her behavior constitutes a violation of *dharma*:

> There is no prohibition against a woman performing sati because she is a Brahmin. However, there is one against a Brahmin woman performing sati because she is grief-stricken. Prohibitions having a specific scope restrict the scope of those statements of Virāj and Aṅgiras that seemingly prohibit sati for Brahmin women in general. Therefore, a Brahmin woman does not sin if she performs sati because scripture enjoins it, but she certainly does sin if she performs it because of grief or the like.
>
> *kiṃ ca na brāhmaṇītvena nimittenānugamananiṣedho bhavati | kiṃ tv asau brāhmaṇyāḥ śokanimittikaḥ | yat tu vairājam āṅgirasaṃ ca vacanaṃ brāhmaṇyā anugamanamātrapratiṣedhakam iva pratibhāti tad viśeṣaviṣayaiḥ pratiṣedhair upasaṃhriyate | tasmād vidhitaḥ pravartamānāyā brāhmaṇyā anugamanād doṣo na vidyate | śokādipravṛttāyās tu bhavaty eveti |*

In order to understand Aparārka's argument here, it is necessary to recall a passage of his commentary cited earlier in this chapter, which essentially repeats an argument of Vijñāneśvara. There Aparārka cites Smṛti passages ascribed to four different authors that seemingly prohibit Brahmin women from performing sati. These authors are Paiṭhīnasi, Virāj, Aṅgiras, and Vyāghrapad. He then argues that these authors really only prohibit Brahmin women from ascending pyres other than those of their husbands and cites a statement of Uśanas that says as much. Hence, in his view, a more specific prohibition, such as that of Uśanas, allows us to narrow the scope of more general prohibitions, such as those of Virāj and Aṅgiras. In all this Aparārka is effectively no different from his predecessor Vijñāneśvara. Unlike Vijñāneśvara, however, he recognizes that while Aṅgiras and Virāj appear to prohibit Brahmin women in general from performing sati, Paiṭhīnasi and Vyāghrapad speak specifically of Brahmin women who are consumed with grief. From this he concludes that although Brahmin women are not generally forbidden from performing sati, they are forbidden from doing so out of sorrow. In making this point, Aparārka may be simply playing the pedant or wishing to display his exegetical acumen. It is distinctly possible, however, that he genuinely believes that sati must be a solemn dispassionate affair.

Whatever the case may be, it is noteworthy that no other Dharmaśāstra author expresses a line of reasoning similar to Aparārka's in this regard.

Lastly, before moving on from Aparārka, it is worth examining his discussion of the unusual soteriological rewards of sati as stated in certain Smṛtis and his attempt to explain how these rewards do not, in fact, violate the accepted laws of *karma*:

> Because of the scriptural statement that a woman who performs sati "rejoices with her husband," such a woman enjoys heaven together with her husband. There might seem to be a conflict between the fact that the reward for performing sati applies only to the widow and the fact that her husband, who did nothing, receives the reward of her entering the fire, which she alone did. But this is easily resolved. The husband's experience of heavenly bliss results from the meritorious deeds that he himself performed. The meritorious deed performed by his wife simply removes the sin that obstructs him from heavenly bliss. And it is not the case that removing an obstruction is tantamount to producing an effect. As for those scriptures that speak of the destruction of the husband's sins as the reward of the meritorious deed done by his wife, their meaning should not to be taken literally, but rather metaphorically. The "destruction" that is spoken of is merely like destruction in that it takes the form of an obstruction blocking her husband's sins from bearing immediate fruit on account of his wife's meritorious deed.
>
> *modate patinā sārdham iti vacanāt saha patyā svargopabhogaḥ | patnīgāmy eva phalam iti tatkṛtasyāgnipraveśasya phalam akartā bhartā bhuṅkta iti virodhaḥ suparih[a]raḥ | yas tu bhartari sukhasamavāyaḥ sa bhartṛgatād eva dharmāt | tatpratibandhakaṃ pāpaṃ patnīkṛto dharma uddharati | na ca pratibandhakoddhārakaḥ kāryaparaḥ | ya[t] tu patyuḥ pāpakṣayaḥ patnīkṛtasya dharmasya phalam iti śrūyate tasyāpi na mukhyo 'rthaḥ | kiṃ tu gauṇah | kṣaya iva kṣayaḥ patnīdharmeṇa patipāpasyānantaraṃ phaladānapratibandharūpaḥ* | (Aparārka on YDh 1.87)

Here Aparārka argues that by performing sati the wife of a sinful man does not actually lead her husband to heaven; he gets there purely through his own past good deeds. His wife's act of self-immolation simply removes for a time the sin that blocks him from experiencing such a happy rebirth. And, according to an influential strand of classical Brahmanical thought, to remove an obstacle is not the same thing as to produce an effect.[37] Hence, because sati does not technically cause a husband's heavenly rebirth, it does not violate the accepted laws of *karma*. Via this argument Aparārka attempts to rationalize the rather unique soteriological power that sati is held to possess.

The *Smṛticandrikā*

After Vijñāneśvara the argument against sati on the grounds that it contradicts the Veda quickly falls out of favor. Indeed, no Dharmaśāstra commentator after him supports this argument, while several attempt to refute it, as we have seen. However, the other argument against sati accepted by Vijñāneśvara—namely, that sati is an inferior option to celibacy, because it yields the inferior result of heaven—has at least one later supporter: Devaṇa Bhaṭṭa, who probably wrote his *Smṛticandrikā* in South India sometime between 1175 and 1225. His statement on the legitimacy of sati reads as follows:

> There is, however, another law, which Viṣṇu (25.14) lays down: "When a woman's husband has died, she should either practice lifelong celibacy or ascend after him." Here the phrase "ascend after him" means that she should ascend the funerary fire after her husband. And likewise Aṅgiras states:
>
> > A woman who ascends the funerary fire when her husband has died behaves like Arundhatī and is honored in heaven.
>
> This other law, however, is lowlier than the law of lifelong celibacy, for it yields a lesser reward (i.e., heaven).
>
> *yat tu viṣṇunā dharmāntaram uktaṃ mṛte bhartari brahmacaryaṃ tadanvārohaṇaṃ veti | tadanvārohaṇaṃ bhartāram anu ārohaṇam agnyārohaṇam | tathā cāṅgirāḥ*
>
> > *mṛte bhartari yā nārī samārohed dhutāśanam |*
> > *sārundhatīsamācārā svargaloke mahīyate ||*
>
> *tad etad dharmāntaram api brahmacaryadharmāj jaghanyaṃ nikṛṣṭaphalatvāt* | (*Smṛticandrikā*, *Vyavahārakāṇḍa*, pp. 596–97)

[37] On this notion in Advaita Vedānta philosophy, see Potter (1981, 32–33).

Following Devaṇa, however, even support for this weakened position against sati seems to cease, as he is apparently the last Dharmaśāstra writer to subscribe to it.[38]

Interestingly, however, although Devaṇa seemingly disapproves of sati, his *Smṛticandrikā* contains a lengthy passage (*Āśaucakāṇḍa*, pp. 89–90) that explains in straightforward prose how to perform the rite:

> Entering the fire, i.e., sati, is enjoined for women. In the case of Śūdras, however, the rite of entering the fire is prescribed without mantras.
>
> When the time of the death of some Brahmin or other has arrived, his wife should take an auspicious bath; put on clean clothes; sip water; take hold of sandalwood powder, flowers, and the like; go to her husband's presence; summon Brahmins; and make the following resolution: "On an auspicious day characterized by the aforementioned characteristics, I will perform sati together with my husband, who is a form of Viṣṇu, so that I might attain residence in Brahmā's world with him." Then, after taking hold of some water mixed with *darbha* grass and unhusked grains, that devoted wife, sitting facing eastward, should offer the gift of her life, saying:
>
> "I will give my body to Viṣṇu here in the form of my husband, who grants all desires, so that I might stay in his heavenly abode. Earth, space, water, fire, and wind, the lords of the world, the seven seers, and time—all deities are my witnesses. May all the sins that I have committed in thought, word, or action perish! I consign my body to the fire. Seeking to attain residence in the world of Brahmā, I give my body to you, my husband here, a member of such-and-such clan, who has the nature of great and glorious Viṣṇu. It does not belong to me."
>
> The officiating priest should then strew *darbha* grass with the tips facing southward upon a bier; place the man's corpse upon that; place his wife to his left; bind her with a rope of *darbha* grass, saying "Go together!"; follow the deceased as he is led by pallbearers (to the cremation ground); establish a fire to the south of the pyre there; place the corpse facing southward in the middle of the pyre after the *ājyabhāga* offerings[39]; lay his wife down to his left; and place a fire in the middle of each of their arms, reciting the mantra that starts "Don't burn him, O fire!" (TĀ 6.1.4).[40] Then, wearing his sacred

[38] In spite of this, however, this argument is central to the case against sati made by Rammohan Roy during the early nineteenth century (see, e.g., Ghose 1901, 130–34).

[39] The *ājyabhāgas* are offerings of ghee that occur in certain Vedic rites called *iṣṭis* prior to the primary offering. For a detailed description of these offerings, see Kane (1962, 2:1059–61).

[40] This is the same as ṚV 10.16.1.

thread over his right shoulder,[41] the officiating priest should join his palms together with *darbha* grass in his hands; recite the mantra that starts "May your eyes go to the sun!" (TĀ 6.1.4); scoop up ghee with a small sacrificial ladle; offer it as an oblation with the words "Svāhā to those who guard the path of these two!" (TĀ 6.2.1); and cremate the couple. This is the rite of sati.

> *praveśaś cānugamanaṃ strīṇām eva vidhīyate |*
> *amantrakaṃ tu śūdrāṇāṃ praveśavidhir ucyate ||*
> *yasya kasyacid brāhmaṇasya maraṇakāle saṃprāpte tatpatnī maṅgalasnānaṃ kṛtvā dhautavastraṃ paridhāyācamya gandhapuṣpādīni dhṛtvā bhartuḥ samīpaṃ gatvā brāhmaṇān āhūya pūrvoktaivaṃguṇa-viśeṣaṇaviśiṣṭāyāṃ puṇyatithau viṣṇurūpeṇa bhartrā saha brahmaloke nivāsasiddhyarthaṃ bhartrā sahānugamanaṃ kariṣya iti saṃkalpya darbhākṣatasahitaṃ jalaṃ dhṛtvā pativratā pūrvābhimukhī samāsīnā—*
> *sarvakāmapradāyāsmai patirūpāya viṣṇave |*
> *mama dehaṃ pradāsyāmi sthātuṃ vai svargamandire ||*
> *bhūmir viyaj jalaṃ tejo vāyuś ca jagadīśvarāḥ |*
> *saptarṣayaś ca kālaś ca sākṣiṇaḥ sarvadevatāḥ ||*
> *matkṛtaṃ pātakaṃ yac ca manovākkāyasaṃbhavam |*
> *tat sarvaṃ nāśam āpnotu vahnau dehaṃ visarjaye ||*
> *asmai bhartre śrīmahāviṣṇusvarūpāya madīyabrahmalokanivāsasiddhiṃ kāmayamānāmukagotrāya tubhyam ahaṃ saṃpradade na mameti prāṇadānaṃ kuryāt | kartā āsandyāṃ dakṣiṇāgrān darbhān āstīrya tatra śavaṃ nidhāya śavasya vāmabhāge tatpatnīṃ nidhāya saṃgacchadhvam iti darbharajjunā pretapatnīṃ cābadhya vāhakair nīyamānaṃ pretam anugatvā citer dakṣiṇabhāge 'gniṃ pratiṣṭhāpya ājyabhāgānte citimadhye dakṣiṇaśirasaṃ śavaṃ nidhāya patnīṃ tasya vāmabhāge nikṣipya tayor bhujayor madhye mainam agne ity* (TĀ 6.1.4) *agniṃ dattvā tataḥ kartā prācīnāvītī darbhapāṇir añjaliṃ baddhvā sūryaṃ te cakṣuḥ śarīrair agne ity* (TĀ 6.1.4) *anumantrya sruveṇājyaṃ gṛhītvā ya etayoḥ patho goptāras [tebhyaḥ] svāhā iti* (TĀ 6.2.1) *hutvā dahet | ity anugamanavidhiḥ |*

Immediately after this passage, the *Smṛticandrikā* contains another one of roughly the same length addressing the case of a woman who desires

[41] Normally, a twice-born man wears his sacred thread (*upavīta*) over his left shoulder. However, it is worn over the right shoulder during rites involving death or ancestor worship. On this, see Kane (1962, 2:287–88).

to perform sati, but apparently cannot bear to lie alongside her husband's corpse and wait there for the cremation fire to burn her alive. Similar to the passage cited above, this passage describes in detail a sati rite, only one where a woman enters her husband's funerary fire after it is set ablaze. Passages like these, which explain in practical terms how to perform particular rituals, are a common feature of the *nibandha* literature, typically referred to as *prayoga* ("performance") sections. Several later digests, for instance, contain similar *prayoga* sections on sati.[42]

Given that Devaṇa Bhaṭṭa is personally rather opposed to sati, however, it is unclear why his work includes a *prayoga* section on the rite. One possible answer is that originally it did not and that the relevant passages constitute a later addition to his text. One finds some support for this hypothesis in the fact that the entire *prayoga* section on sati is apparently missing from one of the two manuscripts used in creating the printed edition of the *Āśaucakāṇḍa* of the *Smṛticandrikā*. Another possible explanation is that Devaṇa felt compelled to include a *prayoga* section on sati in his work, because it was an established practice in his day and one that he did not consider to be actually sinful, but instead simply inferior and unwise. One piece of evidence in favor of this second explanation comes from a lengthy passage of the *Śrāddhakāṇḍa* (pp. 161–69), whose presence in the original *Smṛticandrikā* is not subject to serious doubt. There Devaṇa discusses how the rules for ancestral Śrāddha rites apply specifically to a woman who has performed sati[43] and, thereby, seemingly confirms that his personal opposition to the practice was rather tempered.

The *Madanapārijāta*

Let us turn now to Madanapāla's fourteenth-century legal digest, the *Madanaparijāta*. Special discussion of this text is necessary, as it makes several notable contributions to the treatment of sati within the Dharmaśāstra tradition.

[42] See *Nirṇayasindhu*, p. 438; *Śuddhitattva*, pp. 242–43; and *Dharmasindhu*, pp. 385–86.

[43] The basic position of the *Smṛticandrikā* (*Śrāddhakāṇḍa*, pp. 162) seems to be that if a woman performs sati, one should perform the particular Śrāddha rite known as *sapiṇḍīkaraṇa* for her separately from her husband's *sapiṇḍīkaraṇa*, if one is able to do so. However, one may perform them jointly, if necessary. Moreover, one has the option to perform the Śrāddha rites for such a woman separately from her husband's rites either at a time specifically connected with her death or at the same time as her husband's Śrāddha rites (*Śrāddhakāṇḍa*, pp. 163–64).

Like all Dharmaśāstra authors who support sati, Madanapāla clearly regards it as an optional practice. Unlike other authors, however, he notes that one might conceivably interpret certain Smṛti passages as portraying sati as mandatory. And he devotes a significant passage of his work (*Madanapārijāta*, pp. 198–99) to refuting such an interpretation of these texts:

> [Objection:] This act of sati is surely mandatory for a devoted wife (*pativratā*). And, thus, Hārīta states:
>
> > A woman should be known as a devoted wife if she is pained when her husband is pained, rejoices when he's happy, becomes wretched and emaciated when he's gone abroad, and dies when he dies.
>
> Therefore, the mandatory nature of sati is made clear by this statement, which says that a woman is a devoted wife if she dies when her husband dies. Hence, it is inappropriate to describe the practice as non-mandatory.
>
> [Reply:] This is incorrect, for Manu (5.160) prescribes a course of action other than sati for a devoted wife:
>
> > A virtuous woman who remains celibate after her husband has died goes to heaven, even if sonless, just like those men who have remained celibate.
>
> The phrase "virtuous woman" (*sādhvī*) in this statement expresses that the woman is a devoted wife, for otherwise it would be redundant with the stipulation that she "remains celibate." And, thus, in the *Mahābhārata* (12.144.9–10), Lord Vyāsa shows a woman who is already a devoted wife entering the fire rather than becoming a devoted wife by entering fire:
>
> > That devoted wife entered the blazing fire. There she followed her husband, who was adorned with glittering armbands.

nanu ca pativratāyā idam anugamanaṃ nityam eva | tathā ca hārītaḥ

ārtārte mudite hṛṣṭā proṣite malinā kṛśā |
mṛte mriyeta yā patyau sā strī jñeyā pativratā ||

ato mṛte yā mriyeta pativratety anena nityatvaṃ dyotyate | ataḥ anityatvavarṇanam ayuktam iti cen maivam |

mṛte bhartari sādhvī strī brahmacarye vyavasthitā |
svargaṃ gacched aputrāpi yathā te brahmacāriṇaḥ || (MDh 5.160)

iti manunā pativratāyā ananugamanasyābhihitatvāt | atra sādhvīty anena pativratābhidhīyate anyathā brahmacarye vyavasthitety anena paunaruktyaprasakteḥ | tathā mahābhārate bhagavān vyāsaḥ pativratāyāḥ satyā agnipraveśaṃ darśayati na cāgnipraveśena pativratātvam

pativratā saṃpradīptaṃ praviveśa hutāśanam |
tatra citrāṅgadadharaṃ bhartāraṃ sānupadyate || (MBh 12.144.9–10)

Here the objection is raised that sati must be obligatory for a devoted wife (*pativratā*), since Hārītā, the author of a well-known Smṛti, says that a devoted wife is a woman who, among other things, dies when her husband dies. Madanapāla refutes this objection on the grounds that Manu (5.160) also prescribes a life of celibacy for a devoted wife. But in order for this refutation to work, he must establish that the "virtuous woman" (*sādhvī*) mentioned in Manu is identical with the "devoted wife" (*pativratā*) mentioned in Hārīta. Madanapāla does this by arguing that if Manu's "virtuous woman" were not the same as Hārīta's "devoted wife," it would be redundant for Manu to speak of a "virtuous woman who remains celibate." The point here is that if a devoted wife is required to perform sati, then in order for a virtuous woman to be different, she must by definition be a woman that remains celibate after her husband's death (remarriage and *niyoga* were not options by this time). Therefore, it would be redundant to mention a virtuous woman that remains celibate. Hence, the "virtuous woman" in Manu's statement must be identical with a "devoted wife." One crucial implication of this is that since a devoted wife who is widowed can either perform sati or remain celibate, these acts cannot make a woman a devoted wife. That is, a woman must be a devoted wife prior to making the decision to either remain celibate or perform sati. This, according to Madanapāla, is why the *Mahābhārata* (12.144.9–10) speaks of a woman (actually a female dove) who is already a devoted wife before entering her husband's cremation fire. In this way, the *Madanapārijāta* refutes one possible objection to the position, consistently held by authors in the Dharmaśāstra tradition, that sati was strictly optional.

Nevertheless, although Madanapāla takes exceptional pains to clarify the optional nature of sati, he also effectively weakens at least one earlier restriction on the practice: the prohibition against Brahmin women performing sati on separate pyres from those of their husbands. As readers may recall, this is a prohibition first proposed by Vijñāneśvara in order to explain away those Smṛtis that generally forbid Brahmin women from performing sati; and it is a prohibition that Madanapāla himself (pp. 197–98) explicitly endorses. However, he also notably reduces the impact of this prohibition by allowing a Brahmin woman to perform sati with her husband's bones, if he died abroad:

> When her husband has died in another country, a Brahmin woman can certainly perform sati with his bones. A woman of another class, however, can perform sati even in the absence of her husband's bones by taking some emblem of him, such as his sandals, or even perform sati in the absence of such an emblem, for she is permitted to ascend a separate pyre.
>
> *deśāntaramṛte patyau brāhmaṇyās tadasthibhiḥ sahānugamanaṃ bhavaty eva | itarāsāṃ tv asthyabhāve 'pi patipādukādikacihnaṃ kim api gṛhītvā cihnābhāve 'pi bhavati pṛthakcityanujñānāt |*

Hence, Madanapāla not only supports the practice of sati, as all Dharmaśāstra authors of the fourteenth and later centuries do, but also explicitly weakens an established restriction on the practice, if only a rather minor one and that only slightly.

Lastly, like Aparārka, Madanapāla strives to explain why certain Smṛtis present sati as salvific for both a widow and her husband, although this would seemingly violate the immutable law of *karma* that allows only the performer of an action to enjoy its otherworldly results. However, the passage of the *Madanapārijāta* where this discussion takes place is significantly longer than the corresponding passage of Aparārka and differs from it substantively as well. It begins:

> [Objection:] But there are statements such as the following one of Hārīta:
>
> Whether her husband murdered a Brahmin, was an ingrate, or murdered a friend, a woman purifies him, if she does not remain a widow, but instead dies embracing him.
>
> Don't such statements declare that sati nullifies a man's sins, including even Brahmin-murder? But this is improper, for the power generated by an act and its result are inherently connected to the act's performer in accordance with the maxim: "The result stated in scripture applies to the performer, as scripture indicates as much." (PMS 3.7.18) So the power generated by a husband's sinful acts cannot be nullified by his wife's act of sati. And if one admits to such nullification, the fact that a cause and its effect inhere in the same subject, which is established in scripture, is negated.
>
> [Author:] This is correct. However, statements such as the one about a husband who has murdered a Brahmin merely describe how praiseworthy it is to perform sati through exhortatory expression as they supplement the scriptural injunction to perform sati. Hence, they are not authoritative

in and of themselves. Indeed, the fact that such statements constitute mere exhortatory expressions is fitting, for a man defiled by a sin such as Brahmin-murder becomes an outcaste and, thus, is unworthy of a funeral much less sati. Hence, the aim of the statements in question is merely to express how praiseworthy sati is. Consequently, there is nothing improper about them.

nanu
brahmaghno vā kṛtaghno vā mitraghno vā bhavet patiḥ |
punāty avidhavā nārī tam ādāya mriyeta yā ||
ity evamādihārītādivākyāni brahmahatyādidoṣanivṛttim anugamanenābhidadhāti | etad anupapannaṃ śāstraphalaṃ prayokt[ari tal] lakṣaṇatvād[44] *iti* (PMS 3.7.18) *nyāyenāpūrvaphalayoḥ kartṛsamavetatvāt | patigataduritāpūrvasya patnīgatānugamanenānivṛttiḥ | nivṛttyabhyupagame tu kāryakāraṇayoḥ sāmānādhikaraṇyaṃ śāstrasiddhaṃ vyāhanyeteti ced bāḍham | brahmaghno vety ādīni vākyāni anugamanavidhiśeṣatvenārthavādād anugamanasya prāśastyaṃ varṇayanti | ato na svārthe pramāṇāni | yuktam evārthavādatvam | brahmahananādidoṣaduṣṭasya patitatvenāsau saṃskāram eva tāvan nārhati dūre 'nugamanam | ataḥ prāśastyaparāṇīti na kadā cid anupapattiḥ |* (*Madanapārijāta*, pp. 199–200)

Understanding Madanapāla's argument here requires an understanding of the crucial concept of *arthavāda* or "exhortatory expression" in medieval Dharmaśāstra.[45] Drawing upon ideas developed within the Mīmāṃsā tradition, Dharmaśāstra commentators classify all scriptural statements into a number of categories. Of these by far the most important are the injunction (*vidhi*), which issues a positive command, and the prohibition (*pratiṣedha*), which issues a negative command. An exhortatory expression or *arthavāda* is a statement that is neither an injunction nor a prohibition, but instead supplements an injunction or prohibition by encouraging people to obey it. An *arthavāda* typically does this by lauding the rewards of following a particular injunction or warning of the grave consequences of violating a certain prohibition. This is the theoretical conception of an *arthavāda*. In practice, however, a Dharmaśāstra commentator generally identifies a statement as an *arthavāda*, because it says some inconvenient things that he wishes to ignore

[44] The printed edition reads as *prayoktṛvilakṣaṇatvād*.
[45] On *arthavāda*, see Jha (1964, 177–82) and Kane (1962, 5:1238–44).

or at least to not take literally. And this is precisely what Madanapāla is doing in the above passage, for there he argues that those Smṛtis that portray sati as a means of salvation for a woman's husband are mere *arthavādas*, intended to supplement the injunction to perform sati. As such, one need not take their contents literally. Hence, they are entirely consistent with the accepted laws of *karma*.

Beyond this, after offering the previous explanation, Madanapāla goes on to offer a different one that accepts sati as actually salvific for a woman's husband:

> Alternatively, there are two kinds of *karma*: that which has commenced to yield results and that which has not. Of these, commenced *karma* can only be destroyed by experiencing it. Therefore, although it has commenced to yield results, such *karma* is blocked by the obstruction that is sati. And although it exists, it remains passive as though it does not exist. However, after experiencing heaven and the like as a result of sati, the man subsequently experiences the rest of his commenced *karma*. Uncommenced *karma* is of two kinds: that which is about to yield results and that which is not about to. Just like a penance, sati removes uncommenced *karma* that is not about to yield results, for otherwise it would not be right for a virtuous woman to attain heaven through sati, which is taught to be a means of attaining heaven for both husband and wife.[46] And, thus, the verb "purifies" in the statement that "a woman purifies him, if she does not remain a widow, but instead dies embracing him" is appropriate. As for uncommenced *karma* that is about to yield results, sati nullifies it. It is with this very thought in mind that Vyāsa states:
>
> > If a man has entered hell, bound with terribly cruel fetters, reached the place of his punishment, seized by Yama's henchmen, and stands powerless and depressed, enveloped by his own past deeds, through sati his wife forcefully takes him to heaven, just as a snake-catcher forcefully lifts a snake up out of its hole.
>
> After experiencing heaven as result of sati, however, a man will experience his *karma* that was about to yield results and that had commenced to yields results. Thus, there is no conflict here.

[46] The apparent idea here is that a virtuous woman (*sādhvī*) is by definition a woman who suffers when her husband suffers. Hence, she would never seek to go to heaven, when her husband resides in hell.

evaṃ vā dvividhaṃ karma prāṛabdham aprārabdhaṃ ceti | tatra prārabdhakarmaṇāṃ bhogād eva kṣayāt prārabdham apy anugamanarūpapratibandhakena pratibaddham | vidyamānam apy avidyamānam iva sad udāste | tathā cānugamanasvargādikam anubhūya paścāt prārabdhaśeṣam upabhuṅkte | aprārabdhakarma dvividhaṃ phaladānonmukham anunmukhaṃ ca | yad [an]unmukham [a]prarābdhaṃ[47] *karma tad anugamanenāpanudyate prāyaścitteneva anyathā patipatnyoḥ svargasādhanatvenopadiśyamānānugamanena sādhvyāḥ svargānupapatteḥ | punāty avidhavā nārī tam ādāya mriyeta yety atra ca punāty etad apy upapadyate*[48] *| yat tu dānāyonmukham aprārabdhaṃ karma tasya nivṛttir anugamane bhavatīty etad eva manasi kṛtvā vyāso 'py āha—*

> *yadi praviṣṭo narakaṃ baddhaḥ pāśaiḥ sudāruṇaiḥ |*
> *saṃprāpto yātanāsthānaṃ gṛhīto yamakiṃkaraiḥ |*
> *tiṣṭhate vivaśo dīno veṣṭyamānaḥ svakarmabhiḥ ||*
> *vyālagrāhī yathā vyālaṃ balād uddharate bilāt |*
> *tadvad bhartāram ādāya divaṃ yāti ca sā balād iti ||*

phaladānonmukhaprārabdhaṃ karmānugamanasādhyasvargopabhogānantaram upabhujyata iti na virodhaḥ | (*Madanapārijāta*, pp. 200–201)

Here Madanapāla divides a person's *karma*, that is, the active otherworldly power of his past deeds, into three types: that which has started to yield results, that which is about to yield results, and that which will yield results at a more distant time. He then explains that sati temporarily nullifies a man's negative *karma* that is either currently bearing fruit or about to bear fruit. After his time in heaven as a result of his wife's act of sati, however, he must still experience the results of such bad *karma*. By contrast, sati simply destroys a man's bad *karma* that is far from bearing fruit so that he will never experience its results at all. And in destroying the effects of such bad *karma*, sati works just like a penance.

Of course, all of this fails to answer the really pressing question, which is how sati does not violate the accepted laws of *karma*. Thus, in order to answer this and defend its position that sati can either destroy or temporarily nullify all of a man's sins, the *Madanapārijāta* (pp. 201–2) states:

[47] The printed edition reads as *unmukhaṃ prārabdhaṃ*.
[48] The printed edition reads as *anupapadyate*.

The objection that it is improper for the sins of someone other than the performer of sati to cease is ridiculous, for the husband and wife perform sati together and, thus, their reward for the act is appropriate, just like, for instance, their joint attainment of heaven for performing the Agnihotra rite. And the sin that is caused to cease is only sin committed in previous lives, for a man tainted by sins committed in this life becomes an outcaste and, thus, his wife has no right to perform sati with him.

anyagataduritanivṛttir ayukteti tad apeśalaṃ patipatnyoḥ sahakartṛtvenāgnihotrādisādhyasvargādivad upapatteḥ | idaṃ ca duritaṃ janmāntarakṛtam eva nivartyam | etajjanmakṛtaduritayuktasya patitatvena tena sahānugamanānadhikārāt | (*Madanapārijāta*, pp. 201–2)

Here Madanapāla defends his position that sati can fully expiate some of a husband's sins and temporarily nullify others by arguing that, as in other rituals, a husband and wife jointly perform sati and, thus, jointly enjoy its rewards. Crucially, however, he adds that sati can only affect the sins that a man committed in his previous lives, for a man guilty of serious sins in his current life would become an outcaste and, thus, lack all rights to a proper funeral, much less one involving sati.

Mādhava

As we have seen, numerous Dharmaśāstra commentators explicitly stipulate that sati is prohibited for women who either are pregnant or have children who are very young.[49] Indeed, the general principle that a woman cannot perform sati if it would directly harm her born or unborn children goes unchallenged throughout Dharmaśāstra literature. Perhaps somewhat surprisingly, however, none of the earliest commentators to make this stipulation cites any scriptural passage in support of it. From this, we might infer that its justification lies not in specific scriptural prohibitions, but rather in the basic ethical principle that sati may harm only the widow herself and no one else. In other words, the prohibition against pregnant women and women

[49] See, e.g., the unpublished Nepalese commentary on YDh 1.87; the *Mitākṣarā* on YDh 1.86; *Kṛtyakalpataru*, *Vyavahārakāṇḍa*, p. 635; and *Madanapārijāta*, p. 196.

with small children performing sati is essentially an application of the general prohibition against violence.

The fourteenth-century author Mādhava, however, differs from all of his predecessors in that he cites and comments upon a pair of verses that provide an explicit scriptural basis for the prohibition against women performing sati, if they are pregnant or have small children.[50] The relevant portion of his work (on PSm 4.33) reads:

> And this right to perform sati is blocked if a woman is menstruating or the like. Thus, Bṛhaspati states:
>
> > A woman who has young children should not depart, thereby forsaking raising her young children; nor should a woman who is menstruating or has just given birth; and a pregnant woman should protect her fetus.
>
> Here, by saying "thereby forsaking raising her young children," the author shows that even a woman with young children is entitled to perform sati, if she entrusts other people to raise them. And by emphasizing protection in his statement that a woman "should protect her fetus," he denies the right to perform sati to any woman who might even possibly be suspected to be pregnant. And, thus, it is said in the *Nārada Purāṇa*:
>
> > O beautiful princess, women do not ascend the funeral pyre when they have young children, when they are pregnant, when their menses have failed to appear at the regular time, and while they are menstruating.
>
> The phrase "when their menses have failed to appear at the regular time" denotes women who might possibly be suspected to be pregnant, because their menses have failed to appear at the regular time.
>
> *ayaṃ cādhikāro rajaādibhiḥ pratibadhyate | tathā bṛhaspatiḥ—*
>
> > *bālasaṃvardhanaṃ tyaktvā bālāpatyā na gacchati |*
> > *rajasvalā sūtikā ca rakṣed garbhaṃ garbhiṇīti ||*
>
> *atra bālasaṃvardhanaṃ tyaktveti vadan saṃvardhayitṛjanāntaravisrambhe bālāpātyāyā apy adhikāro 'stīti darśayan rakṣed garbhaṃ ca garbhiṇīti rakṣāṃ darśayan saṃbhāvitagarbhasaṃdehāyā apy adhikāraṃ vārayati | tathā ca nāradīye—*
>
> > *bālāpatyāś ca garbhiṇya adṛṣṭarṭavas tathā |*
> > *rajasvalā rājasūte nārohanti citāṃ śubha iti ||*
>
> *adṛṣṭarṭava ṛtvadarśanena saṃbhāvitagarbhasaṃdehāḥ |*

[50] The *Nirṇayasindhu* (p. 439) also cites these verses.

Mādhava's interpretation of the first verse, ascribed to Bṛhaspati, makes it clear that he accepts the general principle that sati is permissible except in cases where a woman would thereby bring harm to her children. Consequently, women who are pregnant or even may be pregnant, such as those whose menses have failed to appear at the regular time, are strictly forbidden from performing sati. A woman with small children, however, may carry out the rite provided specifically that she entrusts the caretaking of her children to other people.

Regarding Bṛhaspati's prohibition against menstruating women performing sati, this obviously has nothing to do with the principle that through sati a woman should cause harm to no one other than herself. Instead, it undoubtedly stems from the deeply held Brahmanical view that menstrual blood is extremely impure and, therefore, menstruating women must be assiduously excluded from social and ritual life. Interestingly, although Mādhava himself is silent on the matter of menstruating women, the *Smṛticandrikā* cites a text that explains a procedure for delaying a man's cremation in the event that his wife is menstruating and desires to perform sati.[51]

The *Nirṇayasindhu* and *Dharmasindhu*

Finally, let us turn to two late digests: the *Nirṇayasindhu* of Kamalākara Bhaṭṭa, written in Benares in 1612, and the *Dharmasindhu* of Kāśīnātha Upādhyāya, written in Maharashtra in 1790–1791.[52] These works are important to a discussion of sati within Dharmaśāstra, because they effectively take the final steps in eliminating all lingering opposition to the practice within the Hindu legal tradition, although after the thirteenth century no Dharmaśāstra author actually opposes it.

To this end, both the *Nirṇayasindhu* (p. 438) and the *Dharmasindhu* (p. 384) cite the following, a previously unquoted Smṛti passage that lists liberation (*mukti*) as an explicit result of sati:

> When a woman ascends the pyre after her husband, it destroys all her and her husband's sins, leads to deliverance from hell, bestows the reward of

[51] *Śrāddhakāṇḍa*, p. 164: "If a woman intending to follow her husband in death is menstruating, then his relatives should place her dead husband in a vat of oil or in salt and burn him along with her after three nights." (*bhartāram anugacchantī patnī cet sārtavā yadi | tailadroṇyāṃ vinikṣipya lavaṇe vā mṛtaṃ patim || trirātrād dahanaṃ kuryuḥ bāndhavās tu tayā saha |*)

[52] On the provenance of these works, see Kane (1962, 1:932, 977–78).

many heavens, grants liberation, and gives good fortune, wealth, sons, prosperity, etc. in another rebirth.

athānvārohaṇaṃ strīṇām ātmano bhartur eva ca |
sarvapāpakṣayakaraṃ nirayottāraṇāya ca ||
anekasvargaphaladaṃ muktidaṃ ca tathaiva ca |
janmāntare ca saubhāgyadhanaputrādivṛddhidam ||

In light of the earlier commentarial debate, this passage appears tailor-made as a refutation of the last unanswered objection to sati, namely, that it is an inferior option to celibacy, because it yields only the inferior reward of heaven. That is, the content of the above Smṛti and its absence as a cited scripture in the preceding literature combine to strongly suggest that it is a relatively recent creation of the Dharmaśāstra tradition, a creation whose purpose was to refute claims regarding the inferiority of sati vis-à-vis celibacy.[53] Moreover, this hypothesis finds notable confirmation in the *Dharmasindhu*'s explicit position that the practice of sati results in liberation for a woman who lacks desires and rewards, such as heaven, for a woman who possesses desires.[54]

In a similar vein, it is also significant that both the *Nirṇayasindhu* and the *Dharmasindhu* attest to the use within the sati rite of the previously discussed verse of the *Ṛgveda* (10.18.7) that some Dharmaśāstra authors have taken as a positive reference to sati. In particular, the earlier of these two works, the *Nirṇayasindhu*, describes the recitation of this verse in the sati rite as a practice peculiar to Bengal,[55] while the *Dharmasindhu* cites it as part of the standard ritual.[56] Hence, these texts suggest that the verse may have been a

[53] It is noteworthy that the creation of new Smṛtis, which is most clearly demonstrable in this particular case, may also have played a role in other aspects of the Dharmaśāṣtric debate on sati. For instance, there is the verse ascribed to Uśanas that explicitly prohibits a Brahmin widow from mounting a separate funeral pyre and is, therefore, used by commentators to limit the more general prohibition placed on such women in other Smṛtis. Authors within the Dharmaśāstra tradition may well have created this verse with the intention of achieving precisely this end.

[54] *Dharmasindhu*, p. 385: "The established position is that when a woman lacks desire, she attains liberation, but when she possesses desire, she attains rewards such as heaven." (*atra niṣkāmatve muktiḥ sakāmatve svargādiphalānīti vyavasthā* |)

[55] *Nirṇayasindhu*, p. 438: "But the Bengalis say that a Brahmin should recite the verse beginning, 'Let these women . . .' (ṚV 10.18.7), and also the following verse: 'Oṃ, may these auspicious, sinless, most beautiful women, who are devoted to their husband, enter the fire together with their husband's body!'" (*gauḍās tu imā nārīr avidhavā iti oṃ imāḥ pativratāḥ puṇyāḥ striyo 'pāpāḥ suśobhanāḥ | saha bhartuḥ śarīreṇa saṃviśantu vibhāvasum iti ca vipraḥ paṭhed ity āhuḥ* |)

[56] The *Dharmasindhu*, p. 385, contains a passage virtually identical to that given in the preceding note, only lacking the phrase: "But the Bengalis say that . . ." (*gauḍās tu . . . ity āhuḥ* |) Thus, this text,

rather late addition to the sati rite in much of India. Whether or not this was the case, their testimony further indicates that certain elements within the Brahmanical community were not content to refute through strictly exegetical arguments the objection to sati on the grounds that it contradicts the Veda. Instead, by including this verse of the *Ṛgveda* as a mantra, they appear also to have constructed the sati rite itself in such a way that it conveys an aura of Vedic authority. And if this is in fact so, we have here a further Brahmanical argument in favor of sati, albeit one of an oblique and unconventional sort.

Lastly, the *Nirṇayasindhu* (p. 439) even goes so far as to get rid of the restriction that Brahmin widows ascend the same funeral pyres as their husbands:

> Some even say that the statements prohibiting a Brahmin woman from performing sati really mean to prohibit her from dying together with her husband if he died for the sake of a penance or was an outcaste. When either her husband's bones or a piece of *palāśa* wood is burned with her, she does not incur the sin of dying on a separate pyre, for these things are equal to his body as they either constitute a part of him (= the bones) or stand in his place (= the *palāśa* wood).
>
> *niṣedhavākyāni prāyaścittārthaṃ mṛtena patitena vā saha maraṇaniṣedhaparāṇīty apy āhuḥ* | *asthidāhe palāśadāhe vā na pṛthakcitidoṣaḥ aṅgatvena sthānāpattyā vā śarīratulyatvāt* |

In the opening sentence of this passage, Kamalākara introduces a novel interpretation of those scriptures that issue prohibitions against Brahmin women performing sati: instead of referring to separate funeral pyres, they could refer to cases where a woman's husband either was an outcaste or had died in the process of repenting for some grievous sin.[57] If accepted, such an interpretation would virtually eliminate any special restrictions placed on Brahmin widows. Beyond this, Kamalākara proceeds to explain that, in any case, a woman can avoid the sin of ascending a separate funeral pyre by

which was composed in Maharashtra (not Bengal), understands the recitation of RV 10.18.7 to be a standard part of the sati rite rather than a regional peculiarity.

[57] Note that the successful performance of certain penances prescribed in the Dharmaśāstras entails the death of the person performing them. See, e.g., MDh 11.74, 100–101, 105–6.

immolating herself together with either the bones of her dead husband or a *palāśa* wood replacement for him. Furthermore, both the *Śuddhimayūkha* (p. 69) and *Dharmasindhu* (p. 385) make this very same argument. And although Madanapāla allowed a Brahmin woman to perform sati with her husband's bones centuries earlier, as we saw, the use of an entirely artificial replacement for him appears to be a new development. Hence, Kamalākara, even more so than Vijñāneśvara and Aparārka, effectively eliminates any special restrictions placed on Brahmin widows. Hence, taken in their historical and literary contexts, the *Nirṇayasindhu* and *Dharmasindhu* reflect the final weakening of earlier restrictions on sati.

Conclusion

To summarize, one can loosely arrange Dharmaśāstra writings on sati into three historical periods. In the first of these, which roughly corresponds to the second half of the first millennium CE, Smṛti texts that prescribe sati (e.g., ViDh 25.14, PSm 4.32–33) begin to appear. However, during approximately this same period, other Brahmanical authors also compose a number of Smṛtis that proscribe this practice specifically in the case of Brahmin widows. Moreover, Medhātithi, our earliest surviving commentator to address the issue, strongly opposes the practice for all women, yet an early unpublished commentary on Yājñavalkya, composed perhaps a century later, supports it. Taken together, this textual evidence suggests that although practiced by some Brahmins during the second half of the first millennium, sati was still relatively new and quite controversial in many Brahmin communities. In the second period, comprising the eleventh to thirteenth centuries, opposition to this custom starts to weaken, as none of the later commentators fully endorses Medhātithi's position on sati. Indeed, after Vijñāneśvara around the turn of the twelfth century, the strongest position taken against the practice is that it is an inferior option to lifelong celibacy, since its result is only heaven rather than liberation from the cycle of rebirth altogether. Finally, in the third period, starting around the fourteenth century, all opposition to sati within the Dharmaśāstra tradition has in effect disappeared. Beyond this, the *Nirṇayasindhu* (p. 438) and *Dharmasindhu* (p. 384) refute even the attenuated objection to sati on the grounds that, unlike celibacy, it cannot result in liberation, for they cite a previously unquoted Smṛti passage that specifically lists liberation as a reward for performing the rite. These texts thereby claim that sati is at least as beneficial an option for widows as celibacy and perhaps even more so, given the especially lavish praise it sometimes receives. Furthermore, they also effectively do away with the long-standing prohibition against Brahmin women ascending separate pyres from those of their husbands. Nevertheless, all authors within the Dharmaśāstra tradition consistently stop short of making sati an obligatory act. Hence, in short, Dharmaśāstra literature attests to a gradual shift from strict prohibition to complete endorsement in its attitude toward sati, a shift that took place c. 500–1400 CE.

This then raises the question: Does this shift in the attitudes of Dharmaśāstra authors toward sati reflect a broader shift in the attitudes and social practices of Brahmins in premodern India? I believe that the answer is yes, for it is worth noting that while scriptural exegesis generally presents itself as an endeavor to uncover the true meanings of sacred texts, the set of normative assumptions and moral intuitions that form a part of any exegete's background tend to have a major impact on the process of exegesis. In other words, commentators do not simply study scripture to learn the truth; they also study scripture to confirm the truth they already know from their social contexts. As a result, it is reasonable to assume that for the commentators under discussion, one of these already-known truths, which would guide their interpretations, was the relative morality or immorality of sati. And indeed, the *Śuddhimayūkha* of Nīlakaṇṭha (c. 1610–1650) provides some evidence that supports this assumption, when it states:

> From this other verse quoted in the *Kalpataru*, "A Brahmin woman ought not to depart by mounting a separate pyre,"[58] Vijñāneśvara and others correctly deduce that the prohibition against Brahmin widows performing sati applies only to ascending separate funeral pyres. The custom of all peoples supports this position as well.
>
> *kalpatarau pṛthakcitiṃ samāruhya na viprā gantum arhatīti vacontarān niṣedho bhinnacitipara iti vijñāneśvarādayo yuktam utpaśyanti | sārvajanīna ācāro 'py amum eva pakṣam anugṛhṇāti |* (*Śuddhimayūkha*, p. 69)

Here Nīlakaṇṭha unambiguously cites popular custom (*sārvajānīna ācāraḥ*) as additional support for his position on sati. In broad agreement with

[58] I have been unable to locate this verse in the extant edition of the *Kṛtyakalpataru*.

Richard Lariviere's (1997, 98) provocative thesis that "*dharmaśāstra* literature represents a peculiarly Indian record of local social norms," I believe that Nīlakaṇṭha is not alone among Dharmaśāstra writers in his reliance on custom when analyzing sati, only in his explicit statement to this effect. And if this is in fact the case, then by following the intricate details of this Dharmaśāstric debate one can trace a shifting moral attitude toward this practice within the greater Brahmanical community.

This, in turn, leads one to ask why Brahmins chose to adopt the custom of sati specifically during the period 500–1400 CE. That they adopted it from Indian kings, whose wives appear to have engaged in the practice at least occasionally since before the Common Era, is all but certain. In his masterful analysis of widow burning as a cross-cultural phenomenon, Joerg Fisch (2006, 251–54) proposes that Brahmins adopted the custom of sati or widow burning from kings, because it was deemed a prestigious practice and they sought to vie with the ruling elites for social prestige. A similar, but more broadly framed explanation would be to connect the Brahmanical adoption of sati with my earlier hypothesis that, in the hypergamous society that was classical India, there was a fundamental incentive for men to place tighter and tighter restrictions on the women to whom they were related in the hope of acquiring greater social status and prestige. If such an incentive was, in fact, operative in premodern India, then it is easy to understand why orthodox Brahmins came to adopt the practice of sati, for it is plainly an especially severe means of controlling women—specifically women who had fallen outside of the usually controlling bonds of marriage. While certainly plausible, however, a significant shortcoming of both of these explanations is that they fail to link the Brahmanical adoption of sati to specific historical developments in South Asia during the relevant period. That is, they fail to explain why Brahmins adopted the practice of sati during the specific period that it appears they did.

In order to come up with such an explanation, it is helpful to note the conspicuous chronological link between the increasing inheritance rights of widows within Dharmaśāstra, on the one hand, and the Brahmanical adoption of sati, on the other. If the two pivotal texts of Hindu law in the history of a widow's right to inherit are the *Yājñavalkya Dharmaśāstra* and the *Mitākṣarā*, as I argued in Chapter 2, then it would seem to be significant that shortly following each of these texts, the practice of sati apparently becomes markedly more accepted within Brahmanical society. Specifically, as we have seen, the first Dharmaśāstra texts to make any mention at all of sati are those of Viṣṇu (25.14) and Parāśara (4.32–33), which prescribe it as a legitimate option to lifelong celibacy for widows. Hence, the introduction of sati into the Dharmaśāstra tradition conspicuously follows the first Brahmanical text to strongly advocate a widow's right to inherit, namely, the *Yājñavalkya Dharmaśāstra*. Furthermore, as I have shown, the *Mitākṣarā* (on YDh 1.86) rejects the legitimacy of sati, although not as vehemently as his predecessor Medhātithi (on MDh 5.157) does, but after the *Mitākṣarā*, the practice becomes widely accepted within the Dharmaśāstra tradition, and all opposition to it quickly fades. Similarly, the *Mitākṣarā* is also the earliest surviving commentary to grant widows strong rights of inheritance; and all subsequent Dharmaśāstra works grant widows at least equally strong rights. Thus, textual chronology supports the conjecture that at least one major reason for the spread of sati in Brahmanical society was the increasing financial independence of sonless widows in the medieval period, as they became more and more often the sole inheritors of their husbands' estates.[59] And, indeed, it is easy to understand how objections to sati on moral and exegetical grounds might begin to feel less persuasive to many Brahmin men, when substantial amounts of land and money were at stake.

Moreover, it is worth recalling from Chapter 3 that the Dharmaśāstra tradition provides no evidence of mandatory lifelong widow asceticism until the twelfth century and that the fourteenth-century *Madanaparijāta* (pp. 202–3) is the first Brahmanical text to prescribe for widows most of the distinctive ascetic practices that characterize the classical Hindu widow ascetic. Therefore, classical widow asceticism seems to have developed specifically as a complement to sati, that is, as a way of ensuring a family's honor and status whatever option its widowed women chose to follow. Given the social isolation and material deprivation of widow ascetic life, it may even have functioned as a subtle—or not so subtle—inducement to perform sati. Hence, it is distinctly possible that the rise within Brahmanical culture of sati and classical widow asceticism constitutes something of a backlash against the markedly increased inheritance rights of widows within Dharmaśāstra literature and, by implication, Brahmanical society.

[59] A related, yet distinct argument holds the comparatively strong rights of inheritance granted to widows by the *Dāyabhāga* to account for the apparently greater incidence of sati in colonial Bengal relative to other regions of India. On this, see Mani (1998, 59).

Summary

We have now seen how the Hindu legal tradition's views regarding widows evolved over the roughly two millennia during which the tradition was a thriving source of literary production. Specifically, we have examined in fairly exhaustive detail how the views of Dharmaśāstra authors changed over time on the only four widow-related issues that they ever treated at great length and, for periods, contentiously debated, namely, widow remarriage and *niyoga*, widows' rights of inheritance, widow asceticism, and widow self-immolation, or sati. Up to this point, each of these issues has been treated largely in isolation. Consequently, it is worth devoting some space here to bringing them all together and to presenting a broad account of how the overall treatment of widows under Hindu law evolved historically during the two millennia prior to British colonialism.

From the earliest beginnings of Dharmaśāstra literature in perhaps the third century BCE until around 400 CE, the dominant position within the tradition was that widows could simply not inherit their husbands' property but were merely entitled to maintenance, which their affines were ideally supposed to provide. Such opposition to widows' rights of inheritance seems to be just one instantiation of a general Brahmanical opposition to women owning property at that time. The major exception to this opposition to women's ownership of property, of course, is the category of property known as *strīdhana*, or "women's wealth," which comprised wealth owned, controlled, and inherited almost exclusively by women. Wealth of this sort, however, consisted nearly entirely of movable property and would, therefore, likely have been marginal to a family's total wealth in most cases.

During this same early period, when widow's rights of inheritance were at their weakest, the sexual restrictions placed upon widows were also at their weakest, as we have seen. This is most obvious in the case of *niyoga*, which most early Dharmaśāstra authors permitted, although two of them—Āpastamba (2.27.2–7) and Manu (9.64–68)—strongly opposed the practice. However, true widow remarriage was widely prohibited within the Dharmaśāstra tradition throughout its history. The only unambiguous exception to this is Nārada (12.97–102), who clearly allows widows to remarry.

In addition, a number of passages in the works of a few other early authors (e.g., VaDh 17.75–80) seemingly support widow remarriage, although other passages in these same works (e.g., VaDh 17.72–74) implicitly disparage it. Indeed, the development of the institution of *niyoga* itself apparently reflects an underlying Brahmanical apprehension about widow remarriage even in the earliest period of Dharmaśāstra. For *niyoga* seems to be effectively a reformed version of widow remarriage, specifically widow remarriage of the type that anthropologists term "widow inheritance," that is, the practice of a widow remarrying primarily or even exclusively within the family of her dead husband. In other words, certain Brahmin thinkers appear to have intentionally designed *niyoga* so that it was terminologically and conceptually distinct from remarriage and yet served as a viable means for families to avoid the unwanted burden of indefinitely supporting childless women. Thus, although in the earliest period of Dharmaśāstra sexual restrictions on widows were not as severe as they would later become, we can already discern the impulse within orthodox Brahmanical culture to control widows sexually. This, I have suggested, is likely a result of the hypergamous character of early Indian society, for in hypergamous societies a prominent marker of high social status is a high level of sexual restriction of the women within one's social group (i.e., family, caste, clan, etc.).

Nevertheless, although the sexual control of widows was clearly a concern of Hindu jurists from the earliest period, these jurists place notably few nonsexual restrictions on widows. Thus, although widows were expected to observe a period of ascetic mourning lasting either six months or a year according to Baudhāyana (2.4.7–8) and Vasiṣṭha (17.55–56), there does not appear to have been any form of lifelong asceticism required of widows. At the same time, however, it is noteworthy that an optional form of widow asceticism, closely akin to typical forms of male world renunciation and connected with the rare common noun *kātyāyanī*, appears to have existed by at least the middle of the first millennium of the Common Era and possibly much earlier (see VaDh 19.33–34). Moreover, although sati was undoubtedly practiced in diverse areas of South Asia from quite early (c. 400 BCE–300 CE), it was almost certainly not a Brahmanical custom, but rather restricted only to the ruling classes. Hence, the two major institutions characteristic of the high-caste Hindu widow as known from the eighteenth and early nineteenth centuries—that is, classical Hindu widow asceticism and sati—are conspicuously absent from the earliest Dharmaśāstra literature.

The first major developments in the treatment and status of widows under Hindu law begin around the fifth century CE and take place especially during the second half of the first millennium. The first of these is Yājñavalkya's bold move to make a sonless man's widow the primary heir to his entire estate (2.139–40) and also to grant even the wives of men with sons the right to a share of their husbands' estates (2.119, 127). The reasons behind Yājñavalkya's decision to break so sharply from the preceding tradition remain a mystery. However, his decision clearly inaugurates a period of intense debate and controversy within Brahmanical society over a widow's rights of inheritance.

Following the inauguration of this debate, Hindu jurists turned decisively against not merely widow remarriage, which was always widely condemned, but also *niyoga*, which most early Dharmaśāstra writers endorsed. The major texts reflecting this change in Brahmanical attitudes are the commentaries, for after Bhāruci (on MDh 9.68)—the earliest surviving exegete to address these issues—all extant Dharmaśāstra commentators effectively deny the legitimacy of *niyoga*. The seed for this development in Hindu juridical thought, I have argued, was long planted and lies in the underlying logic of hypergamy, which almost inescapably incentivizes the sexual control of women as a marker of high social status, honor, and prestige.

It is difficult to attribute the increasing inheritance rights of widows within Dharmaśāstra to the rejection of *niyoga*, as Altekar (1938, 6–7) long ago suggested, primarily because the decisive rejection of *niyoga* within the tradition appears to have taken place well after authors first began to advocate for widows' increased rights of inheritance. Consequently, the disappearance of *niyoga* and a resulting increase in the number of childless and, therefore, indigent widows in Brahmanical society can hardly explain why certain Hindu jurists began to grant widows greater rights of inheritance. Conversely, the increasing inheritance rights of widows seem to have had no bearing on the rejection of *niyoga*, for the practice appears to have fallen completely out of favor within the Dharmaśāstra tradition while a widow's right to inherit was still being hotly contested. Moreover, both opponents and proponents of a widow's right to inherit reject *niyoga*.[1]

What the increasing inheritance rights of widows seem to have directly contributed to, however, is the Brahmanical adoption of sati, for Viṣṇu (25.14) in perhaps the seventh century is the first Dharmaśāstra author to mention sati. In particular, as we have seen, he prescribes it as a legitimate

[1] See, e.g., Viśvarūpa on YDh 1.68–69 and 2.139–40 and Medhātithi on MDh 9.64 and 8.3.

alternative to lifelong celibacy for widows. Therefore, the introduction of sati into the Dharmaśāstra tradition neatly follows the granting of markedly stronger rights of inheritance to widows. Following Viṣṇu, there is a period of intense controversy over the legitimacy of sati within Brahmanical society.

Furthermore, alongside sati, some sort of mandatory widow asceticism likely developed into a custom within at least segments of Brahmanical society during the second half of the first millennium. For although the twelfth-century *Kṛtyakalpataru* (*Vyavahārakāṇḍa*, pp. 635–38) is the first Dharmaśāstra work to prescribe mandatory lifelong widow asceticism, its discussion of the topic is based entirely upon earlier Smṛtis, many of which plausibly date to the second half of the first millennium. Moreover, in his reading of Manu (5.157), Medhātithi argues against the practice of widow asceticism.

Thus, the second half of the first millennium is a period of deep and contentious debate concerning the treatment and status of widows within Brahmanical society. There is initially the debate over a widow's right to inherit, wherein the established position that widows had no right whatsoever to their husband's property is seriously challenged. And, thereafter, there is the adoption by certain Brahmins of the originally royal practice of widow self-immolation and an ensuing debate on the practice's legitimacy. Moreover, the practice of mandatory widow asceticism of something like the classical type—also perhaps a royal institution in origin—is adopted by certain Brahmins, but rejected by others during this time. In contrast to the new and ongoing debates on these widow-related issues, however, the custom of *niyoga*, which had earlier been the subject of considerable disagreement, becomes effectively a settled issue and is uniformly rejected by Dharmaśāstra authors after the seventh century CE.

The debates within the Dharmaśāstra tradition on sati, widow asceticism, and the inheritance rights of widows are all settled between roughly the twelfth and fourteenth centuries. Just as it was the first of these debates to begin, the debate on a widow's right to inherit her husband's estate is the first one to be settled. Here the decisive text appears to have been the *Mitākṣarā* of Vijñāneśvara (on YDh 2.139–40), which makes the wife of a sonless man the heir to his entire estate, provided only that he had received his inheritance prior to his death and not reunited with his coparceners. For after Vijñāneśvara virtually every Dharmaśāstra author to address the issue grants widows equally strong rights of inheritance. Beyond this, Jīmūtavāhana and subsequent Hindu jurists of Bengal even go so far as to eliminate the

Mitākṣarā's requirement that, in order for a woman to inherit her husband's estate, he must have received his paternal inheritance and not reunited with his coparceners. And, regarding this development, it is noteworthy that evidence from both Jain texts and inscriptions confirms that widows' rights of inheritance actually increased substantially during the course of the twelfth century.

In seeming reaction to this development, opposition to sati within the Hindu legal tradition conspicuously weakens, as we have seen. Thus, after the *Mitākṣarā*, the only Dharmaśāstra text to oppose sati is the *Smṛticandrikā* (*Vyavahārakāṇḍa*, pp. 596–97)—a work composed around the turn of the thirteenth century. And even it does not prohibit sati, but merely relegates it to the status of an inferior option to lifelong celibacy. Furthermore, mandatory widow asceticism of something approaching the classical Hindu type is first clearly attested in digests dating to the twelfth century. Then, beginning with the fourteenth-century *Madanapārijāta* (pp. 202–3), the character of Hindu widow asceticism markedly changes, becoming both harsher and more socially marginalizing, and is first attested within Dharmaśāstra literature in its full classical form. Thereafter, this form of widow asceticism, involving the perpetual shaving of a widow's head, her avoidance of beds, and so on, becomes universally accepted within Brahmanical works. Therefore, it is plausible to view classical Hindu widow asceticism, like sati, as a reaction to widows' increased rights of inheritance within Brahmanical society—specifically as a reaction designed either to deny widows the ability to enjoy their inherited wealth or to eliminate them as heirs so that their husbands' estates might pass on to their male relatives (i.e., brothers, patrilineal cousins, etc.).

Therefore, the most striking feature of the high-caste Hindu widow in early colonial times—her stark choice between either self-immolation or an unrelentingly hard life of material deprivation and social exclusion—only became established in the thirteenth and fourteenth centuries. Moreover, although the logic of hypergamy may well have played a role in this development, given that sati and widow asceticism both involve the strict control of widows, evidence indicates that the increasing inheritance rights of widows played a decisive role.

Appendix: A Widow's Right to Adopt

The first chapter of this book explored one means by which a woman might obtain a son for her deceased husband if he died without sons: *niyoga*, which is the ancient Brahmanical version of levirate. Within the system of classical Hindu law, however, there is another conceivable means by which a sonless man's widow might acquire a son for him, which I have not discussed. This means is adoption, for Dharmaśāstra texts widely allow for the adoption of sons. There is, however, the problem that these texts generally lay down rules for a man to adopt a son and leave it unclear whether a woman is similarly entitled to adopt, specifically a woman whose husband has died. It is perhaps partly for this reason that the issue of a Hindu widow's right to adopt a son became a significant point of legal disputation during the colonial period.[1] Nevertheless, the foundational Dharmaśāstra texts are virtually silent on the topic, suggesting that, unlike *niyoga*, adoption was not a common strategy whereby a Brahmanical widow might obtain a son in the ancient and early medieval periods.

Indeed, the following passage of Vasiṣṭha (15.5) is the only one from a Smṛti text that bears upon a widow's right to adopt:

> A woman can neither give away nor adopt a son without her husband's permission.
>
> *na strī putraṃ dadyāt pratigṛhṇīyād vānyatrānujñānād bhartuḥ* |

Here, alone among Smṛti authors, Vasiṣṭha grants a woman the right to adopt a son. However, he requires her husband's permission in order for this to happen and, thus, leaves unanswered a crucial question: Does the requirement of a husband's permission rule out the possibility of widows adopting sons, since they have no husbands to grant them permission, or does it apply only to women who have living husbands?

So far as I have been able to determine, this question goes not only unanswered but also unasked in all of the early Dharmaśāstra commentaries and digests. Instead, the topic seems to be first addressed only in works of the fifteenth century.

Perhaps the earliest exegete to address the issue is Rudradhara, a Hindu jurist of the Mithilā region whose literary activity Kane (1962, 1:842) has dated to 1425–1460 CE. It is in his *Śuddhiviveka* (p. 100) that Rudradhara takes up the issue of a widow's right to adopt. There, after citing the above passage of Vasiṣṭha, he explains:

> If her husband lives, a woman has the right to give their son away with her husband's permission, but if her husband does not live, she has no such right.
>
> *patyau sati striyāḥ patyanumatyā putradāne 'dhikāraḥ | patyabhāve nādhikāraḥ* |

Here Rudradhara denies a widow the right to give away her son, as she has no husband to grant her permission to do so. From this one can draw the conclusion that widows

[1] On this, see Derrett (1976, 3:45–51, 247–52) and Kane (1962, 3:667–74).

similarly lack the right to adopt sons in Rudradhara's view. And, indeed, Rudradhara goes on to explicitly deny the right to adopt not only to widows, but to women in general. After citing Vasiṣṭha's description of the adoption rite (15.6) and explaining certain details of it, he presents his argument against women's right to adopt as follows:

> Furthermore, because an oblation accompanied by the recitation of the *vyāhṛtis*[2] is part of the adoption of a son and women and Śūdras have no right to recite a mantra such as the *vyāhṛtis*, they certainly cannot adopt a son.
>
> *evaṃ ca vyāhṛtihomasya putrapratigrahaṇāṅgatvād vyāhṛtimantrapāṭhe strīśūdrayor anadhikārāt strīśūdrayor dattakaputro na bhavaty eveti* |

Thus, Rudradhara holds that, as women, widows are unable to adopt sons, since the performance of the adoption rite requires the recitation of a certain Vedic mantra and women lack the right to recite any such mantras. Hence, in short, he interprets Vasiṣṭha (15.5) as saying that women can give their sons away with the permission of their husbands, but they can under no circumstances adopt a son.

This same basic argument is also found in a slightly later work composed in Mithilā, namely, the *Vivādacintāmaṇi* (p. 55) of Vācaspati Miśra, a prolific author active during the second half of the fifteenth century:[3]

> [Author:] Even if her husband grants her permission, a woman has no right to adopt, for that would nullify the recitation of the *vyāhṛtis* and the offering of an oblation that are parts of adoption. This would be the effective meaning of Vasiṣṭha's statement (15.5).
>
> [Objection:] But because it states without qualification that a woman cannot adopt "without her husband's permission," her right to adopt, like her right to give away a son, is established, provided that her husband permits it. And if this is the case, one can assume that she also has the right to employ the Vedic knowledge that is an essential part of the adoption rite.
>
> [Author:] It is true that a woman has a right to employ such knowledge when she acts jointly with her husband, as in a Vedic rite, but not when she acts separately, for that would result in an injunction to adopt that requires the nullification of certain prohibitions.
>
> *bhartur anujñāne 'pi striyā na grahaṇādhikāras tadaṅgavyāhṛtihomabādhād iti vartulārthaḥ | nanv anyatrānujñānād bhartur ity aviśeṣeṇa śravaṇād bhartur anujñāyāṃ dānavad grahaṇe 'pi stryadhikārasiddhau tadaṅgavidyāprayuktir api tasyāḥ kalpyeteti cet satyaṃ sahatvena tasyā adhikāra iṣṭivan na tu pṛthaktvena bādhasāpekṣavidhyāpatteḥ* |

Here, like his predecessor Rudradhara, Vācaspati denies all women, not just widows, the right to adopt independently of their husbands, because the recitation of a particular Vedic mantra and the offering of an oblation are required for the performance of the adoption rite. Therefore, if women were able to adopt sons on their own, it would nullify

[2] The *vyāhṛtis* or "calls" are a set of three sacred words—*bhūr bhuvaḥ svaḥ* ("earth, sky, heaven")—that, among other things, serve as a preamble to the ritual recitation of the famous Sāvitrī mantra (ṚV 3.62.10).

[3] On Vācaspati Miśra and his many Dharmaśāstra writings, see Kane (1962, 1:844–54).

either necessary ritual elements of adoption or scriptural prohibitions against women reciting Vedic mantras and offering oblations.

A slight variant of this argument is found again in the *Dattakamīmāṃsā* of Nandapaṇḍita—an early seventeenth-century digest devoted entirely to the topic of adoption.[4] The relevant section of this work (pp. 19–20) reads:

> Moreover, there is the scripture (VaDh 15.6): "Having offered an oblation while reciting the *vyāhṛtis*, one should adopt only a boy whose relatives do not live far away, that is, who lives close to his relatives." And one hears in this the grammatical form "having offered," the agent of which must be the same as that of the finite verb (i.e., "should adopt"). Thus, it is established that only the person who offers the oblation can adopt. Therefore, since women have no right to offer oblations, they have no right to adopt—so argues Vācaspati.
>
> *kiṃ ca vyāhṛtibhir hutvādūrabāndhavaṃ bandhusaṃnikṛṣṭam eva pratigṛhṇīyād iti* (VaDh 15.6) *samānakartṛkatābodhakatvāpratyayaśravaṇād dhomakartur eva pratigrahasiddheḥ strīṇāṃ homānadhikāritvāt pratigrahānadhikāra iti vācaspatiḥ* |

Here Nandapaṇḍita argues that widows are ineligible to adopt sons, because the adoption rite requires the offering of an oblation—a ritual act that women are barred from performing in classical Brahmanical sources. And, as one can see, Nandapaṇḍita ascribes this particular argument against a widow's right to adopt to Vācaspati, although Rudradhara appears to have been its historical originator. Nandapaṇḍita, however, introduces a new element into this old argument by referring to a pertinent fact of Sanskrit grammar: the agent of a gerund must be the same as the agent of the finite verb in a sentence. Thus, the agent of the finite verb *pratigṛhṇīyāt* ("should adopt") must also be the agent of the gerund *hutvā* ("having offered") in Vasiṣṭha's description of the adoption rite (15.6). Therefore, according to Nandapaṇḍita, only the person who offers the oblation in this rite can adopt a son. The fact that he explicitly makes this point is important, because it is perhaps intended to overcome the objection, found in the *Nirṇayasindhu* (p. 184), that a widow who wishes to adopt can simply have a Brahmin recite the necessary mantra and offer the necessary oblation on her behalf, as is done in other ritual contexts.

Beyond this, earlier in his *Dattakamīmāṃsā* (pp. 12–17), Nandapaṇḍita makes his own wholly new argument against a widow's right to adopt:

> When scripture says that "a sonless man should always arrange a substitute son,"[5] it indicates specifically a man. From this it is understood that a woman has no right to adopt. This is why Vasiṣṭha (15.5) states: "A woman can neither give away nor adopt a son without her husband's permission." Through this it is understood that a widow has no right to adopt, since it is impossible for her to receive her husband's permission. And one should not object that only a woman with a living husband requires her husband's permission, since only she is dependent, not a widow. For Vasiṣṭha (15.5) speaks generically of "a woman" (i.e., not a wife) and, therefore, dependence cannot provide the motive for requiring a husband's permission. Besides a widow is still dependent upon her relatives, as explained in Yājñavalkya's statement (1.84) that, failing sons, a woman's relatives should protect her. If one responds, "Then

[4] Kane (1962, 1:923–25) assigns the date of 1580–1630 to Nandapaṇḍita.

[5] The verse alluded to here is cited earlier in the *Dattakamīmāṃsā* (p. 3), where it is attributed to Atri. The relevant portion of it reads in Sanskrit: *aputreṇaiva kartavyaḥ putrapratinidhiḥ sadā* |

let a widow adopt only with her relatives' permission," that will not work, because the word "husband" in Vasiṣṭha's statement then becomes a synecdoche for other relatives and because a motive for requiring permission is then not established. The motive for requiring a husband's permission is to establish that an adopted boy has become a man's son, even though the rite of adoption was carried out by his wife.

aputreṇeti puṃstvaśravaṇān na striyā adhikāra iti gamyate | *ata eva vasiṣṭhaḥ* (15.5)—*na strī putraṃ dadyāt pratigṛhṇīyād vānyatrānujñānād bhartur iti* | *anena vidhavāyā bhartranujñānāsaṃbhavād anadhikāro gamyate* | *na ca sadhavāyāḥ svabhartranujñāpekṣā pāratantryān na vidhavāyā iti vācyam* | *strīsāmānyopādānena pāratantryasyāprayojakatvāt* | *abhāve jñātayas teṣām iti* (YDh 1.84) *jñātipāratantryasya sadbhāvāc ca* | *tarhi jñātyanujñayaiva tasyāḥ putrīkaraṇam astv iti cen na bhartṛpadasyopalakṣaṇatāpatteḥ prayojanāsiddheś ca* | *prayojanaṃ tu bhartranujñānasya strīkṛtaparigraheṇāpi bhartṛputratvasiddhiḥ* |

There is a crucial ambiguity in this passage regarding Nandapaṇḍita's position on a woman's right to adopt, for at the start of the passage he denies women the right to adopt and yet at the end explains that Vasiṣṭha (15.5) requires a husband's permission, because a boy can thereby become a man's legal son, even when the adoption was performed by his wife—suggesting that women can adopt, if their husbands allow them. Therefore, it is unclear whether Nandapaṇḍita accepts a woman's right to adopt with her husband's permission. What is clear, however, is that he denies widows the right to adopt, because they obviously lack husbands capable of granting them permission.

Having established this, Nandapaṇḍita then addresses the possible objection that the reason a woman needs her husband's permission to adopt is that she is a dependent and, thus, since widows are clearly not dependent upon their husbands, this reason cannot apply to them. Nandapaṇḍita answers this objection by noting that although widows are not dependent upon their husbands, they are still dependent upon other relatives, according to certain scriptures. Moreover, he addresses the possibility that widows should then be able to adopt with the permission of these other relatives upon whom they are dependent and dismisses it on two grounds: (a) such a possibility entails rejecting a plausible literal interpretation of the word "husband" in Vasiṣṭha's statement (15.5) in favor of a nonliteral one, and (b) it fails to explain the reason why a husband's permission is required for a woman to adopt. As Nandapaṇḍita goes on to explain, the real reason for this requirement, in his view, is that an adoptee can become a man's son only if the man agrees to it.[6] The underlying assumption here is that the whole purpose of adoption, like *niyoga* in earlier times, is to provide a sonless man with a legitimate son and heir. Thus, the first commentators within the Dharmaśāstra tradition to address the issue of a widow's right to adopt—Rudradhara, Vācaspati, and Nandapaṇḍita—all oppose this right.

However, there are several later Hindu jurists who advocate for a widow's right to adopt. The earliest of these are two paternal cousins of the famous Bhaṭṭa family of Benares whom we have previously encountered, namely, Kamalākara and Nīlakaṇṭha. The apparently older of these two cousins, Kamalākara, in his *Nirṇayasindhu* (p. 184) defends a widow's right to adopt as follows:

[6] The *Dattakamīmāṃsā* elaborates on this in the subsequent passage (pp. 17–19), stating at one point: "The state of being a son comes about only through the father permitting it, not through adoption, since that can be performed by a woman." (*putratvaṃ ca pitranujñānenaiva na parigraheṇa tasya tatra strīkartṛtvāt* |)

> And this statement (VaDh 15.5) applies when a woman has a living husband. Otherwise it would conflict with the statement of Vatsa and Vyāsa:
>
> A son that a mother or father gives is held to be an adopted son.
>
> Here giving is a synecdoche for giving and adopting. There is, however, the argument made by Rudradhara in the *Śuddhiviveka* that since an oblation accompanied by mantras is part of adopting a son and women and Śūdras have no right to recite mantras, such as the *vyāhṛtis*, they certainly cannot adopt a son. And Vācaspati also argues precisely this. But this argument is incorrect, for Vasiṣṭha states that a woman can also adopt a son with her husband's permission. Although Medhātithi says that, like taking a wife, adopting a son has an otherworldly purpose and must be completed through an oblation[7] and although it is impossible for women to offer oblations, nevertheless, according to Harinātha and others,[8] a woman can have a Brahmin perform oblations and the like for her, just as she does when performing a vow.

idaṃ ca bhartṛsattve | anyathā dadyān mātā pitā vā yaṃ sa putro dattrimaḥ smṛta iti vatsavyāsavacovirodhaḥ syāt | dānaṃ pratigrahopalakṣaṇam | yat tu samantrakahomasya putrapratigrahāṅgatvād vyāhṛtyādimantrapāṭhe ca strīśūdrayor anadhikārāt tayor dattakaḥ putro na bhavaty eveti śuddhiviveke rudradhareṇoktam | vācaspatiś caivam evāha | tan na bhartur anujñayā striyā api pratigrahokteḥ | yady api medhātithinā bhāryātvavad adṛṣṭarūpaṃ dattakatvaṃ homasādhyam uktaṃ striyāś ca homāsaṃbhavas tathāpi vratādivad vipradvārā homādi kārayed iti harināthādayaḥ |

Here Kamalākara interprets Vasiṣṭha's statement (15.5) that prohibits women from giving away or adopting a son without their husbands' permission as applicable only to women who have living husbands. The implication of this is that widows have a right to adopt sons, in his view. And Kamalākara proceeds to defend this right on the basis of a scriptural statement ascribed to Vatsa and Vyāsa that defines an adopted son as a boy given away by either his mother or his father, the implication being that a mother is entitled to give away her son. To find support in this statement for a woman's right to adopt, Kamalākara interprets the act of giving mentioned in it as a synecdoche for both giving and adopting.

After this, he refutes the argument of Rudradhara, Vācaspati Miśra, and Nandapaṇḍita that a widow cannot adopt, because she cannot recite Vedic mantras and offer oblations, which are acts required in the adoption rite. He does this by noting that Vasiṣṭha allows a woman to adopt with her husband's permission. Thus, it cannot be correct that women simply have no right to adopt. Besides—Kamalākara points out—when performing rites that require oblations and the recitation of mantras, women can have Brahmin men perform these acts on their behalf. This is, for instance, the accepted practice when women carry out *vratas* or religious vows.[9] Hence, unlike earlier authors in the Dharmaśāstra tradition, Kamalākara grants widows the same rights of adoption as men.

While agreeing with his cousin on the basic point that widows can adopt sons, Nīlakaṇṭha in his *Vyavahāramayūkha* (p. 70) places a special restriction on their ability to do so:

> Only a woman with a living husband needs her husband's permission to adopt, for such permission has a perceptible purpose (i.e., her dependence). A widow, by

[7] I have been unable to identify a passage of Medhātithi that expresses this view.

[8] According to Kane (1962, 1:776–77), Harinātha is the author of an unpublished Dharmaśāstra worked entitled *Smṛtisāra* and was active from c. 1300 to 1400 CE.

[9] For a detailed study of women's involvement in the performance of vows (*vrata*), see McGee (1987).

> contrast, can adopt even without that, by the command of her father or, failing him, her relatives. Hence, Yājñavalkya (1.84) has explained that a woman is dependent upon her husband only in a particular stage of life:
>
> Her father should protect her as a girl, her husband after marriage, and her sons in old age or, failing them, her relatives. A woman should never be independent.
>
> If she has no husband or he is unable to watch over her due to old age or the like, then a woman is instead dependent upon her sons and so forth.
>
> *bhartranujñā tu sadhavāyā eva dṛṣṭārthatvāt | vidhavāyās tu tāṃ vināpi pitus tadabhāve jñātīnām ājñayā bhavati | ata eva—*
>
> *rakṣet kanyāṃ pitā vinnāṃ patiḥ putrās tu vārddhike |*
> *abhāve jñātayas teṣāṃ na svātantryaṃ kvacit striyāḥ* || (YDh 1.84)
>
> *iti yājñavalkyenāvasthāviśeṣa eva bhartuḥ pāratantryam uktam| tadabhāve vārddhikādinā tasyākṣamatāyāṃ vā putrādīnām api |*

Here, as one can see, Nīlakaṇṭha requires a widow who wishes to adopt a son to first obtain permission to do so from those relatives of hers upon whom she has become dependent after her husband's death. Therefore, he places a significant restriction upon a widow's right to adopt that is not found in Kamalākara's work. Moreover, he justifies this restriction on the basis of what he considers to be the obvious reason behind Vasiṣṭha's requirement that a woman must secure her husband's permission in order to adopt: a wife is dependent upon her husband in all her actions. Hence, having identified dependence as the relevant factor restricting a woman's right to adopt, he holds that, like women with living husbands, widows can also adopt, but only with the permission of those relatives charged with watching over them. Here it bears noting that this position of Nīlakaṇṭha is the same as one that we saw Nandapaṇḍita refute in his *Dattakamīmāṃsā* (pp. 14–17) and that Nīlakaṇṭha offers no rebuttal to Nandapaṇḍita's argument.

Following Nīlakaṇṭha and Kamalākara, several later jurists similarly support a widow's right to inherit. For instance, Kāśīnātha in his *Dharmasindhu* (p. 137) argues for a widow's right to inherit as follows:

> A woman with a living husband can adopt or give away a son with her husband's permission. Without her husband's permission, however, she can neither give away nor adopt a son. Likewise, even a widowed woman can adopt a son if her husband died after telling her that she should adopt a son. Clearly everyone would agree that, in the absence of such permission, a widow can also adopt a son, if she knew of her husband's intention to adopt a son while he was still alive or learned of it from the mouth of a trustworthy individual after his death. Even in the absence of permission from her husband of both of these types, a widow still has the right to adopt a son on the basis of the general scriptural statement that "a sonless man has no world," just as she has the right to perform meritorious acts, such as mandatory and optional vows, on the basis of various scriptures. Vasiṣṭha (15.5) states: "A woman can neither give away nor adopt a son without her husband's permission." But the purpose of this statement is to permit a woman not to adopt a son when she does not have her husband's permission, not to prohibit such a woman from adopting a son, for it makes no sense that such a prohibition would come from the scriptures. Hence, anyone who destroys a man's livelihood, cuts off his ancestral offerings, and the like by obstructing his wife from adopting a son goes to hell, for scripture states:

Anyone who does anything to hinder a Brahmin's livelihood will become one of the dung-eating insects for many years.

This is all elaborated in the *Saṃskārakaustubha*. When adopting sons, women can have the oblations and the like performed by Brahmins, just as they do when performing vows.

sadhavayā striyā patyanujñayā putro grahītavyo dātavyaś ca | bhartranujñābhāve tu na grāhyo na deyaḥ | evaṃ vidhavayāpi striyā tvayā putraḥ svīkārya ity uktvā bhartari mṛte grāhyaḥ | spaṣṭam īdṛśānujñābhāve bhartṛjīvanadaśāyāṃ tanmaraṇottaram āptamukhād vā putrasvīkāraviṣayakabhartrabhiprāyaṃ jñātavatyāpi grāhya iti sarvasaṃmatam | etadubhayavidhabhartranujñābhāve 'pi tattacchāstrān nityakāmyavratādidharmācaraṇa iva putrapratigrahe 'pi nāputrasya loko 'stīty ādisāmānyaśāstrād eva vidhavāyā adhikāraḥ | na strī putraṃ dadyāt pratigṛhṇīyād vānyatra bhartranujñānād iti (VaDh 15.5) *vasiṣṭhavākyaṃ tu bhartranujñārahitāṃ prati putrāpratigrahābhyanujñāparaṃ na tu putrapratigrahaniṣedhaparaṃ śāstraprāptaniṣedhāyogāt | atas tādṛśastriyāḥ putrapratigrahapratibandhena vṛttilopapiṇḍavicchedādi kurvan narakabhāg bhavati |*
yo brāhmaṇasya vṛttau tu pratikūlaṃ samācaret |
viḍbhujāṃ tu kṛmīṇāṃ syād [ekaḥ saṃvatsarān bahūn][10] *||*
iti śāstrād iti kaustubhe vistaraḥ | strībhiḥ putrasvīkāre vratādivad vipradvārā homādikaṃ kāryam |

Kāśīnātha concludes this passage by repeating Kamalākara's position that women can have Brahmins recite mantras and offer oblations for them when adopting sons and, thus, women's lack of entitlement to perform these acts does not bar them from adopting. However, as Kāśīnātha himself states, the bulk of the passage essentially repeats arguments found in much more elaborate form in the *Saṃskārakaustubha* of Anantadeva—an author whom Kane (1962, 1:961–63) dates to the third quarter of the seventeenth century.[11] As one can see, Kāśīnātha's central argument, which he borrows from Anantadeva, is that widows must have a right to adopt, because sons provide crucial assistance to their fathers in the hereafter through the performance of Śrāddha rites. Consequently, to bar a widow from adopting is to deprive a man of sustenance in his next life and, therefore, to act in violation of authoritative scriptures. From the existence of passages such as that above and the dearth of contradicting ones,[12] it would seem that a widow's right to adopt became more widely accepted within Brahmanical society during the seventeenth and eighteenth centuries.

Thus, to summarize, the Dharmaśāstra tradition seems not to have addressed the issue of widows' rights of adoption until the fifteenth century. Given the massive literary output of the tradition prior to this period, this suggests that, at least in orthodox Brahmanical communities, widows seldom, if ever, adopted sons. During the fifteenth century, however, two Hindu jurists from Mithilā—Rudradhara and Vācaspati Miśra—composed works that explicitly oppose a widow's right to adopt; and Nandapaṇḍita followed suit

[10] This *pāda* is missing in the *Dharmasindhu* (p. 137) and has been supplied on the basis of the *Saṃskārakaustubha* (p. 47).

[11] See *Saṃskārakaustubha*, pp. 45–47.

[12] I have been unable to find any Dharmaśāstra work composed after the *Dattakamīmāṃsā* (c. 1580–1630) that opposes a widow's right to adopt. It is distinctly possible, however, that such works exist, given the number of late unpublished digests on adoption. For a reference to these, see Kane (1962, 1:1039–40).

roughly a century later in his *Dattakamīmāṃsā*. This implies that the prospect, if not the actual practice, of widows adopting sons first arose within Brahmanical communities during approximately this period and was controversial. Despite initial opposition to the idea, however, widows' rights of adoption seem to have become increasingly accepted within the Hindu legal tradition throughout the seventeenth and eighteenth centuries, as reflected in the works of Kamalākara, Nīlakaṇṭha, Anantadeva, and Kāśīnātha.

Consequently, by way of conclusion, it is worth considering why the idea of widows adopting sons first arose within Brahmanical communities around the fifteenth century; why the earliest Hindu jurists to address the idea opposed it; and why later ones endorsed it. The initial opposition to a widow's right to adopt within the Dharmaśāstra tradition is perhaps the easiest part to explain. To begin with, the adoption of sons by widows would have been a new practice and, as such, inherently suspect, given the deeply conservative character of orthodox Brahmanical culture in general and Dharmaśāstra in particular. Secondly, it would have constituted a step toward women's independence—something that Brahmanical actors had been striving to curtail during the preceding centuries, as evidenced by the spread of widow asceticism and sati within their communities during the first half of the second millennium. And, finally, it is possible to imagine that certain members of Brahmanical society conceived of adoption as a kind of legalistic procreation akin to sexual procreation. If so, they might well have viewed the practice of widows adopting sons as a breach of female chastity unbefitting of women of respectable families, even if no sexual intercourse was involved.

As to why the idea of widows adopting sons first gained traction within Brahmanical society and why later Dharmaśāstra writers tend to support widows' rights of adoption, I believe that the underlying explanation is likely the same for both phenomena. In order to grasp it, however, we must accept that, contrary to what the *Dharmasindhu* (p. 137) might suggest, the practice of adoption by widows did not arise out of the simple desire to provide sonless men with legal sons and heirs, who would then aid them in the hereafter by performing Śrāddha rites and the like. For by the fifteenth century the notion that sons were essential to a happy and prosperous afterlife had been a ubiquitous feature of Brahmanical society for millennia. Therefore, it is hard to explain why it only led to the practice of widows adopting sons at so late a date.

Instead, if one wants to explain why the prospect of widows adopting first arose and why proponents of the idea increased over time within the Dharmaśāstra tradition, I believe that one must look at certain developments within Brahmanical society specific to the first half of the second millennium—developments that were brought to light in Chapters 2, 3, and 4 of this book. The first of these is that, by around the twelfth century, the wife of a sonless man had become the primary heir to his entire estate throughout much of South Asia. Thereafter, as I argue in Chapters 3 and 4, certain Brahmin men, who were deeply unsettled by the resulting emergence of a class of independently wealthy women within their communities, developed new ways to exert control over such women. Thus, sati and widow asceticism became increasingly accepted between the twelfth and fourteenth centuries within Brahmanical society. Nevertheless, although these strategies of control might have been effective, it is likely that only a small minority of widows ever performed sati.[13] Moreover, while those that did not would have been compelled to

[13] Our evidence on the prevalence of sati in premodern India is poor, but evidence from the colonial period suggests that most widows, even among the higher castes, did not engage in the practice. For a discussion of the relevant colonial data, see Fisch (2006, 255–60).

engage in a life of harsh austerities under the new prevailing orthodoxy, this would have done nothing to alter the fact that they could still be quite wealthy.

Bearing this in mind, one can see how adoption would have been useful to those hoping to deprive widows of their inherited wealth, for an adopted son is a son and, as such, inherits a man's estate before his wife under standard Dharmaśāstra rules.[14] Thus, if a widow were to adopt a son, it would deprive her of most of the property that she inherited from her husband. One might imagine that while this would have had the desired effect of depriving widows of wealth, it would also have resulted in property leaving a man's family as it devolved to his adopted son and his adopted son's sons rather than to his brothers, their sons, and the like. Therefore, one might assume that the prospect of a widow adopting would have held no appeal to members of her husband's family, who would then lose out on significant wealth. However, works of Dharmaśāstra are clear that, if possible, a man who desires to adopt must adopt his brother's son and, failing any such child, another *sapiṇḍa* relative.[15] Hence, if a widow were to adopt a son, this son would be a child born within her husband's close family in most cases. And if a widow needed her relatives' permission in order to adopt, as Nīlakaṇṭha argues in the *Vyavahāramayūkha* (p. 70), then it could effectively be guaranteed that a widow would only adopt the child of a close male relative of her husband. As a result, if a widow adopted a son, this son would not only take possession of her inherited property when he came of age, but also in most cases keep that property securely within her husband's biological family. Therefore, it is plausible to interpret the acceptance of widows' rights of adoption within Dharmaśāstra as yet another means whereby Hindu jurists sought to control women who had fallen outside of the controlling bonds of marriage.

[14] On this, Kane (1962, 3:698) states: "The adopted son is entitled to inherit in the adoptive family as fully as if he were a natural son."

[15] See Derrett (1976, 3:53–54) and Kane (1962, 3:678–79). This basic position goes back at least as far as the *Mitākṣarā*, which states on YDh 2.132:

> There is the statement:
>
> > If just one brother among several brothers born from a single source has a son, then through that son they all have a son—so Manu has declared. (MDh 9.182)
>
> The purpose of this is to prohibit a man from adopting other boys as sons when he can adopt his brother's son.
>
> *yat tu*
>
> > *bhrātṝṇām ekajātānām ekaś cet putravān bhavet |*
> > *sarve te tena putreṇa putriṇo manur abravīt ||*
>
> *iti tad api bhrātṛputrasya putrīkaraṇasaṃbhave 'nyeṣāṃ putrīkaraṇaniṣedhārtham |*

Bibliography

Primary Literature

Abhidhānaratnamālā of Halāyudha. Edited by Theodor Aufrecht. Delhi: Indian Booksellers & Publishers, 1975 [reprint].

Agni Purāṇa. Edited by Rājendra Nātha Śarman. Delhi: Nag Publishers, 1986.

Aitareya Brāhmaṇa. Edited by Theodor Aufrecht. Bonn: Adolph Marcus, 1879.

Amarakośa (a.k.a. *Nāmaliṅgānuśāsana*) of Amarasiṃha. With the commentary of Kṣīrasvāmin. Edited by Krishnaji Govind Oka. Poona: Law Printing Press, 1913.

Aṅguttara Nikāya. Part 1. Edited by R. Morris. 2nd ed., revised by A. K. Warder. London: Pali Text Society, 1961.

Āpastamba Dharmasūtra. With the commentary *Ujjvalā* of Haradatta. Edited and translated (into Hindi) by Umeśa Chandra Pāṇḍeya. Kashi Sanskrit Series, vol. 93. Varanasi: Chowkhambha Sanskrit Series Office, 1969.

Āpastamba Dharmasūtra. Edited and translated by P. Olivelle, in Olivelle 2000.

Aṣṭādhyāyī of Pāṇini. With the commentary *Vyākaraṇa-Mahābhāṣya* of Patañjali. Edited by F. Kielhorn. 3 vols. 3rd rev. ed. by K. V. Abhyankar. Poona: Bhandarkar Oriental Research Institute, 1962–72.

Atharvaveda Saṃhitā (Śaunaka recension). Edited by R. Roth and W. D. Whitney. Berlin: F. Dümmler, 1856.

Baudhāyana Dharmasūtra. Edited and translated by P. Olivelle, in Olivelle 2000.

Brahma Purāṇa. Edited by Peter Schreiner and Renate Söhnen-Thieme. Wiesbaden: O. Harrassowitz, 1987.

Bṛhadāraṇyaka Upaniṣad. Edited and translated by Patrick Olivelle, in *The Early Upaniṣads*. South Asia Research. New York: Oxford University Press, 1998.

Bṛhaspati Smṛti. Edited by K. V. Rangaswami Aiyangar. Baroda: Oriental Institute, 1941.

Dattakamīmāṃsā of Nandapaṇḍita. Edited by Rājendra Prasāda Pāṇḍeya. Prācyavidyāgranthamālā 2. Vārāṇasī: Kāśī Hindū Vidyālaya, 1980.

Dāyabhāga of Jīmūtavāhana. Edited and translated by L. Rocher, in L. Rocher 2002.

Dāyatattva of Raghunandana. Edited by Caṇḍīcaraṇa Smṛtibhūṣaṇa. Calcutta: Victoria Press, 1913.

Dharmasindhu of Kāśīnātha Upādhyāya. Sri Garibdas Oriental Series 14. Delhi: Sri Satguru Publications, 1986 [reprint].

Dvyāśrayakāvya of Hemacandra. With the commentary of Abhayatilakagaṇi. Edited by Abaji Vishnu Kathavate. 2 vols. Bombay Sanskrit and Prakrit Series, no. 69. Bombay: Government Central Press, 1915–21.

Gautama Dharmasūtra. With the commentary of Maskarin. Edited by L. Srinivasacharya. Bibliotheca Sanskrita, vol. 50. Mysore: Government Branch Press, 1917.

Gautama Dharmasūtra. With the commentary *Mitākṣarā* of Haradatta. Edited and translated (into Hindi) by Umesh Chandra Pandey. Kashi Sanskrit Series, vol. 172. Varanasi: Chowkhambha Sanskrit Series Office, 1966.

Gautama Dharmasūtra. Edited and translated by P. Olivelle, in Olivelle 2000.

Harivaṃśa. Edited by Parushuram Lakshman Vaidya. 2 vols. Poona: Bhandarkar Oriental Research Institute, 1969–71.

Harṣacarita of Bāṇa. Edited by P. V. Kane, in Kane 1986.

Hiraṇyakeśi Pitṛmedhasūtra. Edited by W. Caland, in *The Pitṛmedhasūtras of Baudhāyana, Hiraṇyakeśin, Gautama*. Nendeln: Kraus Reprint Ltd., 1966 [reprint].

Īśa Upaniṣad. Edited and translated by P. Olivelle, in *The Early Upaniṣads*. South Asia Research. New York: Oxford University Press, 1998.

Jātakatthavaṇṇanā (together with its commentary). Vol. 3. Edited by V. Fausbøll. London: Trübner & Co., 1883.

Kathāsaritsāgara of Somadeva. Edited by Paṇḍita Jagadīśa Lāla Śāstrin. Delhi: Motilal Banarsidass, 1977 [reprint].

Kṛtyakalpataru of Lakṣmīdhara. Edited by K. V. Rangaswami Aiyangar. 14 vols. Gaekwad's Oriental Series. Baroda: Oriental Institute, 1941–79.

Kumāravihāraśataka of Rāmacandra. Edited by Muni Ratnabodhivijaya. Mumbaī: Śrī Jinaśāsana Ārādhanā Trust, 2002.

Madanapārijāta of Madanapāla. Edited by Madhusudana Smritiratana. Bibliotheca Indica. Calcutta: Asiatic Society of Bengal, 1893.

Mahābhārata. Edited by V. S. Sukthankar et al. 19 vols. Poona: Bhandarkar Oriental Research Institute, 1927–59.

Mālatīmādhava of Bhavabhūti. Edited and translated by M. R. Kāle. 3rd ed. Delhi: Motilal Banarsidass, 1967.

Mālavikāgnimitra of Kālidāsa. Edited by Shankar Pāṇḍurang Pandit. 2nd ed. Bombay Sanskrit Series, no. 6. Bombay: Government Central Book Depot, 1889.

Mānava Dharmaśāstra. With the commentaries of Medhātithi, Sarvajñanārāyaṇa, Kullūka, Rāghavānanda, Nandana, and Rāmacandra. Edited by V. N. Mandlik. 2 vols. Bombay: Ganpat Krishnaji's Press, 1886.

Mānava Dharmaśāstra. With the commentary of Bhāruci. Edited and translated by J. D. M. Derrett. 2 vols. Wiesbaden: F. Steiner, 1975.

Mānava Dharmaśāstra. With the commentary of Medhātithi. Edited and translated by Ganganath Jha. 10 vols. Delhi: Motilal Banarsidass, 1999 [reprint].

Mānava Dharmaśāstra. Edited and translated by P. Olivelle, in Olivelle 2005.

Mānava Dharmaśāstra. With the commentary of Bhāruci. Edited by S. Jagannnātha. University of Mysore Oriental Research Institute Series 214. Mysore: Oriental Research Institute, 2020.

Mattavilāsa of Mahendravarman. Edited by T. Gaṇapati Śāstrī. Trivandrum Sanskrit Series, no. 55. Trivandrum: Superintendent Government Press, 1917.

Nārada Smṛti. With the commentary of Bhavasvāmin. Edited by K. Sāmbaśiva Śāstrī. Trivandram Sanskrit Series. Trivandrum: The Government of Her Highness the Maharani Regent of Travancore, 1929.

Nārada Smṛti. Edited and translated by R. Lariviere. Delhi: Motilal Banarsidass, 2003.

Nirṇayasindhu of Kamalākara Bhaṭṭa. Edited by Nārāyaṇa Rāma Ācārya. Vidyābhavana Prācyavidyā Granthamālā 31. Vārāṇasī: Caukhambā Vidyābhavana, 1991 [reprint].

Nirukta of Yāska. Edited and translated by Lakshman Sarup. Delhi: Motilal Banarsidass, 1967 [reprint].

Parāśaramādhava of Mādhava, commentary on the *Parāśara Smṛti*. Edited by Vāman Śāstrī Islāmpurkar and R. G. Bhadkamkar. 3 vols. Bombay Sanskrit and Prakrit Series, nos. 47, 48, 59, 64, 68, 74. Bombay: Government Central Press, 1893–1919.

Prabandhacintāmaṇi of Merutuṅga. Edited by Jinavijaya Muni. Siṅghī Jaina Granthamālā 1. Śāntiniketan: Siṅghī Jaina Jñānapīṭha, 1931.

Puṟanāṉūṟu. Translated by G. Hart and H. Heifetz, in Hart and Heifetz 1999.

Ṛgveda Saṃhitā. With Sāyaṇa's commentary. Edited by F. Max Müller. 6 vols. London: Wm. H. Allen & Co., 1849–74.

Śabarabhāṣya of Śabara, commentary on the *Pūrvamīmāṃsā Sūtra*. Edited by Maheśachandra Nyāyaratna. Bibliotheca Indica. Calcutta: The Asiatic Society, 1889.

Ṣaḍviṃśa Brāhmaṇa. Edited by B. R. Sharma. Tirupati: Kendriya Sanskrit Vidyapeetha, 1967.

Saṃskārakaustubha of Anantadeva. Edited by Vāsudeva Śarmā Paṇśīkar. Bombay: Nirnaya Sagar Press, 1913.

Saṃskāramayūkha of Nīlakaṇṭha. Edited by N. S. Shende. Bombay: Gujarati Printing Press, 1913.

Śatapatha Brāhmaṇa in the Mādhyandina recension. Edited by A. Weber. Berlin: F. Dümmler, 1855.

Skanda Purāṇa. Edited by Kṣemarāja Śrīkṛṣṇadāsa. 7 vols. Delhi: Nag Publishers, 1986 [reprint].

Smṛticandrikā of Devaṇa Bhaṭṭa. Edited by L. Srinivasacharya. 5 vols. Bibliotheca Sanskrita. Mysore: Government Branch Press, 1914–21.

Śuddhimayūkha of Nīlakaṇṭha Bhaṭṭa. Edited by Anant Yagneshwar Dhupakar. Bombay: Gujarati Printing Press, 1941.

Śuddhitattva of Raghunandana. Edited by Caṇḍīcaraṇa Smṛtibhūṣaṇa. Calcutta: Victoria Press, 1913.

Śuddhiviveka of Rudradhara. Edited by Oṃkāranātha Pāṭhaka. Delhi: Vidyānidhi Prakāśan, 2015.

Taittirīya Āraṇyaka. Edited by K. V. Abhyankar. 2 vols. Ānandāśrama Sanskrit Series 36. Pune: Ānandāśrama, 1967 [reprint].

Taittirīya Brāhmaṇa. Edited by Rājendralāla Mitra. 3 vols. Bibliotheca Indica. Calcutta: Asiatic Society of Bengal, 1859–90.

Taittirīya Saṃhitā. Edited by A. Weber. 2 vols. Indische Studien 1112. Leipzig: F. A. Brockhaus, 1871–72.

Tantravārttika of Kumārila, commentary on the *Pūrvamīmāṃsā Sūtra*. Edited by Gaṅgādhara Śāstrī. Benares Sanskrit Series 5, 7, 16, 23, 27, 29, 32, 34, 36, 39, 60, 62, 72. Benares: Braj B. Das & Co., 1903.

Vaiṣṇava Dharmaśāstra. Edited and translated by Patrick Olivelle. Harvard Oriental Series 73. Cambridge, MA: Harvard University Press, 2009.

Vasiṣṭha Dharmasūtra. Edited and translated by P. Olivelle, in Olivelle 2000.

Vivādacintāmaṇi of Vācaspati Miśra. Edited by Lakshmīkānta Jha. Patna: United Press, 1937.

Vyavahāramayūkha of Nīlakaṇṭha Bhaṭṭa. Edited by Mahadeva Gangadhar Bakre and Vyankatesha Ramachandra Lele. Bombay: Gujarati Printing Press, 1923.

Yājñavalkya Dharmaśāstra. With the commentary of Aparārka. 2 vols. Ānandāśramasaṃskṛtagranthāvali 46. Pune: Ānandāśrama, 1903.

Yājñavalkya Dharmaśāstra. With the commentaries *Bālakrīḍā* of Viśvarūpa and *Mitākṣarā* of Vijñāneśvara and the sub-commentaries *Subodhinī* and *Bālaṃbhaṭṭī* on the *Mitākṣarā*. Edited by S. S. Setlur. Madras: Brahmavadin Press, 1912.

Yājñavalkya Dharmaśāstra. With the commentary *Bālakrīḍā* of Viśvarūpa. Edited by T. Gaṇapati Śāstrī. 2 vols. Trivandrum Sanskrit Series. Trivandrum: The Government of His Highness the Maharajah of Travancore, 1922–24.

Yājñavalkya Dharmaśāstra. With the commentary *Mitākṣarā* of Vijñāneśvara. Edited by Nārāyaṇa Rāma Ācārya. Delhi: Nag Publishers, 1985 [reprint].

Yājñavalkya Dharmaśāstra. Edited and translated by P. Olivelle, in Olivelle 2019.

Yatidharmasamuccaya of Yādava Prakāśa. Edited and translated by Patrick Olivelle. SUNY Series in Religion. Albany: State University of New York Press, 1995.

Secondary Literature

Adriaensen, R., Hans T. Bakker, and H. Isaacson, ed. 1998. *The Skandapurāṇa: Volume I, Adhyāyas 125-*. Groningen: Egbert Forsten.

Altekar, A. S. 1938. "The History of the Widow's Right of Inheritance." *Journal of the Bihar and Orissa Research Society* 24: 4–27.

Altekar, A. S. (1959) 1989. *The Position of Women in Hindu Civilization from Prehistoric Times to the Present*. 2nd ed. Delhi: Motital Banarsidass.

Bandyopadhyay, Sekhar. 1995. "Caste, Widow Marriage, and the Reform of Popular Culture in Colonial Bengal." In *From the Seams of History: Essays on Indian Women*, edited by Bharati Ray, 8–36. Delhi: Oxford University Press.

Basham, A. L. 1968. *The Wonder That Was India: A Survey of the History and Culture of the Indian Sub-Continent before the Coming of the Muslims*. 3rd rev. ed. New York: Taplinger.

Böthlingk, Otto, and Rudolph Roth. 1855–75. *Sanskrit-Wörterbuch*. 7 vols. St. Petersburg: Kaiserlichen Akademie der Wissenschaften.

Brick, David. 2010. "The Dharmaśāstric Debate on Widow-Burning." *Journal of the American Oriental Society* 130, no. 2: 203–23.

Brick, David. 2014. "The Widow-Ascetic Under Hindu Law." *Indo-Iranian Journal* 57, no. 4: 352–83.

Brick, David, ed. and trans. 2015. *Brahmanical Theories of the Gift: A Critical Edition and Annotated Translation of the Dānakāṇḍa of the Kṛtyakalpataru*. Harvard Oriental Series 77. Cambridge, MA: Harvard University Press.

Brick, David. 2018. "Sati." In *Martyrdom, Self-Sacrifice, and Self-Annihilation: Religious Perspectives on Suicide*, ed. Margo Kitts, 162–81. New York: Oxford University Press.

Brick, David. 2021. "The Debate on Cross-Cousin Marriage in Classical Hindu Law." *International Journal of Hindu Studies* 25, no. 1: 1–54.

Bühler, Georg, trans. (1879–82) 1969. *The Sacred Laws of the Āryas: As Taught in the Schools of Āpastamba, Gautama, Vāsishtha, and Baudhāyana*. 2 vols. Sacred Books of the East 2, 14. Delhi: Motilal Banarsidass.

Bühler, Georg, trans. (1886) 1970. *The Laws of Manu: Translated with Extracts from Seven Commentaries*. Sacred Books of the East 25. Delhi: Motilal Banarsidass.

Colebrooke, Henry Thomas. 1795. "On the Duties of a Hindu Widow". *Asiatick Researches* 4: 205–15.

Cowell, E. B., and F. W. Thomas, trans. 1968. *The Harṣa-Carita of Bāṇa*. Delhi: Motilal Banarsidass.

Davis, Donald, Jr. 2004. *The Boundaries of Hindu Law: Tradition, Custom, and Politics in Medieval Kerala*. Corpus Iuris Sanscriticum 5. Torino: CESMEO.

Davis, Donald, Jr. 2012. "Introduction." In *Studies in Hindu Law and Dharmaśāstra* by Ludo Rocher, 17–36. Anthem South Asian Normative Traditions Studies. New York: Anthem Press.

Derrett, J. Duncan M. 1976–78. *Essays in Classical and Modern Hindu Law*. 4 vols. Leiden: E. J. Brill.

Doniger, Wendy, and Brian K. Smith, trans. 1991. *The Laws of Manu*. New York: Penguin Books.

Dutta, Manomohini. 2016. *Inheritance, Property and Women in the Dāyabhāga*. PhD dissertation, University of Texas at Austin.

Dutta, Manomohini. 2018. "*Upakāra*: The Theory of Spiritual Service and Women's Inheritance in the *Dāyabhāga*." *Journal of Hindu Studies* 11: 260–84.

Fisch, Joerg. 2006. *Burning Women: A Global History of Widow Sacrifice from Ancient Times to the Present*. Translated by Rekha Kamath Rajan. New York: Seagull Books.

Fleming, Christopher T. 2020. *Ownership and Inheritance in Sanskrit Jurisprudence*. Oxford Oriental Monographs. New York: Oxford University Press.

Ganguly, D. C. 1933. *History of the Paramāra Dynasty*. Dacca: University of Dacca.

Garzilli, Enrica. 1997. "First Greek and Latin Documents on *Sahagamana* and Some Connected Problems." 2 parts. *Indo-Iranian Journal* 40: 205–43, 339–65.

Ghose, Jogendra Chunder, ed. 1901. *The English Works of Raja Rammohun Roy*. Vol. 2. Calcutta: Srikanta Roy.

Hall, Fitzgerald. 1868. "The Source of Colebrooke's Essay 'On the Duties of a Faithful Hindu Widow.'" *Journal of the Royal Asiatic Society* n.s.-3: 183–98.

Hart, George L. 1973. "Woman and the Sacred in Ancient Tamilnad." *Journal of Asian Studies* 32, no. 2: 233-50.

Hart, George L., and Hank Heifetz, trans. 1999. *The Four Hundred Songs of War and Wisdom: An Anthology of Poems from Classical Tamil: The Puṟanāṉūṟu*. Translations from the Asian Classics. New York: Columbia University Press.

Hatcher, Brian A. 1996. *Idioms of Improvement: Vidyasagar and Cultural Encounter in Bengal*. New York: Oxford University Press.

Hatcher, Brian, trans. 2012. *Hindu Widow Marriage by Ishvarchandra Vidyasagar: A Complete Translation with an Introduction and Critical Notes*. New York: Columbia University Press.

Inden, Ronald B. 1976. *Marriage and Rank in Bengali Culture: A History of Caste and Clan in Middle Period Bengal*. Berkeley: University of California Press.

Jamison, Stephanie. 1996. *Sacrificed Wife/Sacrificer's Wife: Women, Ritual, and Hospitality in Ancient India*. New York: Oxford University Press.

Jamison, Stephanie. 1998. "Rhinoceros Toes: Manu 5.17–18 and the Development of the Dharma System." *Journal of the American Oriental Society* 118, no. 2: 249–56.

Jamison, Stephanie. 2006. "Women 'Between the Empires' and 'Between the Lines.'" In *Between the Empires: Society in India 300 BCE to 400 CE*, edited by P. Olivelle, 191–214. New York: Oxford University Press.

Jamison, Stephanie. 2014. "The Earliest Evidence for the Inborn Debts of a Brahmin: A New Interpretation of *Ṛgveda* X.135." *Journal Asiatique* 302, no. 2: 245–57.

Jamison, Stephanie, and Joel Brereton, trans. 2014. *The Rigveda: The Earliest Religious Poetry of India*. 3 vols. New York: Oxford University Press.

Jha, Ganganath. 1964. *Pūrva-Mīmāṃsā in Its Sources*. 2nd ed. Varanasi: Banaras Hindu University.

Jyväsjärvi Stuart, Mari. 2013. "Male Guardians of Women's Virtues: A Dharmaśāstric Theme and Its Jain Variations." *Journal of the American Oriental Society* 133, no. 1: 35–56.

Kane, P. V. 1962–75. *History of Dharmaśāstra*. 5 vols. 2nd ed. Poona: Bhandarkar Oriental Research Institute.

Kane, P. V., ed. 1986. *The Harṣacarita of Bāṇabhaṭṭa: Text of Uchchhvāsas I-VIII*. Delhi: Motilal Banarsidass.

Lamb, Sarah. 2000. *White Saris and Sweet Mangoes: Aging, Gender, and Body in North India*. Berkeley: University of California Press.

Lariviere, Richard. 1991. "Matrimonial Remedies for Women in Classical Hindu Law: Alternatives to Divorce." In *Rules and Remedies in Classical Indian Law*, edited by Julia Leslie, 37–45. Leiden: E. J. Brill.

Lariviere, Richard. 1997. "Dharmaśāstra, Custom, 'Real Law' and 'Apocryphal' Smṛtis." In *Recht, Staat und Verwaltung im klassischen Indien*, edited by B. Kölver and E. Müller-Luckner, 97–110. Munich: R. Oldenbourg Verlag.

Lariviere, Richard, ed. and trans. 2003. *The Nāradasmṛti*. Delhi: Motilal Banarsidass.

Leslie, Julia. 1989. *The Perfect Wife: The Orthodox Hindu Woman According to the Strīdharmapaddhati of Tryambakayajvan*. South Asian Studies Series. Oxford: Oxford University Press.

Leslie, Julia. 1991. "A Problem of Choice: The Heroic *Satī* or the Widow-Ascetic." In *Rules and Remedies in Classical Indian Law*, edited by Julia Leslie, 46–61. Leiden: E. J. Brill.

Lingat, Robert. (1973) 1998. *The Classical Law of India*. Translated by J. Duncan M. Derrett. Law in India Series. Delhi: Oxford University Press.

Lubin, Timothy. 2015. "Writing and the Recognition of Customary Law in Premodern India and Java." *Journal of the American Oriental Society* 135, no. 2: 225–60.

Kiparski, Paul. 1979. *Pāṇini as a Variationist*. Cambridge, MA: MIT Press.

Mani, Lata. 1998. *Contentious Traditions: The Debate on Sati in Colonial India*. Berkeley: University of California Press.

McGee, Mary. 1987. *Feasting and Fasting: The Vrata Tradition and Its Significance for Hindu Women*. PhD dissertation, Harvard University.

Mitra, Trailokyanath. 1881. *The Law Relating to the Hindu Widow*. Tagore Law Lectures–1879. Calcutta: Thacker, Spink, and Co.

Monier-Williams, Monier. (1899) 2002. *A Sanskrit-English Dictionary*. Delhi: Motilal Banarsidass.

Nandy, Ashis. 1994. "Sati as Profit Versus Sati as a Spectacle: The Public Debate on Roop Kanwar's Death." In *Sati, the Blessing and the Curse*, edited by John Stratton Hawley, 131–48. New York: Oxford University Press.

Narasimhan, Sakuntala. 1992. *Sati: Widow Burning in India*. New York: Anchar Books.

Oldenburg, Veena Talwar. 1994. "The Roop Kanwar Case: Feminist Responses." In *Sati, the Blessing and the Curse*, edited by John Stratton Hawley, 101–30. New York: Oxford University Press.

Olivelle, Patrick, ed. and trans. 1995. *Rules and Regulations of Brahmanical Asceticism: Yatidharmasamuccaya of Yādava Prakāśa*. SUNY Series on Religion. Albany: State University of New York Press.

Olivelle, Patrick. 1998. "Hair and Society: Social Significance of Hair in South Asian Traditions." In *Hair: Its Power and Meaning in Asian Cultures*, edited by A. Hiltebeitel and B. D. Miller, 11–49. New York: State University of New York Press.

Olivelle, Patrick, ed. and trans. 2000. *Dharmasūtras: The Law Codes of Āpastamba, Gautama, Baudhāyana, and Vasiṣṭha*. Delhi: Motilal Banarsidass.

Olivelle, Patrick, ed. and trans. 2005. *Manu's Code of Law: A Critical Edition and Translation of the Mānava-Dharmaśāstra*. New York: Oxford University Press.

Olivelle, Patrick. 2007. "The Date and Provenance of the *Viṣṇu-Smṛti*: On the Intersection between Text and Iconography." *Indologica Taurinensia* 33: 149–64.

Olivelle, Patrick. 2010. "Dharmaśāstra: A Textual History." In *Hinduism and Law: An Introduction*, edited by T. Lubin, D. R. Davis, Jr., and J. K. Krishnan, 28-57. Cambridge: Cambridge University Press.

Olivelle, Patrick, ed. and trans. 2019. *Yajnavalkya: A Treatise on Dharma*. Murty Classical Library of India. Cambridge, MA: Harvard University Press.

Ortner, Sherry. 1996. *Making Gender: The Politics and Erotics of Culture*. Boston: Beacon Press.

Pollock, Sheldon. 1997. "The 'Revelation' of 'Tradition': *śruti, smṛti*, and the Sanskrit Discourse of Power." In *Lex et Litterae: Studies in Honour of Oscar Botto*, edited by S. Lienhard and I. Piovano, 395–417. Torino: CESMEO.

Potter, Karl H. 1981. *Encyclopedia of Indian Philosophies*. Vol. 3. Princeton, NJ: Princeton University Press.

Rocher, Ludo, ed. and trans. 2002. *Jīmūtavāhana's Dāyabhāga: The Hindu Law of Inheritance in Bengal*. New York: Oxford University Press.

Rocher, Ludo. 2012. *Studies in Hindu Law and Dharmaśāstra: Edited with an Introduction by Donald R. Davis, Jr.* Anthem South Asian Normative Traditions Studies. New York: Anthem Press.

Rocher, Ludo, and Rosane Rocher. 2001. "Ownership by Birth: The *Mitākṣarā* Stand." *Journal of Indian Philosophy* 29, no. 2: 241–55.

Rocher, Rosane. 2010. "The Creation of Anglo-Hindu Law." In *Hinduism and Law: An Introduction*, edited by T. Lubin, D. R. Davis, Jr., and J. K. Krishnan, 78-88. Cambridge: Cambridge University Press.

Rocher, Rosane, and Ludo Rocher. 2007. *The Making of Western Indology: Henry Thomas Colebrooke and the East India Company*. London: Routledge.

Settar, S. and Gunther D. Sontheimer, ed. 1982. *Memorial Stones: A Study of Their Origins, Significance and Variety*. Dharwad: Institute of Indian Art History, Karnatak University.

Srinivas, M. N. (1952) 1965. *Religion and Society among the Coorgs of South India*. London: Asia Publishing House.

Srinivas, M. N. 1956. "A Note on Sanskritization and Westernization." *The Far Eastern Quarterly* 15, no. 4: 481–96.

Srinivasan, Saradha. 1979. *Mensuration in Ancient India*. Delhi: Ajanta Publications.

Trautmann, Thomas R. 1981. *Dravidian Kinship*. Cambridge: Cambridge University Press.

Vajpeyi, Ananya. 2010. "*Śūdradharma* and Legal Treatments of Caste." In *Hinduism and Law: An Introduction*, edited by T. Lubin, D. R. Davis, Jr., and J. K. Krishnan, 154–66. Cambridge: Cambridge University Press.

Weisberg, Dvora E. 2009. *Levirate Marriage and the Family in Ancient Judaism*. Waltham, MA: Brandeis University Press.

Wezler, Albrecht. 2004. "Dharma in the Veda and the Dharmaśāstras." *Journal of Indian Philosophy* 32: 629–65.

Yoshimizu, Kiyotaka. 2015. "Kumārila's Criticism of Buddhism as a Religious Movement in His Views on the Sources of Dharma." *Acta Asiatica (Tōhō Gakkai)* 108: 43–62.

Index

For the benefit of digital users, indexed terms that span two pages (e.g., 52–53) may, on occasion, appear on only one of those pages.